United Nations Office for
Disarmament Affairs

DISARMAMENT AND
RELATED TREATIES

Prepared in cooperation with the Kingdom of the Netherlands

United Nations

THE UNITED NATIONS OFFICE FOR DISARMAMENT AFFAIRS is publishing *Disarmament and Related Treaties* pursuant to the purposes of the United Nations Disarmament Information Programme. The mandate of the Programme is to inform, educate and generate public understanding of the importance of multilateral action, and support for it, in the field of arms limitation and disarmament.

For information on this and other United Nations publications related to disarmament, non-proliferation and arms control, please contact:

Information and Outreach Branch
United Nations Office for Disarmament Affairs
United Nations
New York NY 10017
Telephone 212.963.3022
Email: unoda-web@un.org

This publication is available from

www.un.org/disarmament

Prepared in cooperation with the Kingdom of the Netherlands

Disclaimer

This publication is provided for information only and is not intended as the original text of the treaties contained herein. The United Nations assumes no liability for actions undertaken in reliance on the materials contained in this publication.

UNITED NATIONS PUBLICATION
Sales No. E.15.IX.1

ISBN 978-92-1-142302-0
eISBN 978-92-1-057180-7

Contents

Related Treaties

Preface

Treaties are essential to the maintenance of international law and order, and States depend upon them to provide stability and consistency in international relations.

This publication contains the text of multilateral treaties that focus on nuclear weapons, other weapons of mass destruction, conventional arms, and nuclear-weapon-free zones, all of which are essential for promoting peace and security. It also includes treaties in which disarmament and non-proliferation are important elements within a larger framework of issues, such as the Antarctic Treaty or the Agreement Governing the Activities of States on the Moon and Other Celestial Bodies.

With regard to the sources of text compiled in this publication, the United Nations Office of Legal Affairs supplied the information on the agreements for which the United Nations Secretary-General is the depositary, as well as the text of other agreements which have been registered with and published by the United Nations in the *United Nations Treaty Series*. Where the text of such other agreements is not available from the Office of Legal Affairs, the information is taken from the websites of the treaty depositaries or the international or intergovernmental organizations that have secretariat responsibility for said treaties.

Information in this publication presenting the number of signatories and of parties to agreements is as at 28 November 2014. Actions occurring after that date are reflected in the Disarmament Treaties Database (http://disarmament.un.org/treaties/). Other information available from the online database include lists of States that are signatories or States parties to the agreements; statements, declarations or reservations made by signatory States and States parties; and a summary of agreements, with the dates of deposit, adhered to by each State.

This compilation of legal instruments does not include the Convention on Certain Conventional Weapons (CCW), which has been produced in a separate companion publication that can be downloaded.[1] With its multiple protocols on various conventional weapons as well as remnants of war, it was determined that the CCW merited a separate publication of its own.

The United Nations Office for Disarmament Affairs and the Kingdom of the Netherlands hope this book will be a useful tool for diplomats, researchers, those in the service of States parties to the various treaties and conventions, those States not yet parties, and in promoting and furthering the universalization of these instruments.

---

[1] See http://www.un.org/disarmament/publications/more/ccw/.

NUCLEAR

Treaty on the Non-Proliferation of Nuclear Weapons

OPENED FOR SIGNATURE AT LONDON, MOSCOW AND WASHINGTON:
1 July 1968

ENTERED INTO FORCE:
5 March 1970

DEPOSITARY GOVERNMENTS:
Russian Federation
United Kingdom of Great Britain and Northern Ireland
United States of America

NUMBER OF SIGNATORY STATES: 93*

NUMBER OF STATES PARTIES: 190*

＊ As at 28 November 2014. For the updated adherence status, see http://disarmament.un.org/treaties/.

TEXT:

The States concluding this Treaty, hereinafter referred to as the "Parties to the Treaty",

Considering the devastation that would be visited upon all mankind by a nuclear war and the consequent need to make every effort to avert the danger of such a war and to take measures to safeguard the security of peoples,

Believing that the proliferation of nuclear weapons would seriously enhance the danger of nuclear war,

In conformity with resolutions of the United Nations General Assembly calling for the conclusion of an agreement on the prevention of wider dissemination of nuclear weapons,

Undertaking to co-operate in facilitating the application of International Atomic Energy Agency safeguards on peaceful nuclear activities,

Expressing their support for research, development and other efforts to further the application, within the framework of the International Atomic Energy Agency safeguards system, of the principle of safeguarding effectively the flow of source and special fissionable materials by use of instruments and other techniques at certain strategic points,

Affirming the principle that the benefits of peaceful applications of nuclear technology, including any technological by-products which may be derived by nuclear-weapon States from the development of nuclear explosive devices, should be available for peaceful purposes to all Parties to the Treaty, whether nuclear-weapon or non-nuclear-weapon States,

Convinced that, in furtherance of this principle, all Parties to the Treaty are entitled to participate in the fullest possible exchange of scientific information for, and to contribute alone or in co-operation with other States to, the further development of the applications of atomic energy for peaceful purposes,

Declaring their intention to achieve at the earliest possible date the cessation of the nuclear arms race and to undertake effective measures in the direction of nuclear disarmament,

Urging the co-operation of all States in the attainment of this objective,

Recalling the determination expressed by the Parties to the 1963 Treaty banning nuclear weapons tests in the atmosphere, in outer space and under water in its Preamble to seek to achieve the discontinuance of all test explosions of nuclear weapons for all time and to continue negotiations to this end,

Desiring to further the easing of international tension and the strengthening of trust between States in order to facilitate the cessation of the manufacture of nuclear weapons, the liquidation of all their existing stockpiles, and the elimination from national arsenals of nuclear weapons and the means of their delivery pursuant to a Treaty on general and complete disarmament under strict and effective international control,

Recalling that, in accordance with the Charter of the United Nations, States must refrain in their international relations from the threat or use of force against the territorial integrity or political independence of any State, or in any other manner inconsistent with the Purposes of the United Nations, and that the establishment and maintenance of international peace and security are to be promoted with the least diversion for armaments of the world's human and economic resources,

Have agreed as follows:

Article I

Each nuclear-weapon State Party to the Treaty undertakes not to transfer to any recipient whatsoever nuclear weapons or other nuclear explosive devices or control over such weapons or explosive devices directly, or indirectly; and not in any way to assist, encourage, or induce any non-nuclear-weapon State to manufacture or otherwise acquire nuclear weapons or other nuclear explosive devices, or control over such weapons or explosive devices.

Article II

Each non-nuclear-weapon State Party to the Treaty undertakes not to receive the transfer from any transferor whatsoever of nuclear weapons or other nuclear explosive devices or of control over such weapons or explosive devices directly, or indirectly; not to manufacture or otherwise acquire nuclear weapons or other nuclear explosive devices; and not to seek or receive any assistance in the manufacture of nuclear weapons or other nuclear explosive devices.

Article III

1.   Each non-nuclear-weapon State Party to the Treaty undertakes to accept safeguards, as set forth in an agreement to be negotiated and concluded with the International Atomic Energy Agency in accordance with the Statute of the International Atomic Energy Agency and the Agency's safeguards system, for the exclusive purpose of verification of the fulfilment of its obligations assumed under this Treaty with a view to preventing diversion of nuclear energy from peaceful uses to nuclear weapons or other nuclear explosive devices. Procedures for the safeguards required by this Article shall be followed with respect to source or special fissionable material whether it is being produced, processed or used in any principal nuclear facility or is outside any such facility. The safeguards required by this Article shall be applied on all source or special fissionable material in all peaceful nuclear activities within the territory of such State, under its jurisdiction, or carried out under its control anywhere.

2.   Each State Party to the Treaty undertakes not to provide: (a) source or special fissionable material, or (b) equipment or material especially designed or prepared for the processing, use or production of special fissionable material, to any non-nuclear-weapon State for peaceful purposes, unless the source or special fissionable material shall be subject to the safeguards required by this Article.

3.   The safeguards required by this Article shall be implemented in a manner designed to comply with Article IV of this Treaty, and to avoid hampering the economic or

technological development of the Parties or international co-operation in the field of peaceful nuclear activities, including the international exchange of nuclear material and equipment for the processing, use or production of nuclear material for peaceful purposes in accordance with the provisions of this Article and the principle of safeguarding set forth in the Preamble of the Treaty.

4.   Non-nuclear-weapon States Party to the Treaty shall conclude agreements with the International Atomic Energy Agency to meet the requirements of this Article either individually or together with other States in accordance with the Statute of the International Atomic Energy Agency. Negotiation of such agreements shall commence within 180 days from the original entry into force of this Treaty. For States depositing their instruments of ratification or accession after the 180-day period, negotiation of such agreements shall commence not later than the date of such deposit. Such agreements shall enter into force not later than eighteen months after the date of initiation of negotiations.

Article IV

1.   Nothing in this Treaty shall be interpreted as affecting the inalienable right of all the Parties to the Treaty to develop research, production and use of nuclear energy for peaceful purposes without discrimination and in conformity with Articles I and II of this Treaty.

2.   All the Parties to the Treaty undertake to facilitate, and have the right to participate in, the fullest possible exchange

of equipment, materials and scientific and technological information for the peaceful uses of nuclear energy. Parties to the Treaty in a position to do so shall also co-operate in contributing alone or together with other States or international organizations to the further development of the applications of nuclear energy for peaceful purposes, especially in the territories of non-nuclear-weapon States Party to the Treaty, with due consideration for the needs of the developing areas of the world.

Article V

Each Party to the Treaty undertakes to take appropriate measures to ensure that, in accordance with this Treaty, under appropriate international observation and through appropriate international procedures, potential benefits from any peaceful applications of nuclear explosions will be made available to non-nuclear-weapon States Party to the Treaty on a non-discriminatory basis and that the charge to such Parties for the explosive devices used will be as low as possible and exclude any charge for research and development. Non-nuclear-weapon States Party to the Treaty shall be able to obtain such benefits, pursuant to a special international agreement or agreements, through an appropriate international body with adequate representation of non-nuclear-weapon States. Negotiations on this subject shall commence as soon as possible after the Treaty enters into force. Non-nuclear-weapon States Party to the Treaty so desiring may also obtain such benefits pursuant to bilateral agreements.

Article VI

Each of the Parties to the Treaty undertakes to pursue negotiations in good faith on effective measures relating to cessation of the nuclear arms race at an early date and to nuclear disarmament, and on a treaty on general and complete disarmament under strict and effective international control.

Article VII

Nothing in this Treaty affects the right of any group of States to conclude regional treaties in order to assure the total absence of nuclear weapons in their respective territories.

Article VIII

1. Any Party to the Treaty may propose amendments to this Treaty. The text of any proposed amendment shall be submitted to the Depositary Governments which shall circulate it to all Parties to the Treaty. Thereupon, if requested to do so by one-third or more of the Parties to the Treaty, the Depositary Governments shall convene a conference, to which they shall invite all the Parties to the Treaty, to consider such an amendment.

2. Any amendment to this Treaty must be approved by a majority of the votes of all the Parties to the Treaty, including the votes of all nuclear-weapon States Party to the Treaty and all other Parties which, on the date the amendment is

circulated, are members of the Board of Governors of the International Atomic Energy Agency. The amendment shall enter into force for each Party that deposits its instrument of ratification of the amendment upon the deposit of such instruments of ratification by a majority of all the Parties, including the instruments of ratification of all nuclear-weapon States Party to the Treaty and all other Parties which, on the date the amendment is circulated, are members of the Board of Governors of the International Atomic Energy Agency. Thereafter, it shall enter into force for any other Party upon the deposit of its instrument of ratification of the amendment.

3.   Five years after the entry into force of this Treaty, a conference of Parties to the Treaty shall be held in Geneva, Switzerland, in order to review the operation of this Treaty with a view to assuring that the purposes of the Preamble and the provisions of the Treaty are being realised. At intervals of five years thereafter, a majority of the Parties to the Treaty may obtain, by submitting a proposal to this effect to the Depositary Governments, the convening of further conferences with the same objective of reviewing the operation of the Treaty.

Article IX

1.   This Treaty shall be open to all States for signature. Any State which does not sign the Treaty before its entry into force in accordance with paragraph 3 of this Article may accede to it at any time.

2.   This Treaty shall be subject to ratification by signatory States. Instruments of ratification and instruments of accession shall be deposited with the Governments of the United Kingdom of Great Britain and Northern Ireland, the Union of Soviet Socialist Republics and the United States of America, which are hereby designated the Depositary Governments.

3.   This Treaty shall enter into force after its ratification by the States, the Governments of which are designated Depositaries of the Treaty, and forty other States signatory to this Treaty and the deposit of their instruments of ratification. For the purposes of this Treaty, a nuclear-weapon State is one which has manufactured and exploded a nuclear weapon or other nuclear explosive device prior to 1 January 1967.

4.   For States whose instruments of ratification or accession are deposited subsequent to the entry into force of this Treaty, it shall enter into force on the date of the deposit of their instruments of ratification or accession.

5.   The Depositary Governments shall promptly inform all signatory and acceding States of the date of each signature, the date of deposit of each instrument of ratification or of accession, the date of the entry into force of this Treaty, and the date of receipt of any requests for convening a conference or other notices.

6. This Treaty shall be registered by the Depositary Governments pursuant to Article 102 of the Charter of the United Nations.

Article X

1. Each Party shall in exercising its national sovereignty have the right to withdraw from the Treaty if it decides that extraordinary events, related to the subject matter of this Treaty, have jeopardized the supreme interests of its country. It shall give notice of such withdrawal to all other Parties to the Treaty and to the United Nations Security Council three months in advance. Such notice shall include a statement of the extraordinary events it regards as having jeopardized its supreme interests.

2. Twenty-five years after the entry into force of the Treaty, a conference shall be convened to decide whether the Treaty shall continue in force indefinitely, or shall be extended for an additional fixed period or periods. This decision shall be taken by a majority of the Parties to the Treaty.

Article XI

This Treaty, the English, Russian, French, Spanish and Chinese texts of which are equally authentic, shall be deposited in the archives of the Depositary Governments. Duly certified copies of this Treaty shall be transmitted by the Depositary Governments to the Governments of the signatory and acceding States.

IN WITNESS WHEREOF the undersigned, duly authorized, have signed this Treaty.

DONE in triplicate, at the cities of London, Moscow and Washington, this first day of July, one thousand nine hundred and sixty-eight.

Comprehensive Nuclear-Test-Ban Treaty

OPENED FOR SIGNATURE AT NEW YORK:
    24 September 1996

NOT YET IN FORCE

DEPOSITARY:
    Secretary-General of the United Nations

NUMBER OF SIGNATORY STATES: 183*

NUMBER OF STATES PARTIES: 163*

* As at 28 November 2014. For the updated adherence status, see http://disarmament.un.org/treaties/.

TEXT:

Contents

Preamble

The States Parties to this Treaty (hereinafter referred to as "the States Parties"),

Welcoming the international agreements and other positive measures of recent years in the field of nuclear disarmament, including reductions in arsenals of nuclear weapons, as well as in the field of the prevention of nuclear proliferation in all its aspects,

Underlining the importance of the full and prompt implementation of such agreements and measures,

Convinced that the present international situation provides an opportunity to take further effective measures towards nuclear disarmament and against the proliferation of nuclear weapons in all its aspects, and *declaring* their intention to take such measures,

Stressing therefore the need for continued systematic and progressive efforts to reduce nuclear weapons globally, with the ultimate goal of eliminating those weapons, and of general and complete disarmament under strict and effective international control,

Recognizing that the cessation of all nuclear weapon test explosions and all other nuclear explosions, by constraining the development and qualitative improvement of nuclear weapons and ending the development of advanced new types of nuclear weapons, constitutes an effective measure of nuclear disarmament and non-proliferation in all its aspects,

Further recognizing that an end to all such nuclear explosions will thus constitute a meaningful step in the realization of a systematic process to achieve nuclear disarmament,

Convinced that the most effective way to achieve an end to nuclear testing is through the conclusion of a universal and internationally and effectively verifiable comprehensive nuclear-test-ban treaty, which has long been one of the highest priority objectives of the international community in the field of disarmament and non-proliferation,

Noting the aspirations expressed by the Parties to the 1963 Treaty Banning Nuclear Weapon Tests in the Atmosphere, in Outer Space and Under Water to seek to achieve the discontinuance of all test explosions of nuclear weapons for all time,

Noting also the views expressed that this Treaty could contribute to the protection of the environment,

Affirming the purpose of attracting the adherence of all States to this Treaty and its objective to contribute effectively to the prevention of the proliferation of nuclear weapons in all its aspects, to the process of nuclear disarmament and therefore to the enhancement of international peace and security,

Have agreed as follows:

Article I
Basic Obligations

1.   Each State Party undertakes not to carry out any nuclear weapon test explosion or any other nuclear explosion, and to prohibit and prevent any such nuclear explosion at any place under its jurisdiction or control.

2.   Each State Party undertakes, furthermore, to refrain from causing, encouraging, or in any way participating in the carrying out of any nuclear weapon test explosion or any other nuclear explosion.

Article II
The Organization

A.   General Provisions

1.   The States Parties hereby establish the Comprehensive Nuclear-Test-Ban Treaty Organization (hereinafter referred to as "the Organization") to achieve the object and purpose of this Treaty, to ensure the implementation of its provisions, including those for international verification of compliance with it, and to provide a forum for consultation and cooperation among States Parties.

2.   All States Parties shall be members of the Organization. A State Party shall not be deprived of its membership in the Organization.

3.   The seat of the Organization shall be Vienna, Republic of Austria.

4. There are hereby established as organs of the Organization: the Conference of the States Parties, the Executive Council and the Technical Secretariat, which shall include the International Data Centre.

5. Each State Party shall cooperate with the Organization in the exercise of its functions in accordance with this Treaty. States Parties shall consult, directly among themselves, or through the Organization or other appropriate international procedures, including procedures within the framework of the United Nations and in accordance with its Charter, on any matter which may be raised relating to the object and purpose, or the implementation of the provisions, of this Treaty.

6. The Organization shall conduct its verification activities provided for under this Treaty in the least intrusive manner possible consistent with the timely and efficient accomplishment of their objectives. It shall request only the information and data necessary to fulfil its responsibilities under this Treaty. It shall take every precaution to protect the confidentiality of information on civil and military activities and facilities coming to its knowledge in the implementation of this Treaty and, in particular, shall abide by the confidentiality provisions set forth in this Treaty.

7. Each State Party shall treat as confidential and afford special handling to information and data that it receives in confidence from the Organization in connection with the implementation of this Treaty. It shall treat such information

and data exclusively in connection with its rights and obligations under this Treaty.

8.   The Organization, as an independent body, shall seek to utilize existing expertise and facilities, as appropriate, and to maximize cost efficiencies, through cooperative arrangements with other international organizations such as the International Atomic Energy Agency. Such arrangements, excluding those of a minor and normal commercial and contractual nature, shall be set out in agreements to be submitted to the Conference of the States Parties for approval.

9.   The costs of the activities of the Organization shall be met annually by the States Parties in accordance with the United Nations scale of assessments adjusted to take into account differences in membership between the United Nations and the Organization.

10. Financial contributions of States Parties to the Preparatory Commission shall be deducted in an appropriate way from their contributions to the regular budget.

11. A member of the Organization which is in arrears in the payment of its assessed contribution to the Organization shall have no vote in the Organization if the amount of its arrears equals or exceeds the amount of the contribution due from it for the preceding two full years. The Conference of the States Parties may, nevertheless, permit such a member to vote if it is satisfied that the failure to pay is due to conditions beyond the control of the member.

B.   The Conference of the States Parties

Composition, Procedures and Decision-making

12.   The Conference of the States Parties (hereinafter referred to as "the Conference") shall be composed of all States Parties. Each State Party shall have one representative in the Conference, who may be accompanied by alternates and advisers.

13.   The initial session of the Conference shall be convened by the Depositary no later than 30 days after the entry into force of this Treaty.

14.   The Conference shall meet in regular sessions, which shall be held annually, unless it decides otherwise.

15.   A special session of the Conference shall be convened:

(a)   When decided by the Conference;

(b)   When requested by the Executive Council; or

(c)   When requested by any State Party and supported by a majority of the States Parties.

The special session shall be convened no later than 30 days after the decision of the Conference, the request of the Executive Council, or the attainment of the necessary support, unless specified otherwise in the decision or request.

16.   The Conference may also be convened in the form of an Amendment Conference, in accordance with Article VII.

17.   The Conference may also be convened in the form of a Review Conference, in accordance with Article VIII.

18.   Sessions shall take place at the seat of the Organization unless the Conference decides otherwise.

19.   The Conference shall adopt its rules of procedure. At the beginning of each session, it shall elect its President and such other officers as may be required. They shall hold office until a new President and other officers are elected at the next session.

20.   A majority of the States Parties shall constitute a quorum.

21.   Each State Party shall have one vote.

22.   The Conference shall take decisions on matters of procedure by a majority of members present and voting. Decisions on matters of substance shall be taken as far as possible by consensus. If consensus is not attainable when an issue comes up for decision, the President of the Conference shall defer any vote for 24 hours and during this period of deferment shall make every effort to facilitate achievement of consensus, and shall report to the Conference before the end of this period. If consensus is not possible at the end of 24 hours, the Conference shall take a decision by a two-thirds majority of members present and voting unless specified otherwise in this Treaty. When the issue arises

as to whether the question is one of substance or not, that question shall be treated as a matter of substance unless otherwise decided by the majority required for decisions on matters of substance.

23. When exercising its function under paragraph 26 (k), the Conference shall take a decision to add any State to the list of States contained in Annex 1 to this Treaty in accordance with the procedure for decisions on matters of substance set out in paragraph 22. Notwithstanding paragraph 22, the Conference shall take decisions on any other change to Annex 1 to this Treaty by consensus.

Powers and Functions

24. The Conference shall be the principal organ of the Organization. It shall consider any questions, matters or issues within the scope of this Treaty, including those relating to the powers and functions of the Executive Council and the Technical Secretariat, in accordance with this Treaty. It may make recommendations and take decisions on any questions, matters or issues within the scope of this Treaty raised by a State Party or brought to its attention by the Executive Council.

25. The Conference shall oversee the implementation of, and review compliance with, this Treaty and act in order to promote its object and purpose. It shall also oversee the activities of the Executive Council and the Technical Secretariat and may issue guidelines to either of them for the exercise of their functions.

26.   The Conference shall:

(a)   Consider and adopt the report of the Organization on the implementation of this Treaty and the annual programme and budget of the Organization, submitted by the Executive Council, as well as consider other reports;

(b)   Decide on the scale of financial contributions to be paid by States Parties in accordance with paragraph 9;

(c)   Elect the members of the Executive Council;

(d)   Appoint the Director-General of the Technical Secretariat (hereinafter referred to as "the Director-General");

(e)   Consider and approve the rules of procedure of the Executive Council submitted by the latter;

(f)   Consider and review scientific and technological developments that could affect the operation of this Treaty. In this context, the Conference may direct the Director-General to establish a Scientific Advisory Board to enable him or her, in the performance of his or her functions, to render specialized advice in areas of science and technology relevant to this Treaty to the Conference, to the Executive Council or to States Parties. In that case, the Scientific Advisory Board shall be composed of independent experts serving in their individual capacity and appointed, in accordance with terms of reference adopted by the Conference, on the basis of their expertise and experience in the particular scientific fields relevant to the implementation of this Treaty;

(g)   Take the necessary measures to ensure compliance with this Treaty and to redress and remedy any situation that contravenes the provisions of this Treaty, in accordance with Article V;

(h)   Consider and approve at its initial session any draft agreements, arrangements, provisions, procedures, operational manuals, guidelines and any other documents developed and recommended by the Preparatory Commission;

(i)   Consider and approve agreements or arrangements negotiated by the Technical Secretariat with States Parties, other States and international organizations to be concluded by the Executive Council on behalf of the Organization in accordance with paragraph 38 (h);

(j)   Establish such subsidiary organs as it finds necessary for the exercise of its functions in accordance with this Treaty; and

(k)   Update Annex 1 to this Treaty, as appropriate, in accordance with paragraph 23.

C.   The Executive Council

Composition, Procedures and Decision-making

27.   The Executive Council shall consist of 51 members. Each State Party shall have the right, in accordance with the provisions of this Article, to serve on the Executive Council.

28.   Taking into account the need for equitable geographical distribution, the Executive Council shall comprise:

(a)   Ten States Parties from Africa;

(b)   Seven States Parties from Eastern Europe;

(c)   Nine States Parties from Latin America and the Caribbean;

(d)   Seven States Parties from the Middle East and South Asia;

(e)   Ten States Parties from North America and Western Europe; and

(f)   Eight States Parties from South-East Asia, the Pacific and the Far East.

All States in each of the above geographical regions are listed in Annex 1 to this Treaty. Annex 1 to this Treaty shall be updated, as appropriate, by the Conference in accordance with paragraphs 23 and 26 (k). It shall not be subject to amendments or changes under the procedures contained in Article VII.

29.   The members of the Executive Council shall be elected by the Conference. In this connection, each geographical region shall designate States Parties from that region for election as members of the Executive Council as follows:

(a) At least one-third of the seats allocated to each geographical region shall be filled, taking into account political and security interests by States Parties in that region designated on the basis of the nuclear capabilities relevant to the Treaty as determined by international data as well as all or any of the following indicative criteria in the order of priority determined by each region:

(i) Number of monitoring facilities of the International Monitoring System;

(ii) Expertise and experience in monitoring technology; and

(iii) Contribution to the annual budget of the Organization;

(b) One of the seats allocated to each geographical region shall be filled on a rotational basis by the State Party that is first in the English alphabetical order among the States Parties in that region that have not served as members of the Executive Council for the longest period of time since becoming States Parties or since their last term, whichever is shorter. A State Party designated on this basis may decide to forgo its seat. In that case, such a State Party shall submit a letter of renunciation to the Director-General, and the seat shall be filled by the State Party following next-in-order according to this sub-paragraph; and

(c)   The remaining seats allocated to each geographical region shall be filled by States Parties designated from among all the States Parties in that region by rotation or elections.

30.   Each member of the Executive Council shall have one representative on the Executive Council, who may be accompanied by alternates and advisers.

31.   Each member of the Executive Council shall hold office from the end of the session of the Conference at which that member is elected until the end of the second regular annual session of the Conference thereafter, except that for the first election of the Executive Council, 26 members shall be elected to hold office until the end of the third regular annual session of the Conference, due regard being paid to the established numerical proportions as described in paragraph 28.

32.   The Executive Council shall elaborate its rules of procedure and submit them to the Conference for approval.

33.   The Executive Council shall elect its Chairman from among its members.

34.   The Executive Council shall meet for regular sessions. Between regular sessions it shall meet as may be required for the fulfilment of its powers and functions.

35.   Each member of the Executive Council shall have one vote.

36. The Executive Council shall take decisions on matters of procedure by a majority of all its members. The Executive Council shall take decisions on matters of substance by a two-thirds majority of all its members unless specified otherwise in this Treaty. When the issue arises as to whether the question is one of substance or not, that question shall be treated as a matter of substance unless otherwise decided by the majority required for decisions on matters of substance.

Powers and Functions

37. The Executive Council shall be the executive organ of the Organization. It shall be responsible to the Conference. It shall carry out the powers and functions entrusted to it in accordance with this Treaty. In so doing, it shall act in conformity with the recommendations, decisions and guidelines of the Conference and ensure their continuous and proper implementation.

38. The Executive Council shall:

(a) Promote effective implementation of, and compliance with, this Treaty;

(b) Supervise the activities of the Technical Secretariat;

(c) Make recommendations as necessary to the Conference for consideration of further proposals for promoting the object and purpose of this Treaty;

(d) Cooperate with the National Authority of each State Party;

(e) Consider and submit to the Conference the draft annual programme and budget of the Organization, the draft report of the Organization on the implementation of this Treaty, the report on the performance of its own activities and such other reports as it deems necessary or that the Conference may request;

(f) Make arrangements for the sessions of the Conference, including the preparation of the draft agenda;

(g) Examine proposals for changes, on matters of an administrative or technical nature, to the Protocol or the Annexes thereto, pursuant to Article VII, and make recommendations to the States Parties regarding their adoption;

(h) Conclude, subject to prior approval of the Conference, agreements or arrangements with States Parties, other States and international organizations on behalf of the Organization and supervise their implementation, with the exception of agreements or arrangements referred to in sub-paragraph (i);

(i) Approve and supervise the operation of agreements or arrangements relating to the implementation of verification activities with States Parties and other States; and

(j) Approve any new operational manuals and any changes to the existing operational manuals that may be proposed by the Technical Secretariat.

39. The Executive Council may request a special session of the Conference.

40. The Executive Council shall:

(a) Facilitate cooperation among States Parties, and between States Parties and the Technical Secretariat, relating to the implementation of this Treaty through information exchanges;

(b) Facilitate consultation and clarification among States Parties in accordance with Article IV; and

(c) Receive, consider and take action on requests for, and reports on, on-site inspections in accordance with Article IV.

41. The Executive Council shall consider any concern raised by a State Party about possible non-compliance with this Treaty and abuse of the rights established by this Treaty. In doing so, the Executive Council shall consult with the States Parties involved and, as appropriate, request a State Party to take measures to redress the situation within a specified time. To the extent that the Executive Council considers further action to be necessary, it shall take, inter alia, one or more of the following measures:

(a) Notify all States Parties of the issue or matter;

(b)   Bring the issue or matter to the attention of the Conference;

(c)   Make recommendations to the Conference or take action, as appropriate, regarding measures to redress the situation and to ensure compliance in accordance with Article V.

D.   The Technical Secretariat

42.   The Technical Secretariat shall assist States Parties in the implementation of this Treaty. The Technical Secretariat shall assist the Conference and the Executive Council in the performance of their functions. The Technical Secretariat shall carry out the verification and other function entrusted to it by this Treaty, as well as those functions delegated to it by the Conference or the Executive Council in accordance with this Treaty. The Technical Secretariat shall include, as an integral part, the International Data Centre.

43.   The functions of the Technical Secretariat with regard to verification of compliance with this Treaty shall, in accordance with Article IV and the Protocol, include inter alia:

(a)   Being responsible for supervising and coordinating the operation of the International Monitoring System;

(b)   Operating the International Data Centre;

(c)   Routinely receiving, processing, analysing and reporting on International Monitoring System data;

(d)   Providing technical assistance in, and support for, the installation and operation of monitoring stations;

(e)   Assisting the Executive Council in facilitating consultation and clarification among States Parties;

(f)   Receiving requests for on-site inspections and processing them, facilitating Executive Council consideration of such requests, carrying out the preparations for, and providing technical support during, the conduct of on-site inspections, and reporting to the Executive Council;

(g) Negotiating agreements or arrangements with States Parties, other States and international organizations and concluding, subject to prior approval by the Executive Council, any such agreements or arrangements relating to verification activities with States Parties or other States; and

(h)   Assisting the States Parties through their National Authorities on other issues of verification under this Treaty.

44.   The Technical Secretariat shall develop and maintain, subject to approval by the Executive Council, operational manuals to guide the operation of the various components of the verification regime, in accordance with Article IV and the Protocol. These manuals shall not constitute integral parts of this Treaty or the Protocol and may be changed by the Technical Secretariat subject to approval by the Executive Council. The Technical Secretariat shall promptly inform the States Parties of any changes in the operational manuals.

45. The functions of the Technical Secretariat with respect to administrative matters shall include:

(a) Preparing and submitting to the Executive Council the draft programme and budget of the Organization;

(b) Preparing and submitting to the Executive Council the draft report of the Organization on the implementation of this Treaty and such other reports as the Conference or the Executive Council may request;

(c) Providing administrative and technical support to the Conference, the Executive Council and other subsidiary organs;

(d) Addressing and receiving communications on behalf of the Organization relating to the implementation of this Treaty; and

(e) Carrying out the administrative responsibilities related to any agreements between the Organization and other international organizations.

46. All requests and notifications by States Parties to the Organization shall be transmitted through their National Authorities to the Director-General. Requests and notifications shall be in one of the official languages of this Treaty. In response the Director-General shall use the language of the transmitted request or notification.

47. With respect to the responsibilities of the Technical Secretariat for preparing and submitting to the Executive

Council the draft programme and budget of the Organization, the Technical Secretariat shall determine and maintain a clear accounting of all costs for each facility established as part of the International Monitoring System. Similar treatment in the draft programme and budget shall be accorded to all other activities of the Organization.

48. The Technical Secretariat shall promptly inform the Executive Council of any problems that have arisen with regard to the discharge of its functions that have come to its notice in the performance of its activities and that it has been unable to resolve through consultations with the State Party concerned.

49. The Technical Secretariat shall comprise a Director-General, who shall be its head and chief administrative officer, and such scientific, technical and other personnel as may be required. The Director-General shall be appointed by the Conference upon the recommendation of the Executive Council for a term of four years, renewable for one further term, but not thereafter. The first Director-General shall be appointed by the Conference at its initial session upon the recommendation of the Preparatory Commission.

50. The Director-General shall be responsible to the Conference and the Executive Council for the appointment of the staff and for the organization and functioning of the Technical Secretariat. The paramount consideration in the employment of the staff and in the determination of the conditions of service shall be the necessity of securing the highest standards of professional expertise, experience,

efficiency, competence and integrity. Only citizens of States Parties shall serve as the Director-General, as inspectors or as members of the professional and clerical staff. Due regard shall be paid to the importance of recruiting the staff on as wide a geographical basis as possible. Recruitment shall be guided by the principle that the staff shall be kept to the minimum necessary for the proper discharge of the responsibilities of the Technical Secretariat.

51. The Director-General may, as appropriate, after consultation with the Executive Council, establish temporary working groups of scientific experts to provide recommendations on specific issues.

52. In the performance of their duties, the Director-General, the inspectors, the inspection assistants and the members of the staff shall not seek or receive instructions from any Government or from any other source external to the Organization. They shall refrain from any action that might reflect adversely on their positions as international officers responsible only to the Organization. The Director-General shall assume responsibility for the activities of an inspection team.

53. Each State Party shall respect the exclusively international character of the responsibilities of the Director-General, the inspectors, the inspection assistants and the members of the staff and shall not seek to influence them in the discharge of their responsibilities.

E.   Privileges and Immunities

54. The Organization shall enjoy on the territory and in any other place under the jurisdiction or control of a State Party such legal capacity and such privileges and immunities as are necessary for the exercise of its functions.

55. Delegates of States Parties, together with their alternates and advisers, representatives of members elected to the Executive Council, together with their alternates and advisers, the Director-General, the inspectors, the inspection assistants and the members of the staff of the Organization shall enjoy such privileges and immunities as are necessary in the independent exercise of their functions in connection with the Organization.

56. The legal capacity, privileges and immunities referred to in this Article shall be defined in agreements between the Organization and the States Parties as well as in an agreement between the Organization and the State in which the Organization is seated. Such agreements shall be considered and approved in accordance with paragraph 26 (h) and (i).

57. Notwithstanding paragraphs 54 and 55, the privileges and immunities enjoyed by the Director-General, the inspectors, the inspection assistants and the members of the staff of the Technical Secretariat during the conduct of verification activities shall be those set forth in the Protocol.

Article III
National Implementation Measures

1. Each State Party shall, in accordance with its constitutional processes, take any necessary measures to implement its obligations under this Treaty. In particular, it shall take any necessary measures:

(a) To prohibit natural and legal persons anywhere on its territory or in any other place under its jurisdiction as recognized by international law from undertaking any activity prohibited to a State Party under this Treaty;

(b) To prohibit natural and legal persons from undertaking any such activity anywhere under its control; and

(c) To prohibit, in conformity with international law, natural persons possessing its nationality from undertaking any such activity anywhere.

2. Each State Party shall cooperate with other States Parties and afford the appropriate form of legal assistance to facilitate the implementation of the obligations under paragraph 1.

3. Each State Party shall inform the Organization of the measures taken pursuant to this Article.

4. In order to fulfill its obligations under the Treaty, each State Party shall designate or set up a National Authority and shall so inform the Organization upon entry into force

of the Treaty for it. The National Authority shall serve as the national focal point for liaison with the Organization and with other States Parties.

Article IV
Verification

A. General Provisions

1. In order to verify compliance with this Treaty, a verification regime shall be established consisting of the following elements:

   (a) An International Monitoring System;

   (b) Consultation and clarification;

   (c) On-site inspections; and

   (d) Confidence-building measures.

At entry into force of this Treaty, the verification regime shall be capable of meeting the verification requirements of this Treaty.

2. Verification activities shall be based on objective information, shall be limited to the subject matter of this Treaty, and shall be carried out on the basis of full respect for the sovereignty of States Parties and in the least intrusive manner possible consistent with the effective and timely accomplishment of their objectives. Each State Party shall refrain from any abuse of the right of verification.

3. Each State Party undertakes in accordance with this Treaty to cooperate through its National Authority established pursuant to Article III, paragraph 4, with the Organization and with other States Parties to facilitate the verification of compliance with this Treaty by, inter alia:

(a) Establishing the necessary facilities to participate in these verification measures and establishing the necessary communication;

(b) Providing data obtained from national stations that are part of the International Monitoring System;

(c) Participating, as appropriate, in a consultation and clarification process;

(d) Permitting the conduct of on-site inspections; and

(e) Participating, as appropriate, in confidence-building measures.

4. All States Parties, irrespective of their technical and financial capabilities, shall enjoy the equal right of verification and assume the equal obligation to accept verification.

5. For the purposes of this Treaty, no State Party shall be precluded from using information obtained by national technical means of verification in a manner consistent with generally recognized principles of international law, including that of respect for the sovereignty of States.

6.   Without prejudice to the right of States Parties to protect sensitive installations, activities or locations not related to this Treaty, States Parties shall not interfere with elements of the verification regime of this Treaty or with national technical means of verification operating in accordance with paragraph 5.

7.   Each State Party shall have the right to take measures to protect sensitive installations and to prevent disclosure of confidential information and data not related to this Treaty.

8.   Moreover, all necessary measures shall be taken to protect the confidentiality of any information related to civil and military activities and facilities obtained during verification activities.

9.   Subject to paragraph 8, information obtained by the Organization through the verification regime established by this Treaty shall be made available to all States Parties in accordance with the relevant provisions of this Treaty and the Protocol.

10.   The provisions of this Treaty shall not be interpreted as restricting the international exchange of data for scientific purposes.

11.   Each State Party undertakes to cooperate with the Organization and with other States Parties in the improvement of the verification regime, and in the examination of the verification potential of additional monitoring technologies such as electromagnetic pulse

monitoring or satellite monitoring, with a view to developing, when appropriate, specific measures to enhance the efficient and cost-effective verification of this Treaty. Such measures shall, when agreed, be incorporated in existing provisions in this Treaty, the Protocol or as additional sections of the Protocol, in accordance with Article VII, or, if appropriate, be reflected in the operational manuals in accordance with Article II, paragraph 44.

12. The States Parties undertake to promote cooperation among themselves to facilitate and participate in the fullest possible exchange relating to technologies used in the verification of this Treaty in order to enable all States Parties to strengthen their national implementation of verification measures and to benefit from the application of such technologies for peaceful purposes.

13. The provisions of this Treaty shall be implemented in a manner which avoids hampering the economic and technological development of the States Parties for further development of the application of atomic energy for peaceful purposes.

Verification Responsibilities of the Technical Secretariat

14. In discharging its responsibilities in the area of verification specified in this Treaty and the Protocol, in cooperation with the States Parties the Technical Secretariat shall, for the purpose of this Treaty:

(a) Make arrangements to receive and distribute data and reporting products relevant to the verification of this

Treaty in accordance with its provisions, and to maintain a global communications infrastructure appropriate to this task;

(b) Routinely through its International Data Centre, which shall in principle be the focal point within the Technical Secretariat for data storage and data processing:

(i) Receive and initiate requests for data from the International Monitoring System;

(ii) Receive data, as appropriate, resulting from the process of consultation and clarification, from on-site inspections, and from confidence-building measures; and

(iii) Receive other relevant data from States Parties and international organizations in accordance with this Treaty and the Protocol;

(c) Supervise, coordinate and ensure the operation of the International Monitoring System and its component elements, and of the International Data Centre, in accordance with the relevant operational manuals;

(d) Routinely process, analyse and report on International Monitoring System data according to agreed procedures so as to permit the effective international verification of this Treaty and to contribute to the early resolution of compliance concerns;

(e)   Make available all data, both raw and processed, and any reporting products, to all States Parties, each State Party taking responsibility for the use of International Monitoring System data in accordance with Article II, paragraph 7, and with paragraphs 8 and 13 of this Article;

(f)   Provide to all States Parties equal, open, convenient and timely access to all stored data;

(g)   Store all data, both raw and processed, and reporting products;

(h)   Coordinate and facilitate requests for additional data from the International Monitoring System;

(i)   Coordinate requests for additional data from one State Party to another State Party;

(j)   Provide technical assistance in, and support for, the installation and operation of monitoring facilities and respective communication means, where such assistance and support are required by the State concerned;

(k)   Make available to any State Party, upon its request, techniques utilized by the Technical Secretariat and its International Data Centre in compiling, storing, processing, analysing and reporting on data from the verification regime; and

(l)   Monitor, assess and report on the overall performance of the International Monitoring System and of the International Data Centre.

15. The agreed procedures to be used by the Technical Secretariat in discharging the verification responsibilities referred to in paragraph 14 and detailed in the Protocol shall be elaborated in the relevant operational manuals.

B. The International Monitoring System

16. The International Monitoring System shall comprise facilities for seismological monitoring, radionuclide monitoring including certified laboratories, hydroacoustic monitoring, infrasound monitoring, and respective means of communication, and shall be supported by the International Data Centre of the Technical Secretariat.

17. The International Monitoring System shall be placed under the authority of the Technical Secretariat. All monitoring facilities of the International Monitoring System shall be owned and operated by the States hosting or otherwise taking responsibility for them in accordance with the Protocol.

18. Each State Party shall have the right to participate in the international exchange of data and to have access to all data made available to the International Data Centre. Each State Party shall cooperate with the International Data Centre through its National Authority.

Funding the International Monitoring System

19. For facilities incorporated into the International Monitoring System and specified in Tables 1-A, 2-A, 3 and 4 of Annex 1 to the Protocol, and for their functioning, to the

extent that such facilities are agreed by the relevant State and the Organization to provide data to the International Data Centre in accordance with the technical requirements of the Protocol and relevant operational manuals, the Organization, as specified in agreements or arrangements pursuant to Part I, paragraph 4 of the Protocol, shall meet the costs of:

(a) Establishing any new facilities and upgrading existing facilities unless the State responsible for such facilities meets these costs itself;

(b) Operating and maintaining International Monitoring System facilities, including facility physical security if appropriate, and application of agreed data authentication procedures;

(c) Transmitting International Monitoring System data (raw or processed) to the International Data Centre by the most direct and cost-effective means available, including, if necessary, via appropriate communications nodes, from monitoring stations, laboratories, analytical facilities or from national data centres; or such data (including samples where appropriate) to laboratory and analytical facilities from monitoring stations; and

(d) Analysing samples on behalf of the Organization.

20. For auxiliary network seismic stations specified in Table 1-B of Annex 1 to the Protocol the Organization, as specified

in agreements or arrangements pursuant to Part I, paragraph 4 of the Protocol, shall meet the costs only of:

(a) Transmitting data to the International Data Centre;

(b) Authenticating data from such stations;

(c) Upgrading stations to the required technical standard, unless the State responsible for such facilities meets these costs itself;

(d) If necessary, establishing new stations for the purposes of this Treaty where no appropriate facilities currently exist, unless the State responsible for such facilities meets these costs itself; and

(e) Any other costs related to the provision of data required by the Organization as specified in the relevant operational manuals.

21. The Organization shall also meet the cost of provision to each State Party of its requested selection from the standard range of International Data Centre reporting products and services, as specified in Part I, Section F of the Protocol. The cost of preparation and transmission of any additional data or products shall be met by the requesting State Party.

22. The agreements or, if appropriate, arrangements concluded with States Parties or States hosting or otherwise taking responsibility for facilities of the International Monitoring System shall contain provisions for meeting

these costs. Such provisions may include modalities whereby a State Party meets any of the costs referred to in paragraphs 19 (a) and 20 (c) and (d) for facilities which it hosts or for which it is responsible, and is compensated by an appropriate reduction in its assessed financial contribution to the Organization. Such a reduction shall not exceed 50 percent of the annual assessed financial contribution of a State Party, but may be spread over successive years. A State Party may share such a reduction with another State Party by agreement or arrangement between themselves and with the concurrence of the Executive Council. The agreements or arrangements referred to in this paragraph shall be approved in accordance with Article II, paragraphs 26 (h) and 38 (i).

Changes to the International Monitoring System

23. Any measures referred to in paragraph 11 affecting the International Monitoring System by means of addition or deletion of a monitoring technology shall, when agreed, be incorporated into this Treaty and the Protocol pursuant to Article VII, paragraphs 1 to 6.

24. The following changes to the International Monitoring System, subject to the agreement of those States directly affected, shall be regarded as matters of an administrative or technical nature pursuant to Article VII, paragraphs 7 and 8:

(a) Changes to the number of facilities specified in the Protocol for a given monitoring technology; and

(b) Changes to other details for particular facilities as reflected in the Tables of Annex 1 to the Protocol (including, inter alia, State responsible for the facility; location; name of facility; type of facility; and attribution of a facility between the primary and auxiliary seismic networks).

If the Executive Council recommends, pursuant to Article VII, paragraph 8 (d), that such changes be adopted, it shall as a rule also recommend pursuant to Article VII, paragraph 8 (g), that such changes enter into force upon notification by the Director-General of their approval.

25.   The Director-General, in submitting to the Executive Council and States Parties information and evaluation in accordance with Article VII, paragraph 8 (b), shall include in the case of any proposal made pursuant to paragraph 24:

(a)   A technical evaluation of the proposal;

(b)   A statement on the administrative and financial impact of the proposal; and

(c)   A report on consultations with States directly affected by the proposal, including indication of their agreement.

Temporary Arrangements

26. In cases of significant or irretrievable breakdown of a monitoring facility specified in the Tables of Annex 1 to the Protocol, or in order to cover other temporary reductions of monitoring coverage, the Director-General shall, in consultation and agreement with those States directly affected, and with the approval of the Executive

Council, initiate temporary arrangements of no more than one year's duration, renewable if necessary by agreement of the Executive Council and of the States directly affected for another year. Such arrangements shall not cause the number of operational facilities of the International Monitoring System to exceed the number specified for the relevant network; shall meet as far as possible the technical and operational requirements specified in the operational manual for the relevant network; and shall be conducted within the budget of the Organization. The Director-General shall furthermore take steps to rectify the situation and make proposals for its permanent resolution. The Director-General shall notify all States Parties of any decision taken pursuant to this paragraph.

Cooperating National Facilities

27.   States Parties may also separately establish cooperative arrangements with the Organization, in order to make available to the International Data Centre supplementary data from national monitoring stations that are not formally part of the International Monitoring System.

28.   Such cooperative arrangements may be established as follows:

(a)   Upon request by a State Party, and at the expense of that State, the Technical Secretariat shall take the steps required to certify that a given monitoring facility meets the technical and operational requirements specified in the relevant operational manuals for an International Monitoring System facility, and make arrangements for the authentication of its data. Subject to the agreement of the Executive Council, the Technical Secretariat shall then formally designate such a facility as a cooperating national facility. The Technical Secretariat shall take the steps required to revalidate its certification as appropriate;

(b)   The Technical Secretariat shall maintain a current list of cooperating national facilities and shall distribute it to all States Parties; and

(c)   The International Data Centre shall call upon data from cooperating national facilities, if so requested by a State Party, for the purposes of facilitating consultation and clarification and the consideration of on-site inspection requests, data transmission costs being borne by that State Party.

The conditions under which supplementary data from such facilities are made available, and under which the International Data Centre may request further or expedited reporting, or clarifications, shall be elaborated in the operational manual for the respective monitoring network.

C.   Consultation and Clarification

29. Without prejudice to the right of any State Party to request an on-site inspection, States Parties should, whenever possible, first make every effort to clarify and resolve, among themselves or with or through the Organization, any matter which may cause concern about possible non-compliance with the basic obligations of this Treaty.

30. A State Party that receives a request pursuant to paragraph 29 directly from another State Party shall provide the clarification to the requesting State Party as soon as possible, but in any case no later than 48 hours after the request. The requesting and requested States Parties may keep the Executive Council and the Director-General informed of the request and the response.

31. A State Party shall have the right to request the Director-General to assist in clarifying any matter which may cause concern about possible non-compliance with the basic obligations of this Treaty. The Director-General shall provide appropriate information in the possession of the Technical Secretariat relevant to such a concern. The Director-General shall inform the Executive Council of the request and of the information provided in response, if so requested by the requesting State Party.

32. A State Party shall have the right to request the Executive Council to obtain clarification from another State Party on any matter which may cause concern about possible non-compliance with the basic obligations of this Treaty. In such a case, the following shall apply:

(a) The Executive Council shall forward the request for clarification to the requested State Party through the Director-General no later than 24 hours after its receipt;

(b) The requested State Party shall provide the clarification to the Executive Council as soon as possible, but in any case no later than 48 hours after receipt of the request;

(c) The Executive Council shall take note of the clarification and forward it to the requesting State Party no later than 24 hours after its receipt;

(d) If the requesting State Party deems the clarification to be inadequate, it shall have the right to request the Executive Council to obtain further clarification from the requested State Party.

The Executive Council shall inform without delay all other States Parties about any request for clarification pursuant to this paragraph as well as any response provided by the requested State Party.

33. If the requesting State Party considers the clarification obtained under paragraph 32 (d) to be unsatisfactory, it shall have the right to request a meeting of the Executive Council in which States Parties involved that are not members of the Executive Council shall be entitled to take part. At such a meeting, the Executive Council shall consider the matter and may recommend any measure in accordance with Article V.

D.   On-site Inspections

Request for an On-Site Inspection

34. Each State Party has the right to request an on-site inspection in accordance with the provisions of this Article and Part II of the Protocol in the territory or in any other

place under the jurisdiction or control of any State Party, or in any area beyond the jurisdiction or control of any State.

35.   The sole purpose of an on-site inspection shall be to clarify whether a nuclear weapon test explosion or any other nuclear explosion has been carried out in violation of Article I and, to the extent possible, to gather any facts which might assist in identifying any possible violator.

36.   The requesting State Party shall be under the obligation to keep the on-site inspection request within the scope of this Treaty and to provide in the request information in accordance with paragraph 37. The requesting State Party shall refrain from unfounded or abusive inspection requests.

37.   The on-site inspection request shall be based on information collected by the International Monitoring System, on any relevant technical information obtained by national technical means of verification in a manner consistent with generally recognized principles of international law, or on a combination thereof. The request shall contain information pursuant to Part II, paragraph 41 of the Protocol.

38.   The requesting State Party shall present the on-site inspection request to the Executive Council and at the same time to the Director-General for the latter to begin immediate processing.

*Follow-up After Submission of an On-Site Inspection
Request*

39. The Executive Council shall begin its consideration immediately upon receipt of the on-site inspection request.

40. The Director-General, after receiving the on-site inspection request, shall acknowledge receipt of the request to the requesting State Party within two hours and communicate the request to the State Party sought to be inspected within six hours. The Director-General shall ascertain that the request meets the requirements specified in Part II, paragraph 41 of the Protocol, and, if necessary, shall assist the requesting State Party in filing the request accordingly, and shall communicate the request to the Executive Council and to all other States Parties within 24 hours.

41. When the on-site inspection request fulfils the requirements, the Technical Secretariat shall begin preparations for the on-site inspection without delay.

42. The Director-General, upon receipt of an on-site inspection request referring to an inspection area under the jurisdiction or control of a State Party, shall immediately seek clarification from the State Party sought to be inspected in order to clarify and resolve the concern raised in the request.

43. A State Party that receives a request for clarification pursuant to paragraph 42 shall provide the Director-General with explanations and with other relevant information

available as soon as possible, but no later than 72 hours after receipt of the request for clarification.

44. The Director-General, before the Executive Council takes a decision on the on-site inspection request, shall transmit immediately to the Executive Council any additional information available from the International Monitoring System or provided by any State Party on the event specified in the request, including any clarification provided pursuant to paragraphs 42 and 43, as well as any other information from within the Technical Secretariat that the Director-General deems relevant or that is requested by the Executive Council.

45. Unless the requesting State Party considers the concern raised in the on-site inspection request to be resolved and withdraws the request, the Executive Council shall take a decision on the request in accordance with paragraph 46.

Executive Council Decisions

46. The Executive Council shall take a decision on the on-site inspection request no later than 96 hours after receipt of the request from the requesting State Party. The decision to approve the on-site inspection shall be made by at least 30 affirmative votes of members of the Executive Council. If the Executive Council does not approve the inspection, preparations shall be stopped and no further action on the request shall be taken.

47. No later than 25 days after the approval of the on-site inspection in accordance with paragraph 46, the inspection

team shall transmit to the Executive Council, through the Director-General, a progress inspection report. The continuation of the inspection shall be considered approved unless the Executive Council, no later than 72 hours after receipt of the progress inspection report, decides by a majority of all its members not to continue the inspection. If the Executive Council decides not to continue the inspection, the inspection shall be terminated, and the inspection team shall leave the inspection area and the territory of the inspected State Party as soon as possible in accordance with Part II, paragraphs 109 and 110 of the Protocol.

48. In the course of the on-site inspection, the inspection team may submit to the Executive Council, through the Director-General, a proposal to conduct drilling. The Executive Council shall take a decision on such a proposal no later than 72 hours after receipt of the proposal. The decision to approve drilling shall be made by a majority of all members of the Executive Council.

49. The inspection team may request the Executive Council, through the Director-General, to extend the inspection duration by a maximum of 70 days beyond the 60-day time-frame specified in Part II, paragraph 4 of the Protocol, if the inspection team considers such an extension essential to enable it to fulfil its mandate. The inspection team shall indicate in its request which of the activities and techniques listed in Part II, paragraph 69 of the Protocol it intends to carry out during the extension period. The Executive Council shall take a decision on the extension request no later than 72 hours after receipt of the request. The decision to approve

an extension of the inspection duration shall be made by a majority of all members of the Executive Council.

50. Any time following the approval of the continuation of the on-site inspection in accordance with paragraph 47, the inspection team may submit to the Executive Council, through the Director-General, a recommendation to terminate the inspection. Such a recommendation shall be considered approved unless the Executive Council, no later than 72 hours after receipt of the recommendation, decides by a two-thirds majority of all its members not to approve the termination of the inspection. In case of termination of the inspection, the inspection team shall leave the inspection area and the territory of the inspected State Party as soon as possible in accordance with Part II, paragraphs 109 and 110 of the Protocol.

51. The requesting State Party and the State Party sought to be inspected may participate in the deliberations of the Executive Council on the on-site inspection request without voting. The requesting State Party and the inspected State Party may also participate without voting in any subsequent deliberations of the Executive Council related to the inspection.

52. The Director-General shall notify all States Parties within 24 hours about any decision by and reports, proposals, requests and recommendations to the Executive Council pursuant to paragraphs 46 to 50.

Follow-up After Executive Council Approval of an
On-Site Inspection

53. An on-site inspection approved by the Executive Council shall be conducted without delay by an inspection team designated by the Director-General and in accordance with the provisions of this Treaty and the Protocol. The inspection team shall arrive at the point of entry no later than six days following the receipt by the Executive Council of the on-site inspection request from the requesting State Party.

54. The Director-General shall issue an inspection mandate for the conduct of the on-site inspection. The inspection mandate shall contain the information specified in Part II, paragraph 42 of the Protocol.

55. The Director-General shall notify the inspected State Party of the inspection no less than 24 hours before the planned arrival of the inspection team at the point of entry, in accordance with Part II, paragraph 43 of the Protocol.

The Conduct of an On-Site Inspection

56. Each State Party shall permit the Organization to conduct an on-site inspection on its territory or at places under its jurisdiction or control in accordance with the provisions of this Treaty and the Protocol. However, no State Party shall have to accept simultaneous on-site inspections on its territory or at places under its jurisdiction or control.

57. In accordance with the provisions of this Treaty and the Protocol, the inspected State Party shall have:

(a) The right and the obligation to make every reasonable effort to demonstrate its compliance with this Treaty and, to this end, to enable the inspection team to fulfil its mandate;

(b) The right to take measures it deems necessary to protect national security interests and to prevent disclosure of confidential information not related to the purpose of the inspection;

(c) The obligation to provide access within the inspection area for the sole purpose of determining facts relevant to the purpose of the inspection, taking into account sub-paragraph (b) and any constitutional obligations it may have with regard to proprietary rights or searches and seizures;

(d) The obligation not to invoke this paragraph or Part II, paragraph 88 of the Protocol to conceal any violation of its obligations under Article I; and

(e) The obligation not to impede the ability of the inspection team to move within the inspection area and to carry out inspection activities in accordance with this Treaty and the Protocol.

Access, in the context of an on-site inspection, means both the physical access of the inspection team and the inspection equipment to, and the conduct of inspection activities within, the inspection area.

58. The on-site inspection shall be conducted in the least intrusive manner possible, consistent with the efficient and timely accomplishment of the inspection mandate, and in accordance with the procedures set forth in the Protocol. Wherever possible, the inspection team shall begin with the least intrusive procedures and then proceed to more intrusive procedures only as it deems necessary to collect sufficient information to clarify the concern about possible non-compliance with this Treaty. The inspectors shall seek only the information and data necessary for the purpose of the inspection and shall seek to minimize interference with normal operations of the inspected State Party.

59. The inspected State Party shall assist the inspection team throughout the on-site inspection and facilitate its task.

60. If the inspected State Party, acting in accordance with Part II, paragraphs 86 to 96 of the Protocol, restricts access within the inspection area, it shall make every reasonable effort in consultations with the inspection team to demonstrate through alternative means its compliance with this Treaty.

Observer

61. With regard to an observer, the following shall apply:

(a) The requesting State Party, subject to the agreement of the inspected State Party, may send a representative, who shall be a national either of the requesting State Party or of a third State Party, to observe the conduct of the on-site inspection;

(b) The inspected State Party shall notify its acceptance or non-acceptance of the proposed observer to the Director-General within 12 hours after approval of the on-site inspection by the Executive Council;

(c) In case of acceptance, the inspected State Party shall grant access to the observer in accordance with the Protocol;

(d) The inspected State Party shall, as a rule, accept the proposed observer, but if the inspected State Party exercises a refusal, that fact shall be recorded in the inspection report.

There shall be no more than three observers from an aggregate of requesting States Parties.

Reports of an On-Site Inspection

62. Inspection reports shall contain:

(a) A description of the activities conducted by the inspection team;

(b) The factual findings of the inspection team relevant to the purpose of the inspection;

(c) An account of the cooperation granted during the on-site inspection;

(d)   A factual description of the extent of the access granted, including the alternative means provided to the team, during the on-site inspection; and

(e)   Any other details relevant to the purpose of the inspection.

Differing observations made by inspectors may be attached to the report.

63.   The Director-General shall make draft inspection reports available to the inspected State Party. The inspected State Party shall have the right to provide the Director-General within 48 hours with its comments and explanations, and to identify any information and data which, in its view, are not related to the purpose of the inspection and should not be circulated outside the Technical Secretariat. The Director-General shall consider the proposals for changes to the draft inspection report made by the inspected State Party and shall wherever possible incorporate them. The Director-General shall also annex the comments and explanations provided by the inspected State Party to the inspection report.

64.   The Director-General shall promptly transmit the inspection report to the requesting State Party, the inspected State Party, the Executive Council and to all other States Parties. The Director-General shall further transmit promptly to the Executive Council and to all other States Parties any results of sample analysis in designated laboratories in accordance with Part II, paragraph 104 of the Protocol, relevant data from the International Monitoring

System, the assessments of the requesting and inspected States Parties, as well as any other information that the Director-General deems relevant. In the case of the progress inspection report referred to in paragraph 47, the Director-General shall transmit the report to the Executive Council within the time-frame specified in that paragraph.

65. The Executive Council, in accordance with its powers and functions, shall review the inspection report and any material provided pursuant to paragraph 64, and shall address any concerns as to:

(a) Whether any non-compliance with this Treaty has occurred; and

(b) Whether the right to request an on-site inspection has been abused.

66. If the Executive Council reaches the conclusion, in keeping with its powers and functions, that further action may be necessary with regard to paragraph 65, it shall take the appropriate measures in accordance with Article V.

Frivolous or Abusive On-Site Inspection Requests

67. If the Executive Council does not approve the on-site inspection on the basis that the on-site inspection request is frivolous or abusive, or if the inspection is terminated for the same reasons, the Executive Council shall consider and decide on whether to implement appropriate measures to redress the situation, including the following:

(a)   Requiring the requesting State Party to pay for the cost of any preparations made by the Technical Secretariat;

(b)   Suspending the right of the requesting State Party to request an on-site inspection for a period of time, as determined by the Executive Council; and

(c)   Suspending the right of the requesting State Party to serve on the Executive Council for a period of time.

E.   Confidence-building Measures

68.   In order to:

(a)   Contribute to the timely resolution of any compliance concerns arising from possible misinterpretation of verification data relating to chemical explosions; and

(b)   Assist in the calibration of the stations that are part of the component networks of the International Monitoring System,

each State Party undertakes to cooperate with the Organization and with other States Parties in implementing relevant measures as set out in Part III of the Protocol.

Article V
Measures to Redress a Situation and to Ensure Compliance, Including Sanctions

1.   The Conference, taking into account, inter alia, the recommendations of the Executive Council, shall take the

necessary measures, as set forth in paragraphs 2 and 3, to ensure compliance with this Treaty and to redress and remedy any situation which contravenes the provisions of this Treaty.

2.   In cases where a State Party has been requested by the Conference or the Executive Council to redress a situation raising problems with regard to its compliance and fails to fulfil the request within the specified time, the Conference may, inter alia, decide to restrict or suspend the State Party from the exercise of its rights and privileges under this Treaty until the Conference decides otherwise.

3.   In cases where damage to the object and purpose of this Treaty may result from non-compliance with the basic obligations of this Treaty, the Conference may recommend to States Parties collective measures which are in conformity with international law.

4.   The Conference, or alternatively, if the case is urgent, the Executive Council, may bring the issue, including relevant information and conclusions, to the attention of the United Nations.

Article VI
Settlement of Disputes

1.   Disputes that may arise concerning the application or the interpretation of this Treaty shall be settled in accordance with the relevant provisions of this Treaty and in

conformity with the provisions of the Charter of the United Nations.

2.   When a dispute arises between two or more States Parties, or between one or more States Parties and the Organization, relating to the application or interpretation of this Treaty, the parties concerned shall consult together with a view to the expeditious settlement of the dispute by negotiation or by other peaceful means of the parties' choice, including recourse to appropriate organs of this Treaty and, by mutual consent, referral to the International Court of Justice in conformity with the Statute of the Court. The parties involved shall keep the Executive Council informed of actions being taken.

3.   The Executive Council may contribute to the settlement of a dispute that may arise concerning the application or interpretation of this Treaty by whatever means it deems appropriate, including offering its good offices, calling upon the States Parties to a dispute to seek a settlement through a process of their own choice, bringing the matter to the attention of the Conference and recommending a time-limit for any agreed procedure.

4.   The Conference shall consider questions related to disputes raised by States Parties or brought to its attention by the Executive Council. The Conference shall, as it finds necessary, establish or entrust organs with tasks related to the settlement of these disputes in conformity with Article II, paragraph 26 (j).

5.   The Conference and the Executive Council are separately empowered, subject to authorization from the General Assembly of the United Nations, to request the International Court of Justice to give an advisory opinion on any legal question arising within the scope of the activities of the Organization. An agreement between the Organization and the United Nations shall be concluded for this purpose in accordance with Article II, paragraph 38 (h).

6.   This Article is without prejudice to Articles IV and V.

Article VII
Amendments

1.   At any time after the entry into force of this Treaty, any State Party may propose amendments to this Treaty, the Protocol, or the Annexes to the Protocol. Any State Party may also propose changes, in accordance with paragraph 7, to the Protocol or the Annexes thereto. Proposals for amendments shall be subject to the procedures in paragraphs 2 to 6. Proposals for changes, in accordance with paragraph 7, shall be subject to the procedures in paragraph 8.

2.   The proposed amendment shall be considered and adopted only by an Amendment Conference.

3.   Any proposal for an amendment shall be communicated to the Director-General, who shall circulate it to all States Parties and the Depositary and seek the views of the States Parties on whether an Amendment Conference should be convened to consider the proposal. If a majority of the States

Parties notify the Director-General no later than 30 days after its circulation that they support further consideration of the proposal, the Director-General shall convene an Amendment Conference to which all States Parties shall be invited.

4.   The Amendment Conference shall be held immediately following a regular session of the Conference unless all States Parties that support the convening of an Amendment Conference request that it be held earlier. In no case shall an Amendment Conference be held less than 60 days after the circulation of the proposed amendment.

5.   Amendments shall be adopted by the Amendment Conference by a positive vote of a majority of the States Parties with no State Party casting a negative vote.

6.   Amendments shall enter into force for all States Parties 30 days after deposit of the instruments of ratification or acceptance by all those States Parties casting a positive vote at the Amendment Conference.

7.   In order to ensure the viability and effectiveness of this Treaty, Parts I and III of the Protocol and Annexes 1 and 2 to the Protocol shall be subject to changes in accordance with paragraph 8, if the proposed changes are related only to matters of an administrative or technical nature. All other provisions of the Protocol and the Annexes thereto shall not be subject to changes in accordance with paragraph 8.

8. Proposed changes referred to in paragraph 7 shall be made in accordance with the following procedures:

(a) The text of the proposed changes shall be transmitted together with the necessary information to the Director-General. Additional information for the evaluation of the proposal may be provided by any State Party and the Director-General. The Director-General shall promptly communicate any such proposals and information to all States Parties, the Executive Council and the Depositary;

(b) No later than 60 days after its receipt, the Director-General shall evaluate the proposal to determine all its possible consequences for the provisions of this Treaty and its implementation and shall communicate any such information to all States Parties and the Executive Council;

(c) The Executive Council shall examine the proposal in the light of all information available to it, including whether the proposal fulfils the requirements of paragraph 7. No later than 90 days after its receipt, the Executive Council shall notify its recommendation, with appropriate explanations, to all States Parties for consideration. States Parties shall acknowledge receipt within 10 days;

(d) If the Executive Council recommends to all States Parties that the proposal be adopted, it shall be considered approved if no State Party objects to it within 90 days after receipt of the recommendation. If the Executive Council recommends that the proposal be rejected, it shall be considered rejected if no State Party objects to the rejection within 90 days after receipt of the recommendation;

(e) If a recommendation of the Executive Council does not meet with the acceptance required under sub-paragraph (d), a decision on the proposal, including whether it fulfils the requirements of paragraph 7, shall be taken as a matter of substance by the Conference at its next session;

(f) The Director-General shall notify all States Parties and the Depositary of any decision under this paragraph;

(g) Changes approved under this procedure shall enter into force for all States Parties 180 days after the date of notification by the Director-General of their approval unless another time period is recommended by the Executive Council or decided by the Conference.

Article VIII
Review of the Treaty

1. Unless otherwise decided by a majority of the States Parties, ten years after the entry into force of this Treaty a Conference of the States Parties shall be held to review the operation and effectiveness of this Treaty, with a view to assuring itself that the objectives and purposes in the Preamble and the provisions of the Treaty are being realized. Such review shall take into account any new scientific and technological developments relevant to this Treaty. On the basis of a request by any State Party, the Review Conference shall consider the possibility of permitting the conduct

of underground nuclear explosions for peaceful purposes. If the Review Conference decides by consensus that such nuclear explosions may be permitted, it shall commence work without delay, with a view to recommending to States Parties an appropriate amendment to this Treaty that shall preclude any military benefits of such nuclear explosions. Any such proposed amendment shall be communicated to the Director-General by any State Party and shall be dealt with in accordance with the provisions of Article VII.

2. At intervals of ten years thereafter, further Review Conferences may be convened with the same objective, if the Conference so decides as a matter of procedure in the preceding year. Such Conferences may be convened after an interval of less than ten years if so decided by the Conference as a matter of substance.

3. Normally, any Review Conference shall be held immediately following the regular annual session of the Conference provided for in Article II.

Article IX
Duration and Withdrawal

1. This Treaty shall be of unlimited duration.

2. Each State Party shall, in exercising its national sovereignty, have the right to withdraw from this Treaty if it decides that extraordinary events related to the subject matter of this Treaty have jeopardized its supreme interests.

3.   Withdrawal shall be effected by giving notice six months in advance to all other States Parties, the Executive Council, the Depositary and the United Nations Security Council. Notice of withdrawal shall include a statement of the extraordinary event or events which a State Party regards as jeopardizing its supreme interests.

Article X
Status of the Protocol and the Annexes

The Annexes to this Treaty, the Protocol, and the Annexes to the Protocol form an integral part of the Treaty. Any reference to this Treaty includes the Annexes to this Treaty, the Protocol and the Annexes to the Protocol.

Article XI
Signature

This Treaty shall be open to all States for signature before its entry into force.

Article XII
Ratification

This Treaty shall be subject to ratification by States Signatories according to their respective constitutional processes.

Article XIII
Accession

Any State which does not sign this Treaty before its entry into force may accede to it at any time thereafter.

Article XIV
Entry into Force

1.   This Treaty shall enter into force 180 days after the date of deposit of the instruments of ratification by all States listed in Annex 2 to this Treaty, but in no case earlier than two years after its opening for signature.

2.   If this Treaty has not entered into force three years after the date of the anniversary of its opening for signature, the Depositary shall convene a Conference of the States that have already deposited their instruments of ratification upon the request of a majority of those States. That Conference shall examine the extent to which the requirement set out in paragraph 1 has been met and shall consider and decide by consensus what measures consistent with international law may be undertaken to accelerate the ratification process in order to facilitate the early entry into force of this Treaty.

3.   Unless otherwise decided by the Conference referred to in paragraph 2 or other such conferences, this process shall be repeated at subsequent anniversaries of the opening for signature of this Treaty, until its entry into force.

4.   All States Signatories shall be invited to attend the Conference referred to in paragraph 2 and any subsequent conferences as referred to in paragraph 3, as observers.

5.   For States whose instruments of ratification or accession are deposited subsequent to the entry into force of this Treaty, it shall enter into force on the 30th day following the date of deposit of their instruments of ratification or accession.

Article XV
Reservations

The Articles of and the Annexes to this Treaty shall not be subject to reservations. The provisions of the Protocol to this Treaty and the Annexes to the Protocol shall not be subject to reservations incompatible with the object and purpose of this Treaty.

Article XVI
Depositary

1.   The Secretary-General of the United Nations shall be the Depositary of this Treaty and shall receive signatures, instruments of ratification and instruments of accession.

2.   The Depositary shall promptly inform all States Signatories and acceding States of the date of each signature, the date of deposit of each instrument of ratification or accession, the date of the entry into force of this Treaty and

of any amendments and changes thereto, and the receipt of other notices.

3.   The Depositary shall send duly certified copies of this Treaty to the Governments of the States Signatories and acceding States.

4.   This Treaty shall be registered by the Depositary pursuant to Article 102 of the Charter of the United Nations.

Article XVII
Authentic Texts

This Treaty, of which the Arabic, Chinese, English, French, Russian and Spanish texts are equally authentic, shall be deposited with the Secretary-General of the United Nations.

Annex 1 to the Treaty
List of States Pursuant to Article II,
Paragraph 28

Africa

Algeria, Angola, Benin, Botswana, Burkina Faso, Burundi, Cameroon, Cape Verde, Central African Republic, Chad, Comoros, Congo, Côte d'Ivoire, Djibouti, Egypt, Equatorial Guinea, Eritrea, Ethiopia, Gabon, Gambia, Ghana, Guinea, Guinea-Bissau, Kenya, Lesotho, Liberia, Libyan Arab Jamahiriya, Madagascar, Malawi, Mali, Mauritania, Mauritius, Morocco, Mozambique, Namibia, Niger, Nigeria, Rwanda, Sao Tome & Principe, Senegal, Seychelles, Sierra Leone, Somalia, South Africa, Sudan, Swaziland, Togo, Tunisia, Uganda, United Republic of Tanzania, Zaire, Zambia, Zimbabwe.

Eastern Europe

Albania, Armenia, Azerbaijan, Belarus, Bosnia and Herzegovina, Bulgaria, Croatia, Czech Republic, Estonia, Georgia, Hungary, Latvia, Lithuania, Poland, Republic of Moldova, Romania, Russian Federation, Slovakia, Slovenia, The former Yugoslav Republic of Macedonia, Ukraine, Yugoslavia.

Latin America and the Caribbean

Antigua and Barbuda, Argentina, Bahamas, Barbados, Belize, Bolivia, Brazil, Chile, Colombia, Costa Rica, Cuba, Dominica,

Dominican Republic, Ecuador, El Salvador, Grenada, Guatemala, Guyana, Haiti, Honduras, Jamaica, Mexico, Nicaragua, Panama, Paraguay, Peru, Saint Kitts and Nevis, Saint Lucia, Saint Vincent and the Grenadines, Suriname, Trinidad and Tobago, Uruguay, Venezuela.

Middle East and South Asia

Afghanistan, Bahrain, Bangladesh, Bhutan, India, Iran (Islamic Republic of), Iraq, Israel, Jordan, Kazakhstan, Kuwait, Kyrgyzstan, Lebanon, Maldives, Nepal, Oman, Pakistan, Qatar, Saudi Arabia, Sri Lanka, Syrian Arab Republic, Tajikistan, Turkmenistan, United Arab Emirates, Uzbekistan, Yemen.

North America and Western Europe

Andorra, Austria, Belgium, Canada, Cyprus, Denmark, Finland, France, Germany, Greece, Holy See, Iceland, Ireland, Italy, Liechtenstein, Luxembourg, Malta, Monaco, Netherlands, Norway, Portugal, San Marino, Spain, Sweden, Switzerland, Turkey, United Kingdom of Great Britain and Northern Ireland, United States of America.

South East Asia, the Pacific and the Far East

Australia, Brunei Darussalam, Cambodia, China, Cook Islands, Democratic People's Republic of Korea, Fiji, Indonesia, Japan, Kiribati, Lao People's Democratic Republic, Malaysia, Marshall Islands, Micronesia (Federated

States of), Mongolia, Myanmar, Nauru, New Zealand, Niue, Palau, Papua New Guinea, Philippines, Republic of Korea, Samoa, Singapore, Solomon Islands, Thailand, Tonga, Tuvalu, Vanuatu, Viet Nam.

Annex 2 to the Treaty
List of States Pursuant to Article XIV

List of States members of the Conference on Disarmament as at 18 June 1996 which formally participated in the work of the 1996 session of the Conference and which appear in Table 1 of the International Atomic Energy Agency's April 1996 edition of "Nuclear Power Reactors in the World", and of States members of the Conference on Disarmament as at 18 June 1996 which formally participated in the work of the 1996 session of the Conference and which appear in Table 1 of the International Atomic Energy Agency's December 1995 edition of "Nuclear Research Reactors in the World":

Algeria, Argentina, Australia, Austria, Bangladesh, Belgium, Brazil, Bulgaria, Canada, Chile, China, Colombia, Democratic People's Republic of Korea, Egypt, Finland, France, Germany, Hungary, India, Indonesia, Iran (Islamic Republic of), Israel, Italy, Japan, Mexico, Netherlands, Norway, Pakistan, Peru, Poland, Romania, Republic of Korea, Russian Federation, Slovakia, South Africa, Spain, Sweden, Switzerland, Turkey, Ukraine, United Kingdom of Great Britain and Northern Ireland, United States of America, Viet Nam, Zaire.

Protocol to the Comprehensive Nuclear-Test-Ban Treaty

Part I
The International Monitoring System and International Data Centre Functions

A. General Provisions

1.   The International Monitoring System shall comprise monitoring facilities as set out in Article IV, paragraph 16, and respective means of communication.

2.   The monitoring facilities incorporated into the International Monitoring System shall consist of those facilities specified in Annex 1 to this Protocol. The International Monitoring System shall fulfil the technical and operational requirements specified in the relevant operational manuals.

3.   The Organization, in accordance with Article II, shall, in cooperation and consultation with the States Parties, with other States, and with international organizations as appropriate, establish and coordinate the operation and maintenance, and any future agreed modification or development of the International Monitoring System.

4.   In accordance with appropriate agreements or arrangements and procedures, a State Party or other State hosting or otherwise taking responsibility for International Monitoring System facilities and the Technical Secretariat shall agree and cooperate in establishing, operating, upgrading, financing, and maintaining monitoring facilities,

related certified laboratories and respective means of communication within areas under its jurisdiction or control or elsewhere in conformity with international law. Such cooperation shall be in accordance with the security and authentication requirements and technical specifications contained in the relevant operational manuals. Such a State shall give the Technical Secretariat authority to access a monitoring facility for checking equipment and communication links, and shall agree to make the necessary changes in the equipment and the operational procedures to meet agreed requirements. The Technical Secretariat shall provide to such States appropriate technical assistance as is deemed by the Executive Council to be required for the proper functioning of the facility as part of the International Monitoring System.

5.　Modalities for such cooperation between the Organization and States Parties or States hosting or otherwise taking responsibility for facilities of the International Monitoring System shall be set out in agreements or arrangements as appropriate in each case.

B.　Seismological Monitoring

6.　Each State Party undertakes to cooperate in an international exchange of seismological data to assist in the verification of compliance with this Treaty. This cooperation shall include the establishment and operation of a global network of primary and auxiliary seismological monitoring stations. These stations shall provide data in accordance with agreed procedures to the International Data Centre.

7.   The network of primary stations shall consist of the 50 stations specified in Table 1-A of Annex 1 to this Protocol. These stations shall fulfil the technical and operational requirements specified in the Operational Manual for Seismological Monitoring and the International Exchange of Seismological Data. Uninterrupted data from the primary stations shall be transmitted, directly or through a national data centre, on-line to the International Data Centre.

8.   To supplement the primary network, an auxiliary network of 120 stations shall provide information, directly or through a national data centre, to the International Data Centre upon request. The auxiliary stations to be used are listed in Table 1-B of Annex 1 to this Protocol. The auxiliary stations shall fulfil the technical and operational requirements specified in the Operational Manual for Seismological Monitoring and the International Exchange of Seismological Data. Data from the auxiliary stations may at any time be requested by the International Data Centre and shall be immediately available through on-line computer connections.

C.   Radionuclide Monitoring

9.   Each State Party undertakes to cooperate in an international exchange of data on radionuclides in the atmosphere to assist in the verification of compliance with this Treaty. This cooperation shall include the establishment and operation of a global network of radionuclide monitoring stations and certified laboratories. The network shall

provide data in accordance with agreed procedures to the International Data Centre.

10.   The network of stations to measure radionuclides in the atmosphere shall comprise an overall network of 80 stations, as specified in Table 2-A of Annex 1 to this Protocol. All stations shall be capable of monitoring for the presence of relevant particulate matter in the atmosphere. Forty of these stations shall also be capable of monitoring for the presence of relevant noble gases upon the entry into force of this Treaty. For this purpose the Conference, at its initial session, shall approve a recommendation by the Preparatory Commission as to which 40 stations from Table 2-A of Annex 1 to this Protocol shall be capable of noble gas monitoring. At its first regular annual session, the Conference shall consider and decide on a plan for implementing noble gas monitoring capability throughout the network. The Director-General shall prepare a report to the Conference on the modalities for such implementation. All monitoring stations shall fulfil the technical and operational requirements specified in the Operational Manual for Radionuclide Monitoring and the International Exchange of Radionuclide Data.

11.   The network of radionuclide monitoring stations shall be supported by laboratories, which shall be certified by the Technical Secretariat in accordance with the relevant operational manual for the performance, on contract to the Organization and on a fee-for-service basis, of the analysis of samples from radionuclide monitoring stations. Laboratories specified in Table 2-B of Annex 1 to this Protocol, and appropriately equipped, shall, as required,

also be drawn upon by the Technical Secretariat to perform additional analysis of samples from radionuclide monitoring stations. With the agreement of the Executive Council, further laboratories may be certified by the Technical Secretariat to perform the routine analysis of samples from manual monitoring stations where necessary. All certified laboratories shall provide the results of such analysis to the International Data Centre, and in so doing shall fulfil the technical and operational requirements specified in the Operational Manual on Radionuclide Monitoring and the International Exchange of Radionuclide Data.

D. Hydroacoustic Monitoring

12. Each State Party undertakes to cooperate in an international exchange of hydroacoustic data to assist in the verification of compliance with this Treaty. This cooperation shall include the establishment and operation of a global network of hydroacoustic monitoring stations. These stations shall provide data in accordance with agreed procedures to the International Data Centre.

13. The network of hydroacoustic stations shall consist of the stations specified in Table 3 of Annex 1 to this Protocol, and shall comprise an overall network of six hydrophone and five T-phase stations. These stations shall fulfil the technical and operational requirements specified in the Operational Manual for Hydroacoustic Monitoring and the International Exchange of Hydroacoustic Data.

E. Infrasound Monitoring

14. Each State Party undertakes to cooperate in an international exchange of infrasound data to assist in the verification of compliance with this Treaty. This cooperation shall include the establishment and operation of a global network of infrasound monitoring stations. These stations shall provide data in accordance with agreed procedures to the International Data Centre.

15. The network of infrasound stations shall consist of the stations specified in Table 4 of Annex 1 to this Protocol, and shall comprise an overall network of 60 stations. These stations shall fulfil the technical and operational requirements specified in the Operational Manual for Infrasound Monitoring and the International Exchange of Infrasound Data.

F. International Data Centre Functions

16. The International Data Centre shall receive, collect, process, analyse, report on and archive data from International Monitoring System facilities, including the results of analysis conducted at certified laboratories.

17. The procedures and standard event screening criteria to be used by the International Data Centre in carrying out its agreed functions, in particular for the production of standard reporting products and for the performance of a standard range of services for States Parties, shall be elaborated in the Operational Manual for the International Data Centre and shall be progressively developed. The procedures and criteria

developed initially by the Preparatory Commission shall be approved by the Conference at its initial session.

International Data Centre Standard Products

18. The International Data Centre shall apply on a routine basis automatic processing methods and interactive human analysis to raw International Monitoring System data in order to produce and archive standard International Data Centre products on behalf of all States Parties. These products shall be provided at no cost to States Parties and shall be without prejudice to final judgements with regard to the nature of any event, which shall remain the responsibility of States Parties, and shall include:

(a) Integrated lists of all signals detected by the International Monitoring System, as well as standard event lists and bulletins, including the values and associated uncertainties calculated for each event located by the International Data Centre, based on a set of standard parameters;

(b) Standard screened event bulletins that result from the application to each event by the International Data Centre of standard event screening criteria, making use of the characterisation parameters specified in Annex 2 to this Protocol, with the objective of characterizing, highlighting in the standard event bulletin, and thereby screening out, events considered to be consistent with natural phenomena or non-nuclear, man-made phenomena. The standard event bulletin shall indicate numerically for each event the degree to which that event meets or does not meet the event screening criteria. In applying standard event screening, the International Data Centre shall use both global and supplementary screening criteria to take account of regional variations where applicable. The International Data Centre shall progressively enhance its technical capabilities as experience is gained in the operation of the International Monitoring System;

(c) Executive summaries, which summarize the data acquired and archived by the International Data Centre, the products of the International Data Centre, and the performance and operational status of the International Monitoring System and International Data Centre; and

(d) Extracts or subsets of the standard International Data Centre products specified in sub-paragraphs (a) to (c), selected according to the request of an individual State Party.

19. The International Data Centre shall carry out, at no cost to States Parties, special studies to provide in-depth, technical review by expert analysis of data from the International Monitoring System, if requested by the Organization or by a State Party, to improve the estimated values for the standard signal and event parameters.

International Data Centre Services to States Parties

20. The International Data Centre shall provide States Parties with open, equal, timely and convenient access to all International Monitoring System data, raw or processed, all International Data Centre products, and all other

International Monitoring System data in the archive of the International Data Centre or, through the International Data Centre, of International Monitoring System facilities. The methods for supporting data access and the provision of data shall include the following services:

(a)   Automatic and regular forwarding to a State Party of the products of the International Data Centre or the selection by the State Party thereof, and, as requested, the selection by the State Party of International Monitoring System data;

(b)   The provision of the data or products generated in response to ad hoc requests by States Parties for the retrieval from the International Data Centre and International Monitoring System facility archives of data and products, including interactive electronic access to the International Data Centre database; and

(c)   Assisting individual States Parties, at their request and at no cost for reasonable efforts, with expert technical analysis of International Monitoring System data and other relevant data provided by the requesting State Party, in order to help the State Party concerned to identify the source of specific events. The output of any such technical analysis shall be considered a product of the requesting State Party, but shall be available to all States Parties.

The International Data Centre services specified in sub-paragraphs (a) and (b) shall be made available at no cost to each State Party. The volumes and formats of data shall be set out in the Operational Manual for the International Data Centre.

National Event Screening

21. The International Data Centre shall, if requested by a State Party, apply to any of its standard products, on a regular and automatic basis, national event screening criteria established by that State Party, and provide the results of such analysis to that State Party. This service shall be undertaken at no cost to the requesting State Party. The output of such national event screening processes shall be considered a product of the requesting State Party.

Technical Assistance

22. The International Data Centre shall, where required, provide technical assistance to individual States Parties:

(a) In formulating their requirements for selection and screening of data and products;

(b) By installing at the International Data Centre, at no cost to a requesting State Party for reasonable efforts, computer algorithms or software provided by that State Party to compute new signal and event parameters that are not included in the Operational Manual for the International Data Centre, the output being considered products of the requesting State Party; and

(c)   By assisting States Parties to develop the capability to receive, process and analyse International Monitoring System data at a national data centre.

23. The International Data Centre shall continuously monitor and report on the operational status of the International Monitoring System facilities, of communications links, and of its own processing systems. It shall provide immediate notification to those responsible should the operational performance of any component fail to meet agreed levels set out in the relevant operational manual.

Part II
On-Site Inspections

A.   General Provisions

1.   The procedures in this Part shall be implemented pursuant to the provisions for on-site inspections set out in Article IV.

2.   The on-site inspection shall be carried out in the area where the event that triggered the on-site inspection request occurred.

3.   The area of an on-site inspection shall be continuous and its size shall not exceed 1000 square kilometres. There shall be no linear distance greater than 50 kilometres in any direction.

4.   The duration of an on-site inspection shall not exceed 60 days from the date of the approval of the on-site inspection request in accordance with Article IV, paragraph 46, but may be extended by a maximum of 70 days in accordance with Article IV, paragraph 49.

5.   If the inspection area specified in the inspection mandate extends to the territory or other place under the jurisdiction or control of more than one State Party, the provisions on on-site inspections shall, as appropriate, apply to each of the States Parties to which the inspection area extends.

6.   In cases where the inspection area is under the jurisdiction or control of the inspected State Party but

is located on the territory of another State Party or where the access from the point of entry to the inspection area requires transit through the territory of a State Party other than the inspected State Party, the inspected State Party shall exercise the rights and fulfil the obligations concerning such inspections in accordance with this Protocol. In such a case, the State Party on whose territory the inspection area is located shall facilitate the inspection and shall provide for the necessary support to enable the inspection team to carry out its tasks in a timely and effective manner. States Parties through whose territory transit is required to reach the inspection area shall facilitate such transit.

7. In cases where the inspection area is under the jurisdiction or control of the inspected State Party but is located on the territory of a State not Party to this Treaty, the inspected State Party shall take all necessary measures to ensure that the inspection can be carried out in accordance with this Protocol. A State Party that has under its jurisdiction or control one or more areas on the territory of a State not Party to this Treaty shall take all necessary measures to ensure acceptance by the State on whose territory the inspection area is located of inspectors and inspection assistants designated to that State Party. If an inspected State Party is unable to ensure access, it shall demonstrate that it took all necessary measures to ensure access.

8. In cases where the inspection area is located on the territory of a State Party but is under the jurisdiction or control of a State not Party to this Treaty, the State

Party shall take all necessary measures required of an inspected State Party and a State Party on whose territory the inspection area is located, without prejudice to the rules and practices of international law, to ensure that the on-site inspection can be carried out in accordance with this Protocol. If the State Party is unable to ensure access to the inspection area, it shall demonstrate that it took all necessary measures to ensure access, without prejudice to the rules and practices of international law.

9. The size of the inspection team shall be kept to the minimum necessary for the proper fulfilment of the inspection mandate. The total number of members of the inspection team present on the territory of the inspected State Party at any given time, except during the conduct of drilling, shall not exceed 40 persons. No national of the requesting State Party or the inspected State Party shall be a member of the inspection team.

10. The Director-General shall determine the size of the inspection team and select its members from the list of inspectors and inspection assistants, taking into account the circumstances of a particular request.

11. The inspected State Party shall provide for or arrange the amenities necessary for the inspection team, such as communication means, interpretation services, transportation, working space, lodging, meals, and medical care.

12. The inspected State Party shall be reimbursed by the Organization, in a reasonably short period of time after conclusion of the inspection, for all expenses, including those mentioned in paragraphs 11 and 49, related to the stay and functional activities of the inspection team on the territory of the inspected State Party.

13. Procedures for the implementation of on-site inspections shall be detailed in the Operational Manual for On-Site Inspections.

B. Standing Arrangements

Designation of Inspectors and Inspection Assistants

14. An inspection team may consist of inspectors and inspection assistants. An on-site inspection shall only be carried out by qualified inspectors specially designated for this function. They may be assisted by specially designated inspection assistants, such as technical and administrative personnel, aircrew and interpreters.

15. Inspectors and inspection assistants shall be nominated for designation by the States Parties or, in case of staff of the Technical Secretariat, by the Director-General, on the basis of their expertise and experience relevant to the purpose and functions of on-site inspections. The nominees shall be approved in advance by the States Parties in accordance with paragraph 18.

16. Each State Party, no later than 30 days after the entry into force of this Treaty for it, shall notify the Director-General of the names, dates of birth, sex, ranks,

qualifications and professional experience of the persons proposed by the State Party for designation as inspectors and inspection assistants.

17. No later than 60 days after the entry into force of this Treaty, the Technical Secretariat shall communicate in writing to all States Parties an initial list of the names, nationalities, dates of birth, sex and ranks of the inspectors and inspection assistants proposed for designation by the Director-General and the States Parties, as well as a description of their qualifications and professional experience.

18. Each State Party shall immediately acknowledge receipt of the initial list of inspectors and inspection assistants proposed for designation. Any inspector or inspection assistant included in this list shall be regarded as accepted unless a State Party, no later than 30 days after acknowledgment of receipt of the list, declares its non-acceptance in writing. The State Party may include the reason for the objection. In the case of non-acceptance, the proposed inspector or inspection assistant shall not undertake or participate in on-site inspection activities on the territory or in any other place under the jurisdiction or control of the State Party that has declared its non-acceptance. The Technical Secretariat shall immediately confirm receipt of the notification of objection.

19. Whenever additions or changes to the list of inspectors and inspection assistants are proposed by the Director-General or a State Party, replacement inspectors and

inspection assistants shall be designated in the same manner as set forth with respect to the initial list. Each State Party shall promptly notify the Technical Secretariat if an inspector or inspection assistant nominated by it can no longer fulfil the duties of an inspector or inspection assistant.

20. The Technical Secretariat shall keep the list of inspectors and inspection assistants up to date and notify all States Parties of any additions or changes to the list.

21. A State Party requesting an on-site inspection may propose that an inspector from the list of inspectors and inspection assistants serve as its observer in accordance with Article IV, paragraph 61.

22. Subject to paragraph 23, a State Party shall have the right at any time to object to an inspector or inspection assistant who has already been accepted. It shall notify the Technical Secretariat of its objection in writing and may include the reason for the objection. Such objection shall come into effect 30 days after receipt of the notification by the Technical Secretariat. The Technical Secretariat shall immediately confirm receipt of the notification of the objection and inform the objecting and nominating States Parties of the date on which the inspector or inspection assistant shall cease to be designated for that State Party.

23. A State Party that has been notified of an inspection shall not seek the removal from the inspection team of any of the inspectors or inspection assistants named in the inspection mandate.

24. The number of inspectors and inspection assistants accepted by a State Party must be sufficient to allow for availability of appropriate numbers of inspectors and inspection assistants. If, in the opinion of the Director-General, the non-acceptance by a State Party of proposed inspectors or inspection assistants impedes the designation of a sufficient number of inspectors and inspection assistants or otherwise hampers the effective fulfilment of the purposes of an on-site inspection, the Director-General shall refer the issue to the Executive Council.

25. Each inspector included in the list of inspectors and inspection assistants shall receive relevant training. Such training shall be provided by the Technical Secretariat pursuant to the procedures specified in the Operational Manual for On-Site Inspections. The Technical Secretariat shall co-ordinate, in agreement with the States Parties, a schedule of training for the inspectors.

Privileges and Immunities

26. Following acceptance of the initial list of inspectors and inspection assistants as provided for in paragraph 18 or as subsequently altered in accordance with paragraph 19, each State Party shall be obliged to issue, in accordance with its national procedures and upon application by an inspector or inspection assistant, multiple entry/exit and/or transit visas and other relevant documents to enable each inspector and inspection assistant to enter and to remain on the territory of that State Party for the sole purpose of carrying out inspection activities. Each State Party shall issue the

necessary visa or travel documents for this purpose no later than 48 hours after receipt of the application or immediately upon arrival of the inspection team at the point of entry on the territory of the State Party. Such documents shall be valid for as long as is necessary to enable the inspector or inspection assistant to remain on the territory of the inspected State Party for the sole purpose of carrying out the inspection activities.

27. To exercise their functions effectively, members of the inspection team shall be accorded privileges and immunities as set forth in sub-paragraphs (a) to (i). Privileges and immunities shall be granted to members of the inspection team for the sake of this Treaty and not for the personal benefit of the individuals themselves. Such privileges and immunities shall be accorded to them for the entire period between arrival on and departure from the territory of the inspected State Party, and thereafter with respect to acts previously performed in the exercise of their official functions.

(a) The members of the inspection team shall be accorded the inviolability enjoyed by diplomatic agents pursuant to Article 29 of the Vienna Convention on Diplomatic Relations of 18 April 1961;

(b) The living quarters and office premises occupied by the inspection team carrying out inspection activities pursuant to this Treaty shall be accorded the inviolability and protection accorded to the premises of diplomatic agents pursuant to Article 30, paragraph 1, of the Vienna Convention on Diplomatic Relations;

(c) The papers and correspondence, including records, of the inspection team shall enjoy the inviolability accorded to all papers and correspondence of diplomatic agents pursuant to Article 30, paragraph 2, of the Vienna Convention on Diplomatic Relations. The inspection team shall have the right to use codes for their communications with the Technical Secretariat;

(d) Samples and approved equipment carried by members of the inspection team shall be inviolable subject to provisions contained in this Treaty and exempt from all customs duties. Hazardous samples shall be transported in accordance with relevant regulations;

(e) The members of the inspection team shall be accorded the immunities accorded to diplomatic agents pursuant to Article 31, paragraphs 1, 2 and 3, of the Vienna Convention on Diplomatic Relations;

(f) The members of the inspection team carrying out prescribed activities pursuant to this Treaty shall be accorded the exemption from dues and taxes accorded to diplomatic agents pursuant to Article 34 of the Vienna Convention on Diplomatic Relations;

(g) The members of the inspection team shall be permitted to bring into the territory of the inspected State Party, without payment of any customs duties or related charges, articles for personal use, with the exception of articles the import or export of which is prohibited by law or controlled by quarantine regulations;

(h) The members of the inspection team shall be accorded the same currency and exchange facilities as are accorded to representatives of foreign Governments on temporary official missions; and

(i) The members of the inspection team shall not engage in any professional or commercial activity for personal profit on the territory of the inspected State Party.

28. When transiting the territory of States Parties other than the inspected State Party, the members of the inspection team shall be accorded the privileges and immunities enjoyed by diplomatic agents pursuant to Article 40, paragraph 1, of the Vienna Convention on Diplomatic Relations. Papers and correspondence, including records, and samples and approved equipment carried by them, shall be accorded the privileges and immunities set forth in paragraph 27 (c) and (d).

29. Without prejudice to their privileges and immunities the members of the inspection team shall be obliged to respect the laws and regulations of the inspected State Party and, to the extent that is consistent with the inspection mandate, shall be obliged not to interfere in the internal affairs of that State. If the inspected State Party considers that there has been an abuse of privileges and immunities specified in this Protocol, consultations shall be held between the State

Party and the Director-General to determine whether such an abuse has occurred and, if so determined, to prevent a repetition of such an abuse.

30. The immunity from jurisdiction of members of the inspection team may be waived by the Director-General in those cases when the Director-General is of the opinion that immunity would impede the course of justice and that it can be waived without prejudice to the implementation of the provisions of this Treaty. Waiver must always be express.

31. Observers shall be accorded the same privileges and immunities accorded to members of the inspection team pursuant to this section, except for those accorded pursuant to paragraph 27 (d).

Points of Entry

32. Each State Party shall designate its points of entry and shall supply the required information to the Technical Secretariat no later than 30 days after this Treaty enters into force for it. These points of entry shall be such that the inspection team can reach any inspection area from at least one point of entry within 24 hours. Locations of points of entry shall be provided to all States Parties by the Technical Secretariat. Points of entry may also serve as points of exit.

33. Each State Party may change its points of entry by giving notice of such change to the Technical Secretariat. Changes shall become effective 30 days after the Technical Secretariat receives such notification, to allow appropriate notification to all States Parties.

34. If the Technical Secretariat considers that there are insufficient points of entry for the timely conduct of inspections or that changes to the points of entry proposed by a State Party would hamper such timely conduct of inspections, it shall enter into consultations with the State Party concerned to resolve the problem.

Arrangements for Use of Non-Scheduled Aircraft

35. Where timely travel to the point of entry is not feasible using scheduled commercial flights, an inspection team may utilize non-scheduled aircraft. No later than 30 days after this Treaty enters into force for it, each State Party shall inform the Technical Secretariat of the standing diplomatic clearance number for non-scheduled aircraft transporting an inspection team and equipment necessary for inspection. Aircraft routings shall be along established international airways that are agreed upon between the State Party and the Technical Secretariat as the basis for such diplomatic clearance.

Approved Inspection Equipment

36. The Conference, at its initial session, shall consider and approve a list of equipment for use during on-site inspections. Each State Party may submit proposals for the inclusion of equipment in the list. Specifications for the use of the equipment, as detailed in the Operational Manual for On-Site Inspections, shall take account of safety and confidentiality considerations where such equipment is likely to be used.

37. The equipment for use during on-site inspections shall consist of core equipment for the inspection activities and techniques specified in paragraph 69 and auxiliary equipment necessary for the effective and timely conduct of on-site inspections.

38. The Technical Secretariat shall ensure that all types of approved equipment are available for on-site inspections when required. When required for an on-site inspection, the Technical Secretariat shall duly certify that the equipment has been calibrated, maintained and protected. To facilitate the checking of the equipment at the point of entry by the inspected State Party, the Technical Secretariat shall provide documentation and attach seals to authenticate the certification.

39. Any permanently held equipment shall be in the custody of the Technical Secretariat. The Technical Secretariat shall be responsible for the maintenance and calibration of such equipment.

40. As appropriate, the Technical Secretariat shall make arrangements with States Parties to provide equipment mentioned in the list. Such States Parties shall be responsible for the maintenance and calibration of such equipment.

C.   On-Site Inspection Request, Inspection Mandate and Notification of Inspection

On-Site Inspection Request

41. Pursuant to Article IV, paragraph 37, the on-site inspection request shall contain at least the following information:

   (a) The estimated geographical and vertical co-ordinates of the location of the event that triggered the request with an indication of the possible margin of error;

   (b) The proposed boundaries of the area to be inspected, specified on a map and in accordance with paragraphs 2 and 3;

   (c) The State Party or States Parties to be inspected or an indication that the area to be inspected or part thereof is beyond the jurisdiction or control of any State;

   (d) The probable environment of the event that triggered the request;

   (e) The estimated time of the event that triggered the request, with an indication of the possible margin of error;

   (f) All data upon which the request is based;

   (g) The personal details of the proposed observer, if any; and

   (h) The results of a consultation and clarification process in accordance with Article IV, or an explanation, if relevant, of the reasons why such a consultation and clarification process has not been carried out.

Inspection Mandate

42.   The mandate for an on-site inspection shall contain:

(a)   The decision of the Executive Council on the on-site inspection request;

(b)   The name of the State Party or States Parties to be inspected or an indication that the inspection area or part thereof is beyond the jurisdiction or control of any State;

(c)   The location and boundaries of the inspection area specified on a map, taking into account all information on which the request was based and all other available technical information, in consultation with the requesting State Party;

(d)   The planned types of activity of the inspection team in the inspection area;

(e)   The point of entry to be used by the inspection team;

(f)   Any transit or basing points, as appropriate;

(g)   The name of the head of the inspection team;

(h)   The names of members of the inspection team;

(i)   The name of the proposed observer, if any; and

(j)   The list of equipment to be used in the inspection area.

If a decision by the Executive Council pursuant to Article IV, paragraphs 46 to 49, necessitates a modification of the inspection mandate, the Director-General may update the mandate with respect to sub-paragraphs (d), (h) and (j), as appropriate. The Director-General shall immediately notify the inspected State Party of any such modification.

Notification of Inspection

43.   The notification made by the Director-General pursuant to Article IV, paragraph 55 shall include the following information:

(a)   The inspection mandate;

(b)   The date and estimated time of arrival of the inspection team at the point of entry;

(c)   The means of arrival at the point of entry;

(d)   If appropriate, the standing diplomatic clearance number for non-scheduled aircraft; and

(e)   A list of any equipment which the Director-General requests the inspected State Party to make available to the inspection team for use in the inspection area.

44. The inspected State Party shall acknowledge receipt of the notification by the Director-General no later than 12 hours after having received the notification.

D. Pre-Inspection Activities

Entry into the Territory of the Inspected State Party, Activities at the Point of Entry and Transfer to the Inspection Area

45. The inspected State Party that has been notified of the arrival of the inspection team shall ensure the immediate entry of the inspection team into its territory.

46. When a non-scheduled aircraft is used for travel to the point of entry, the Technical Secretariat shall provide the inspected State Party with a flight plan, through the National Authority, for the flight of the aircraft from the last airfield prior to entering the airspace of that State Party to the point of entry, no less than six hours before the scheduled departure time from that airfield. Such a plan shall be filed in accordance with the procedures of the International Civil Aviation Organization applicable to civil aircraft. The Technical Secretariat shall include in the remarks section of the flight plan the standing diplomatic clearance number and the appropriate notation identifying the aircraft as an inspection aircraft. If a military aircraft is used, the Technical Secretariat shall request prior authorization from the inspected State Party to enter its airspace.

47. No less than three hours before the scheduled departure of the inspection team from the last airfield prior to entering

the airspace of the inspected State Party, the inspected State Party shall ensure that the flight plan filed in accordance with paragraph 46 is approved, so that the inspection team may arrive at the point of entry by the estimated arrival time.

48. Where necessary, the head of the inspection team and the representative of the inspected State Party shall agree on a basing point and a flight plan from the point of entry to the basing point and, if necessary, to the inspection area.

49. The inspected State Party shall provide for or arrange parking, security protection, servicing and fuel as required by the Technical Secretariat for the aircraft of the inspection team at the point of entry and, where necessary, at the basing point and at the inspection area. Such aircraft shall not be liable for landing fees, departure tax, and similar charges. This paragraph shall also apply to aircraft used for overflight during the on-site inspection.

50. Subject to paragraph 51, there shall be no restriction by the inspected State Party on the inspection team bringing approved equipment that is in conformity with the inspection mandate into the territory of that State Party, or on its use in accordance with the provisions of the Treaty and this Protocol.

51. The inspected State Party shall have the right, without prejudice to the time-frame specified in paragraph 54, to check in the presence of inspection team members at the point of entry that the equipment has been approved and certified in accordance with paragraph 38. The inspected

State Party may exclude equipment that is not in conformity with the inspection mandate or that has not been approved and certified in accordance with paragraph 38.

52. Immediately upon arrival at the point of entry and without prejudice to the time-frame specified in paragraph 54, the head of the inspection team shall present to the representative of the inspected State Party the inspection mandate and an initial inspection plan prepared by the inspection team specifying the activities to be carried out by it. The inspection team shall be briefed by representatives of the inspected State Party with the aid of maps and other documentation as appropriate. The briefing shall include relevant natural terrain features, safety and confidentiality issues, and logistical arrangements for the inspection. The inspected State Party may indicate locations within the inspection area that, in its view, are not related to the purpose of the inspection.

53. After the pre-inspection briefing, the inspection team shall, as appropriate, modify the initial inspection plan, taking into account any comments by the inspected State Party. The modified inspection plan shall be made available to the representative of the inspected State Party.

54. The inspected State Party shall do everything in its power to provide assistance and to ensure the safe conduct of the inspection team, the approved equipment specified in paragraphs 50 and 51 and baggage from the point of entry to the inspection area no later than 36 hours after arrival at

the point of entry, if no other timing has been agreed upon within the time-frame specified in paragraph 57.

55. To confirm that the area to which the inspection team has been transported corresponds to the inspection area specified in the inspection mandate, the inspection team shall have the right to use approved location-finding equipment. The inspected State Party shall assist the inspection team in this task.

E. Conduct of Inspections

General Rules

56. The inspection team shall discharge its functions in accordance with the provisions of the Treaty and this Protocol.

57. The inspection team shall begin its inspection activities in the inspection area as soon as possible, but in no case later than 72 hours after arrival at the point of entry.

58. The activities of the inspection team shall be so arranged as to ensure the timely and effective discharge of its functions and the least possible inconvenience to the inspected State Party and disturbance to the inspection area.

59. In cases where the inspected State Party has been requested, pursuant to paragraph 43 (e) or in the course of the inspection, to make available any equipment for use by the inspection team in the inspection area, the inspected State Party shall comply with the request to the extent it can.

60. During the on-site inspection the inspection team shall have, inter alia:

(a) The right to determine how the inspection will proceed, consistent with the inspection mandate and taking into account any steps taken by the inspected State Party consistent with the provisions on managed access;

(b) The right to modify the inspection plan, as necessary, to ensure the effective execution of the inspection;

(c) The obligation to take into account the recommendations and suggested modifications by the inspected State Party to the inspection plan;

(d) The right to request clarifications in connection with ambiguities that may arise during the inspection;

(e) The obligation to use only those techniques specified in paragraph 69 and to refrain from activities that are not relevant to the purpose of the inspection. The team shall collect and document such facts as are related to the purpose of the inspection, but shall neither seek nor document information that is clearly unrelated thereto. Any material collected and subsequently found not to be relevant shall be returned to the inspected State Party;

(f) The obligation to take into account and include in its report data and explanations on the nature of the event that triggered the request, provided by the inspected State Party from the national monitoring networks of the inspected State Party and from other sources;

(g)   The obligation to provide the inspected State Party, at its request, with copies of the information and data collected in the inspection area; and

(h)   The obligation to respect the confidentiality and the safety and health regulations of the inspected State Party.

61.   During the on-site inspection the inspected State Party shall have, inter alia:

(a)   The right to make recommendations at any time to the inspection team regarding possible modification of the inspection plan;

(b)   The right and the obligation to provide a representative to liaise with the inspection team;

(c)   The right to have representatives accompany the inspection team during the performance of its duties and observe all inspection activities carried out by the inspection team. This shall not delay or otherwise hinder the inspection team in the exercise of its functions;

(d)   The right to provide additional information and to request the collection and documentation of additional facts it believes are relevant to the inspection;

(e)   The right to examine all photographic and measurement products as well as samples and to retain any photographs or parts thereof showing sensitive sites not related to the purpose of the inspection. The inspected

State Party shall have the right to receive duplicate copies of all photographic and measurement products. The inspected State Party shall have the right to retain photographic originals and first-generation photographic products and to put photographs or parts thereof under joint seal within its territory. The inspected State Party shall have the right to provide its own camera operator to take still/ video photographs as requested by the inspection team. Otherwise, these functions shall be performed by members of the inspection team;

(f) The right to provide the inspection team, from its national monitoring networks and from other sources, with data and explanations on the nature of the event that triggered the request; and

(g) The obligation to provide the inspection team with such clarification as may be necessary to resolve any ambiguities that arise during the inspection.

Communications

62. The members of the inspection team shall have the right at all times during the on-site inspection to communicate with each other and with the Technical Secretariat. For this purpose they may use their own duly approved and certified equipment with the consent of the inspected State Party, to the extent that the inspected State Party does not provide them with access to other telecommunications.

Observer

63. In accordance with Article IV, paragraph 61, the requesting State Party shall liaise with the Technical Secretariat to co-ordinate the arrival of the observer at the same point of entry or basing point as the inspection team within a reasonable period of the arrival of the inspection team.

64. The observer shall have the right throughout the inspection to be in communication with the embassy of the requesting State Party located in the inspected State Party or, in the case of absence of an embassy, with the requesting State Party itself.

65. The observer shall have the right to arrive at the inspection area and to have access to and within the inspection area as granted by the inspected State Party.

66. The observer shall have the right to make recommendations to the inspection team throughout the inspection.

67. Throughout the inspection, the inspection team shall keep the observer informed about the conduct of the inspection and the findings.

68. Throughout the inspection, the inspected State Party shall provide or arrange for the amenities necessary for the observer similar to those enjoyed by the inspection team as described in paragraph 11. All costs in connection with the

stay of the observer on the territory of the inspected State Party shall be borne by the requesting State Party.

Inspection Activities and Techniques

69. The following inspection activities may be conducted and techniques used, in accordance with the provisions on managed access, on collection, handling and analysis of samples, and on overflights:

(a) Position finding from the air and at the surface to confirm the boundaries of the inspection area and establish co-ordinates of locations therein, in support of the inspection activities;

(b) Visual observation, video and still photography and multi-spectral imaging, including infrared measurements, at and below the surface, and from the air, to search for anomalies or artifacts;

(c) Measurement of levels of radioactivity above, at and below the surface, using gamma radiation monitoring and energy resolution analysis from the air, and at or under the surface, to search for and identify radiation anomalies;

(d) Environmental sampling and analysis of solids, liquids and gases from above, at and below the surface to detect anomalies;

(e) Passive seismological monitoring for aftershocks to localize the search area and facilitate determination of the nature of an event;

(f)   Resonance seismometry and active seismic surveys to search for and locate underground anomalies, including cavities and rubble zones;

(g)   Magnetic and gravitational field mapping, ground penetrating radar and electrical conductivity measurements at the surface and from the air, as appropriate, to detect anomalies or artifacts; and

(h)   Drilling to obtain radioactive samples.

70. Up to 25 days after the approval of the on-site inspection in accordance with Article IV, paragraph 46, the inspection team shall have the right to conduct any of the activities and use any of the techniques listed in paragraph 69 (a) to (e). Following the approval of the continuation of the inspection in accordance with Article IV, paragraph 47, the inspection team shall have the right to conduct any of the activities and use any of the techniques listed in paragraph 69 (a) to (g). The inspection team shall only conduct drilling after the approval of the Executive Council in accordance with Article IV, paragraph 48. If the inspection team requests an extension of the inspection duration in accordance with Article IV, paragraph 49, it shall indicate in its request which of the activities and techniques listed in paragraph 69 it intends to carry out in order to be able to fulfil its mandate.

Overflights

71. The inspection team shall have the right to conduct an overflight over the inspection area during the on-site inspection for the purposes of providing the inspection team

with a general orientation of the inspection area, narrowing down and optimizing the locations for ground-based inspection and facilitating the collection of factual evidence, using equipment specified in paragraph 79.

72. The overflight shall be conducted as soon as practically possible. The total duration of the overflight over the inspection area shall be no more than 12 hours.

73. Additional overflights using equipment specified in paragraphs 79 and 80 may be conducted subject to the agreement of the inspected State Party.

74. The area to be covered by overflights shall not extend beyond the inspection area.

75. The inspected State Party shall have the right to impose restrictions or, in exceptional cases and with reasonable justification, prohibitions on the overflight of sensitive sites not related to the purpose of the inspection. Restrictions may relate to the flight altitude, the number of passes and circling, the duration of hovering, the type of aircraft, the number of inspectors on board, and the type of measurements or observations. If the inspection team considers that the restrictions or prohibitions on the overflight of sensitive sites may impede the fulfilment of its mandate, the inspected State Party shall make every reasonable effort to provide alternative means of inspection.

76. Overflights shall be conducted according to a flight plan duly filed and approved in accordance with aviation rules

and regulations of the inspected State Party. Flight safety regulations of the inspected State Party shall be strictly observed throughout all flying operations.

77. During overflights landing should normally be authorized only for purposes of staging or refuelling.

78. Overflights shall be conducted at altitudes as requested by the inspection team consistent with the activities to be conducted, visibility conditions, as well as the aviation and the safety regulations of the inspected State Party and its right to protect sensitive information not related to the purposes of the inspection. Overflights shall be conducted up to a maximum altitude of 1,500 metres above the surface.

79. For the overflight conducted pursuant to paragraphs 71 and 72, the following equipment may be used on board the aircraft:

(a)   Field glasses;

(b)   Passive location-finding equipment;

(c)   Video cameras; and

(d)   Hand-held still cameras.

80. For any additional overflights conducted pursuant to paragraph 73, inspectors on board the aircraft may also use portable, easily installed equipment for:

(a)   Multi-spectral (including infrared) imagery;

(b) Gamma spectroscopy; and

(c) Magnetic field mapping.

81. Overflights shall be conducted with a relatively slow fixed or rotary wing aircraft. The aircraft shall afford a broad, unobstructed view of the surface below.

82. The inspected State Party shall have the right to provide its own aircraft, pre-equipped as appropriate in accordance with the technical requirements of the relevant operational manual, and crew. Otherwise, the aircraft shall be provided or rented by the Technical Secretariat.

83. If the aircraft is provided or rented by the Technical Secretariat, the inspected State Party shall have the right to check the aircraft to ensure that it is equipped with approved inspection equipment. Such checking shall be completed within the time-frame specified in paragraph 57.

84. Personnel on board the aircraft shall consist of:

(a) The minimum number of flight crew consistent with the safe operation of the aircraft;

(b) Up to four members of the inspection team;

(c) Up to two representatives of the inspected State Party;

(d) An observer, if any, subject to the agreement of the inspected State Party; and

(e) An interpreter, if necessary.

85. Procedures for the implementation of overflights shall be detailed in the Operational Manual for On-Site Inspections.

Managed Access

86. The inspection team shall have the right to access the inspection area in accordance with the provisions of the Treaty and this Protocol.

87. The inspected State Party shall provide access within the inspection area in accordance with the time-frame specified in paragraph 57.

88. Pursuant to Article IV, paragraph 57 and paragraph 86 above, the rights and obligations of the inspected State Party shall include:

(a) The right to take measures to protect sensitive installations and locations in accordance with this Protocol;

(b) The obligation, when access is restricted within the inspection area, to make every reasonable effort to satisfy the requirements of the inspection mandate through alternative means. Resolving any questions regarding one or more aspects of the inspection shall not delay or interfere with the conduct of the inspection team of other aspects of the inspection; and

(c)   The right to make the final decision regarding any access of the inspection team, taking into account its obligations under this Treaty and the provisions on managed access.

89.   Pursuant to Article IV, paragraph 57 (b) and paragraph 88 (a) above, the inspected State Party shall have the right throughout the inspection area to take measures to protect sensitive installations and locations and to prevent disclosure of confidential information not related to the purpose of the inspection. Such measures may include, inter alia:

(a)   Shrouding of sensitive displays, stores, and equipment;

(b)   Restricting measurements of radionuclide activity and nuclear radiation to determining the presence or absence of those types and energies of radiation relevant to the purpose of the inspection;

(c)   Restricting the taking of or analysing of samples to determining the presence or absence of radioactive or other products relevant to the purpose of the inspection;

(d)   Managing access to buildings and other structures in accordance with paragraphs 90 and 91; and

(e)   Declaring restricted-access sites in accordance with paragraphs 92 to 96.

90. Access to buildings and other structures shall be deferred until after the approval of the continuation of the on-site inspection in accordance with Article IV, paragraph 47, except for access to buildings and other structures housing the entrance to a mine, other excavations, or caverns of large volume not otherwise accessible. For such buildings and structures, the inspection team shall have the right only of transit, as directed by the inspected State Party, in order to enter such mines, caverns or other excavations.

91. If, following the approval of the continuation of the inspection in accordance with Article IV, paragraph 47, the inspection team demonstrates credibly to the inspected State Party that access to buildings and other structures is necessary to fulfil the inspection mandate and that the necessary activities authorized in the mandate could not be carried out from the outside, the inspection team shall have the right to gain access to such buildings or other structures. The head of the inspection team shall request access to a specific building or structure indicating the purpose of such access, the specific number of inspectors, as well as the intended activities. The modalities for access shall be subject to negotiation between the inspection team and the inspected State Party. The inspected State Party shall have the right to impose restrictions or, in exceptional cases and with reasonable justification, prohibitions, on the access to buildings and other structures.

92. When restricted-access sites are declared pursuant to paragraph 89 (e), each such site shall be no larger than four square kilometres. The inspected State Party has the right

to declare up to 50 square kilometres of restricted-access sites. If more than one restricted-access site is declared, each such site shall be separated from any other such site by a minimum distance of 20 metres. Each restricted-access site shall have clearly defined and accessible boundaries.

93.   The size, location, and boundaries of restricted-access sites shall be presented to the head of the inspection team no later than the time that the inspection team seeks access to a location that contains all or part of such a site.

94.   The inspection team shall have the right to place equipment and take other steps necessary to conduct its inspection up to the boundary of a restricted-access site.

95.   The inspection team shall be permitted to observe visually all open places within the restricted-access site from the boundary of the site.

96.   The inspection team shall make every reasonable effort to fulfil the inspection mandate outside the declared restricted-access sites prior to requesting access to such sites. If at any time the inspection team demonstrates credibly to the inspected State Party that the necessary activities authorized in the mandate could not be carried out from the outside and that access to a restricted-access site is necessary to fulfil the mandate, some members of the inspection team shall be granted access to accomplish specific tasks within the site. The inspected State Party shall have the right to shroud or otherwise protect sensitive equipment, objects and materials not related to the purpose of the inspection.

The number of inspectors shall be kept to the minimum necessary to complete the tasks related to the inspection. The modalities for such access shall be subject to negotiation between the inspection team and the inspected State Party.

Collection, Handling and Analysis of Samples

97. Subject to paragraphs 86 to 96 and 98 to 100, the inspection team shall have the right to collect and remove relevant samples from the inspection area.

98. Whenever possible, the inspection team shall analyse samples on-site. Representatives of the inspected State Party shall have the right to be present when samples are analysed on-site. At the request of the inspection team, the inspected State Party shall, in accordance with agreed procedures, provide assistance for the analysis of samples on-site. The inspection team shall have the right to transfer samples for off-site analysis at laboratories designated by the Organization only if it demonstrates that the necessary sample analysis can not be performed on-site.

99. The inspected State Party shall have the right to retain portions of all samples collected when these samples are analysed and may take duplicate samples.

100. The inspected State Party shall have the right to request that any unused samples or portions thereof be returned.

101. The designated laboratories shall conduct chemical and physical analysis of the samples transferred for off-site

analysis. Details of such analysis shall be elaborated in the Operational Manual for On-Site Inspections.

102. The Director-General shall have the primary responsibility for the security, integrity and preservation of samples and for ensuring that the confidentiality of samples transferred for off-site analysis is protected. The Director-General shall do so in accordance with procedures contained in the Operational Manual for On-Site Inspections. The Director-General shall, in any case:

(a) Establish a stringent regime governing the collection, handling, transport and analysis of samples;

(b) Certify the laboratories designated to perform different types of analysis;

(c) Oversee the standardization of equipment and procedures at these designated laboratories and of mobile analytical equipment and procedures;

(d) Monitor quality control and overall standards in relation to the certification of these laboratories and in relation to mobile equipment and procedures; and

(e) Select from among the designated laboratories those which shall perform analytical or other functions in relation to specific investigations.

103. When off-site analysis is to be performed, samples shall be analysed in at least two designated laboratories. The Technical Secretariat shall ensure the expeditious processing

of the analysis. The samples shall be accounted for by the Technical Secretariat and any unused samples or portions thereof shall be returned to the Technical Secretariat.

104. The Technical Secretariat shall compile the results of the laboratory analysis of samples relevant to the purpose of the inspection. Pursuant to Article IV, paragraph 63, the Director-General shall transmit any such results promptly to the inspected State Party for comments and thereafter to the Executive Council and to all other States Parties and shall include detailed information concerning the equipment and methodology employed by the designated laboratories.

Conduct of Inspections in Areas beyond the Jurisdiction or Control of Any State

105. In case of an on-site inspection in an area beyond the jurisdiction or control of any State, the Director-General shall consult with the appropriate States Parties and agree on any transit or basing points to facilitate a speedy arrival of the inspection team in the inspection area.

106. The States Parties on whose territory transit or basing points are located shall, as far as possible, assist in facilitating the inspection, including transporting the inspection team, its baggage and equipment to the inspection area, as well as providing the relevant amenities specified in paragraph 11. The Organization shall reimburse assisting States Parties for all costs incurred.

107. Subject to the approval of the Executive Council, the Director-General may negotiate standing arrangements

with States Parties to facilitate assistance in the event of an on-site inspection in an area beyond the jurisdiction or control of any State.

108. In cases where one or more States Parties have conducted an investigation of an ambiguous event in an area beyond the jurisdiction or control of any State before a request is made for an on-site inspection in that area, any results of such investigation may be taken into account by the Executive Council in its deliberations pursuant to Article IV.

Post-Inspection Procedures

109. Upon conclusion of the inspection, the inspection team shall meet with the representative of the inspected State Party to review the preliminary findings of the inspection team and to clarify any ambiguities. The inspection team shall provide the representative of the inspected State Party with its preliminary findings in written form according to a standardized format, together with a list of any samples and other material taken from the inspection area pursuant to paragraph 98. The document shall be signed by the head of the inspection team. In order to indicate that he or she has taken notice of the contents of the document, the representative of the inspected State Party shall countersign the document. The meeting shall be completed no later than 24 hours after the conclusion of the inspection.

Departure

110. Upon completion of the post-inspection procedures, the inspection team and the observer shall leave, as soon as possible, the territory of the inspected State Party. The inspected State Party shall do everything in its power to provide assistance and to ensure the safe conduct of the inspection team, equipment and baggage to the point of exit. Unless agreed otherwise by the inspected State Party and the inspection team, the point of exit used shall be the same as the point of entry.

Part III
Confidence-Building Measures

1.   Pursuant to Article IV, paragraph 68, each State Party shall, on a voluntary basis, provide the Technical Secretariat with notification of any chemical explosion using 300 tonnes or greater of TNT-equivalent blasting material detonated as a single explosion anywhere on its territory, or at any place under its jurisdiction or control. If possible, such notification shall be provided in advance. Such notification shall include details on location, time, quantity and type of explosive used, as well as on the configuration and intended purpose of the blast.

2.   Each State Party shall, on a voluntary basis, as soon as possible after the entry into force of this Treaty provide to the Technical Secretariat, and at annual intervals thereafter update, information related to its national use of all other chemical explosions greater than 300 tonnes TNT-equivalent. In particular, the State Party shall seek to advise:

(a)   The geographic locations of sites where the explosions originate;

(b)   The nature of activities producing them and the general profile and frequency of such explosions;

(c)   Any other relevant detail, if available; and

to assist the Technical Secretariat in clarifying the origins of any such event detected by the International Monitoring System.

3. A State Party may, on a voluntary and mutually-acceptable basis, invite representatives of the Technical Secretariat or of other States Parties to visit sites within its territory referred to in paragraphs 1 and 2.

4. For the purpose of calibrating the International Monitoring System, States Parties may liaise with the Technical Secretariat to carry out chemical calibration explosions or to provide relevant information on chemical explosions planned for other purposes.

Annex 1 to the Protocol

Table 1-A
List of Seismological Stations Comprising the Primary Network

	State responsible for station	Location	Latitude	Longitude	Type
1	Argentina	PLCA Paso Flores	40.7 S	70.6 W	3–C
2	Australia	WRA Warramunga, NT	19.9 S	134.3 E	array
3	Australia	ASAR Alice Springs, NT	23.7 S	133.9 E	array
4	Australia	STKA Stephens Creek, SA	31.9 S	141.6 E	3–C
5	Australia	MAW Mawson, Antarctica	67.6 S	62.9 E	3–C
6	Bolivia	LPAZ La Paz	16.3 S	68.1 W	3–C
7	Brazil	BDFB Brasilia	15.6 S	48.0 W	3–C
8	Canada	ULMC Lac du Bonnet, Man.	50.2 N	95.9 W	3–C
9	Canada	YKAC Yellowknife, N.W.T.	62.5 N	114.6 W	array
10	Canada	SCH Schefferville, Quebec	54.8 N	66.8 W	3–C
11	Central African Republic	BGCA Bangui	05.2 N	18.4 E	3–C
12	China	HAI Hailar	49.3 N	119.7 E	3–C > array
13	China	LZH Lanzhou	36.1 N	103.8 E	3–C > array
14	Colombia	XSA El Rosal	04.9 N	74.3 W	3–C

	State responsible for station	Location	Latitude	Longitude	Type
15	Côte d'Ivoire	DBIC Dimbroko	06.7 N	04.9 W	3–C
16	Egypt	LXEG Luxor	26.0 N	33.0 E	array
17	Finland	FINES Lahti	61.4 N	26.1 E	array
18	France	PPT Tahiti	17.6 S	149.6 W	3–C
19	Germany	GEC2 Freyung	48.9 N	13.7 E	array
20	To be determined	To be determined	To be determined	To be determined	To be determined
21	Iran (Islamic Republic of)	THR Tehran	35.8 N	51.4 E	3–C
22	Japan	MJAR Matsushiro	36.5 N	138.2 E	array
23	Kazakhstan	MAK Makanchi	46.8 N	82.0 E	array
24	Kenya	KMBO Kilimambogo	01.1 S	37.2 E	3–C
25	Mongolia	JAVM Javhlant	48.0 N	106.8 E	3–C > array
26	Niger	New Site	to be determined	to be determined	3–C > array
27	Norway	NAO Hamar	60.8 N	10.8 E	array
28	Norway	ARAO Karasjok	69.5 N	25.5 E	array
29	Pakistan	PRPK Pari	33.7 N	73.3 E	array
30	Paraguay	CPUP Villa Florida	26.3 S	57.3 W	3–C
31	Republic of Korea	KSRS Wonju	37.5 N	127.9 E	array

	State responsible for station	Location	Latitude	Longitude	Type
32	Russian Federation	KBZ Khabaz	43.7 N	42.9 E	3–C
33	Russian Federation	ZAL Zalesovo	53.9 N	84.8 E	3–C > array
34	Russian Federation	NRI Norilsk	69.0 N	88.0 E	3–C
35	Russian Federation	PDY Peleduy	59.6 N	112.6 E	3–C > array
36	Russian Federation	PET Petropavlovsk– Kamchatskiy	53.1 N	157.8 E	3–C > array
37	Russian Federation	USK Ussuriysk	44.2 N	132.0 E	3–C > array
38	Saudi Arabia	New Site	to be deter- mined	to be deter- mined	array
39	South Africa	BOSA Boshof	28.6 S	25.6 E	3–C
40	Spain	ESDC Sonseca	39.7 N	04.0 W	array
41	Thailand	CMTO Chiang Mai	18.8 N	99.0 E	array
42	Tunisia	THA Thala	35.6 N	08.7 E	3–C
43	Turkey	BRTR Belbashi The array is subject to relocation at Keskin	39.9 N	32.8 E	array
44	Turkmenistan	GEYT Alibeck	37.9 N	58.1 E	array
45	Ukraine	AKASG Malin	50.4 N	29.1 E	array
46	United States of America	LJTX Lajitas, TX	29.3 N	103.7 W	array
47	United States of America	MNV Mina, NV	38.4 N	118.2 W	array

	State responsible for station	Location	Latitude	Longitude	Type
48	United States of America	PIWY Pinedale, WY	42.8 N	109.6 W	array
49	United States of America	ELAK Eielson, AK	64.8 N	146.9 W	array
50	United States of America	VNDA Vanda, Antarctica	77.5 S	161.9 E	3–C

Key: 3–C > array: Indicates that the site could start operations in the International Monitoring System as a three-component station and be upgraded to an array at a later time.

Table 1–B
List of Seismological Stations Comprising
the Auxiliary Network

	State responsible for station	Location	Latitude	Longitude	Type
1	Argentina	CFA Coronel Fontana	31.6 S	68.2 W	3–C
2	Argentina	USHA Ushuaia	55.0 S	68.0 W	3–C
3	Armenia	GNI Garni	40.1 N	44.7 E	3–C
4	Australia	CTA Charters Towers, QLD	20.1 S	146.3 E	3–C
5	Australia	FITZ Fitzroy Crossing, WA	18.1 S	125.6 E	3–C
6	Australia	NWAO Narrogin, WA	32.9 S	117.2 E	3–C
7	Bangladesh	CHT Chittagong	22.4 N	91.8 E	3–C
8	Bolivia	SIV San Ignacio	16.0 S	61.1 W	3–C
9	Botswana	LBTB Lobatse	25.0 S	25.6 E	3–C
10	Brazil	PTGA Pitinga	0.7 S	60.0 W	3–C
11	Brazil	RGNB Rio Grande do Norte	6.9 S	37.0 W	3–C
12	Canada	FRB Iqaluit, N.W.T.	63.7 N	68.5 W	3–C
13	Canada	DLBC Dease Lake, B.C.	58.4 N	130.0 W	3–C
14	Canada	SADO Sadowa, Ont.	44.8 N	79.1 W	3–C
15	Canada	BBB Bella Bella, B.C.	52.2 N	128.1 W	3–C

	State responsible for station	Location	Latitude	Longitude	Type
16	Canada	MBC Mould Bay, N.W.T.	76.2 N	119.4 W	3–C
17	Canada	INK Inuvik, N.W.T.	68.3 N	133.5 W	3–C
18	Chile	RPN Easter Island	27.2 S	109.4 W	3–C
19	Chile	LVC Limon Verde	22.6 S	68.9 W	3–C
20	China	BJT Baijiatuan	40.0 N	116.2 E	3–C
21	China	KMI Kunming	25.2 N	102.8 E	3–C
22	China	SSE Sheshan	31.1 N	121.2 E	3–C
23	China	XAN Xi'an	34.0 N	108.9 E	3–C
24	Cook Islands	RAR Rarotonga	21.2 S	159.8 W	3–C
25	Costa Rica	JTS Las Juntas de Abangares	10.3 N	85.0 W	3–C
26	Czech Republic	VRAC Vranov	49.3 N	16.6 E	3–C
27	Denmark	SFJ Søndre Strømfjord, Greenland	67.0 N	50.6 W	3–C
28	Djibouti	ATD Arta Tunnel	11.5 N	42.9 E	3–C
29	Egypt	KEG Kottamya	29.9 N	31.8 E	3–C
30	Ethiopia	FURI Furi	8.9 N	38.7 E	3–C
31	Fiji	MSVF Monasavu, Viti Levu	17.8 S	178.1 E	3–C
32	France	NOUC Port Laguerre, New Caledonia	22.1 S	166.3 E	3–C

	State responsible for station	Location	Latitude	Longitude	Type
33	France	KOG Kourou, French Guiana	5.2 N	52.7 W	3–C
34	Gabon	BAMB Bambay	1.7 S	13.6 E	3–C
35	Germany/ South Africa	--- SANAE Station, Antarctica	71.7 S	2.9 W	3–C
36	Greece	IDI Anogia, Crete	35.3 N	24.9 E	3–C
37	Guatemala	RDG Rabir	15.0 N	90.5 W	3–C
38	Iceland	BORG Borgarnes	64.8 N	21.3 W	3–C
39	To be determined	To be determined	To be determined	To be determined	To be determined
40	Indonesia	PACI Cibinong, Jawa Barat	6.5 S	107.0 E	3–C
41	Indonesia	JAY Jayapura, Irian Jaya	2.5 S	140.7 E	3–C
42	Indonesia	SWI Sorong, Irian Jaya	0.9 S	131.3 E	3–C
43	Indonesia	PSI Parapat, Sumatera	2.7 N	98.9 E	3–C
44	Indonesia	KAPI Kappang, Sulawesi Selatan	5.0 S	119.8 E	3–C
45	Indonesia	KUG Kupang, Nusatenggara Timur	10.2 S	123.6 E	3–C
46	Iran (Islamic Republic of)	KRM Kerman	30.3 N	57.1 E	3–C
47	Iran (Islamic Republic of)	MSN Masjed–e–Soleyman	31.9 N	49.3 E	3–C
48	Israel	MBH Eilath	29.8 N	34.9 E	3–C

	State responsible for station	Location	Latitude	Longitude	Type
49	Israel	PARD Parod	32.6 N	35.3 E	array
50	Italy	ENAS Enna, Sicily	37.5 N	14.3 E	3–C
51	Japan	JNU Ohita, Kyushu	33.1 N	130.9 E	3–C
52	Japan	JOW Kunigami, Okinawa	26.8 N	128.3 E	3–C
53	Japan	JHJ Hachijojima, Izu Islands	33.1 N	139.8 E	3–C
54	Japan	JKA Kamikawa–asahi, Hokkaido	44.1 N	142.6 E	3–C
55	Japan	JCJ Chichijima, Ogasawara	27.1 N	142.2 E	3–C
56	Jordan	---- Ashqof	32.5 N	37.6 E	3–C
57	Kazakstan	BRVK Borovoye	53.1 N	70.3 E	array
58	Kazakstan	KURK Kurchatov	50.7 N	78.6 E	array
59	Kazakstan	AKTO Aktyubinsk	50.4 N	58.0 E	3–C
60	Kyrgyzstan	AAK Ala–Archa	42.6 N	74.5 E	3–C
61	Madagascar	TAN Antananarivo	18.9 S	47.6 E	3–C
62	Mali	KOWA Kowa	14.5 N	4.0 W	3–C
63	Mexico	TEYM Tepich, Yucatan	20.2 N	88.3 W	3–C
64	Mexico	TUVM Tuzandepeti, Veracruz	18.0 N	94.4 W	3–C

	State responsible for station	Location	Latitude	Longitude	Type
65	Mexico	LPBM La Paz, Baja California Sur	24.2 N	110.2 W	3–C
66	Morocco	MDT Midelt	32.8 N	4.6 W	3–C
67	Namibia	TSUM Tsumeb	19.1 S	17.4 E	3–C
68	Nepal	EVN Everest	28.0 N	86.8 E	3–C
69	New Zealand	EWZ Erewhon, South Island	43.5 S	170.9 E	3–C
70	New Zealand	RAO Raoul Island	29.2 S	177.9 W	3–C
71	New Zealand	URZ Urewera, North Island	38.3 S	177.1 E	3–C
72	Norway	SPITS Spitsbergen	78.2 N	16.4 E	array
73	Norway	JMI Jan Mayen	70.9 N	8.7 W	3–C
74	Oman	WSAR Wadi Sarin	23.0 N	58.0 E	3–C
75	Papua New Guinea	PMG Port Moresby	9.4 S	147.2 E	3–C
76	Papua New Guinea	BIAL Bialla	5.3 S	151.1 E	3–C
77	Peru	CAJP Cajamarca	7.0 S	78.0 W	3–C
78	Peru	NNA Nana	12.0 S	76.8 W	3–C
79	Philippines	DAV Davao, Mindanao	7.1 N	125.6 E	3–C
80	Philippines	TGY Tagaytay, Luzon	14.1 N	120.9 E	3–C
81	Romania	MLR Muntele Rosu	45.5 N	25.9 E	3–C

	State responsible for station	Location	Latitude	Longitude	Type
82	Russian Federation	KIRV Kirov	58.6 N	49.4 E	3–C
83	Russian Federation	KIVO Kislovodsk	44.0 N	42.7 E	array
84	Russian Federation	OBN Obninsk	55.1 N	36.6 E	3–C
85	Russian Federation	ARU Arti	56.4 N	58.6 E	3–C
86	Russian Federation	SEY Seymchan	62.9 N	152.4 E	3–C
87	Russian Federation	TLY Talaya	51.7 N	103.6 E	3–C
88	Russian Federation	YAK Yakutsk	62.0N	129.7 E	3–C
89	Russian Federation	URG Urgal	51.1N	132.3 E	3–C
90	Russian Federation	BIL Bilibino	68.0 N	166.4 E	3–C
91	Russian Federation	TIXI Tiksi	71.6 N	128.9 E	3–C
92	Russian Federation	YSS Yuzhno–Sakhalinsk	47.0 N	142.8 E	3–C
93	Russian Federation	MA2 Magadan	59.6 N	150.8 E	3–C
94	Russian Federation	ZIL Zilim	53.9 N	57.0 E	3–C
95	Samoa	AFI Afiamalu	13.9 S	171.8 W	3–C
96	Saudi Arabia	RAYN Ar Rayn	23.6 N	45.6 E	3–C
97	Senegal	MBO Mbour	14.4 N	17.0 W	3–C
98	Solomon Islands	HNR Honiara, Guadalcanal	9.4 S	160.0 E	3–C

	State responsible for station	Location	Latitude	Longitude	Type
99	South Africa	SUR Sutherland	32.4 S	20.8 E	3–C
100	Sri Lanka	COC Colombo	6.9 N	79.9 E	3–C
101	Sweden	HFS Hagfors	60.1 N	13.7 E	array
102	Switzerland	DAVOS Davos	46.8 N	9.8 E	3–C
103	Uganda	MBRU Mbarara	0.4 S	30.4 E	3–C
104	United Kingdom	EKA Eskdalemuir	55.3 N	3.2 W	array
105	United States of America	GUMO Guam, Marianas Islands	13.6 N	144.9 E	3–C
106	United States of America	PMSA Palmer Station, Antarctica	64.8 S	64.1 W	3–C
107	United States of America	TKL Tuckaleechee Caverns, TN	35.7 N	83.8 W	3–C
108	United States of America	PFCA Piñon Flat, CA	33.6 N	116.5 W	3–C
109	United States of America	YBH Yreka, CA	41.7 N	122.7 W	3–C
110	United States of America	KDC Kodiak Island, AK	57.8 N	152.5 W	3–C
111	United States of America	ALQ Albuquerque, NM	35.0 N	106.5 W	3–C
112	United States of America	ATTU Attu Island, AK	52.8 N	172.7 E	3–C
113	United States of America	ELK Elko, NV	40.7 N	115.2 W	3–C
114	United States of America	SPA South Pole, Antarctica	90.0 S	– –	3–C

	State responsible for station	Location	Latitude	Longitude	Type
115	United States of America	NEW Newport, WA	48.3 N	117.1 W	3–C
116	United States of America	SJG San Juan, PR	18.1 N	66.2 W	3–C
117	Venezuela	SDV Santo Domingo	8.9 N	70.6 W	3–C
118	Venezuela	PCRV Puerto la Cruz	10.2 N	64.6 W	3–C
119	Zambia	LSZ Lusaka	15.3 S	28.2 E	3–C
120	Zimbabwe	BUL Bulawayo	to be advised	to be advised	3–C

Table 2–A
List of Radionuclide Stations

	State responsible for station	Location	Latitude	Longitude
1	Argentina	Buenos Aires	34.0 S	58.0 W
2	Argentina	Salta	24.0 S	65.0 W
3	Argentina	Bariloche	41.1 S	71.3 W
4	Australia	Melbourne, VIC	37.5 S	144.6 E
5	Australia	Mawson, Antarctica	67.6 S	62.5 E
6	Australia	Townsville, QLD	19.2 S	146.8 E
7	Australia	Macquarie Island	54.0 S	159.0 E
8	Australia	Cocos Islands	12.0 S	97.0 E
9	Australia	Darwin, NT	12.4 S	130.7 E
10	Australia	Perth, WA	31.9 S	116.0 E
11	Brazil	Rio de Janeiro	22.5 S	43.1 W
12	Brazil	Recife	8.0 S	35.0 W
13	Cameroon	Douala	4.2 N	9.9 E
14	Canada	Vancouver, B.C.	49.3 N	123.2 W
15	Canada	Resolute, N.W.T.	74.7 N	94.9 W
16	Canada	Yellowknife, N.W.T.	62.5 N	114.5 W
17	Canada	St. John's, N.L.	47.0 N	53.0 W
18	Chile	Punta Arenas	53.1 S	70.6 W
19	Chile	Hanga Roa, Easter Island	27.1 S	108.4 W
20	China	Beijing	39.8 N	116.2 E
21	China	Lanzhou	35.8 N	103.3 E
22	China	Guangzhou	23.0 N	113.3 E
23	Cook Islands	Rarotonga	21.2 S	159.8 W
24	Ecuador	Isla San Cristóbal, Galápagos Islands	1.0 S	89.2 W
25	Ethiopia	Filtu	5.5 N	42.7 E
26	Fiji	Nadi	18.0 S	177.5 E

	State responsible for station	Location	Latitude	Longitude
27	France	Papeete, Tahiti	17.0 S	150.0 W
28	France	Pointe–à–Pitre, Guadeloupe	17.0 N	62.0 W
29	France	Réunion	21.1 S	55.6 E
30	France	Port–aux–Français, Kerguelen	49.0 S	70.0 E
31	France	Cayenne, French Guiana	5.0 N	52.0 W
32	France	Dumont d'Urville, Antarctica	66.0 S	140.0 E
33	Germany	Schauinsland/ Freiburg	47.9 N	7.9 E
34	Iceland	Reykjavik	64.4 N	21.9 W
35	To be determined	To be determined	To be determined	To be determined
36	Iran (Islamic Republic of)	Tehran	35.0 N	52.0 E
37	Japan	Okinawa	26.5 N	127.9 E
38	Japan	Takasaki, Gunma	36.3 N	139.0 E
39	Kiribati	Kiritimati	2.0 N	157.0 W
40	Kuwait	Kuwait City	29.0 N	48.0 E
41	Libya	Misratah	32.5 N	15.0 E
42	Malaysia	Kuala Lumpur	2.6 N	101.5 E
43	Mauritania	Nouakchott	18.0 N	17.0 W
44	Mexico	Baja California	28.0 N	113.0 W
45	Mongolia	Ulaanbaatar	47.5 N	107.0 E
46	New Zealand	Chatham Island	44.0 S	176.5 W
47	New Zealand	Kaitaia	35.1 S	173.3 E
48	Niger	Bilma	18.0 N	13.0 E
49	Norway	Spitsbergen	78.2 N	16.4 E
50	Panama	Panama City	8.9 N	79.6 W
51	Papua New Guinea	New Hanover	3.0 S	150.0 E

	State responsible for station	Location	Latitude	Longitude
52	Philippines	Quezon City	14.5 N	121.0 E
53	Portugal	Ponta Delgada, São Miguel, Azores	37.4 N	25.4 W
54	Russian Federation	Kirov	58.6 N	49.4 E
55	Russian Federation	Norilsk	69.0 N	88.0E
56	Russian Federation	Peleduy	59.6 N	112.6 E
57	Russian Federation	Bilibino	68.0 N	166.4 E
58	Russian Federation	Ussuriysk	43.7 N	131.9 E
59	Russian Federation	Zalesovo	53.9 N	84.8 E
60	Russian Federation	Petropavlovsk–Kamchatskiy	53.1 N	158.8 E
61	Russian Federation	Dubna	56.7 N	37.3 E
62	South Africa	Marion Island	46.5 S	37.0 E
63	Sweden	Stockholm	59.4 N	18.0 E
64	Tanzania	Dar es Salaam	6.0 S	39.0 E
65	Thailand	Bangkok	13.8 N	100.5 E
66	United Kingdom	BIOT/Chagos Archipelago	7.0 S	72.0 E
67	United Kingdom	St. Helena	16.0 S	6.0 W
68	United Kingdom	Tristan da Cunha	37.0 S	12.3 W
69	United Kingdom	Halley, Antarctica	76.0 S	28.0 W
70	United States of America	Sacramento, CA	38.7 N	121.4 W
71	United States of America	Sand Point, AK	55.0 N	160.0 W
72	United States of America	Melbourne, FL	28.3 N	80.6 W
73	United States of America	Palmer Station, Antarctica	64.5 S	64.0 W
74	United States of America	Ashland, KS	37.2 N	99.8 W

	State responsible for station	Location	Latitude	Longitude
75	United States of America	Charlottesville, VA	38.0 N	78.0 W
76	United States of America	Salchaket, AK	64.4 N	147.1 W
77	United States of America	Wake Island	19.3 N	166.6 E
78	United States of America	Midway Islands	28.0 N	177.0 W
79	United States of America	Oahu, HI	21.5 N	158.0 W
80	United States of America	Upi, Guam	13.7 N	144.9 E

Table 2–B
List of Radionuclide Laboratories

	State responsible for laboratory	Name and place of laboratory
1	Argentina	National Board of Nuclear Regulation Buenos Aires
2	Australia	Australian Radiation Laboratory Melbourne, VIC
3	Austria	Austrian Research Center Seibersdorf
4	Brazil	Institute of Radiation Protection and Dosimetry Rio de Janeiro
5	Canada	Health Canada Ottawa, Ont.
6	China	Beijing
7	Finland	Centre for Radiation and Nuclear Safety Helsinki
8	France	Atomic Energy Commission Montlhéry
9	Israel	Soreq Nuclear Research Centre Yavne
10	Italy	Laboratory of the National Agency for the Protection of the Environment Rome
11	Japan	Japan Atomic Energy Research Institute Tokai, Ibaraki
12	New Zealand	National Radiation Laboratory Christchurch
13	Russian Federation	Central Radiation Control Laboratory, Ministry of Defence Special Verification Service Moscow
14	South Africa	Atomic Energy Corporation Pelindaba
15	United Kingdom	AWE Blacknest Chilton
16	United States of America	McClellan Central Laboratories Sacramento, CA

Table 3
List of Hydroacoustic Stations

	State responsible for station	Location	Latitude	Longitude	Type
1	Australia	Cape Leeuwin, WA	34.4 S	115.1 E	Hydrophone
2	Canada	Queen Charlotte Islands, B.C.	53.3 N	132.5 W	T–phase
3	Chile	Juan Fernández Island	33.7 S	78.8 W	Hydrophone
4	France	Crozet Islands	46.5 S	52.2 E	Hydrophone
5	France	Guadeloupe	16.3 N	61.1 W	T–phase
6	Mexico	Clarión Island	18.2 N	114.6 W	T–phase
7	Portugal	Flores	39.3 N	31.3 W	T–phase
8	United Kingdom	BIOT/Chagos Archipelago	7.3 S	72.4 E	Hydrophone
9	United Kingdom	Tristan da Cunha	37.2 S	12.5 W	T–phase
10	United States of America	Ascension	8.0 S	14.4 W	Hydrophone
11	United States of America	Wake Island	19.3 N	166.6 E	Hydrophone

Table 4
List of Infrasound Stations

	State responsible for station	Location	Latitude	Longitude
1	Argentina	Paso Flores	40.7 S	70.6 W
2	Argentina	Ushuaia	55.0 S	68.0 W
3	Australia	Davis Base, Antarctica	68.4 S	77.6 E
4	Australia	Narrogin, WA	32.9 S	117.2 E
5	Australia	Hobart, TAS	42.1 S	147.2 E
6	Australia	Cocos Islands	12.3 S	97.0 E
7	Australia	Warramunga, NT	19.9 S	134.3 E
8	Bolivia	La Paz	16.3 S	68.1 W
9	Brazil	Brasilia	15.6 S	48.0 W
10	Canada	Lac du Bonnet, Man.	50.2 N	95.9 W
11	Cape Verde	Cape Verde Islands	16.0 N	24.0 W
12	Central African Republic	Bangui	5.2 N	18.4 E
13	Chile	Easter Island	27.0 S	109.2 W
14	Chile	Juan Fernández Island	33.8 S	80.7 W
15	China	Beijing	40.0 N	116.0 E
16	China	Kunming	25.0 N	102.8 E
17	Côte d'Ivoire	Dimbokro	6.7 N	4.9 W
18	Denmark	Dundas, Greenland	76.5 N	68.7 W
19	Djibouti	Djibouti	11.3 N	43.5 E
20	Ecuador	Galápagos Islands	0.0 N	91.7 W
21	France	Marquesas Islands	10.0 S	140.0 W
22	France	Port LaGuerre, New Caledonia	22.1 S	166.3 E
23	France	Kerguelen	49.2 S	69.1 E
24	France	Tahiti	17.6 S	149.6 W
25	France	Kourou, French Guiana	5.2 N	52.7 W
26	Germany	Freyung	48.9 N	13.7 E

	State responsible for station	Location	Latitude	Longitude
27	Germany	Georg von Neumayer, Antarctica	70.6 S	8.4 W
28	To be determined	To be determined	To be determined	To be determined
29	Iran (Islamic Republic of)	Tehran	35.7 N	51.4 E
30	Japan	Tsukuba	36.0 N	140.1 E
31	Kazakstan	Aktyubinsk	50.4 N	58.0 E
32	Kenya	Kilimanbogo	1.3 S	36.8 E
33	Madagascar	Antananarivo	18.8 S	47.5 E
34	Mongolia	Javhlant	48.0 N	106.8 E
35	Namibia	Tsumeb	19.1 S	17.4 E
36	New Zealand	Chatham Island	44.0 S	176.5 W
37	Norway	Karasjok	69.5 N	25.5 E
38	Pakistan	Rahimyar Khan	28.2 N	70.3 E
39	Palau	Palau	7.5 N	134.5 E
40	Papua New Guinea	Rabaul	4.1 S	152.1 E
41	Paraguay	Villa Florida	26.3 S	57.3 W
42	Portugal	Azores	37.8 N	25.5 W
43	Russian Federation	Dubna	56.7 N	37.3 E
44	Russian Federation	Petropavlovsk–Kamchatskiy	53.1 N	158.8 E
45	Russian Federation	Ussuriysk	43.7 N	131.9 E
46	Russian Federation	Zalesovo	53.9 N	84.8 E
47	South Africa	Boshof	28.6 S	25.4 E
48	Tunisia	Thala	35.6 N	8.7 E
49	United Kingdom	Tristan da Cunha	37.0 S	12.3 W
50	United Kingdom	Ascension	8.0 S	14.3 W
51	United Kingdom	Bermuda	32.0 N	64.5 W
52	United Kingdom	BIOT/Chagos Archipelago	5.0 S	72.0 E

	State responsible for station	Location	Latitude	Longitude
53	United States of America	Eielson, AK	64.8 N	146.9 W
54	United States of America	Siple Station, Antarctica	75.5 S	83.6 W
55	United States of America	Windless Bight, Antarctica	77.5 S	161.8 E
56	United States of America	Newport, WA	48.3 N	117.1 W
57	United States of America	Piñon Flat, CA	33.6 N	116.5 W
58	United States of America	Midway Islands	28.1N	177.2 W
59	United States of America	Hawaii, HI	19.6 N	155.3 W
60	United States of America	Wake Island	19.3 N	166.6 E

Annex 2 to the Protocol
List of Characterisation Parameters for International Data Centre Standard Event Screening

1. The International Data Centre standard event screening criteria shall be based on the standard event characterisation parameters determined during the combined processing of data from all the monitoring technologies in the International Monitoring System. Standard event screening shall make use of both global and supplementary screening criteria to take account of regional variations where applicable.

2. For events detected by the International Monitoring System seismic component, the following parameters, inter alia, may be used:

- location of the event;

- depth of the event;

- ratio of the magnitude of surface waves to body waves;

- signal frequency content;

- spectral ratios of phases;

- spectral scalloping;

- first motion of the P-wave;

- focal mechanism;

- relative excitation of seismic phases;

- comparative measures to other events and groups of events; and

- regional discriminants where applicable.

3. For events detected by the International Monitoring System hydroacoustic component, the following parameters, inter alia, may be used:

- signal frequency content including corner frequency, wide-band energy, and mean centre frequency and bandwidth;
- frequency-dependent duration of signals;
- spectral ratio; and
- indications of bubble-pulse signals and bubble-pulse delay.

4. For events detected by the International Monitoring System infrasound component, the following parameters, inter alia, may be used:

- signal frequency content and dispersion;
- signal duration; and
- peak amplitude.

5. For events detected by the International Monitoring System radionuclide component, the following parameters, inter alia, may be used:

- concentration of background natural and man-made radionuclides;
- concentration of specific fission and activation products outside normal observations; and
- ratios of one specific fission and activation product to another.

Treaty Banning Nuclear Weapon Tests in the Atmosphere, in Outer Space and Under Water (Partial Test Ban Treaty)

SIGNED BY THE ORIGINAL PARTIES, THE UNION OF SOVIET SOCIALIST REPUBLICS, THE UNITED KINGDOM OF GREAT BRITAIN AND NORTHERN IRELAND AND THE UNITED STATES OF AMERICA AT MOSCOW:
5 August 1963

OPENED FOR SIGNATURE AT LONDON, MOSCOW AND WASHINGTON:
8 August 1963

ENTERED INTO FORCE:
10 October 1963

DEPOSITARY GOVERNMENTS:
Russian Federation
United Kingdom of Great Britain and Northern Ireland
United States of America

NUMBER OF SIGNATORY STATES: 105*

NUMBER OF STATES PARTIES: 126*

* As at 28 November 2014. For the updated adherence status, see http://disarmament.un.org/treaties/.

TEXT:

The Governments of the United States of America, the United Kingdom of Great Britain and Northern Ireland, and the Union of Soviet Socialist Republics, hereinafter referred to as the "Original Parties",

Proclaiming as their principal aim the speediest possible achievement of an agreement on general and complete disarmament under strict international control in accordance with the objectives of the United Nations which would put an end to the armaments race and eliminate the incentive to the production and testing of all kinds of weapons, including nuclear weapons,

Seeking to achieve the discontinuance of all test explosions of nuclear weapons for all time, determined to continue negotiations to this end, and desiring to put an end to the contamination of man's environment by radioactive substances,

Have agreed as follows:

Article I

1.   Each of the Parties to this Treaty undertakes to prohibit, to prevent, and not to carry out any nuclear weapon test explosion, or any other nuclear explosion, at any place under its jurisdiction or control:

(a)   in the atmosphere; beyond its limits, including outer space; or under water, including territorial waters or high seas; or

(b)   in any other environment if such explosion causes radioactive debris to be present outside the territorial limits of the State under whose jurisdiction or control such explosion is conducted. It is understood in this connection that the provisions of this subparagraph are without prejudice to the conclusion of a Treaty resulting in the permanent banning of all nuclear test explosions, including all such explosions underground, the conclusion of which, as the Parties have stated in the Preamble to this Treaty, they seek to achieve.

2. Each of the Parties to this Treaty undertakes furthermore to refrain from causing, encouraging, or in any way participating in, the carrying out of any nuclear weapon test explosion, or any other nuclear explosion, anywhere which would take place in any of the environments described, or have the effect referred to, in paragraph 1 of this Article.

Article II

1. Any Party may propose amendments to this Treaty. The text of any proposed amendment shall be submitted to the Depositary Governments which shall circulate it to all Parties to this Treaty. Thereafter, if requested to do so by one-third or more of the Parties, the Depositary Governments shall convene a conference, to which they shall invite all the Parties, to consider such amendment.

2. Any amendment to this Treaty must be approved by a majority of the votes of all the Parties to this Treaty, including the votes of all of the Original Parties. The amendment shall enter into force for all Parties upon the deposit of instruments of ratification by a majority of all the

Parties, including the instruments of ratification of all of the Original Parties.

Article III

1.   This Treaty shall be open to all States for signature. Any State which does not sign this Treaty before its entry into force in accordance with paragraph 3 of this Article may accede to it at any time.

2.   This Treaty shall be subject to ratification by signatory States. Instruments of ratification and instruments of accession shall be deposited with the Governments of the Original Parties -- the United States of America, the United Kingdom of Great Britain and Northern Ireland, and the Union of Soviet Socialist Republics -- which are hereby designated the Depositary Governments.

3.   This Treaty shall enter into force after its ratification by all the Original Parties and the deposit of their instruments of ratification.

4.   For States whose instruments of ratification or accession are deposited subsequent to the entry into force of this Treaty, it shall enter into force on the date of the deposit of their instruments of ratification or accession.

5.   The Depositary Governments shall promptly inform all signatory and acceding States of the date of each signature, the date of deposit of each instrument of ratification of and accession to this Treaty, the date of its entry into force, and

the date of receipt of any requests for conferences or other notices.

6.   This Treaty shall be registered by the Depositary Governments pursuant to Article 102 of the Charter of the United Nations.

Article IV

This Treaty shall be of unlimited duration.

Each Party shall in exercising its national sovereignty have the right to withdraw from the Treaty if it decides that extraordinary events, related to the subject matter of this Treaty, have jeopardized the supreme interests of its country. It shall give notice of such withdrawal to all other Parties to the Treaty three months in advance.

Article V

This Treaty, of which the English and Russian texts are equally authentic, shall be deposited in the archives of the Depositary Governments. Duly certified copies of this Treaty shall be transmitted by the Depositary Governments to the Governments of the signatory and acceding States.

IN WITNESS WHEREOF the undersigned, duly authorized, have signed this Treaty.

DONE in triplicate at the city of Moscow the fifth day of August, one thousand nine hundred and sixty-three.

OTHER WEAPONS
OF MASS DESTRUCTION

Protocol for the Prohibition of the Use in War of Asphyxiating, Poisonous or Other Gases, and of Bacteriological Methods of Warfare (1925 Geneva Protocol)

SIGNED AT GENEVA: 17 June 1925

ENTERED INTO FORCE:
For each signatory as from the date of deposit of its ratification; accessions take effect on the date of the notification by the depositary Government

DEPOSITARY:
Government of France

NUMBER OF SIGNATORY STATES: 36*

NUMBER OF STATES PARTIES: 138*

* As at 28 November 2014. For the updated adherence status, see http://disarmament.un.org/treaties/.

TEXT:

THE UNDERSIGNED PLENIPOTENTIARIES, in the name of their respective Governments:

WHEREAS the use in war of asphyxiating, poisonous or other gases, and of all analogous liquids, materials or devices, has been justly condemned by the general opinion of the civilised world; and

WHEREAS the prohibition of such use has been declared in Treaties to which the majority of Powers of the world are Parties; and

TO THE END that this prohibition shall be universally accepted as a part of International Law, binding alike the conscience and the practice of nations;

DECLARE:

That the High Contracting Parties, so far as they are not already Parties to Treaties prohibiting such use, accept this prohibition, agree to extend this prohibition to the use of bacteriological methods of warfare and agree to be bound as between themselves according to the terms of this declaration.

The High Contracting Parties will exert every effort to induce other States to accede to the present Protocol. Such accession will be notified to the Government of the French Republic, and by the latter to all signatory and acceding Powers, and will take effect on the date of the notification by the Government of the French Republic.

The present Protocol, of which the French and English texts are both authentic, shall be ratified as soon as possible. It shall bear today's date.

The ratifications of the present Protocol shall be addressed to the Government of the French Republic, which will at once notify the deposit of such ratification to each of the signatory and acceding Powers.

The instruments of ratification of and accession to the present Protocol will remain deposited in the archives of the Government of the French Republic.

The present Protocol will come into force for each signatory Power as from the date of deposit of its ratification, and, from that moment, each Power will be bound as regards other Powers which have already deposited their ratifications.

IN WITNESS WHEREOF the Plenipotentiaries have signed the present Protocol.

DONE at Geneva in a single copy, this seventeenth day of June, One Thousand Nine Hundred and Twenty-Five.

Convention on the Prohibition of the Development, Production and Stockpiling of Bacteriological (Biological) and Toxin Weapons and on their Destruction (Biological Weapons Convention)

OPENED FOR SIGNATURE AT LONDON, MOSCOW AND WASHINGTON:
10 April 1972

ENTERED INTO FORCE:
26 March 1975

DEPOSITARY GOVERNMENTS:
Russian Federation
United Kingdom of Great Britain and Northern Ireland
United States of America

NUMBER OF SIGNATORY STATES: 110*

NUMBER OF STATES PARTIES: 168*

* As at 28 November 2014. For the updated adherence status, see http://disarmament.un.org/treaties/.

TEXT:

The States Parties to this Convention,

Determined to act with a view to achieving effective progress towards general and complete disarmament, including the prohibition and elimination of all types of weapons of mass destruction, and convinced that the prohibition of the development, production and stockpiling of chemical and bacteriological (biological) weapons and their elimination, through effective measures, will facilitate the achievement of general and complete disarmament under strict and effective international control,

Recognising the important significance of the Protocol for the Prohibition of the Use in War of Asphyxiating, Poisonous or Other Gases, and of Bacteriological Methods of Warfare, signed at Geneva on 17 June 1925, and conscious also of the contribution which the said Protocol has already made and continues to make, to mitigating the horrors of war,

Reaffirming their adherence to the principles and objectives of that Protocol and calling upon all States to comply strictly with them,

Recalling that the General Assembly of the United Nations has repeatedly condemned all actions contrary to the principles and objectives of the Geneva Protocol of 17 June 1925,

Desiring to contribute to the strengthening of confidence between peoples and the general improvement of the international atmosphere,

Desiring also to contribute to the realisation of the purposes and principles of the Charter of the United Nations,

Convinced of the importance and urgency of eliminating from the arsenals of States, through effective measures, such dangerous weapons of mass destruction as those using chemical or bacteriological (biological) agents,

Recognising that an agreement on the prohibition of bacteriological (biological) and toxin weapons represents a first possible step towards the achievement of agreement on effective measures also for the prohibition of the development, production and stockpiling of chemical weapons, and determined to continue negotiations to that end,

Determined, for the sake of all mankind, to exclude completely the possibility of bacteriological (biological) agents and toxins being used as weapons,

Convinced that such use would be repugnant to the conscience of mankind and that no effort should be spared to minimise this risk,

Have agreed as follows:

Article I

Each State Party to this Convention undertakes never in any circumstances to develop, produce, stockpile or otherwise acquire or retain:

(1) microbial or other biological agents, or toxins whatever their origin or method of production, of types and in

quantities that have no justification for prophylactic, protective or other peaceful purposes;

(2) weapons, equipment or means of delivery designed to use such agents or toxins for hostile purposes or in armed conflict.

Article II

Each State Party to this Convention undertakes to destroy, or to divert to peaceful purposes, as soon as possible but not later than nine months after the entry into force of the Convention, all agents, toxins, weapons, equipment and means of delivery specified in Article I of the Convention, which are in its possession or under its jurisdiction or control. In implementing the provisions of this Article all necessary safety precautions shall be observed to protect populations and the environment.

Article III

Each State Party to this Convention undertakes not to transfer to any recipient whatsoever, directly or indirectly, and not in any way to assist, encourage, or induce any State, group of States or international organisations to manufacture or otherwise acquire any of the agents, toxins, weapons, equipment or means of delivery specified in Article I of the Convention.

Article IV

Each State Party to this Convention shall, in accordance with its constitutional processes, take any necessary measures to prohibit and prevent the development, production, stockpiling, acquisition or retention of the agents, toxins, weapons, equipment and means of delivery specified in Article I of the Convention, within the territory of such State, under its jurisdiction or under its control anywhere.

Article V

The States Parties to this Convention undertake to consult one another and to co-operate in solving any problems which may arise in relation to the objective of, or in the application of the provisions of, the Convention. Consultation and co-operation pursuant to this Article may also be undertaken through appropriate international procedures within the framework of the United Nations and in accordance with its Charter.

Article VI

(1)   Any State Party to this Convention which finds that any other State Party is acting in breach of obligations deriving from the provisions of the Convention may lodge a complaint with the Security Council of the United Nations. Such a complaint should include all possible evidence confirming its validity, as well as a request for its consideration by the Security Council.

(2) Each State Party to this Convention undertakes to co-operate in carrying out any investigation which the Security Council may initiate, in accordance with the provisions of the Charter of the United Nations, on the basis of the complaint received by the Council. The Security Council shall inform the States Parties to the Convention of the results of the investigation.

Article VII

Each State Party to this Convention undertakes to provide or support assistance, in accordance with the United Nations Charter, to any Party to the Convention which so requests, if the Security Council decides that such Party has been exposed to danger as a result of violation of the Convention.

Article VIII

Nothing in this Convention shall be interpreted as in any way limiting or detracting from the obligations assumed by any State under the Protocol for the Prohibition of the Use in War of Asphyxiating, Poisonous or Other Gases, and of Bacteriological Methods of Warfare, signed at Geneva on 17 June 1925.

Article IX

Each State Party to this Convention affirms the recognised objective of effective prohibition of chemical weapons and, to this end, undertakes to continue negotiations in good faith with a view to reaching early agreement on effective measures for the prohibition of their development, production and stockpiling and for their destruction, and on appropriate measures concerning equipment and means of delivery specifically designed for the production or use of chemical agents for weapons purposes.

Article X

(1) The States Parties to this Convention undertake to facilitate, and have the right to participate in, the fullest possible exchange of equipment, materials and scientific and technological information for the use of bacteriological (biological) agents and toxins for peaceful purposes. Parties to the Convention in a position to do so shall also co-operate in contributing individually or together with other States or international organisations to the further development and application of scientific discoveries in the field of bacteriology (biology) for the prevention of disease, or for other peaceful purposes.

(2) This Convention shall be implemented in a manner designed to avoid hampering the economic or technological development of States Parties to the Convention or international co-operation in the field of peaceful bacteriological (biological) activities, including the international exchange of bacteriological (biological) agents and toxins and equipment for the processing, use or production of bacteriological (biological) agents and toxins

for peaceful purposes in accordance with the provisions of the Convention.

Article XI

Any State Party may propose amendments to this Convention. Amendments shall enter into force for each State Party accepting the amendments upon their acceptance by a majority of the States Parties to the Convention and thereafter for each remaining State Party on the date of acceptance by it.

Article XII

Five years after the entry into force of this Convention, or earlier if it is requested by a majority of Parties to the Convention by submitting a proposal to this effect to the Depositary Governments, a conference of States Parties to the Convention shall be held at Geneva, Switzerland, to review the operation of the Convention, with a view to assuring that the purposes of the preamble and the provisions of the Convention, including the provisions concerning negotiations on chemical weapons, are being realised. Such review shall take into account any new scientific and technological developments relevant to the Convention.

Article XIII

(1) This Convention shall be of unlimited duration.

(2)   Each State Party to this Convention shall in exercising its national sovereignty have the right to withdraw from the Convention if it decides that extraordinary events, related to the subject matter of the Convention, have jeopardised the supreme interests of its country. It shall give notice of such withdrawal to all other States Parties to the Convention and to the United Nations Security Council three months in advance. Such notice shall include a statement of the extraordinary events it regards as having jeopardised its supreme interests.

Article XIV

(1)   This Convention shall be open to all States for signature. Any State which does not sign the Convention before its entry into force in accordance with paragraph 3 of this Article may accede to it at any time.

(2)   This Convention shall be subject to ratification by signatory States. Instruments of ratification and instruments of accession shall be deposited with the Governments of the United Kingdom of Great Britain and Northern Ireland, the Union of Soviet Socialist Republics and the United States of America, which are hereby designated the Depositary Governments.

(3)   This Convention shall enter into force after the deposit of instruments of ratification by twenty-two Governments, including the Governments designated as Depositaries of the Convention.

(4) For States whose instruments of ratification or accession are deposited subsequent to the entry into force of this Convention, it shall enter into force on the date of the deposit of their instruments of ratification or accession.

(5) The Depositary Governments shall promptly inform all signatory and acceding States of the date of each signature, the date of deposit of each instrument of ratification or of accession and the date of the entry into force of this Convention, and of the receipt of other notices.

(6) This Convention shall be registered by the Depositary Governments pursuant to Article 102 of the Charter of the United Nations.

Article XV

This Convention, the English, Russian, French, Spanish and Chinese texts of which are equally authentic, shall be deposited in the archives of the Depositary Governments. Duly certified copies of the Convention shall be transmitted by the Depositary Governments to the Governments of the signatory and acceding States.

Convention on the Prohibition of the Development, Production, Stockpiling and Use of Chemical Weapons and on their Destruction (Chemical Weapons Convention)

SIGNED AT PARIS:
13 January 1993

ENTERED INTO FORCE:
29 April 1997

DEPOSITARY:
Secretary-General of the United Nations

NUMBER OF SIGNATORY STATES: 165*

NUMBER OF STATES PARTIES: 190*

* As at 28 November 2014. For the updated adherence status, see http://disarmament.un.org/treaties/.

TEXT:

Preamble

The States Parties to this Convention,

Determined to act with a view to achieving effective progress towards general and complete disarmament under strict and effective international control, including the prohibition and elimination of all types of weapons of mass destruction,

Desiring to contribute to the realization of the purposes and principles of the Charter of the United Nations,

Recalling that the General Assembly of the United Nations has repeatedly condemned all actions contrary to the principles and objectives of the Protocol for the Prohibition of the Use in War of Asphyxiating, Poisonous or Other Gases, and of Bacteriological Methods of Warfare, signed at Geneva on 17 June 1925 (the Geneva Protocol of 1925),

Recognizing that this Convention reaffirms principles and objectives of and obligations assumed under the Geneva Protocol of 1925, and the Convention on the Prohibition of the Development, Production and Stockpiling of Bacteriological (Biological) and Toxin Weapons and on their Destruction signed at London, Moscow and Washington on 10 April 1972,

Bearing in mind the objective contained in Article IX of the Convention on the Prohibition of the Development, Production and Stockpiling of Bacteriological (Biological) and Toxin Weapons and on their Destruction,

Determined for the sake of all mankind, to exclude completely the possibility of the use of chemical weapons, through the implementation of the provisions of this Convention, thereby complementing the obligations assumed under the Geneva Protocol of 1925,

Recognizing the prohibition, embodied in the pertinent agreements and relevant principles of international law, of the use of herbicides as a method of warfare,

Considering that achievements in the field of chemistry should be used exclusively for the benefit of mankind,

Desiring to promote free trade in chemicals as well as international cooperation and exchange of scientific and technical information in the field of chemical activities for purposes not prohibited under this Convention in order to enhance the economic and technological development of all States Parties,

Convinced that the complete and effective prohibition of the development, production, acquisition, stockpiling, retention, transfer and use of chemical weapons, and their destruction, represent a necessary step towards the achievement of these common objectives,

Have agreed as follows:

Article I
General obligations

1.   Each State Party to this Convention undertakes never under any circumstances:

(a)   To develop, produce, otherwise acquire, stockpile or retain chemical weapons, or transfer, directly or indirectly, chemical weapons to anyone;

(b)   To use chemical weapons;

(c)   To engage in any military preparations to use chemical weapons;

(d)   To assist, encourage or induce, in any way, anyone to engage in any activity prohibited to a State Party under this Convention.

2.   Each State Party undertakes to destroy chemical weapons it owns or possesses, or that are located in any place under its jurisdiction or control, in accordance with the provisions of this Convention.

3.   Each State Party undertakes to destroy all chemical weapons it abandoned on the territory of another State Party, in accordance with the provisions of this Convention.

4.   Each State Party undertakes to destroy any chemical weapons production facilities it owns or possesses, or that are located in any place under its jurisdiction or control, in accordance with the provisions of this Convention.

5.   Each State Party undertakes not to use riot control agents as a method of warfare.

Article II
Definitions and criteria

For the purposes of this Convention:

1.   "Chemical Weapons" means the following, together or separately:

(a)   Toxic chemicals and their precursors, except where intended for purposes not prohibited under this Convention, as long as the types and quantities are consistent with such purposes;

(b)   Munitions and devices, specifically designed to cause death or other harm through the toxic properties of those toxic chemicals specified in subparagraph (a), which would be released as a result of the employment of such munitions and devices;

(c)   Any equipment specifically designed for use directly in connection with the employment of munitions and devices specified in subparagraph (b).

2.   "Toxic Chemical" means:

Any chemical which through its chemical action on life processes can cause death, temporary incapacitation or permanent harm to humans or animals. This includes all such chemicals, regardless of their origin or of their method of production, and regardless of whether they are produced in facilities, in munitions or elsewhere.

(For the purpose of implementing this Convention, toxic chemicals which have been identified for the application of verification measures are listed in Schedules contained in the Annex on Chemicals.)

3.   "Precursor" means:

Any chemical reactant which takes part at any stage in the production by whatever method of a toxic chemical. This includes any key component of a binary or multicomponent chemical system.

(For the purpose of implementing this Convention, precursors which have been identified for the application of verification measures are listed in Schedules contained in the Annex on Chemicals.)

4.   "Key Component of Binary or Multicomponent Chemical Systems" (hereinafter referred to as "key component") means:

The precursor which plays the most important role in determining the toxic properties of the final product and reacts rapidly with other chemicals in the binary or multicomponent system.

5.   "Old Chemical Weapons" means:

(a)   Chemical weapons which were produced before 1925; or

(b)   Chemical weapons produced in the period between 1925 and 1946 that have deteriorated to such extent that they can no longer be used as chemical weapons.

6.   "Abandoned Chemical Weapons" means:

Chemical weapons, including old chemical weapons, abandoned by a State after 1 January 1925 on the territory of another State without the consent of the latter.

7.   "Riot Control Agent" means:

Any chemical not listed in a Schedule, which can produce rapidly in humans sensory irritation or disabling physical effects which disappear within a short time following termination of exposure.

8.   "Chemical Weapons Production Facility":

(a)   Means any equipment, as well as any building housing such equipment, that was designed, constructed or used at any time since 1 January 1946:

(i)   As part of the stage in the production of chemicals ("final technological stage") where the material flows would contain, when the equipment is in operation:

(1)   Any chemical listed in Schedule 1 in the Annex on Chemicals; or

(2)   Any other chemical that has no use, above 1 tonne per year on the territory of a State Party or in any other place under the jurisdiction or control of a State Party, for purposes not prohibited under this Convention, but can be used for chemical weapons purposes;

or

(ii) For filling chemical weapons, including, inter alia, the filling of chemicals listed in Schedule 1 into munitions, devices or bulk storage containers; the filling of chemicals into containers that form part of assembled binary munitions and devices or into chemical submunitions that form part of assembled unitary munitions and devices, and the loading of the containers and chemical submunitions into the respective munitions and devices;

(b)   Does not mean:

(i)   Any facility having a production capacity for synthesis of chemicals specified in subparagraph (a) (i) that is less than 1 tonne;

(ii) Any facility in which a chemical specified in subparagraph (a) (i) is or was produced as an unavoidable by-product of activities for purposes not prohibited under this Convention, provided that the chemical does not exceed 3 per cent of the total product and that the facility is subject to declaration and inspection under the Annex on Implementation and Verification (hereinafter referred to as "Verification Annex"); or

(iii) The single small-scale facility for production of chemicals listed in Schedule 1 for purposes not prohibited under this Convention as referred to in Part VI of the Verification Annex.

9. "Purposes Not Prohibited Under this Convention" means:

(a) Industrial, agricultural, research, medical, pharmaceutical or other peaceful purposes;

(b) Protective purposes, namely those purposes directly related to protection against toxic chemicals and to protection against chemical weapons;

(c) Military purposes not connected with the use of chemical weapons and not dependent on the use of the toxic properties of chemicals as a method of warfare;

(d) Law enforcement including domestic riot control purposes.

10. "Production Capacity" means:

The annual quantitative potential for manufacturing a specific chemical based on the technological process actually used or, if the process is not yet operational, planned to be used at the relevant facility. It shall be deemed to be equal to the nameplate capacity or, if the nameplate capacity is not available, to the design capacity. The nameplate capacity is the product output under conditions optimized for maximum quantity for the production facility, as demonstrated by one or more test-runs. The design capacity is the corresponding theoretically calculated product output.

11. "Organization" means the Organization for the Prohibition of Chemical Weapons established pursuant to Article VIII of this Convention.

12. For the purposes of Article VI:

(a) "Production" of a chemical means its formation through chemical reaction;

(b) "Processing" of a chemical means a physical process, such as formulation, extraction and purification, in which a chemical is not converted into another chemical;

(c) "Consumption" of a chemical means its conversion into another chemical via a chemical reaction.

Article III
Declarations

1. Each State Party shall submit to the Organization, not later than 30 days after this Convention enters into force for it, the following declarations, in which it shall:

(a) With respect to chemical weapons:

(i) Declare whether it owns or possesses any chemical weapons, or whether there are any chemical weapons located in any place under its jurisdiction or control;

(ii) Specify the precise location, aggregate quantity and detailed inventory of chemical weapons it owns or possesses, or that are located in any place under its jurisdiction or control, in accordance with Part IV (A), paragraphs 1 to 3, of the Verification Annex, except for those chemical weapons referred to in sub-subparagraph (iii);

(iii) Report any chemical weapons on its territory that are owned and possessed by another State and located in any place under the jurisdiction or control of another State, in accordance with Part IV (A), paragraph 4, of the Verification Annex;

(iv) Declare whether it has transferred or received, directly or indirectly, any chemical weapons since 1 January 1946 and specify the transfer or receipt of such weapons, in accordance with Part IV (A), paragraph 5, of the Verification Annex;

(v)   Provide its general plan for destruction of chemical weapons that it owns or possesses, or that are located in any place under its jurisdiction or control, in accordance with Part IV (A), paragraph 6, of the Verification Annex;

(b) With respect to old chemical weapons and abandoned chemical weapons:

(i)   Declare whether it has on its territory old chemical weapons and provide all available information in accordance with Part IV (B), paragraph 3, of the Verification Annex;

(ii) Declare whether there are abandoned chemical weapons on its territory and provide all available information in accordance with Part IV (B), paragraph 8, of the Verification Annex;

(iii) Declare whether it has abandoned chemical weapons on the territory of other States and provide all available information in accordance with Part IV (B), paragraph 10, of the Verification Annex;

(c) With respect to chemical weapons production facilities:

(i) Declare whether it has or has had any chemical weapons production facility under its ownership or possession, or that is or has been located in any place under its jurisdiction or control at any time since 1 January 1946;

(ii) Specify any chemical weapons production facility it has or has had under its ownership or possession or that is or has been located in any place under its jurisdiction or control at any time since 1 January 1946, in accordance with Part V, paragraph 1, of the Verification Annex, except for those facilities referred to in sub-subparagraph (iii);

(iii) Report any chemical weapons production facility on its territory that another State has or has had under its ownership and possession and that is or has been located in any place under the jurisdiction or control of another State at any time since 1 January 1946, in accordance with Part V, paragraph 2, of the Verification Annex;

(iv) Declare whether it has transferred or received, directly or indirectly, any equipment for the production of chemical weapons since 1 January 1946 and specify the transfer or receipt of such equipment, in accordance with Part V, paragraphs 3 to 5, of the Verification Annex;

(v) Provide its general plan for destruction of any chemical weapons production facility it owns or possesses, or that is located in any place under its jurisdiction or control, in accordance with Part V, paragraph 6, of the Verification Annex;

(vi) Specify actions to be taken for closure of any chemical weapons production facility it owns or possesses, or that is located in any place under its jurisdiction or control, in accordance with Part V, paragraph 1 (i), of the Verification Annex;

(vii) Provide its general plan for any temporary conversion of any chemical weapons production facility it owns or possesses, or that is located in any place under its jurisdiction or control, into a chemical weapons destruction facility, in accordance with Part V, paragraph 7, of the Verification Annex;

(d)   With respect to other facilities:

Specify the precise location, nature and general scope of activities of any facility or establishment under its ownership or possession, or located in any place under its jurisdiction or control, and that has been designed, constructed or used since 1 January 1946 primarily for development of chemical weapons. Such declaration shall include, inter alia, laboratories and test and evaluation sites;

(e)   With respect to riot control agents: Specify the chemical name, structural formula and Chemical Abstracts Service (CAS) registry number, if assigned, of each chemical it holds for riot control purposes. This declaration shall be updated not later than 30 days after any change becomes effective.

2.   The provisions of this Article and the relevant provisions of Part IV of the Verification Annex shall not, at the discretion of a State Party, apply to chemical weapons buried on its territory before 1 January 1977 and which remain buried, or which had been dumped at sea before 1 January 1985.

Article IV
Chemical weapons

1.   The provisions of this Article and the detailed procedures for its implementation shall apply to all chemical weapons owned or possessed by a State Party, or that are located in any place under its jurisdiction or control, except old chemical weapons and abandoned chemical weapons to which Part IV (B) of the Verification Annex applies.

2. Detailed procedures for the implementation of this Article are set forth in the Verification Annex.

3. All locations at which chemical weapons specified in paragraph 1 are stored or destroyed shall be subject to systematic verification through on-site inspection and monitoring with on-site instruments, in accordance with Part IV (A) of the Verification Annex.

4. Each State Party shall, immediately after the declaration under Article III, paragraph 1 (a), has been submitted, provide access to chemical weapons specified in paragraph 1 for the purpose of systematic verification of the declaration through on-site inspection. Thereafter, each State Party shall not remove any of these chemical weapons, except to a chemical weapons destruction facility. It shall provide access to such chemical weapons, for the purpose of systematic on-site verification.

5. Each State Party shall provide access to any chemical weapons destruction facilities and their storage areas, that it owns or possesses, or that are located in any place under its jurisdiction or control, for the purpose of systematic verification through on-site inspection and monitoring with on-site instruments.

6. Each State Party shall destroy all chemical weapons specified in paragraph 1 pursuant to the Verification Annex and in accordance with the agreed rate and sequence of destruction (hereinafter referred to as "order of destruction"). Such destruction shall begin not later than

two years after this Convention enters into force for it and shall finish not later than 10 years after entry into force of this Convention. A State Party is not precluded from destroying such chemical weapons at a faster rate.

7.   Each State Party shall:

(a) Submit detailed plans for the destruction of chemical weapons specified in paragraph 1 not later than 60 days before each annual destruction period begins, in accordance with Part IV (A), paragraph 29, of the Verification Annex; the detailed plans shall encompass all stocks to be destroyed during the next annual destruction period;

(b) Submit declarations annually regarding the implementation of its plans for destruction of chemical weapons specified in paragraph 1, not later than 60 days after the end of each annual destruction period; and

(c)   Certify, not later than 30 days after the destruction process has been completed, that all chemical weapons specified in paragraph 1 have been destroyed.

8.   If a State ratifies or accedes to this Convention after the 10-year period for destruction set forth in paragraph 6, it shall destroy chemical weapons specified in paragraph 1 as soon as possible. The order of destruction and procedures for stringent verification for such a State Party shall be determined by the Executive Council.

9.   Any chemical weapons discovered by a State Party after the initial declaration of chemical weapons shall be reported,

secured and destroyed in accordance with Part IV (A) of the
Verification Annex.

10. Each State Party, during transportation, sampling,
storage and destruction of chemical weapons, shall assign
the highest priority to ensuring the safety of people and to
protecting the environment. Each State Party shall transport,
sample, store and destroy chemical weapons in accordance
with its national standards for safety and emissions.

11. Any State Party which has on its territory chemical
weapons that are owned or possessed by another State, or
that are located in any place under the jurisdiction or control
of another State, shall make the fullest efforts to ensure that
these chemical weapons are removed from its territory not
later than one year after this Convention enters into force
for it. If they are not removed within one year, the State
Party may request the Organization and other States Parties
to provide assistance in the destruction of these chemical
weapons.

12. Each State Party undertakes to cooperate with other
States Parties that request information or assistance on a
bilateral basis or through the Technical Secretariat regarding
methods and technologies for the safe and efficient
destruction of chemical weapons.

13. In carrying out verification activities pursuant to
this Article and Part IV (A) of the Verification Annex, the
Organization shall consider measures to avoid unnecessary
duplication of bilateral or multilateral agreements on

verification of chemical weapons storage and their destruction among States Parties.

To this end, the Executive Council shall decide to limit verification to measures complementary to those undertaken pursuant to such a bilateral or multilateral agreement, if it considers that:

(a) Verification provisions of such an agreement are consistent with the verification provisions of this Article and Part IV (A) of the Verification Annex;

(b) Implementation of such an agreement provides for sufficient assurance of compliance with the relevant provisions of this Convention; and

(c) Parties to the bilateral or multilateral agreement keep the Organization fully informed about their verification activities.

14. If the Executive Council takes a decision pursuant to paragraph 13, the Organization shall have the right to monitor the implementation of the bilateral or multilateral agreement.

15. Nothing in paragraphs 13 and 14 shall affect the obligation of a State Party to provide declarations pursuant to Article III, this Article and Part IV (A) of the Verification Annex.

16. Each State Party shall meet the costs of destruction of chemical weapons it is obliged to destroy. It shall also

meet the costs of verification of storage and destruction of these chemical weapons unless the Executive Council decides otherwise. If the Executive Council decides to limit verification measures of the Organization pursuant to paragraph 13, the costs of complementary verification and monitoring by the Organization shall be paid in accordance with the United Nations scale of assessment, as specified in Article VIII, paragraph 7.

17. The provisions of this Article and the relevant provisions of Part IV of the Verification Annex shall not, at the discretion of a State Party, apply to chemical weapons buried on its territory before 1 January 1977 and which remain buried, or which had been dumped at sea before 1 January 1985.

Article V
Chemical weapons production facilities

1. The provisions of this Article and the detailed procedures for its implementation shall apply to any and all chemical weapons production facilities owned or possessed by a State Party, or that are located in any place under its jurisdiction or control.

2. Detailed procedures for the implementation of this Article are set forth in the Verification Annex.

3. All chemical weapons production facilities specified in paragraph 1 shall be subject to systematic verification through on-site inspection and monitoring with on-site

instruments in accordance with Part V of the Verification Annex.

4.   Each State Party shall cease immediately all activity at chemical weapons production facilities specified in paragraph 1, except activity required for closure.

5.   No State Party shall construct any new chemical weapons production facilities or modify any existing facilities for the purpose of chemical weapons production or for any other activity prohibited under this Convention.

6.   Each State Party shall, immediately after the declaration under Article III, paragraph 1 (c), has been submitted, provide access to chemical weapons production facilities specified in paragraph 1, for the purpose of systematic verification of the declaration through on-site inspection.

7.   Each State Party shall:

    (a)   Close, not later than 90 days after this Convention enters into force for it, all chemical weapons production facilities specified in paragraph 1, in accordance with Part V of the Verification Annex, and give notice thereof; and

    (b)   Provide access to chemical weapons production facilities specified in paragraph 1, subsequent to closure, for the purpose of systematic verification through on-site inspection and monitoring with on-site instruments in order to ensure that the facility remains closed and is subsequently destroyed.

8.   Each State Party shall destroy all chemical weapons production facilities specified in paragraph 1 and related facilities and equipment, pursuant to the Verification Annex and in accordance with an agreed rate and sequence of destruction (hereinafter referred to as "order of destruction"). Such destruction shall begin not later than one year after this Convention enters into force for it, and shall finish not later than 10 years after entry into force of this Convention. A State Party is not precluded from destroying such facilities at a faster rate.

9.   Each State Party shall:

(a)   Submit detailed plans for destruction of chemical weapons production facilities specified in paragraph 1, not later than 180 days before the destruction of each facility begins;

(b)   Submit declarations annually regarding the implementation of its plans for the destruction of all chemical weapons production facilities specified in paragraph 1, not later than 90 days after the end of each annual destruction period; and

(c)   Certify, not later than 30 days after the destruction process has been completed, that all chemical weapons production facilities specified in paragraph 1 have been destroyed.

10.   If a State ratifies or accedes to this Convention after the 10-year period for destruction set forth in paragraph 8, it

shall destroy chemical weapons production facilities specified in paragraph 1 as soon as possible. The order of destruction and procedures for stringent verification for such a State Party shall be determined by the Executive Council.

11. Each State Party, during the destruction of chemical weapons production facilities, shall assign the highest priority to ensuring the safety of people and to protecting the environment. Each State Party shall destroy chemical weapons production facilities in accordance with its national standards for safety and emissions.

12. Chemical weapons production facilities specified in paragraph 1 may be temporarily converted for destruction of chemical weapons in accordance with Part V, paragraphs 18 to 25, of the Verification Annex. Such a converted facility must be destroyed as soon as it is no longer in use for destruction of chemical weapons but, in any case, not later than 10 years after entry into force of this Convention.

13. A State Party may request, in exceptional cases of compelling need, permission to use a chemical weapons production facility specified in paragraph 1 for purposes not prohibited under this Convention. Upon the recommendation of the Executive Council, the Conference of the States Parties shall decide whether or not to approve the request and shall establish the conditions upon which approval is contingent in accordance with Part V, Section D, of the Verification Annex.

14. The chemical weapons production facility shall be converted in such a manner that the converted facility is not more capable of being reconverted into a chemical weapons production facility than any other facility used for industrial, agricultural, research, medical, pharmaceutical or other peaceful purposes not involving chemicals listed in Schedule 1.

15. All converted facilities shall be subject to systematic verification through on-site inspection and monitoring with on-site instruments in accordance with Part V, Section D, of the Verification Annex.

16. In carrying out verification activities pursuant to this Article and Part V of the Verification Annex, the Organization shall consider measures to avoid unnecessary duplication of bilateral or multilateral agreements on verification of chemical weapons production facilities and their destruction among States Parties.

To this end, the Executive Council shall decide to limit the verification to measures complementary to those undertaken pursuant to such a bilateral or multilateral agreement, if it considers that:

(a) Verification provisions of such an agreement are consistent with the verification provisions of this Article and Part V of the Verification Annex;

(b) Implementation of the agreement provides for sufficient assurance of compliance with the relevant provisions of this Convention; and

(c) Parties to the bilateral or multilateral agreement keep the Organization fully informed about their verification activities.

17. If the Executive Council takes a decision pursuant to paragraph 16, the Organization shall have the right to monitor the implementation of the bilateral or multilateral agreement.

18. Nothing in paragraphs 16 and 17 shall affect the obligation of a State Party to make declarations pursuant to Article III, this Article and Part V of the Verification Annex.

19. Each State Party shall meet the costs of destruction of chemical weapons production facilities it is obliged to destroy. It shall also meet the costs of verification under this Article unless the Executive Council decides otherwise. If the Executive Council decides to limit verification measures of the Organization pursuant to paragraph 16, the costs of complementary verification and monitoring by the Organization shall be paid in accordance with the United Nations scale of assessment, as specified in Article VIII, paragraph 7.

Article VI
Activities not prohibited under this Convention

1.   Each State Party has the right, subject to the provisions of this Convention, to develop, produce, otherwise acquire, retain, transfer and use toxic chemicals and their precursors for purposes not prohibited under this Convention.

2.   Each State Party shall adopt the necessary measures to ensure that toxic chemicals and their precursors are only developed, produced, otherwise acquired, retained, transferred, or used within its territory or in any other place under its jurisdiction or control for purposes not prohibited under this Convention. To this end, and in order to verify that activities are in accordance with obligations under this Convention, each State Party shall subject toxic chemicals and their precursors listed in Schedules 1, 2 and 3 of the Annex on Chemicals, facilities related to such chemicals, and other facilities as specified in the Verification Annex, that are located on its territory or in any other place under its jurisdiction or control, to verification measures as provided in the Verification Annex.

3.   Each State Party shall subject chemicals listed in Schedule 1 (hereinafter referred to as "Schedule 1 chemicals") to the prohibitions on production, acquisition, retention, transfer and use as specified in Part VI of the Verification Annex. It shall subject Schedule 1 chemicals and facilities specified in Part VI of the Verification Annex to systematic verification through on-site inspection and monitoring with

on-site instruments in accordance with that Part of the Verification Annex.

4.   Each State Party shall subject chemicals listed in Schedule 2 (hereinafter referred to as "Schedule 2 chemicals") and facilities specified in Part VII of the Verification Annex to data monitoring and on-site verification in accordance with that Part of the Verification Annex.

5.   Each State Party shall subject chemicals listed in Schedule 3 (hereinafter referred to as "Schedule 3 chemicals") and facilities specified in Part VIII of the Verification Annex to data monitoring and on-site verification in accordance with that Part of the Verification Annex.

6.   Each State Party shall subject facilities specified in Part IX of the Verification Annex to data monitoring and eventual on-site verification in accordance with that Part of the Verification Annex unless decided otherwise by the Conference of the States Parties pursuant to Part IX, paragraph 22, of the Verification Annex.

7.   Not later than 30 days after this Convention enters into force for it, each State Party shall make an initial declaration on relevant chemicals and facilities in accordance with the Verification Annex.

8.   Each State Party shall make annual declarations regarding the relevant chemicals and facilities in accordance with the Verification Annex.

9. For the purpose of on-site verification, each State Party shall grant to the inspectors access to facilities as required in the Verification Annex.

10. In conducting verification activities, the Technical Secretariat shall avoid undue intrusion into the State Party's chemical activities for purposes not prohibited under this Convention and, in particular, abide by the provisions set forth in the Annex on the Protection of Confidential Information (hereinafter referred to as "Confidentiality Annex").

11. The provisions of this Article shall be implemented in a manner which avoids hampering the economic or technological development of States Parties, and international cooperation in the field of chemical activities for purposes not prohibited under this Convention including the international exchange of scientific and technical information and chemicals and equipment for the production, processing or use of chemicals for purposes not prohibited under this Convention.

Article VII
National implementation measures

General undertakings

1. Each State Party shall, in accordance with its constitutional processes, adopt the necessary measures to implement its obligations under this Convention. In particular, it shall:

(a) Prohibit natural and legal persons anywhere on its territory or in any other place under its jurisdiction as recognized by international law from undertaking any activity prohibited to a State Party under this Convention, including enacting penal legislation with respect to such activity;

(b) Not permit in any place under its control any activity prohibited to a State Party under this Convention; and

(c) Extend its penal legislation enacted under subparagraph (a) to any activity prohibited to a State Party under this Convention undertaken anywhere by natural persons, possessing its nationality, in conformity with international law.

2. Each State Party shall cooperate with other States Parties and afford the appropriate form of legal assistance to facilitate the implementation of the obligations under paragraph 1.

3. Each State Party, during the implementation of its obligations under this Convention, shall assign the highest priority to ensuring the safety of people and to protecting the environment, and shall cooperate as appropriate with other States Parties in this regard.

Relations between the State Party and the Organization

4.   In order to fulfil its obligations under this Convention, each State Party shall designate or establish a National Authority to serve as the national focal point for effective liaison with the Organization and other States Parties. Each State Party shall notify the Organization of its National Authority at the time that this Convention enters into force for it.

5.   Each State Party shall inform the Organization of the legislative and administrative measures taken to implement this Convention.

6.   Each State Party shall treat as confidential and afford special handling to information and data that it receives in confidence from the Organization in connection with the implementation of this Convention. It shall treat such information and data exclusively in connection with its rights and obligations under this Convention and in accordance with the provisions set forth in the Confidentiality Annex.

7.   Each State Party undertakes to cooperate with the Organization in the exercise of all its functions and in particular to provide assistance to the Technical Secretariat.

Article VIII
The Organization

A.   General provisions

1.   The States Parties to this Convention hereby establish the Organization for the Prohibition of Chemical Weapons to achieve the object and purpose of this Convention, to ensure the implementation of its provisions, including those for international verification of compliance with it, and to provide a forum for consultation and cooperation among States Parties.

2.   All States Parties to this Convention shall be members of the Organization. A State Party shall not be deprived of its membership in the Organization.

3.   The seat of the Headquarters of the Organization shall be The Hague, Kingdom of the Netherlands.

4.   There are hereby established as the organs of the Organization: the Conference of the States Parties, the Executive Council, and the Technical Secretariat.

5.   The Organization shall conduct its verification activities provided for under this Convention in the least intrusive manner possible consistent with the timely and efficient accomplishment of their objectives. It shall request only the information and data necessary to fulfil its responsibilities under this Convention. It shall take every precaution to protect the confidentiality of information on civil and military activities and facilities coming to its knowledge in the implementation of this Convention and, in particular,

shall abide by the provisions set forth in the Confidentiality Annex.

6. In undertaking its verification activities the Organization shall consider measures to make use of advances in science and technology.

7. The costs of the Organization's activities shall be paid by States Parties in accordance with the United Nations scale of assessment adjusted to take into account differences in membership between the United Nations and this Organization, and subject to the provisions of Articles IV and V. Financial contributions of States Parties to the Preparatory Commission shall be deducted in an appropriate way from their contributions to the regular budget. The budget of the Organization shall comprise two separate chapters, one relating to administrative and other costs, and one relating to verification costs.

8. A member of the Organization which is in arrears in the payment of its financial contribution to the Organization shall have no vote in the Organization if the amount of its arrears equals or exceeds the amount of the contribution due from it for the preceding two full years. The Conference of the States Parties may, nevertheless, permit such a member to vote if it is satisfied that the failure to pay is due to conditions beyond the control of the member.

B. The Conference of the States Parties

Composition, procedures and decision-making

9. The Conference of the States Parties (hereinafter referred to as "the Conference") shall be composed of all members of this Organization. Each member shall have one representative in the Conference, who may be accompanied by alternates and advisers.

10. The first session of the Conference shall be convened by the depositary not later than 30 days after the entry into force of this Convention.

11. The Conference shall meet in regular sessions which shall be held annually unless it decides otherwise.

12. Special sessions of the Conference shall be convened:

(a) When decided by the Conference;

(b) When requested by the Executive Council;

(c) When requested by any member and supported by one third of the members; or

(d) In accordance with paragraph 22 to undertake reviews of the operation of this Convention.

Except in the case of subparagraph (d), the special session shall be convened not later than 30 days after receipt of the request by the Director-General of the Technical Secretariat, unless specified otherwise in the request.

13. The Conference shall also be convened in the form of an Amendment Conference in accordance with Article XV, paragraph 2.

14. Sessions of the Conference shall take place at the seat of the Organization unless the Conference decides otherwise.

15. The Conference shall adopt its rules of procedure. At the beginning of each regular session, it shall elect its Chairman and such other officers as may be required. They shall hold office until a new Chairman and other officers are elected at the next regular session.

16. A majority of the members of the Organization shall constitute a quorum for the Conference.

17. Each member of the Organization shall have one vote in the Conference.

18. The Conference shall take decisions on questions of procedure by a simple majority of the members present and voting. Decisions on matters of substance should be taken as far as possible by consensus. If consensus is not attainable when an issue comes up for decision, the Chairman shall defer any vote for 24 hours and during this period of deferment shall make every effort to facilitate achievement of consensus, and shall report to the Conference before the end of this period. If consensus is not possible at the end of 24 hours, the Conference shall take the decision by a two-thirds majority of members present and voting unless specified otherwise in this Convention. When the issue

arises as to whether the question is one of substance or not, that question shall be treated as a matter of substance unless otherwise decided by the Conference by the majority required for decisions on matters of substance.

Powers and functions

19. The Conference shall be the principal organ of the Organization. It shall consider any questions, matters or issues within the scope of this Convention, including those relating to the powers and functions of the Executive Council and the Technical Secretariat. It may make recommendations and take decisions on any questions, matters or issues related to this Convention raised by a State Party or brought to its attention by the Executive Council.

20. The Conference shall oversee the implementation of this Convention, and act in order to promote its object and purpose. The Conference shall review compliance with this Convention. It shall also oversee the activities of the Executive Council and the Technical Secretariat and may issue guidelines in accordance with this Convention to either of them in the exercise of their functions.

21. The Conference shall:

(a) Consider and adopt at its regular sessions the report, programme and budget of the Organization, submitted by the Executive Council, as well as consider other reports;

(b)   Decide on the scale of financial contributions to be paid by States Parties in accordance with paragraph 7;

(c)   Elect the members of the Executive Council;

(d)   Appoint the Director-General of the Technical Secretariat (hereinafter referred to as "the Director-General");

(e)   Approve the rules of procedure of the Executive Council submitted by the latter;

(f)   Establish such subsidiary organs as it finds necessary for the exercise of its functions in accordance with this Convention;

(g)   Foster international cooperation for peaceful purposes in the field of chemical activities;

(h)   Review scientific and technological developments that could affect the operation of this Convention and, in this context, direct the Director-General to establish a Scientific Advisory Board to enable him, in the performance of his functions, to render specialized advice in areas of science and technology relevant to this Convention, to the Conference, the Executive Council or States Parties. The Scientific Advisory Board shall be composed of independent experts appointed in accordance with terms of reference adopted by the Conference;

(i) Consider and approve at its first session any draft agreements, provisions and guidelines developed by the Preparatory Commission;

(j) Establish at its first session the voluntary fund for assistance in accordance with Article X;

(k) Take the necessary measures to ensure compliance with this Convention and to redress and remedy any situation which contravenes the provisions of this Convention, in accordance with Article XII.

22. The Conference shall not later than one year after the expiry of the fifth and the tenth year after the entry into force of this Convention, and at such other times within that time period as may be decided upon, convene in special sessions to undertake reviews of the operation of this Convention. Such reviews shall take into account any relevant scientific and technological developments. At intervals of five years thereafter, unless otherwise decided upon, further sessions of the Conference shall be convened with the same objective.

C. The Executive Council

Composition, procedure and decision-making

23. The Executive Council shall consist of 41 members. Each State Party shall have the right, in accordance with the principle of rotation, to serve on the Executive Council. The members of the Executive Council shall be elected by the Conference for a term of two years. In order to ensure the effective functioning of this Convention, due regard being

specially paid to equitable geographical distribution, to the importance of chemical industry, as well as to political and security interests, the Executive Council shall be composed as follows:

(a)　Nine States Parties from Africa to be designated by States Parties located in this region. As a basis for this designation it is understood that, out of these nine States Parties, three members shall, as a rule, be the States Parties with the most significant national chemical industry in the region as determined by internationally reported and published data; in addition, the regional group shall agree also to take into account other regional factors in designating these three members;

(b)　Nine States Parties from Asia to be designated by States Parties located in this region. As a basis for this designation it is understood that, out of these nine States Parties, four members shall, as a rule, be the States Parties with the most significant national chemical industry in the region as determined by internationally reported and published data; in addition, the regional group shall agree also to take into account other regional factors in designating these four members;

(c)　Five States Parties from Eastern Europe to be designated by States Parties located in this region. As a basis for this designation it is understood that, out of these five States Parties, one member shall, as a rule, be the State Party with the most significant national chemical industry in the region as determined by internationally reported and published data; in addition, the regional group shall agree also to take into account other regional factors in designating this one member;

(d) Seven States Parties from Latin America and the Caribbean to be designated by States Parties located in this region. As a basis for this designation it is understood that, out of these seven States Parties, three members shall, as a rule, be the States Parties with the most significant national chemical industry in the region as determined by internationally reported and published data; in addition, the regional group shall agree also to take into account other regional factors in designating these three members;

(e) Ten States Parties from among Western European and other States to be designated by States Parties located in this region. As a basis for this designation it is understood that, out of these 10 States Parties, 5 members shall, as a rule, be the States Parties with the most significant national chemical industry in the region as determined by internationally reported and published data; in addition, the regional group shall agree also to take into account other regional factors in designating these five members;

(f) One further State Party to be designated consecutively by States Parties located in the regions of Asia and Latin America and the Caribbean. As a basis for this designation it is understood that this State Party shall be a rotating member from these regions.

24. For the first election of the Executive Council 20 members shall be elected for a term of one year, due regard being paid to the established numerical proportions as described in paragraph 23.

25. After the full implementation of Articles IV and V the Conference may, upon the request of a majority of the members of the Executive Council, review the composition of the Executive Council taking into account developments related to the principles specified in paragraph 23 that are governing its composition.

26. The Executive Council shall elaborate its rules of procedure and submit them to the Conference for approval.

27. The Executive Council shall elect its Chairman from among its members.

28. The Executive Council shall meet for regular sessions. Between regular sessions it shall meet as often as may be required for the fulfilment of its powers and functions.

29. Each member of the Executive Council shall have one vote. Unless otherwise specified in this Convention, the Executive Council shall take decisions on matters of substance by a two-thirds majority of all its members. The Executive Council shall take decisions on questions of procedure by a simple majority of all its members. When the issue arises as to whether the question is one of substance or not, that question shall be treated as a matter of substance

unless otherwise decided by the Executive Council by the majority required for decisions on matters of substance.

Powers and functions

30. The Executive Council shall be the executive organ of the Organization. It shall be responsible to the Conference. The Executive Council shall carry out the powers and functions entrusted to it under this Convention, as well as those functions delegated to it by the Conference. In so doing, it shall act in conformity with the recommendations, decisions and guidelines of the Conference and assure their proper and continuous implementation.

31. The Executive Council shall promote the effective implementation of, and compliance with, this Convention. It shall supervise the activities of the Technical Secretariat, cooperate with the National Authority of each State Party and facilitate consultations and cooperation among States Parties at their request.

32. The Executive Council shall:

(a) Consider and submit to the Conference the draft programme and budget of the Organization;

(b) Consider and submit to the Conference the draft report of the Organization on the implementation of this Convention, the report on the performance of its own activities and such special reports as it deems necessary or which the Conference may request;

(c) Make arrangements for the sessions of the Conference including the preparation of the draft agenda.

33. The Executive Council may request the convening of a special session of the Conference.

34. The Executive Council shall:

(a) Conclude agreements or arrangements with States and international organizations on behalf of the Organization, subject to prior approval by the Conference;

(b) Conclude agreements with States Parties on behalf of the Organization in connection with Article X and supervise the voluntary fund referred to in Article X;

(c) Approve agreements or arrangements relating to the implementation of verification activities, negotiated by the Technical Secretariat with States Parties.

35. The Executive Council shall consider any issue or matter within its competence affecting this Convention and its implementation, including concerns regarding compliance, and cases of non-compliance, and, as appropriate, inform States Parties and bring the issue or matter to the attention of the Conference.

36. In its consideration of doubts or concerns regarding compliance and cases of non-compliance, including, inter alia, abuse of the rights provided for under this Convention, the Executive Council shall consult with the States Parties involved and, as appropriate, request the State Party to take

measures to redress the situation within a specified time. To the extent that the Executive Council considers further action to be necessary, it shall take, inter alia, one or more of the following measures:

(a) Inform all States Parties of the issue or matter;

(b) Bring the issue or matter to the attention of the Conference;

(c) Make recommendations to the Conference regarding measures to redress the situation and to ensure compliance.

The Executive Council shall, in cases of particular gravity and urgency, bring the issue or matter, including relevant information and conclusions, directly to the attention of the United Nations General Assembly and the United Nations Security Council. It shall at the same time inform all States Parties of this step.

D.   The Technical Secretariat

37. The Technical Secretariat shall assist the Conference and the Executive Council in the performance of their functions. The Technical Secretariat shall carry out the verification measures provided for in this Convention. It shall carry out the other functions entrusted to it under this Convention as well as those functions delegated to it by the Conference and the Executive Council.

38. The Technical Secretariat shall:

(a)   Prepare and submit to the Executive Council the draft programme and budget of the Organization;

(b)   Prepare and submit to the Executive Council the draft report of the Organization on the implementation of this Convention and such other reports as the Conference or the Executive Council may request;

(c)   Provide administrative and technical support to the Conference, the Executive Council and subsidiary organs;

(d)   Address and receive communications on behalf of the Organization to and from States Parties on matters pertaining to the implementation of this Convention;

(e)   Provide technical assistance and technical evaluation to States Parties in the implementation of the provisions of this Convention, including evaluation of scheduled and unscheduled chemicals.

39.   The Technical Secretariat shall:

(a)   Negotiate agreements or arrangements relating to the implementation of verification activities with States Parties, subject to approval by the Executive Council;

(b)   Not later than 180 days after entry into force of this Convention, coordinate the establishment and maintenance of permanent stockpiles of emergency and humanitarian assistance by States Parties in accordance with Article X, paragraphs 7 (b) and (c). The Technical Secretariat may inspect the items maintained for serviceability. Lists of items to be stockpiled shall be considered and approved by the Conference pursuant to paragraph 21 (i) above;

(c) Administer the voluntary fund referred to in Article X, compile declarations made by the States Parties and register, when requested, bilateral agreements concluded between States Parties or between a State Party and the Organization for the purposes of Article X.

40. The Technical Secretariat shall inform the Executive Council of any problem that has arisen with regard to the discharge of its functions, including doubts, ambiguities or uncertainties about compliance with this Convention that have come to its notice in the performance of its verification activities and that it has been unable to resolve or clarify through its consultations with the State Party concerned.

41. The Technical Secretariat shall comprise a Director-General, who shall be its head and chief administrative officer, inspectors and such scientific, technical and other personnel as may be required.

42. The Inspectorate shall be a unit of the Technical Secretariat and shall act under the supervision of the Director-General.

43. The Director-General shall be appointed by the Conference upon the recommendation of the Executive Council for a term of four years, renewable for one further term, but not thereafter.

44. The Director-General shall be responsible to the Conference and the Executive Council for the appointment of the staff and the organization and functioning of the Technical Secretariat. The paramount consideration in the employment of the staff and in the determination of the conditions of service shall be the necessity of securing the highest standards of efficiency, competence and integrity. Only citizens of States Parties shall serve as the Director-General, as inspectors or as other members of the professional and clerical staff. Due regard shall be paid to the importance of recruiting the staff on as wide a geographical basis as possible. Recruitment shall be guided by the principle that the staff shall be kept to a minimum necessary for the proper discharge of the responsibilities of the Technical Secretariat.

45. The Director-General shall be responsible for the organization and functioning of the Scientific Advisory Board referred to in paragraph 21 (h). The Director-General shall, in consultation with States Parties, appoint members of the Scientific Advisory Board, who shall serve in their individual capacity. The members of the Board shall be appointed on the basis of their expertise in the particular scientific fields relevant to the implementation of this Convention. The Director-General may also, as appropriate, in consultation with members of the Board, establish temporary working groups of scientific experts to provide recommendations on specific issues. In regard to the above, States Parties may submit lists of experts to the Director-General.

46. In the performance of their duties, the Director-General, the inspectors and the other members of the staff shall not seek or receive instructions from any Government or from any other source external to the Organization. They shall refrain from any action that might reflect on their positions as international officers responsible only to the Conference and the Executive Council.

47. Each State Party shall respect the exclusively international character of the responsibilities of the Director-General, the inspectors and the other members of the staff and not seek to influence them in the discharge of their responsibilities.

E. Privileges and immunities

48. The Organization shall enjoy on the territory and in any other place under the jurisdiction or control of a State Party such legal capacity and such privileges and immunities as are necessary for the exercise of its functions.

49. Delegates of States Parties, together with their alternates and advisers, representatives appointed to the Executive Council together with their alternates and advisers, the Director-General and the staff of the Organization shall enjoy such privileges and immunities as are necessary in the independent exercise of their functions in connection with the Organization.

50. The legal capacity, privileges, and immunities referred to in this Article shall be defined in agreements between the Organization and the States Parties as well as in an

agreement between the Organization and the State in which the headquarters of the Organization is seated. These agreements shall be considered and approved by the Conference pursuant to paragraph 21 (i).

51. Notwithstanding paragraphs 48 and 49, the privileges and immunities enjoyed by the Director-General and the staff of the Technical Secretariat during the conduct of verification activities shall be those set forth in Part II, Section B, of the Verification Annex.

Article IX
Consultations, cooperation and fact-finding

1. States Parties shall consult and cooperate, directly among themselves, or through the Organization or other appropriate international procedures, including procedures within the framework of the United Nations and in accordance with its Charter, on any matter which may be raised relating to the object and purpose, or the implementation of the provisions, of this Convention.

2. Without prejudice to the right of any State Party to request a challenge inspection, States Parties should, whenever possible, first make every effort to clarify and resolve, through exchange of information and consultations among themselves, any matter which may cause doubt about compliance with this Convention, or which gives rise to concerns about a related matter which may be considered ambiguous. A State Party which receives a request from another State Party for clarification of any matter which

the requesting State Party believes causes such a doubt or concern shall provide the requesting State Party as soon as possible, but in any case not later than 10 days after the request, with information sufficient to answer the doubt or concern raised along with an explanation of how the information provided resolves the matter. Nothing in this Convention shall affect the right of any two or more States Parties to arrange by mutual consent for inspections or any other procedures among themselves to clarify and resolve any matter which may cause doubt about compliance or gives rise to a concern about a related matter which may be considered ambiguous. Such arrangements shall not affect the rights and obligations of any State Party under other provisions of this Convention.

Procedure for requesting clarification

3.   A State Party shall have the right to request the Executive Council to assist in clarifying any situation which may be considered ambiguous or which gives rise to a concern about the possible non-compliance of another State Party with this Convention. The Executive Council shall provide appropriate information in its possession relevant to such a concern.

4.   A State Party shall have the right to request the Executive Council to obtain clarification from another State Party on any situation which may be considered ambiguous or which gives rise to a concern about its possible non-compliance with this Convention. In such a case, the following shall apply:

(a) The Executive Council shall forward the request for clarification to the State Party concerned through the Director-General not later than 24 hours after its receipt;

(b) The requested State Party shall provide the clarification to the Executive Council as soon as possible, but in any case not later than 10 days after the receipt of the request;

(c) The Executive Council shall take note of the clarification and forward it to the requesting State Party not later than 24 hours after its receipt;

(d) If the requesting State Party deems the clarification to be inadequate, it shall have the right to request the Executive Council to obtain from the requested State Party further clarification;

(e) For the purpose of obtaining further clarification requested under subparagraph (d), the Executive Council may call on the Director-General to establish a group of experts from the Technical Secretariat, or if appropriate staff are not available in the Technical Secretariat, from elsewhere, to examine all available information and data relevant to the situation causing the concern. The group of experts shall submit a factual report to the Executive Council on its findings;

(f) If the requesting State Party considers the clarification obtained under subparagraphs (d) and (e) to be unsatisfactory, it shall have the right to request a special session of the Executive Council in which States Parties involved that are not members of the Executive Council shall be entitled to take part. In such a special session, the Executive Council shall consider the matter and may recommend any measure it deems appropriate to resolve the situation.

5.   A State Party shall also have the right to request the Executive Council to clarify any situation which has been considered ambiguous or has given rise to a concern about its possible non-compliance with this Convention. The Executive Council shall respond by providing such assistance as appropriate.

6.   The Executive Council shall inform the States Parties about any request for clarification provided in this Article.

7.   If the doubt or concern of a State Party about a possible non-compliance has not been resolved within 60 days after the submission of the request for clarification to the Executive Council, or it believes its doubts warrant urgent consideration, notwithstanding its right to request a challenge inspection, it may request a special session of the Conference in accordance with Article VIII, paragraph 12 (c). At such a special session, the Conference shall consider the matter and may recommend any measure it deems appropriate to resolve the situation.

Procedures for challenge inspections

8.   Each State Party has the right to request an on-site challenge inspection of any facility or location in the

territory or in any other place under the jurisdiction or control of any other State Party for the sole purpose of clarifying and resolving any questions concerning possible non-compliance with the provisions of this Convention, and to have this inspection conducted anywhere without delay by an inspection team designated by the Director-General and in accordance with the Verification Annex.

9.   Each State Party is under the obligation to keep the inspection request within the scope of this Convention and to provide in the inspection request all appropriate information on the basis of which a concern has arisen regarding possible non-compliance with this Convention as specified in the Verification Annex. Each State Party shall refrain from unfounded inspection requests, care being taken to avoid abuse. The challenge inspection shall be carried out for the sole purpose of determining facts relating to the possible non-compliance.

10.   For the purpose of verifying compliance with the provisions of this Convention, each State Party shall permit the Technical Secretariat to conduct the on-site challenge inspection pursuant to paragraph 8.

11.   Pursuant to a request for a challenge inspection of a facility or location, and in accordance with the procedures provided for in the Verification Annex, the inspected State Party shall have:

(a)   The right and the obligation to make every reasonable effort to demonstrate its compliance with this

Convention and, to this end, to enable the inspection team to fulfil its mandate;

(b) The obligation to provide access within the requested site for the sole purpose of establishing facts relevant to the concern regarding possible non-compliance; and

(c) The right to take measures to protect sensitive installations, and to prevent disclosure of confidential information and data, not related to this Convention.

12. With regard to an observer, the following shall apply:

(a) The requesting State Party may, subject to the agreement of the inspected State Party, send a representative who may be a national either of the requesting State Party or of a third State Party, to observe the conduct of the challenge inspection.

(b) The inspected State Party shall then grant access to the observer in accordance with the Verification Annex.

(c) The inspected State Party shall, as a rule, accept the proposed observer, but if the inspected State Party exercises a refusal, that fact shall be recorded in the final report.

13. The requesting State Party shall present an inspection request for an on-site challenge inspection to the Executive Council and at the same time to the Director-General for immediate processing.

14. The Director-General shall immediately ascertain that the inspection request meets the requirements specified in Part X, paragraph 4, of the Verification Annex, and, if necessary, assist the requesting State Party in filing the inspection request accordingly. When the inspection request fulfils the requirements, preparations for the challenge inspection shall begin.

15. The Director-General shall transmit the inspection request to the inspected State Party not less than 12 hours before the planned arrival of the inspection team at the point of entry.

16. After having received the inspection request, the Executive Council shall take cognizance of the Director-General's actions on the request and shall keep the case under its consideration throughout the inspection procedure. However, its deliberations shall not delay the inspection process.

17. The Executive Council may, not later than 12 hours after having received the inspection request, decide by a three-quarter majority of all its members against carrying out the challenge inspection, if it considers the inspection request to be frivolous, abusive or clearly beyond the scope of this Convention as described in paragraph 8. Neither the requesting nor the inspected State Party shall participate in such a decision. If the Executive Council decides against the challenge inspection, preparations shall be stopped, no further action on the inspection request shall be taken, and the States Parties concerned shall be informed accordingly.

18. The Director-General shall issue an inspection mandate for the conduct of the challenge inspection. The inspection mandate shall be the inspection request referred to in paragraphs 8 and 9 put into operational terms, and shall conform with the inspection request.

19. The challenge inspection shall be conducted in accordance with Part X or, in the case of alleged use, in accordance with Part XI of the Verification Annex. The inspection team shall be guided by the principle of conducting the challenge inspection in the least intrusive manner possible, consistent with the effective and timely accomplishment of its mission.

20. The inspected State Party shall assist the inspection team throughout the challenge inspection and facilitate its task. If the inspected State Party proposes, pursuant to Part X, Section C, of the Verification Annex, arrangements to demonstrate compliance with this Convention, alternative to full and comprehensive access, it shall make every reasonable effort, through consultations with the inspection team, to reach agreement on the modalities for establishing the facts with the aim of demonstrating its compliance.

21. The final report shall contain the factual findings as well as an assessment by the inspection team of the degree and nature of access and cooperation granted for the satisfactory implementation of the challenge inspection. The Director-General shall promptly transmit the final report of the inspection team to the requesting State Party, to the inspected State Party, to the Executive Council and to

all other States Parties. The Director-General shall further transmit promptly to the Executive Council the assessments of the requesting and of the inspected States Parties, as well as the views of other States Parties which may be conveyed to the Director-General for that purpose, and then provide them to all States Parties.

22. The Executive Council shall, in accordance with its powers and functions, review the final report of the inspection team as soon as it is presented, and address any concerns as to:

(a) Whether any non-compliance has occurred;

(b) Whether the request had been within the scope of this Convention; and

(c) Whether the right to request a challenge inspection had been abused.

23. If the Executive Council reaches the conclusion, in keeping with its powers and functions, that further action may be necessary with regard to paragraph 22, it shall take the appropriate measures to redress the situation and to ensure compliance with this Convention, including specific recommendations to the Conference. In the case of abuse, the Executive Council shall examine whether the requesting State Party should bear any of the financial implications of the challenge inspection.

24. The requesting State Party and the inspected State Party shall have the right to participate in the review process. The

Executive Council shall inform the States Parties and the next session of the Conference of the outcome of the process.

25. If the Executive Council has made specific recommendations to the Conference, the Conference shall consider action in accordance with Article XII.

Article X
Assistance and protection against chemical weapons

1. For the purposes of this Article, "Assistance" means the coordination and delivery to States Parties of protection against chemical weapons, including, inter alia, the following: detection equipment and alarm systems; protective equipment; decontamination equipment and decontaminants; medical antidotes and treatments; and advice on any of these protective measures.

2. Nothing in this Convention shall be interpreted as impeding the right of any State Party to conduct research into, develop, produce, acquire, transfer or use means of protection against chemical weapons, for purposes not prohibited under this Convention.

3. Each State Party undertakes to facilitate, and shall have the right to participate in, the fullest possible exchange of equipment, material and scientific and technological information concerning means of protection against chemical weapons.

4. For the purposes of increasing the transparency of national programmes related to protective purposes, each State Party shall provide annually to the Technical Secretariat information on its programme, in accordance with procedures to be considered and approved by the Conference pursuant to Article VIII, paragraph 21 (i).

5. The Technical Secretariat shall establish, not later than 180 days after entry into force of this Convention and maintain, for the use of any requesting State Party, a data bank containing freely available information concerning various means of protection against chemical weapons as well as such information as may be provided by States Parties.

The Technical Secretariat shall also, within the resources available to it, and at the request of a State Party, provide expert advice and assist the State Party in identifying how its programmes for the development and improvement of a protective capacity against chemical weapons could be implemented.

6. Nothing in this Convention shall be interpreted as impeding the right of States Parties to request and provide assistance bilaterally and to conclude individual agreements with other States Parties concerning the emergency procurement of assistance.

7. Each State Party undertakes to provide assistance through the Organization and to this end to elect to take one or more of the following measures:

(a)   To contribute to the voluntary fund for assistance to be established by the Conference at its first session;

(b)   To conclude, if possible not later than 180 days after this Convention enters into force for it, agreements with the Organization concerning the procurement, upon demand, of assistance;

(c)   To declare, not later than 180 days after this Convention enters into force for it, the kind of assistance it might provide in response to an appeal by the Organization. If, however, a State Party subsequently is unable to provide the assistance envisaged in its declaration, it is still under the obligation to provide assistance in accordance with this paragraph.

8.   Each State Party has the right to request and, subject to the procedures set forth in paragraphs 9, 10 and 11, to receive assistance and protection against the use or threat of use of chemical weapons if it considers that:

(a)   Chemical weapons have been used against it;

(b)   Riot control agents have been used against it as a method of warfare; or

(c)   It is threatened by actions or activities of any State that are prohibited for States Parties by Article I.

9.   The request, substantiated by relevant information, shall be submitted to the Director-General, who shall transmit it immediately to the Executive Council and to

all States Parties. The Director-General shall immediately forward the request to States Parties which have volunteered, in accordance with paragraphs 7 (b) and (c), to dispatch emergency assistance in case of use of chemical weapons or use of riot control agents as a method of warfare, or humanitarian assistance in case of serious threat of use of chemical weapons or serious threat of use of riot control agents as a method of warfare to the State Party concerned not later than 12 hours after receipt of the request. The Director-General shall initiate, not later than 24 hours after receipt of the request, an investigation in order to provide foundation for further action. He shall complete the investigation within 72 hours and forward a report to the Executive Council. If additional time is required for completion of the investigation, an interim report shall be submitted within the same time-frame. The additional time required for investigation shall not exceed 72 hours. It may, however, be further extended by similar periods. Reports at the end of each additional period shall be submitted to the Executive Council. The investigation shall, as appropriate and in conformity with the request and the information accompanying the request, establish relevant facts related to the request as well as the type and scope of supplementary assistance and protection needed.

10. The Executive Council shall meet not later than 24 hours after receiving an investigation report to consider the situation and shall take a decision by simple majority within the following 24 hours on whether to instruct the Technical Secretariat to provide supplementary assistance. The Technical Secretariat shall immediately transmit to all

States Parties and relevant international organizations the investigation report and the decision taken by the Executive Council. When so decided by the Executive Council, the Director-General shall provide assistance immediately. For this purpose, the Director-General may cooperate with the requesting State Party, other States Parties and relevant international organizations. The States Parties shall make the fullest possible efforts to provide assistance.

11. If the information available from the ongoing investigation or other reliable sources would give sufficient proof that there are victims of use of chemical weapons and immediate action is indispensable, the Director-General shall notify all States Parties and shall take emergency measures of assistance, using the resources the Conference has placed at his disposal for such contingencies. The Director-General shall keep the Executive Council informed of actions undertaken pursuant to this paragraph.

Article XI
Economic and technological development

1.   The provisions of this Convention shall be implemented in a manner which avoids hampering the economic or technological development of States Parties, and international cooperation in the field of chemical activities for purposes not prohibited under this Convention including the international exchange of scientific and technical information and chemicals and equipment for the production, processing or use of chemicals for purposes not prohibited under this Convention.

2.   Subject to the provisions of this Convention and without prejudice to the principles and applicable rules of international law, the States Parties shall:

(a)   Have the right, individually or collectively, to conduct research with, to develop, produce, acquire, retain, transfer, and use chemicals;

(b)   Undertake to facilitate, and have the right to participate in, the fullest possible exchange of chemicals, equipment and scientific and technical information relating to the development and application of chemistry for purposes not prohibited under this Convention;

(c)   Not maintain among themselves any restrictions, including those in any international agreements, incompatible with the obligations undertaken under this Convention, which would restrict or impede trade and the development and promotion of scientific and technological knowledge in the field of chemistry for industrial, agricultural, research, medical, pharmaceutical or other peaceful purposes;

(d)   Not use this Convention as grounds for applying any measures other than those provided for, or permitted, under this Convention nor use any other international agreement for pursuing an objective inconsistent with this Convention;

(e)   Undertake to review their existing national regulations in the field of trade in chemicals in order to render them consistent with the object and purpose of this Convention.

Article XII
Measures to redress a situation and to ensure compliance, including sanctions

1.   The Conference shall take the necessary measures, as set forth in paragraphs 2, 3 and 4, to ensure compliance with this Convention and to redress and remedy any situation which contravenes the provisions of this Convention. In considering action pursuant to this paragraph, the Conference shall take into account all information and recommendations on the issues submitted by the Executive Council.

2.   In cases where a State Party has been requested by the Executive Council to take measures to redress a situation raising problems with regard to its compliance, and where the State Party fails to fulfil the request within the specified time, the Conference may, inter alia, upon the recommendation of the Executive Council, restrict or suspend the State Party's rights and privileges under this Convention until it undertakes the necessary action to conform with its obligations under this Convention.

3.   In cases where serious damage to the object and purpose of this Convention may result from activities prohibited under this Convention, in particular by Article I, the Conference may recommend collective measures to States Parties in conformity with international law.

4.   The Conference shall, in cases of particular gravity, bring the issue, including relevant information and conclusions, to the attention of the United Nations General Assembly and the United Nations Security Council.

Article XIII
Relation to other international agreements

Nothing in this Convention shall be interpreted as in any way limiting or detracting from the obligations assumed by any State under the Protocol for the Prohibition of the Use in War of Asphyxiating, Poisonous or Other Gases, and of Bacteriological Methods of Warfare, signed at Geneva on 17 June 1925, and under the Convention on the Prohibition of the Development, Production and Stockpiling of Bacteriological (Biological) and Toxin Weapons and on Their Destruction, signed at London, Moscow and Washington on 10 April 1972.

Article XIV
Settlement of disputes

1.   Disputes that may arise concerning the application or the interpretation of this Convention shall be settled in accordance with the relevant provisions of this Convention and in conformity with the provisions of the Charter of the United Nations.

2.   When a dispute arises between two or more States Parties, or between one or more States Parties and the Organization, relating to the interpretation or application of

this Convention, the parties concerned shall consult together with a view to the expeditious settlement of the dispute by negotiation or by other peaceful means of the parties' choice, including recourse to appropriate organs of this Convention and, by mutual consent, referral to the International Court of Justice in conformity with the Statute of the Court. The States Parties involved shall keep the Executive Council informed of actions being taken.

3.   The Executive Council may contribute to the settlement of a dispute by whatever means it deems appropriate, including offering its good offices, calling upon the States Parties to a dispute to start the settlement process of their choice and recommending a time-limit for any agreed procedure.

4.   The Conference shall consider questions related to disputes raised by States Parties or brought to its attention by the Executive Council. The Conference shall, as it finds necessary, establish or entrust organs with tasks related to the settlement of these disputes in conformity with Article VIII, paragraph 21 (f).

5.   The Conference and the Executive Council are separately empowered, subject to authorization from the General Assembly of the United Nations, to request the International Court of Justice to give an advisory opinion on any legal question arising within the scope of the activities of the Organization. An agreement between the Organization and the United Nations shall be concluded for this purpose in accordance with Article VIII, paragraph 34 (a).

6.   This Article is without prejudice to Article IX or to the provisions on measures to redress a situation and to ensure compliance, including sanctions.

Article XV
Amendments

1.   Any State Party may propose amendments to this Convention. Any State Party may also propose changes, as specified in paragraph 4, to the Annexes of this Convention. Proposals for amendments shall be subject to the procedures in paragraphs 2 and 3. Proposals for changes, as specified in paragraph 4, shall be subject to the procedures in paragraph 5.

2.   The text of a proposed amendment shall be submitted to the Director-General for circulation to all States Parties and to the Depositary. The proposed amendment shall be considered only by an Amendment Conference. Such an Amendment Conference shall be convened if one third or more of the States Parties notify the Director-General not later than 30 days after its circulation that they support further consideration of the proposal. The Amendment Conference shall be held immediately following a regular session of the Conference unless the requesting States Parties ask for an earlier meeting. In no case shall an Amendment Conference be held less than 60 days after the circulation of the proposed amendment.

3.   Amendments shall enter into force for all States Parties 30 days after deposit of the instruments of ratification

or acceptance by all the States Parties referred to under subparagraph (b) below:

(a)   When adopted by the Amendment Conference by a positive vote of a majority of all States Parties with no State Party casting a negative vote; and

(b)   Ratified or accepted by all those States Parties casting a positive vote at the Amendment Conference.

4.   In order to ensure the viability and the effectiveness of this Convention, provisions in the Annexes shall be subject to changes in accordance with paragraph 5, if proposed changes are related only to matters of an administrative or technical nature. All changes to the Annex on Chemicals shall be made in accordance with paragraph 5. Sections A and C of the Confidentiality Annex, Part X of the Verification Annex, and those definitions in Part I of the Verification Annex which relate exclusively to challenge inspections, shall not be subject to changes in accordance with paragraph 5.

5.   Proposed changes referred to in paragraph 4 shall be made in accordance with the following procedures:

(a)   The text of the proposed changes shall be transmitted together with the necessary information to the Director-General. Additional information for the evaluation of the proposal may be provided by any State Party and the Director-General. The Director-General shall promptly communicate any such proposals and information to all States Parties, the Executive Council and the Depositary;

(b)   Not later than 60 days after its receipt, the Director-General shall evaluate the proposal to determine all its possible consequences for the provisions of this Convention and its implementation and shall communicate any such information to all States Parties and the Executive Council;

(c)   The Executive Council shall examine the proposal in the light of all information available to it, including whether the proposal fulfils the requirements of paragraph 4. Not later than 90 days after its receipt, the Executive Council shall notify its recommendation, with appropriate explanations, to all States Parties for consideration. States Parties shall acknowledge receipt within 10 days;

(d)   If the Executive Council recommends to all States Parties that the proposal be adopted, it shall be considered approved if no State Party objects to it within 90 days after receipt of the recommendation. If the Executive Council recommends that the proposal be rejected, it shall be considered rejected if no State Party objects to the rejection within 90 days after receipt of the recommendation;

(e)   If a recommendation of the Executive Council does not meet with the acceptance required under subparagraph (d), a decision on the proposal, including whether it fulfils the requirements of paragraph 4, shall be taken as a matter of substance by the Conference at its next session;

(f)   The Director-General shall notify all States Parties and the Depositary of any decision under this paragraph;

(g) Changes approved under this procedure shall enter into force for all States Parties 180 days after the date of notification by the Director-General of their approval unless another time period is recommended by the Executive Council or decided by the Conference.

Article XVI
Duration and withdrawal

1. This Convention shall be of unlimited duration.

2. Each State Party shall, in exercising its national sovereignty, have the right to withdraw from this Convention if it decides that extraordinary events, related to the subject-matter of this Convention, have jeopardized the supreme interests of its country. It shall give notice of such withdrawal 90 days in advance to all other States Parties, the Executive Council, the Depositary and the United Nations Security Council. Such notice shall include a statement of the extraordinary events it regards as having jeopardized its supreme interests.

3. The withdrawal of a State Party from this Convention shall not in any way affect the duty of States to continue fulfilling the obligations assumed under any relevant rules of international law, particularly the Geneva Protocol of 1925.

Article XVII
Status of the Annexes

The Annexes form an integral part of this Convention. Any reference to this Convention includes the Annexes.

Article XVIII
Signature

This Convention shall be open for signature for all States before its entry into force.

Article XIX
Ratification

This Convention shall be subject to ratification by States Signatories according to their respective constitutional processes.

Article XX
Accession

Any State which does not sign this Convention before its entry into force may accede to it at any time thereafter.

Article XXI
Entry into force

1.   This Convention shall enter into force 180 days after the date of the deposit of the 65th instrument of ratification,

but in no case earlier than two years after its opening for signature.

2.   For States whose instruments of ratification or accession are deposited subsequent to the entry into force of this Convention, it shall enter into force on the 30th day following the date of deposit of their instrument of ratification or accession.

Article XXII
Reservations

The Articles of this Convention shall not be subject to reservations. The Annexes of this Convention shall not be subject to reservations incompatible with its object and purpose.

Article XXIII
Depositary

The Secretary-General of the United Nations is hereby designated as the Depositary of this Convention and shall, inter alia:

(a)   Promptly inform all signatory and acceding States of the date of each signature, the date of deposit of each instrument of ratification or accession and the date of the entry into force of this Convention, and of the receipt of other notices;

(b)   Transmit duly certified copies of this Convention to the Governments of all signatory and acceding States; and

(c)   Register this Convention pursuant to Article 102 of the Charter of the United Nations.

Article XXIV
Authentic texts

This Convention, of which the Arabic, Chinese, English, French, Russian and Spanish texts are equally authentic, shall be deposited with the Secretary-General of the United Nations.

IN WITNESS WHEREOF the undersigned, being duly authorized to that effect, have signed this Convention.

Done at Paris on the thirteenth day of January, one thousand nine hundred and ninety-three.

Annex on chemicals

Contents

A. Guidelines for schedules of chemicals

Guidelines for Schedule 1

1. The following criteria shall be taken into account in considering whether a toxic chemical or precursor should be included in Schedule 1:

(a) It has been developed, produced, stockpiled or used as a chemical weapon as defined in Article II;

(b) It poses otherwise a high risk to the object and purpose of this Convention by virtue of its high potential for use in activities prohibited under this Convention because one or more of the following conditions are met:

(i) It possesses a chemical structure closely related to that of other toxic chemicals listed in Schedule 1, and has, or can be expected to have, comparable properties;

(ii) It possesses such lethal or incapacitating toxicity as well as other properties that would enable it to be used as a chemical weapon;

(iii) It may be used as a precursor in the final single technological stage of production of a toxic chemical listed in Schedule 1, regardless of whether this stage takes place in facilities, in munitions or elsewhere;

(c) It has little or no use for purposes not prohibited under this Convention.

Guidelines for Schedule 2

2.   The following criteria shall be taken into account in considering whether a toxic chemical not listed in Schedule 1 or a precursor to a Schedule 1 chemical or to a chemical listed in Schedule 2, part A, should be included in Schedule 2:

(a)   It poses a significant risk to the object and purpose of this Convention because it possesses such lethal or incapacitating toxicity as well as other properties that could enable it to be used as a chemical weapon;

(b)   It may be used as a precursor in one of the chemical reactions at the final stage of formation of a chemical listed in Schedule 1 or Schedule 2, part A;

(c)   It poses a significant risk to the object and purpose of this Convention by virtue of its importance in the production of a chemical listed in Schedule 1 or Schedule 2, part A;

(d)   It is not produced in large commercial quantities for purposes not prohibited under this Convention.

Guidelines for Schedule 3

3.   The following criteria shall be taken into account in considering whether a toxic chemical or precursor, not listed in other Schedules, should be included in Schedule 3:

(a)   It has been produced, stockpiled or used as a chemical weapon;

(b) It poses otherwise a risk to the object and purpose of this Convention because it possesses such lethal or incapacitating toxicity as well as other properties that might enable it to be used as a chemical weapon;

(c) It poses a risk to the object and purpose of this Convention by virtue of its importance in the production of one or more chemicals listed in Schedule 1 or Schedule 2, part B;

(d) It may be produced in large commercial quantities for purposes not prohibited under this Convention.

B. Schedules of chemicals

The following Schedules list toxic chemicals and their precursors. For the purpose of implementing this Convention, these Schedules identify chemicals for the application of verification measures according to the provisions of the Verification Annex. Pursuant to Article II, subparagraph 1 (a), these Schedules do not constitute a definition of chemical weapons.

(Whenever reference is made to groups of dialkylated chemicals, followed by a list of alkyl groups in parentheses, all chemicals possible by all possible combinations of alkyl groups listed in the parentheses are considered as listed in the respective Schedule as long as they are not explicitly exempted. A chemical marked "*" on Schedule 2, part A, is subject to special thresholds for declaration and verification, as specified in Part VII of the Verification Annex.)

Schedule 1

(CAS registry number)

A.   *Toxic chemicals:*

(1)   O-Alkyl ($\_C_{10}$, incl. cycloalkyl) alkyl
      (Me, Et, n-Pr or i-Pr)-phosphonofluoridates

  e.g. Sarin: O-Isopropyl methylphosphonofluoridate (107-44-8)
    Soman: O-Pinacolyl methylphosphonofluoridate (96-64-0)

(2)   O-Alkyl ($\_C_{10}$, incl. cycloalkyl) N,N-dialkyl
      (Me, Et, n-Pr or i-Pr) phosphoramidocyanidates

  e.g. Tabun: O-Ethyl N,N-dimethyl
    phosphoramidocyanidate (77-81-6)

(3)   O-Alkyl (H or $\_C_{10}$, incl. cycloalkyl) S-2-dialkyl
      (Me, Et, n-Pr or i-Pr)-aminoethyl alkyl
      (Me, Et, n-Pr or i-Pr) phosphonothiolates and
      corresponding alkylated or protonated salts

  e.g. VX: O-Ethyl S-2-diisopropylaminoethyl
    methyl phosphonothiolate (50782-69-9)

(4)   Sulfur mustards:
      2-Chloroethylchloromethylsulfide (2625-76-5)
      Mustard gas: Bis(2-chloroethyl)sulfide (505-60-2)
      Bis(2-chloroethylthio)methane (63869-13-6)
      Sesquimustard: 1,2-Bis(2-chloroethylthio)ethane (3563-36-8)
      1,3-Bis(2-chloroethylthio)-n-propane (63905-10-2)
      1,4-Bis(2-chloroethylthio)-n-butane (142868-93-7)
      1,5-Bis(2-chloroethylthio)-n-pentane (42868-94-8)

Bis(2-chloroethylthiomethyl)ether		(63918-90-1)
O-Mustard: Bis(2-chloroethylthioethyl)ether		(63918-89-8)

(5) Lewisites:

Lewisite 1: 2-Chlorovinyldichloroarsine	(541-25-3)
Lewisite 2: Bis(2-chlorovinyl)chloroarsine	(40334-69-8)
Lewisite 3: Tris(2-chlorovinyl)arsine	(40334-70-1)

(6) Nitrogen mustards:

HN1: Bis(2-chloroethyl)ethylamine	(538-07-8)
HN2: Bis(2-chloroethyl)methylamine	(51-75-2)
HN3: Tris(2-chloroethyl)amine	(555-77-1)

(7) Saxitoxin	(35523-89-8)
(8) Ricin	(9009-86-3)

B. *Precursors:*

(9) Alkyl (Me, Et, n-Pr or i-Pr) phosphonyldifluorides

e.g.   DF: Methylphosphonyldifluoride,   (676-99-3)

(10) O-Alkyl (H or $\_C_{10}$, incl. cycloalkyl) O-2-dialkyl
(Me, Et, n-Pr or i-Pr)-aminoethyl alkyl
(Me, Et, n-Pr or i-Pr) phosphonites
and corresponding alkylated or protonated salts

e.g.   QL: O-Ethyl O-2-diisopropylaminoethyl
methylphosphonite   (57856-11-8)

(11) Chlorosarin: O-Isopropyl methylphosphonochloridate   (1445-76-7)

(12) Chlorosoman: O-Pinacolyl methylphosphonochloridate   (7040-57-5)

Schedule 2

A.   *Toxic chemicals*

(1)   Amiton: O,O-Diethyl S-[2-(diethylamino)ethyl]
       phosphorothiolate   (78-53-5)
       and corresponding alkylated or protonated salts

(2)   PFIB: 1,1,3,3,3-Pentafluoro-2-(trifluoromethyl)-
       1-propene   (382-21-8)

(3)   BZ: 3-Quinuclidinyl benzilate (*)   (6581-06-2)

B.   *Precursors:*

(4)   Chemicals, except for those listed in Schedule 1,
       containing a phosphorus atom to which is bonded
       one methyl, ethyl or propyl (normal or iso) group
       but not further carbon atoms,

       e.g.   Methylphosphonyl dichloride   (676-97-1)
              Dimethyl methylphosphonate   (756-79-6)

       Exemption: Fonofos: O-Ethyl S-phenyl
              ethylphosphonothiolothionate   (944-22-9)

(5)   N, N-Dialkyl (Me Et n-Pr or i-Pr) phosphoramidic
       dihalides

(6)   Dialkyl (Me, Et, n-Pr or i-Pr) N,N-dialkyl
       (Me, Et, n-Pr or i-Pr)-phosphoramidates

(7)   Arsenic trichloride   (7784-34-1)

(8) 2,2-Diphenyl-2-hydroxyacetic acid   (76-93-7)

(9) Quinuclidine-3-ol   (1619-34-7)

(10) N,N-Dialkyl (Me, Et, n-Pr or i-Pr) aminoethyl-2-chlorides
     and corresponding protonated salts

(11) N,N-Dialkyl (Me, Et, n-Pr or i-Pr) aminoethane-2-ols
     and corresponding protonated salts

     Exemptions: N,N-Dimethylaminoethanol   (108-01-0)
        and corresponding protonated salts
        N,N-Diethylaminoethanol   (100-37-8)
        and corresponding protonated salts

(12) N,N-Dialkyl (Me, Et, n-Pr or i-Pr) aminoethane-2-thiols
     and corresponding protonated salts

(13) Thiodiglycol: Bis(2-hydroxyethyl)sulfide   (111-48-8)

(14) Pinacolyl alcohol: 3,3-Dimethylbutane-2-ol   (464-07-3)

Schedule 3

A. *Toxic chemicals:*

(1) Phosgene: Carbonyl dichloride   (75-44-5)

(2) Cyanogen chloride   (506-77-4)

(3) Hydrogen cyanide   (74-90-8)

(4) Chloropicrin: Trichloronitromethane   (76-06-2)

B. *Precursors:*

(5) Phosphorus oxychloride   (10025-87-3)

(6) Phosphorus trichloride   (7719-12-2)

(7) Phosphorus pentachloride   (10026-13-8)

(8) Trimethyl phosphite   (121-45-9)

(9) Triethyl phosphite   (122-52-1)

(10) Dimethyl phosphite   (868-85-9)

(11) Diethyl phosphite   (762-04-9)

(12) Sulfur monochloride   (10025-67-9)

(13) Sulfur dichloride   (10545-99-0)

(14) Thionyl chloride   (7719-09-7)

(15) Ethyldiethanolamine   (139-87-7)

(16) Methyldiethanolamine   (105-59-9)

(17) Triethanolamine   (102-71-6)

Annex on implementation and verification ("Verification Annex")

Contents

Part XI
Investigations in cases of alleged use of chemical weapons. . 436

Part I
Definitions

1. "Approved Equipment" means the devices and instruments necessary for the performance of the inspection team's duties that have been certified by the Technical Secretariat in accordance with regulations prepared by the Technical Secretariat pursuant to Part II, paragraph 27 of this Annex. Such equipment may also refer to the administrative supplies or recording materials that would be used by the inspection team.

2. "Building" as referred to in the definition of chemical weapons production facility in Article II comprises specialized buildings and standard buildings.

   (a) "Specialized Building" means:

   (i) Any building, including underground structures, containing specialized equipment in a production or filling configuration;

   (ii) Any building, including underground structures, which has distinctive features which distinguish it from buildings normally used for chemical production or filling activities not prohibited under this Convention.

   (b) "Standard Building" means any building, including underground structures, constructed to prevailing industry standards for facilities not producing any chemical specified in Article II, paragraph 8 (a) (i), or corrosive chemicals.

3.   "Challenge Inspection" means the inspection of any facility or location in the territory or in any other place under the jurisdiction or control of a State Party requested by another State Party pursuant to Article IX, paragraphs 8 to 25.

4.   "Discrete Organic Chemical" means any chemical belonging to the class of chemical compounds consisting of all compounds of carbon except for its oxides, sulfides and metal carbonates, identifiable by chemical name, by structural formula, if known, and by Chemical Abstracts Service registry number, if assigned.

5.   "Equipment" as referred to in the definition of chemical weapons production facility in Article II comprises specialized equipment and standard equipment.

(a)   "Specialized Equipment" means:

(i)   The main production train, including any reactor or equipment for product synthesis, separation or purification, any equipment used directly for heat transfer in the final technological stage, such as in reactors or in product separation, as well as any other equipment which has been in contact with any chemical specified in Article II, paragraph 8 (a) (i), or would be in contact with such a chemical if the facility were operated;

(ii)   Any chemical weapon filling machines;

(iii) Any other equipment specially designed, built or installed for the operation of the facility as a chemical weapons production facility, as distinct from a facility constructed according to prevailing commercial industry standards for facilities not producing any chemical specified in Article II, paragraph 8 (a) (i), or corrosive chemicals, such as: equipment made of high-nickel alloys or other special corrosion-resistant material; special equipment for waste control, waste treatment, air filtering, or solvent recovery; special containment enclosures and safety shields; non-standard laboratory equipment used to analyse toxic chemicals for chemical weapons purposes; custom-designed process control panels; or dedicated spares for specialized equipment.

(b) "Standard Equipment" means:

(i) Production equipment which is generally used in the chemical industry and is not included in the types of specialized equipment;

(ii) Other equipment commonly used in the chemical industry, such as: fire-fighting equipment; guard and security/safety surveillance equipment; medical facilities, laboratory facilities; or communications equipment.

6. "Facility" in the context of Article VI means any of the industrial sites as defined below ("plant site","plant" and "unit").

(a) "Plant Site" (Works, Factory) means the local integration of one or more plants, with any intermediate administrative levels, which are under one operational control, and includes common infrastructure, such as:

    (i)   Administration and other offices;

    (ii) Repair and maintenance shops;

    (iii) Medical centre;

    (iv) Utilities;

    (v)   Central analytical laboratory;

    (vi) Research and development laboratories;

    (vii) Central effluent and waste treatment area; and

    (viii)Warehouse storage.

(b) "Plant" (Production facility, Workshop) means a relatively self-contained area, structure or building containing one or more units with auxiliary and associated infrastructure, such as:

    (i)   Small administrative section;

    (ii) Storage/handling areas for feedstock and products;

    (iii) Effluent/waste handling/treatment area;

    (iv) Control/analytical laboratory;

(v)   First aid service/related medical section; and

(vi) Records associated with the movement into, around and from the site, of declared chemicals and their feedstock or product chemicals formed from them, as appropriate.

(c)   "Unit" (Production unit, Process unit) means the combination of those items of equipment, including vessels and vessel set up, necessary for the production, processing or consumption of a chemical.

7.   "Facility Agreement" means an agreement or arrangement between a State Party and the Organization relating to a specific facility subject to on-site verification pursuant to Articles IV, V and VI.

8.   "Host State" means the State on whose territory lie facilities or areas of another State, Party to this Convention, which are subject to inspection under this Convention.

9.   "In-Country Escort" means individuals specified by the inspected State Party and, if appropriate, by the Host State, if they so wish, to accompany and assist the inspection team during the in-country period.

10.   "In-Country Period" means the period from the arrival of the inspection team at a point of entry until its departure from the State at a point of entry.

11. "Initial Inspection" means the first on-site inspection of facilities to verify declarations submitted pursuant to Articles III, IV, V and VI and this Annex.

12. "Inspected State Party" means the State Party on whose territory or in any other place under its jurisdiction or control an inspection pursuant to this Convention takes place, or the State Party whose facility or area on the territory of a Host State is subject to such an inspection; it does not, however, include the State Party specified in Part II, paragraph 21 of this Annex.

13. "Inspection Assistant" means an individual designated by the Technical Secretariat as set forth in Part II, Section A, of this Annex to assist inspectors in an inspection or visit, such as medical, security and administrative personnel and interpreters.

14. "Inspection Mandate" means the instructions issued by the Director-General to the inspection team for the conduct of a particular inspection.

15. "Inspection Manual" means the compilation of additional procedures for the conduct of inspections developed by the Technical Secretariat.

16. "Inspection Site" means any facility or area at which an inspection is carried out and which is specifically defined in the respective facility agreement or inspection request or mandate or inspection request as expanded by the alternative or final perimeter.

17. "Inspection Team" means the group of inspectors and inspection assistants assigned by the Director-General to conduct a particular inspection.

18. "Inspector" means an individual designated by the Technical Secretariat according to the procedures as set forth in Part II, Section A, of this Annex, to carry out an inspection or visit in accordance with this Convention.

19. "Model Agreement" means a document specifying the general form and content for an agreement concluded between a State Party and the Organization for fulfilling the verification provisions specified in this Annex.

20. "Observer" means a representative of a requesting State Party or a third State Party to observe a challenge inspection.

21. "Perimeter" in case of challenge inspection means the external boundary of the inspection site, defined by either geographic coordinates or description on a map.

(a) "Requested Perimeter" means the inspection site perimeter as specified in conformity with Part X, paragraph 8, of this Annex;

(b) "Alternative Perimeter" means the inspection site perimeter as specified, alternatively to the requested perimeter, by the inspected State Party; it shall conform to the requirements specified in Part X, paragraph 17, of this Annex;

(c) "Final Perimeter" means the final inspection site perimeter as agreed in negotiations between the inspection team and the inspected State Party, in accordance with Part X, paragraphs 16 to 21, of this Annex;

(d) "Declared Perimeter" means the external boundary of the facility declared pursuant to Articles III, IV, V and VI.

22. "Period of Inspection", for the purposes of Article IX, means the period of time from provision of access to the inspection team to the inspection site until its departure from the inspection site, exclusive of time spent on briefings before and after the verification activities.

23. "Period of Inspection", for the purposes of Articles IV, V and VI, means the period of time from arrival of the inspection team at the inspection site until its departure from the inspection site, exclusive of time spent on briefings before and after the verification activities.

24. "Point of Entry"/"Point of Exit" means a location designated for the in-country arrival of inspection teams for inspections pursuant to this Convention or for their departure after completion of their mission.

25. "Requesting State Party" means a State Party which has requested a challenge inspection pursuant to Article IX.

26. "Tonne" means metric ton, i.e. 1,000 kg.

Part II
General rules of verification

A. Designation of inspectors and inspection assistants

1.   Not later than 30 days after entry into force of this Convention the Technical Secretariat shall communicate, in writing, to all States Parties the names, nationalities and ranks of the inspectors and inspection assistants proposed for designation, as well as a description of their qualifications and professional experiences.

2.   Each State Party shall immediately acknowledge receipt of the list of inspectors and inspection assistants, proposed for designation communicated to it. The State Party shall inform the Technical Secretariat in writing of its acceptance of each inspector and inspection assistant, not later than 30 days after acknowledgement of receipt of the list. Any inspector and inspection assistant included in this list shall be regarded as designated unless a State Party, not later than 30 days after acknowledgement of receipt of the list, declares its non-acceptance in writing. The State Party may include the reason for the objection.

In the case of non-acceptance, the proposed inspector or inspection assistant shall not undertake or participate in verification activities on the territory or in any other place under the jurisdiction or control of the State Party which has declared its non-acceptance. The Technical Secretariat shall, as necessary, submit further proposals in addition to the original list.

3. Verification activities under this Convention shall only be performed by designated inspectors and inspection assistants.

4. Subject to the provisions of paragraph 5, a State Party has the right at any time to object to an inspector or inspection assistant who has already been designated. It shall notify the Technical Secretariat of its objection in writing and may include the reason for the objection. Such objection shall come into effect 30 days after receipt by the Technical Secretariat. The Technical Secretariat shall immediately inform the State Party concerned of the withdrawal of the designation of the inspector or inspection assistant.

5. A State Party that has been notified of an inspection shall not seek to have removed from the inspection team for that inspection any of the designated inspectors or inspection assistants named in the inspection team list.

6. The number of inspectors or inspection assistants accepted by and designated to a State Party must be sufficient to allow for availability and rotation of appropriate numbers of inspectors and inspection assistants.

7. If, in the opinion of the Director-General, the non-acceptance of proposed inspectors or inspection assistants impedes the designation of a sufficient number of inspectors or inspection assistants or otherwise hampers the effective fulfilment of the tasks of the Technical Secretariat, the Director-General shall refer the issue to the Executive Council.

8.   Whenever amendments to the above-mentioned lists of inspectors and inspection assistants are necessary or requested, replacement inspectors and inspection assistants shall be designated in the same manner as set forth with respect to the initial list.

9.   The members of the inspection team carrying out an inspection of a facility of a State Party located on the territory of another State Party shall be designated in accordance with the procedures set forth in this Annex as applied both to the inspected State Party and the Host State Party.

B.   Privileges and immunities

10.   Each State Party shall, not later than 30 days after acknowledgement of receipt of the list of inspectors and inspection assistants or of changes thereto, provide multiple entry/exit and/or transit visas and other such documents to enable each inspector or inspection assistant to enter and to remain on the territory of that State Party for the purpose of carrying out inspection activities. These documents shall be valid for at least two years after their provision to the Technical Secretariat.

11.   To exercise their functions effectively, inspectors and inspection assistants shall be accorded privileges and immunities as set forth in subparagraphs (a) to (i). Privileges and immunities shall be granted to members of the inspection team for the sake of this Convention and not for the personal benefit of the individuals themselves. Such privileges and immunities shall be accorded to them

for the entire period between arrival on and departure from the territory of the inspected State Party or Host State, and thereafter with respect to acts previously performed in the exercise of their official functions.

(a) The members of the inspection team shall be accorded the inviolability enjoyed by diplomatic agents pursuant to Article 29 of the Vienna Convention on Diplomatic Relations of 18 April 1961.

(b) The living quarters and office premises occupied by the inspection team carrying out inspection activities pursuant to this Convention shall be accorded the inviolability and protection accorded to the premises of diplomatic agents pursuant to Article 30, paragraph 1, of the Vienna Convention on Diplomatic Relations.

(c) The papers and correspondence, including records, of the inspection team shall enjoy the inviolability accorded to all papers and correspondence of diplomatic agents pursuant to Article 30, paragraph 2, of the Vienna Convention on Diplomatic Relations. The inspection team shall have the right to use codes for their communications with the Technical Secretariat.

(d) Samples and approved equipment carried by members of the inspection team shall be inviolable subject to provisions contained in this Convention and exempt from all customs duties. Hazardous samples shall be transported in accordance with relevant regulations.

(e) The members of the inspection team shall be accorded the immunities accorded to diplomatic agents pursuant to Article 31, paragraphs 1, 2 and 3, of the Vienna Convention on Diplomatic Relations.

(f) The members of the inspection team carrying out prescribed activities pursuant to this Convention shall be accorded the exemption from dues and taxes accorded to diplomatic agents pursuant to Article 34 of the Vienna Convention on Diplomatic Relations.

(g) The members of the inspection team shall be permitted to bring into the territory of the inspected State Party or Host State Party, without payment of any customs duties or related charges, articles for personal use, with the exception of articles the import or export of which is prohibited by law or controlled by quarantine regulations.

(h) The members of the inspection team shall be accorded the same currency and exchange facilities as are accorded to representatives of foreign Governments on temporary official missions.

(i) The members of the inspection team shall not engage in any professional or commercial activity for personal profit on the territory of the inspected State Party or the Host State.

12. When transiting the territory of non-inspected States Parties, the members of the inspection team shall be accorded the privileges and immunities enjoyed by

diplomatic agents pursuant to Article 40, paragraph 1, of the Vienna Convention on Diplomatic Relations. Papers and correspondence, including records, and samples and approved equipment, carried by them, shall be accorded the privileges and immunities set forth in paragraph 11 (c) and (d).

13. Without prejudice to their privileges and immunities the members of the inspection team shall be obliged to respect the laws and regulations of the inspected State Party or Host State and, to the extent that is consistent with the inspection mandate, shall be obliged not to interfere in the internal affairs of that State. If the inspected State Party or Host State Party considers that there has been an abuse of privileges and immunities specified in this Annex, consultations shall be held between the State Party and the Director-General to determine whether such an abuse has occurred and, if so determined, to prevent a repetition of such an abuse.

14. The immunity from jurisdiction of members of the inspection team may be waived by the Director-General in those cases when the Director-General is of the opinion that immunity would impede the course of justice and that it can be waived without prejudice to the implementation of the provisions of this Convention. Waiver must always be express.

15. Observers shall be accorded the same privileges and immunities accorded to inspectors pursuant to this section, except for those accorded pursuant to paragraph 11 (d).

C. Standing arrangements

Points of entry

16. Each State Party shall designate the points of entry and shall supply the required information to the Technical Secretariat not later than 30 days after this Convention enters into force for it. These points of entry shall be such that the inspection team can reach any inspection site from at least one point of entry within 12 hours. Locations of points of entry shall be provided to all States Parties by the Technical Secretariat.

17. Each State Party may change the points of entry by giving notice of such change to the Technical Secretariat. Changes shall become effective 30 days after the Technical Secretariat receives such notification to allow appropriate notification to all States Parties.

18. If the Technical Secretariat considers that there are insufficient points of entry for the timely conduct of inspections or that changes to the points of entry proposed by a State Party would hamper such timely conduct of inspections, it shall enter into consultations with the State Party concerned to resolve the problem.

19. In cases where facilities or areas of an inspected State Party are located on the territory of a Host State Party or where the access from the point of entry to the facilities or areas subject to inspection requires transit through the territory of another State Party, the inspected State Party shall exercise the rights and fulfil the obligations concerning such inspections in accordance with this Annex. The Host

State Party shall facilitate the inspection of those facilities or areas and shall provide for the necessary support to enable the inspection team to carry out its tasks in a timely and effective manner. States Parties through whose territory transit is required to inspect facilities or areas of an inspected State Party shall facilitate such transit.

20. In cases where facilities or areas of an inspected State Party are located on the territory of a State not Party to this Convention, the inspected State Party shall take all necessary measures to ensure that inspections of those facilities or areas can be carried out in accordance with the provisions of this Annex. A State Party that has one or more facilities or areas on the territory of a State not Party to this Convention shall take all necessary measures to ensure acceptance by the Host State of inspectors and inspection assistants designated to that State Party. If an inspected State Party is unable to ensure access, it shall demonstrate that it took all necessary measures to ensure access.

21. In cases where the facilities or areas sought to be inspected are located on the territory of a State Party, but in a place under the jurisdiction or control of a State not Party to this Convention, the State Party shall take all necessary measures as would be required of an inspected State Party and a Host State Party to ensure that inspections of such facilities or areas can be carried out in accordance with the provisions of this Annex. If the State Party is unable to ensure access to those facilities or areas, it shall demonstrate that it took all necessary measures to ensure access. This

paragraph shall not apply where the facilities or areas sought to be inspected are those of the State Party.

Arrangements for use of non-scheduled aircraft

22. For inspections pursuant to Article IX and for other inspections where timely travel is not feasible using scheduled commercial transport, an inspection team may need to utilize aircraft owned or chartered by the Technical Secretariat. Not later than 30 days after this Convention enters into force for it, each State Party shall inform the Technical Secretariat of the standing diplomatic clearance number for non-scheduled aircraft transporting inspection teams and equipment necessary for inspection into and out of the territory in which an inspection site is located. Aircraft routings to and from the designated point of entry shall be along established international airways that are agreed upon between the States Parties and the Technical Secretariat as the basis for such diplomatic clearance.

23. When a non-scheduled aircraft is used, the Technical Secretariat shall provide the inspected State Party with a flight plan, through the National Authority, for the aircraft's flight from the last airfield prior to entering the airspace of the State in which the inspection site is located to the point of entry, not less than six hours before the scheduled departure time from that airfield. Such a plan shall be filed in accordance with the procedures of the International Civil Aviation Organization applicable to civil aircraft. For its owned or chartered flights, the Technical Secretariat shall include in the remarks section of each flight plan the

standing diplomatic clearance number and the appropriate notation identifying the aircraft as an inspection aircraft.

24. Not less than three hours before the scheduled departure of the inspection team from the last airfield prior to entering the airspace of the State in which the inspection is to take place, the inspected State Party or Host State Party shall ensure that the flight plan filed in accordance with paragraph 23 is approved so that the inspection team may arrive at the point of entry by the estimated arrival time.

25. The inspected State Party shall provide parking, security protection, servicing and fuel as required by the Technical Secretariat for the aircraft of the inspection team at the point of entry when such aircraft is owned or chartered by the Technical Secretariat. Such aircraft shall not be liable for landing fees, departure tax, and similar charges. The Technical Secretariat shall bear the cost of such fuel, security protection and servicing.

Administrative arrangements

26. The inspected State Party shall provide or arrange for the amenities necessary for the inspection team such as communication means, interpretation services to the extent necessary for the performance of interviewing and other tasks, transportation, working space, lodging, meals and medical care. In this regard, the inspected State Party shall be reimbursed by the Organization for such costs incurred by the inspection team.

Approved equipment

27. Subject to paragraph 29, there shall be no restriction by the inspected State Party on the inspection team bringing onto the inspection site such equipment, approved in accordance with paragraph 28, which the Technical Secretariat has determined to be necessary to fulfil the inspection requirements. The Technical Secretariat shall prepare and, as appropriate, update a list of approved equipment, which may be needed for the purposes described above, and regulations governing such equipment which shall be in accordance with this Annex. In establishing the list of approved equipment and these regulations, the Technical Secretariat shall ensure that safety considerations for all the types of facilities at which such equipment is likely to be used, are taken fully into account. A list of approved equipment shall be considered and approved by the Conference pursuant to Article VIII, paragraph 21 (i).

28. The equipment shall be in the custody of the Technical Secretariat and be designated, calibrated and approved by the Technical Secretariat. The Technical Secretariat shall, to the extent possible, select that equipment which is specifically designed for the specific kind of inspection required. Designated and approved equipment shall be specifically protected against unauthorized alteration.

29. The inspected State Party shall have the right, without prejudice to the prescribed time-frames, to inspect the equipment in the presence of inspection team members at the point of entry, i.e., to check the identity of the equipment brought in or removed from the territory of the inspected

State Party or the Host State. To facilitate such identification, the Technical Secretariat shall attach documents and devices to authenticate its designation and approval of the equipment. The inspection of the equipment shall also ascertain to the satisfaction of the inspected State Party that the equipment meets the description of the approved equipment for the particular type of inspection. The inspected State Party may exclude equipment not meeting that description or equipment without the above-mentioned authentication documents and devices. Procedures for the inspection of equipment shall be considered and approved by the Conference pursuant to Article VIII, paragraph 21 (i).

30. In cases where the inspection team finds it necessary to use equipment available on site not belonging to the Technical Secretariat and requests the inspected State Party to enable the team to use such equipment, the inspected State Party shall comply with the request to the extent it can.

D. Pre-inspection activities

Notification

31. The Director-General shall notify the State Party before the planned arrival of the inspection team at the point of entry and within the prescribed time-frames, where specified, of its intention to carry out an inspection.

32. Notifications made by the Director-General shall include the following information:

    (a) The type of inspection;

(b)   The point of entry;

(c)   The date and estimated time of arrival at the point of entry;

(d)   The means of arrival at the point of entry;

(e)   The site to be inspected;

(f)   The names of inspectors and inspection assistants;

(g)   If appropriate, aircraft clearance for special flights.

33.   The inspected State Party shall acknowledge the receipt of a notification by the Technical Secretariat of an intention to conduct an inspection, not later than one hour after receipt of such notification.

34.   In the case of an inspection of a facility of a State Party located on the territory of another State Party, both States Parties shall be simultaneously notified in accordance with paragraphs 31 and 32.

Entry into the territory of the inspected State Party or Host State and transfer to the inspection site

35.   The inspected State Party or Host State Party which has been notified of the arrival of an inspection team, shall ensure its immediate entry into the territory and shall through an in-country escort or by other means do everything in its power to ensure the safe conduct of the

inspection team and its equipment and supplies, from its point of entry to the inspection site(s) and to a point of exit.

36. The inspected State Party or Host State Party shall, as necessary, assist the inspection team in reaching the inspection site not later than 12 hours after the arrival at the point of entry.

Pre-inspection briefing

37. Upon arrival at the inspection site and before the commencement of the inspection, the inspection team shall be briefed by facility representatives, with the aid of maps and other documentation as appropriate, on the facility, the activities carried out there, safety measures and administrative and logistic arrangements necessary for the inspection. The time spent for the briefing shall be limited to the minimum necessary and in any event not exceed three hours.

E.   Conduct of inspections

General rules

38. The members of the inspection team shall discharge their functions in accordance with the provisions of this Convention, as well as rules established by the Director-General and facility agreements concluded between States Parties and the Organization.

39. The inspection team shall strictly observe the inspection mandate issued by the Director-General. It shall refrain from activities going beyond this mandate.

40. The activities of the inspection team shall be so arranged as to ensure the timely and effective discharge of its functions and the least possible inconvenience to the inspected State Party or Host State and disturbance to the facility or area inspected. The inspection team shall avoid unnecessarily hampering or delaying the operation of a facility and avoid affecting its safety. In particular, the inspection team shall not operate any facility. If inspectors consider that, to fulfil their mandate, particular operations should be carried out in a facility, they shall request the designated representative of the inspected facility to have them performed. The representative shall carry out the request to the extent possible.

41. In the performance of their duties on the territory of an inspected State Party or Host State, the members of the inspection team shall, if the inspected State Party so requests, be accompanied by representatives of the inspected State Party, but the inspection team must not thereby be delayed or otherwise hindered in the exercise of its functions.

42. Detailed procedures for the conduct of inspections shall be developed for inclusion in the inspection manual by the Technical Secretariat, taking into account guidelines to be considered and approved by the Conference pursuant to Article VIII, paragraph 21 (i).

Safety

43. In carrying out their activities, inspectors and inspection assistants shall observe safety regulations

established at the inspection site, including those for the protection of controlled environments within a facility and for personal safety. In order to implement these requirements, appropriate detailed procedures shall be considered and approved by the Conference pursuant to Article VIII, paragraph 21 (i).

Communications

44. Inspectors shall have the right throughout the in-country period to communicate with the Headquarters of the Technical Secretariat. For this purpose they may use their own, duly certified, approved equipment and may request that the inspected State Party or Host State Party provide them with access to other telecommunications. The inspection team shall have the right to use its own two-way system of radio communications between personnel patrolling the perimeter and other members of the inspection team.

Inspection team and inspected State Party rights

45. The inspection team shall, in accordance with the relevant Articles and Annexes of this Convention as well as with facility agreements and procedures set forth in the inspection manual, have the right to unimpeded access to the inspection site. The items to be inspected will be chosen by the inspectors.

46. Inspectors shall have the right to interview any facility personnel in the presence of representatives of the inspected State Party with the purpose of establishing relevant facts.

Inspectors shall only request information and data which are necessary for the conduct of the inspection, and the inspected State Party shall furnish such information upon request. The inspected State Party shall have the right to object to questions posed to the facility personnel if those questions are deemed not relevant to the inspection. If the head of the inspection team objects and states their relevance, the questions shall be provided in writing to the inspected State Party for reply. The inspection team may note any refusal to permit interviews or to allow questions to be answered and any explanations given, in that part of the inspection report that deals with the cooperation of the inspected State Party.

47.   Inspectors shall have the right to inspect documentation and records they deem relevant to the conduct of their mission.

48.   Inspectors shall have the right to have photographs taken at their request by representatives of the inspected State Party or of the inspected facility. The capability to take instant development photographic prints shall be available. The inspection team shall determine whether photographs conform to those requested and, if not, repeat photographs shall be taken. The inspection team and the inspected State Party shall each retain one copy of every photograph.

49.   The representatives of the inspected State Party shall have the right to observe all verification activities carried out by the inspection team.

50. The inspected State Party shall receive copies, at its request, of the information and data gathered about its facility(ies) by the Technical Secretariat.

51. Inspectors shall have the right to request clarifications in connection with ambiguities that arise during an inspection. Such requests shall be made promptly through the representative of the inspected State Party. The representative of the inspected State Party shall provide the inspection team, during the inspection, with such clarification as may be necessary to remove the ambiguity. If questions relating to an object or a building located within the inspection site are not resolved, the object or building shall, if requested, be photographed for the purpose of clarifying its nature and function. If the ambiguity cannot be removed during the inspection, the inspectors shall notify the Technical Secretariat immediately. The inspectors shall include in the inspection report any such unresolved question, relevant clarifications, and a copy of any photographs taken.

Collection, handling and analysis of samples

52. Representatives of the inspected State Party or of the inspected facility shall take samples at the request of the inspection team in the presence of inspectors. If so agreed in advance with the representatives of the inspected State Party or of the inspected facility, the inspection team may take samples itself.

53. Where possible, the analysis of samples shall be performed on-site. The inspection team shall have the right to perform on-site analysis of samples using approved equipment brought by it. At the request of the inspection team, the inspected State Party shall, in accordance with agreed procedures, provide assistance for the analysis of samples on-site. Alternatively, the inspection team may request that appropriate analysis on-site be performed in its presence.

54. The inspected State Party has the right to retain portions of all samples taken or take duplicate samples and be present when samples are analysed on-site.

55. The inspection team shall, if it deems it necessary, transfer samples for analysis off-site at laboratories designated by the Organization.

56. The Director-General shall have the primary responsibility for the security, integrity and preservation of samples and for ensuring that the confidentiality of samples transferred for analysis off-site is protected. The Director-General shall do so in accordance with procedures, to be considered and approved by the Conference pursuant to Article VIII, paragraph 21 (i), for inclusion in the inspection manual. He shall:

(a) Establish a stringent regime governing the collection, handling, transport and analysis of samples;

(b) Certify the laboratories designated to perform different types of analysis;

(c) Oversee the standardization of equipment and procedures at these designated laboratories, mobile analytical equipment and procedures, and monitor quality control and overall standards in relation to the certification of these laboratories, mobile equipment and procedures; and

(d) Select from among the designated laboratories those which shall perform analytical or other functions in relation to specific investigations.

57. When off-site analysis is to be performed, samples shall be analysed in at least two designated laboratories. The Technical Secretariat shall ensure the expeditious processing of the analysis. The samples shall be accounted for by the Technical Secretariat and any unused samples or portions thereof shall be returned to the Technical Secretariat.

58. The Technical Secretariat shall compile the results of the laboratory analysis of samples relevant to compliance with this Convention and include them in the final inspection report. The Technical Secretariat shall include in the report detailed information concerning the equipment and methodology employed by the designated laboratories.

Extension of inspection duration

59. Periods of inspection may be extended by agreement with the representative of the inspected State Party.

Debriefing

60. Upon completion of an inspection the inspection team shall meet with representatives of the inspected State Party and the personnel responsible for the inspection site to review the preliminary findings of the inspection team and to clarify any ambiguities. The inspection team shall provide to the representatives of the inspected State Party its preliminary findings in written form according to a standardized format, together with a list of any samples and copies of written information and data gathered and other material to be taken off-site. The document shall be signed by the head of the inspection team. In order to indicate that he has taken notice of the contents of the document, the representative of the inspected State Party shall countersign the document. This meeting shall be completed not later than 24 hours after the completion of the inspection.

F. Departure

61. Upon completion of the post-inspection procedures, the inspection team shall leave, as soon as possible, the territory of the inspected State Party or the Host State.

G. Reports

62. Not later than 10 days after the inspection, the inspectors shall prepare a factual, final report on the activities conducted by them and on their findings. It shall only contain facts relevant to compliance with this Convention, as provided for under the inspection mandate. The report shall also provide information as to the manner in which the State Party inspected cooperated with the

inspection team. Differing observations made by inspectors may be attached to the report. The report shall be kept confidential.

63. The final report shall immediately be submitted to the inspected State Party. Any written comments, which the inspected State Party may immediately make on its findings shall be annexed to it. The final report together with annexed comments made by the inspected State Party shall be submitted to the Director-General not later than 30 days after the inspection.

64. Should the report contain uncertainties, or should cooperation between the National Authority and the inspectors not measure up to the standards required, the Director-General shall approach the State Party for clarification.

65. If the uncertainties cannot be removed or the facts established are of a nature to suggest that obligations undertaken under this Convention have not been met, the Director-General shall inform the Executive Council without delay.

H. Application of general provisions

66. The provisions of this Part shall apply to all inspections conducted pursuant to this Convention, except where the provisions of this Part differ from the provisions set forth for specific types of inspections in Parts III to XI of this Annex, in which case the latter provisions shall take precedence.

Part III
General provisions for verification measures pursuant to Articles IV, V and VI, paragraph 3

A.   Initial inspections and facility agreements

1.   Each declared facility subject to on-site inspection pursuant to Articles IV, V, and VI, paragraph 3, shall receive an initial inspection promptly after the facility is declared. The purpose of this inspection of the facility shall be to verify information provided and to obtain any additional information needed for planning future verification activities at the facility, including on-site inspections and continuous monitoring with on-site instruments, and to work on the facility agreements.

2.   States Parties shall ensure that the verification of declarations and the initiation of the systematic verification measures can be accomplished by the Technical Secretariat at all facilities within the established time-frames after this Convention enters into force for them.

3.   Each State Party shall conclude a facility agreement with the Organization for each facility declared and subject to on-site inspection pursuant to Articles IV, V, and VI, paragraph 3.

4.   Facility agreements shall be completed not later than 180 days after this Convention enters into force for the State Party or after the facility has been declared for the first time, except for a chemical weapons destruction facility to which paragraphs 5 to 7 shall apply.

5.   In the case of a chemical weapons destruction facility that begins operations more than one year after this Convention enters into force for the State Party, the facility agreement shall be completed not less than 180 days before the facility begins operation.

6.   In the case of a chemical weapons destruction facility that is in operation when this Convention enters into force for the State Party, or begins operation not later than one year thereafter, the facility agreement shall be completed not later than 210 days after this Convention enters into force for the State Party, except that the Executive Council may decide that transitional verification arrangements, approved in accordance with Part IV (A), paragraph 51, of this Annex and including a transitional facility agreement, provisions for verification through on-site inspection and monitoring with on-site instruments, and the time-frame for application of the arrangements, are sufficient.

7.   In the case of a facility, referred to in paragraph 6, that will cease operations not later than two years after this Convention enters into force for the State Party, the Executive Council may decide that transitional verification arrangements, approved in accordance with Part IV (A), paragraph 51, of this Annex and including a transitional facility agreement, provisions for verification through on-site inspection and monitoring with on-site instruments, and the time-frame for application of the arrangements, are sufficient.

8.   Facility agreements shall be based on models for such agreements and provide for detailed arrangements which shall govern inspections at each facility. The model agreements shall include provisions to take into account future technological developments and shall be considered and approved by the Conference pursuant to Article VIII, paragraph 21 (i).

9.   The Technical Secretariat may retain at each site a sealed container for photographs, plans and other information that it may wish to refer to in the course of subsequent inspections.

B.   Standing arrangements

10.   Where applicable, the Technical Secretariat shall have the right to have continuous monitoring instruments and systems and seals installed and to use them, in conformity with the relevant provisions in this Convention and the facility agreements between States Parties and the Organization.

11.   The inspected State Party shall, in accordance with agreed procedures, have the right to inspect any instrument used or installed by the inspection team and to have it tested in the presence of representatives of the inspected State Party. The inspection team shall have the right to use the instruments that were installed by the inspected State Party for its own monitoring of the technological process of the destruction of chemical weapons. To this end, the inspection team shall have the right to inspect those instruments that it

intends to use for purposes of verification of the destruction of chemical weapons and to have them tested in its presence.

12. The inspected State Party shall provide the necessary preparation and support for the establishment of continuous monitoring instruments and systems.

13. In order to implement paragraphs 11 and 12, appropriate detailed procedures shall be considered and approved by the Conference pursuant to Article VIII, paragraph 21 (i).

14. The inspected State Party shall immediately notify the Technical Secretariat if an event occurs or may occur at a facility where monitoring instruments are installed, which may have an impact on the monitoring system. The inspected State Party shall coordinate subsequent actions with the Technical Secretariat with a view to restoring the operation of the monitoring system and establishing interim measures, if necessary, as soon as possible.

15. The inspection team shall verify during each inspection that the monitoring system functions correctly and that emplaced seals have not been tampered with. In addition, visits to service the monitoring system may be required to perform any necessary maintenance or replacement of equipment, or to adjust the coverage of the monitoring system as required.

16. If the monitoring system indicates any anomaly, the Technical Secretariat shall immediately take action

to determine whether this resulted from equipment malfunction or activities at the facility. If, after this examination, the problem remains unresolved, the Technical Secretariat shall immediately ascertain the actual situation, including through immediate on-site inspection of, or visit to, the facility if necessary. The Technical Secretariat shall report any such problem immediately after its detection to the inspected State Party which shall assist in its resolution.

C.   Pre-inspection activities

17. The inspected State Party shall, except as specified in paragraph 18, be notified of inspections not less than 24 hours in advance of the planned arrival of the inspection team at the point of entry.

18. The inspected State Party shall be notified of initial inspections not less than 72 hours in advance of the estimated time of arrival of the inspection team at the point of entry.

Part IV (A)
Destruction of chemical weapons and its verification pursuant to Article IV

A. Declarations

Chemical weapons

1.   The declaration of chemical weapons by a State Party pursuant to Article III, paragraph 1 (a) (ii), shall include the following:

(a)   The aggregate quantity of each chemical declared;

(b)   The precise location of each chemical weapons storage facility, expressed by:

(i)   Name;

(ii)   Geographical coordinates; and

(iii)   A detailed site diagram, including a boundary map and the location of bunkers/storage areas within the facility.

(c)   The detailed inventory for each chemical weapons storage facility including:

(i)   Chemicals defined as chemical weapons in accordance with Article II;

(ii)   Unfilled munitions, sub-munitions, devices and equipment defined as chemical weapons;

(iii) Equipment specially designed for use directly in connection with the employment of munitions, sub-munitions, devices or equipment specified in sub-subparagraph (ii);

(iv) Chemicals specifically designed for use directly in connection with the employment of munitions, sub-munitions, devices or equipment specified in sub-subparagraph (ii).

2.   For the declaration of chemicals referred to in paragraph 1 (c) (i) the following shall apply:

(a)   Chemicals shall be declared in accordance with the Schedules specified in the Annex on Chemicals;

(b)   For a chemical not listed in the Schedules in the Annex on Chemicals the information required for possible assignment of the chemical to the appropriate Schedule shall be provided, including the toxicity of the pure compound. For a precursor, the toxicity and identity of the principal final reaction product(s) shall be provided;

(c)   Chemicals shall be identified by chemical name in accordance with current International Union of Pure and Applied Chemistry (IUPAC) nomenclature, structural formula and Chemical Abstracts Service registry number, if assigned. For a precursor, the toxicity and identity of the principal final reaction product(s) shall be provided;

(d)   In cases involving mixtures of two or more chemicals, each chemical shall be identified and the percentage of each shall be provided, and the mixture shall be declared under the category of the most toxic chemical. If a component of a binary chemical weapon consists of a mixture of two or more chemicals, each chemical shall be identified and the percentage of each provided;

(e) Binary chemical weapons shall be declared under the relevant end product within the framework of the categories of chemical weapons referred to in paragraph 16. The following supplementary information shall be provided for each type of binary chemical munition/device:

(i) The chemical name of the toxic end-product;

(ii) The chemical composition and quantity of each component;

(iii) The actual weight ratio between the components;

(iv) Which component is considered the key component;

(v) The projected quantity of the toxic end-product calculated on a stoichiometric basis from the key component, assuming 100 per cent yield. A declared quantity (in tonnes) of the key component intended for a specific toxic end-product shall be considered equivalent to the quantity (in tonnes) of this toxic end-product calculated on a stoichiometric basis assuming 100 per cent yield.

(f) For multicomponent chemical weapons, the declaration shall be analogous to that envisaged for binary chemical weapons;

(g) For each chemical the form of storage, i.e. munitions, sub-munitions, devices, equipment or bulk containers and other containers shall be declared. For each form of storage the following shall be listed:

(i) Type;

(ii) Size or calibre;

(iii) Number of items; and

(iv) Nominal weight of chemical fill per item.

(h) For each chemical the total weight present at the storage facility shall be declared;

(i) In addition, for chemicals stored in bulk, the percentage purity shall be declared, if known.

3. For each type of unfilled munitions, sub-munitions, devices or equipment, referred to in paragraph 1 (c) (ii), the information shall include:

(a) The number of items;

(b) The nominal fill volume per item;

(c) The intended chemical fill.

Declarations of chemical weapons pursuant to Article
III, paragraph 1 (a) (iii)

4.   The declaration of chemical weapons pursuant to
Article III, paragraph 1 (a) (iii), shall contain all information
specified in paragraphs 1 to 3 above. It is the responsibility
of the State Party on whose territory the chemical weapons
are located to make appropriate arrangements with the other
State to ensure that the declarations are made. If the State
Party on whose territory the chemical weapons are located is
not able to fulfil its obligations under this paragraph, it shall
state the reasons therefor.

Declarations of past transfers and receipts

5.   A State Party that has transferred or received chemical
weapons since 1 January 1946 shall declare these transfers
or receipts pursuant to Article III, paragraph 1 (a) (iv),
provided the amount transferred or received exceeded 1
tonne per chemical per year in bulk and/or munition form.
This declaration shall be made according to the inventory
format specified in paragraphs 1 and 2. This declaration shall
also indicate the supplier and recipient countries, the dates
of the transfers or receipts and, as precisely as possible, the
current location of the transferred items. When not all the
specified information is available for transfers or receipts of
chemical weapons for the period between 1 January 1946
and 1 January 1970, the State Party shall declare whatever
information is still available to it and provide an explanation
as to why it cannot submit a full declaration.

Submission of the general plan for destruction of
chemical weapons

6.   The general plan for destruction of chemical weapons submitted pursuant to Article III, paragraph 1 (a) (v), shall provide an overview of the entire national chemical weapons destruction programme of the State Party and information on the efforts of the State Party to fulfil the destruction requirements contained in this Convention. The plan shall specify:

(a)   A general schedule for destruction, giving types and approximate quantities of chemical weapons planned to be destroyed in each annual destruction period for each existing chemical weapons destruction facility and, if possible, for each planned chemical weapons destruction facility;

(b)   The number of chemical weapons destruction facilities existing or planned to be operated over the destruction period;

(c)   For each existing or planned chemical weapons destruction facility:

(i)   Name and location; and

(ii)   The types and approximate quantities of chemical weapons, and the type (for example, nerve agent or blister agent) and approximate quantity of chemical fill, to be destroyed;

(d)   The plans and programmes for training personnel for the operation of destruction facilities;

(e)   The national standards for safety and emissions that the destruction facilities must satisfy;

(f)   Information on the development of new methods for destruction of chemical weapons and on the improvement of existing methods;

(g)   The cost estimates for destroying the chemical weapons; and

(h)   Any issues which could adversely impact on the national destruction programme.

B.   Measures to secure the storage facility and storage facility preparation

7.   Not later than when submitting its declaration of chemical weapons, a State Party shall take such measures as it considers appropriate to secure its storage facilities and shall prevent any movement of its chemical weapons out of the facilities, except their removal for destruction.

8.   A State Party shall ensure that chemical weapons at its storage facilities are configured to allow ready access for verification in accordance with paragraphs 37 to 49.

9.   While a storage facility remains closed for any movement of chemical weapons out of the facility other than their removal for destruction, a State Party may

continue at the facility standard maintenance activities, including standard maintenance of chemical weapons; safety monitoring and physical security activities; and preparation of chemical weapons for destruction.

10. Maintenance activities of chemical weapons shall not include:

(a) Replacement of agent or of munition bodies;

(b) Modification of the original characteristics of munitions, or parts or components thereof.

11. All maintenance activities shall be subject to monitoring by the Technical Secretariat.

C.   Destruction

Principles and methods for destruction
of chemical weapons

12. "Destruction of chemical weapons" means a process by which chemicals are converted in an essentially irreversible way to a form unsuitable for production of chemical weapons, and which in an irreversible manner renders munitions and other devices unusable as such.

13. Each State Party shall determine how it shall destroy chemical weapons, except that the following processes may not be used: dumping in any body of water, land burial or open-pit burning. It shall destroy chemical weapons only at specifically designated and appropriately designed and equipped facilities.

14.   Each State Party shall ensure that its chemical weapons destruction facilities are constructed and operated in a manner to ensure the destruction of the chemical weapons; and that the destruction process can be verified under the provisions of this Convention.

Order of destruction

15.   The order of destruction of chemical weapons is based on the obligations specified in Article I and the other Articles, including obligations regarding systematic on-site verification. It takes into account interests of States Parties for undiminished security during the destruction period; confidence-building in the early part of the destruction stage; gradual acquisition of experience in the course of destroying chemical weapons; and applicability irrespective of the actual composition of the stockpiles and the methods chosen for the destruction of the chemical weapons. The order of destruction is based on the principle of levelling out.

16.   For the purpose of destruction, chemical weapons declared by each State Party shall be divided into three categories:

Category 1:   Chemical weapons on the basis of Schedule 1 chemicals and their parts and components;

Category 2:   Chemical weapons on the basis of all other chemicals and their parts and components;

Category 3: Unfilled munitions and devices, and equipment specifically designed for use directly in connection with employment of chemical weapons.

17. A State Party shall start:

(a) The destruction of Category 1 chemical weapons not later than two years after this Convention enters into force for it, and shall complete the destruction not later than 10 years after entry into force of this Convention. A State Party shall destroy chemical weapons in accordance with the following destruction deadlines:

(i) Phase 1: Not later than two years after entry into force of this Convention, testing of its first destruction facility shall be completed. Not less than 1 per cent of the Category 1 chemical weapons shall be destroyed not later than three years after the entry into force of this Convention;

(ii) Phase 2: Not less than 20 per cent of the Category 1 chemical weapons shall be destroyed not later than five years after the entry into force of this Convention;

(iii) Phase 3: Not less than 45 per cent of the Category 1 chemical weapons shall be destroyed not later than seven years after the entry into force of this Convention;

(iv) Phase 4: All Category 1 chemical weapons shall be destroyed not later than 10 years after the entry into force of this Convention.

(b) The destruction of Category 2 chemical weapons not later than one year after this Convention enters into force for it and shall complete the destruction not later than five years after the entry into force of this Convention. Category 2 chemical weapons shall be destroyed in equal annual increments throughout the destruction period. The comparison factor for such weapons is the weight of the chemicals within Category 2; and

(c) The destruction of Category 3 chemical weapons not later than one year after this Convention enters into force for it, and shall complete the destruction not later than five years after the entry into force of this Convention. Category 3 chemical weapons shall be destroyed in equal annual increments throughout the destruction period. The comparison factor for unfilled munitions and devices is expressed in nominal fill volume (m3) and for equipment in number of items.

18. For the destruction of binary chemical weapons the following shall apply:

(a) For the purposes of the order of destruction, a declared quantity (in tonnes) of the key component intended for a specific toxic end-product shall be considered equivalent to the quantity (in tonnes) of this toxic end-product calculated on a stoichiometric basis assuming 100 per cent yield.

(b) A requirement to destroy a given quantity of the key component shall entail a requirement to destroy a corresponding quantity of the other component, calculated from the actual weight ratio of the components in the relevant type of binary chemical munition/device.

(c) If more of the other component is declared than is needed, based on the actual weight ratio between components, the excess shall be destroyed over the first two years after destruction operations begin.

(d) At the end of each subsequent operational year a State Party may retain an amount of the other declared component that is determined on the basis of the actual weight ratio of the components in the relevant type of binary chemical munition/device.

19. For multicomponent chemical weapons the order of destruction shall be analogous to that envisaged for binary chemical weapons.

Modification of intermediate destruction deadlines

20. The Executive Council shall review the general plans for destruction of chemical weapons, submitted pursuant to Article III, paragraph 1 (a) (v), and in accordance with paragraph 6, inter alia, to assess their conformity with the order of destruction set forth in paragraphs 15 to 19. The Executive Council shall consult with any State Party whose

plan does not conform, with the objective of bringing the plan into conformity.

21. If a State Party, due to exceptional circumstances beyond its control, believes that it cannot achieve the level of destruction specified for Phase 1, Phase 2 or Phase 3 of the order of destruction of Category 1 chemical weapons, it may propose changes in those levels. Such a proposal must be made not later than 120 days after the entry into force of this Convention and shall contain a detailed explanation of the reasons for the proposal.

22. Each State Party shall take all necessary measures to ensure destruction of Category 1 chemical weapons in accordance with the destruction deadlines set forth in paragraph 17 (a) as changed pursuant to paragraph 21. However, if a State Party believes that it will be unable to ensure the destruction of the percentage of Category 1 chemical weapons required by an intermediate destruction deadline, it may request the Executive Council to recommend to the Conference to grant an extension of its obligation to meet that deadline. Such a request must be made not less than 180 days before the intermediate destruction deadline and shall contain a detailed explanation of the reasons for the request and the plans of the State Party for ensuring that it will be able to fulfil its obligation to meet the next intermediate destruction deadline.

23. If an extension is granted, the State Party shall still be under the obligation to meet the cumulative destruction requirements set forth for the next destruction deadline.

Extensions granted pursuant to this Section shall not, in any way, modify the obligation of the State Party to destroy all Category 1 chemical weapons not later than 10 years after the entry into force of this Convention.

Extension of the deadline for completion of destruction

24. If a State Party believes that it will be unable to ensure the destruction of all Category 1 chemical weapons not later than 10 years after the entry into force of this Convention, it may submit a request to the Executive Council for an extension of the deadline for completing the destruction of such chemical weapons. Such a request must be made not later than nine years after the entry into force of this Convention.

25. The request shall contain:

(a) The duration of the proposed extension;

(b) A detailed explanation of the reasons for the proposed extension; and

(c) A detailed plan for destruction during the proposed extension and the remaining portion of the original 10-year period for destruction.

26. A decision on the request shall be taken by the Conference at its next session, on the recommendation of the Executive Council. Any extension shall be the minimum necessary, but in no case shall the deadline for a State Party to complete its destruction of all chemical weapons

be extended beyond 15 years after the entry into force of this Convention. The Executive Council shall set conditions for the granting of the extension, including the specific verification measures deemed necessary as well as specific actions to be taken by the State Party to overcome problems in its destruction programme. Costs of verification during the extension period shall be allocated in accordance with Article IV, paragraph 16.

27. If an extension is granted, the State Party shall take appropriate measures to meet all subsequent deadlines.

28. The State Party shall continue to submit detailed annual plans for destruction in accordance with paragraph 29 and annual reports on the destruction of Category 1 chemical weapons in accordance with paragraph 36, until all Category 1 chemical weapons are destroyed. In addition, not later than at the end of each 90 days of the extension period, the State Party shall report to the Executive Council on its destruction activity. The Executive Council shall review progress towards completion of destruction and take the necessary measures to document this progress. All information concerning the destruction activities during the extension period shall be provided by the Executive Council to States Parties, upon request.

Detailed annual plans for destruction

29. The detailed annual plans for destruction shall be submitted to the Technical Secretariat not less than 60 days

before each annual destruction period begins pursuant to Article IV, paragraph 7 (a), and shall specify:

(a) The quantity of each specific type of chemical weapon to be destroyed at each destruction facility and the inclusive dates when the destruction of each specific type of chemical weapon will be accomplished;

(b) The detailed site diagram for each chemical weapons destruction facility and any changes to previously submitted diagrams; and

(c) The detailed schedule of activities for each chemical weapons destruction facility for the upcoming year, identifying time required for design, construction or modification of the facility, installation of equipment, equipment check-out and operator training, destruction operations for each specific type of chemical weapon, and scheduled periods of inactivity.

30. A State Party shall provide, for each of its chemical weapons destruction facilities, detailed facility information to assist the Technical Secretariat in developing preliminary inspection procedures for use at the facility.

31. The detailed facility information for each destruction facility shall include the following information:

(a) Name, address and location;

(b) Detailed, annotated facility drawings;

(c)   Facility design drawings, process drawings, and piping and instrumentation design drawings;

(d)   Detailed technical descriptions, including design drawings and instrument specifications, for the equipment required for: removing the chemical fill from the munitions, devices, and containers; temporarily storing the drained chemical fill; destroying the chemical agent; and destroying the munitions, devices, and containers;

(e)   Detailed technical descriptions of the destruction process, including material flow rates, temperatures and pressures, and designed destruction efficiency;

(f)   Design capacity for each specific type of chemical weapon;

(g)   A detailed description of the products of destruction and the method of their ultimate disposal;

(h)   A detailed technical description of measures to facilitate inspections in accordance with this Convention;

(i)   A detailed description of any temporary holding area at the destruction facility that will be used to provide chemical weapons directly to the destruction facility, including site and facility drawings and information on the storage capacity for each specific type of chemical weapon to be destroyed at the facility;

(j)   A detailed description of the safety and medical measures in force at the facility;

(k)   A detailed description of the living quarters and working premises for the inspectors; and

(l)   Suggested measures for international verification.

32. A State Party shall provide, for each of its chemical weapons destruction facilities, the plant operations manuals, the safety and medical plans, the laboratory operations and quality assurance and control manuals, and the environmental permits that have been obtained, except that this shall not include material previously provided.

33. A State Party shall promptly notify the Technical Secretariat of any developments that could affect inspection activities at its destruction facilities.

34. Deadlines for submission of the information specified in paragraphs 30 to 32 shall be considered and approved by the Conference pursuant to Article VIII, paragraph 21 (i).

35. After a review of the detailed facility information for each destruction facility, the Technical Secretariat, if the need arises, shall enter into consultation with the State Party concerned in order to ensure that its chemical weapons destruction facilities are designed to assure the destruction of chemical weapons, to allow advanced planning on how verification measures may be applied and to ensure that the application of verification measures is consistent with proper facility operation, and that the facility operation allows appropriate verification.

Annual reports on destruction

36. Information regarding the implementation of plans for destruction of chemical weapons shall be submitted to the Technical Secretariat pursuant to Article IV, paragraph 7 (b), not later than 60 days after the end of each annual destruction period and shall specify the actual amounts of chemical weapons which were destroyed during the previous year at each destruction facility. If appropriate, reasons for not meeting destruction goals should be stated.

D. Verification

Verification of declarations of chemical weapons through on-site inspection

37. The purpose of the verification of declarations of chemical weapons shall be to confirm through on-site inspection the accuracy of the relevant declarations made pursuant to Article III.

38. The inspectors shall conduct this verification promptly after a declaration is submitted. They shall, inter alia, verify the quantity and identity of chemicals, types and number of munitions, devices and other equipment.

39. The inspectors shall employ, as appropriate, agreed seals, markers or other inventory control procedures to facilitate an accurate inventory of the chemical weapons at each storage facility.

40. As the inventory progresses, inspectors shall install such agreed seals as may be necessary to clearly indicate if

any stocks are removed, and to ensure the securing of the storage facility during the inventory. After completion of the inventory, such seals will be removed unless otherwise agreed.

Systematic verification of storage facilities

41. The purpose of the systematic verification of storage facilities shall be to ensure that no undetected removal of chemical weapons from such facilities takes place.

42. The systematic verification shall be initiated as soon as possible after the declaration of chemical weapons is submitted and shall continue until all chemical weapons have been removed from the storage facility. It shall in accordance with the facility agreement, combine on-site inspection and monitoring with on-site instruments.

43. When all chemical weapons have been removed from the storage facility, the Technical Secretariat shall confirm the declaration of the State Party to that effect. After this confirmation, the Technical Secretariat shall terminate the systematic verification of the storage facility and shall promptly remove any monitoring instruments installed by the inspectors.

Inspections and visits

44. The particular storage facility to be inspected shall be chosen by the Technical Secretariat in such a way as to preclude the prediction of precisely when the facility is to be inspected. The guidelines for determining the frequency

of systematic on-site inspections shall be elaborated by the Technical Secretariat, taking into account the recommendations to be considered and approved by the Conference pursuant to Article VIII, paragraph 21 (i).

45. The Technical Secretariat shall notify the inspected State Party of its decision to inspect or visit the storage facility 48 hours before the planned arrival of the inspection team at the facility for systematic inspections or visits. In cases of inspections or visits to resolve urgent problems, this period may be shortened. The Technical Secretariat shall specify the purpose of the inspection or visit.

46. The inspected State Party shall make any necessary preparations for the arrival of the inspectors and shall ensure their expeditious transportation from their point of entry to the storage facility. The facility agreement will specify administrative arrangements for inspectors.

47. The inspected State Party shall provide the inspection team upon its arrival at the chemical weapons storage facility to carry out an inspection, with the following data on the facility:

(a) The number of storage buildings and storage locations;

(b) For each storage building and storage location, the type and the identification number or designation, shown on the site diagram; and

(c) For each storage building and storage location at the facility, the number of items of each specific type of chemical weapon, and, for containers that are not part of binary munitions, the actual quantity of chemical fill in each container.

48. In carrying out an inventory, within the time available, inspectors shall have the right:

(a) To use any of the following inspection techniques:

(i) inventory all the chemical weapons stored at the facility;

(ii) inventory all the chemical weapons stored in specific buildings or locations at the facility, as chosen by the inspectors; or

(iii) inventory all the chemical weapons of one or more specific types stored at the facility, as chosen by the inspectors; and

(b) To check all items inventoried against agreed records.

49. Inspectors shall, in accordance with facility agreements:

(a) Have unimpeded access to all parts of the storage facilities including any munitions, devices, bulk containers, or other containers therein. While conducting their activity, inspectors shall comply with the safety regulations at the facility. The items to be inspected will be chosen by the inspectors; and

(b) Have the right, during the first and any subsequent inspection of each chemical weapons storage facility, to designate munitions, devices, and containers from which samples are to be taken, and to affix to such munitions, devices, and containers a unique tag that will indicate an attempt to remove or alter the tag. A sample shall be taken from a tagged item at a chemical weapons storage facility or a chemical weapons destruction facility as soon as it is practically possible in accordance with the corresponding destruction programmes, and, in any case, not later than by the end of the destruction operations.

Systematic verification of the destruction of chemical weapons

50. The purpose of verification of destruction of chemical weapons shall be:

(a) To confirm the identity and quantity of the chemical weapons stocks to be destroyed; and

(b) To confirm that these stocks have been destroyed.

51. Chemical weapons destruction operations during the first 390 days after the entry into force of this Convention shall be governed by transitional verification arrangements. Such arrangements, including a transitional facility agreement, provisions for verification through on-site inspection and monitoring with on-site instruments, and

the time-frame for application of the arrangements, shall be agreed between the Organization and the inspected State Party. These arrangements shall be approved by the Executive Council not later than 60 days after this Convention enters into force for the State Party, taking into account the recommendations of the Technical Secretariat, which shall be based on an evaluation of the detailed facility information provided in accordance with paragraph 31 and a visit to the facility. The Executive Council shall, at its first session, establish the guidelines for such transitional verification arrangements, based on recommendations to be considered and approved by the Conference pursuant to Article VIII, paragraph 21 (i). The transitional verification arrangements shall be designed to verify, throughout the entire transitional period, the destruction of chemical weapons in accordance with the purposes set forth in paragraph 50, and to avoid hampering ongoing destruction operations.

52. The provisions of paragraphs 53 to 61 shall apply to chemical weapons destruction operations that are to begin not earlier than 390 days after the entry into force of this Convention.

53. On the basis of this Convention and the detailed destruction facility information, and as the case may be, on experience from previous inspections, the Technical Secretariat shall prepare a draft plan for inspecting the destruction of chemical weapons at each destruction facility. The plan shall be completed and provided to the inspected State Party for comment not less than 270 days before the facility begins destruction operations pursuant

to this Convention. Any differences between the Technical Secretariat and the inspected State Party should be resolved through consultations. Any unresolved matter shall be forwarded to the Executive Council for appropriate action with a view to facilitating the full implementation of this Convention.

54. The Technical Secretariat shall conduct an initial visit to each chemical weapons destruction facility of the inspected State Party not less than 240 days before each facility begins destruction operations pursuant to this Convention, to allow it to familiarize itself with the facility and assess the adequacy of the inspection plan.

55. In the case of an existing facility where chemical weapons destruction operations have already been initiated, the inspected State Party shall not be required to decontaminate the facility before the Technical Secretariat conducts an initial visit. The duration of the visit shall not exceed five days and the number of visiting personnel shall not exceed 15.

56. The agreed detailed plans for verification, with an appropriate recommendation by the Technical Secretariat, shall be forwarded to the Executive Council for review. The Executive Council shall review the plans with a view to approving them, consistent with verification objectives and obligations under this Convention. It should also confirm that verification schemes for destruction are consistent with verification aims and are efficient and practical. This review

should be completed not less than 180 days before the destruction period begins.

57. Each member of the Executive Council may consult with the Technical Secretariat on any issues regarding the adequacy of the plan for verification. If there are no objections by any member of the Executive Council, the plan shall be put into action.

58. If there are any difficulties, the Executive Council shall enter into consultations with the State Party to reconcile them. If any difficulties remain unresolved they shall be referred to the Conference.

59. The detailed facility agreements for chemical weapons destruction facilities shall specify, taking into account the specific characteristics of the destruction facility and its mode of operation:

(a) Detailed on-site inspection procedures; and

(b) Provisions for verification through continuous monitoring with on-site instruments and physical presence of inspectors.

60. Inspectors shall be granted access to each chemical weapons destruction facility not less than 60 days before the commencement of the destruction, pursuant to this Convention, at the facility. Such access shall be for the purpose of supervising the installation of the inspection equipment, inspecting this equipment and testing its operation, as well as for the purpose of carrying out a final

engineering review of the facility. In the case of an existing facility where chemical weapons destruction operations have already been initiated, destruction operations shall be stopped for the minimum amount of time required, not to exceed 60 days, for installation and testing of the inspection equipment. Depending on the results of the testing and review, the State Party and the Technical Secretariat may agree on additions or changes to the detailed facility agreement for the facility.

61. The inspected State Party shall notify, in writing, the inspection team leader at a chemical weapons destruction facility not less than four hours before the departure of each shipment of chemical weapons from a chemical weapons storage facility to that destruction facility. This notification shall specify the name of the storage facility, the estimated times of departure and arrival, the specific types and quantities of chemical weapons being transported, whether any tagged items are being moved, and the method of transportation. This notification may include notification of more than one shipment. The inspection team leader shall be promptly notified, in writing, of any changes in this information.

Chemical weapons storage facilities at chemical weapons destruction facilities

62. The inspectors shall verify the arrival of the chemical weapons at the destruction facility and the storing of these chemical weapons. The inspectors shall verify the inventory of each shipment, using agreed procedures consistent with

facility safety regulations, prior to the destruction of the chemical weapons. They shall employ, as appropriate, agreed seals, markers or other inventory control procedures to facilitate an accurate inventory of the chemical weapons prior to destruction.

63. As soon and as long as chemical weapons are stored at chemical weapons storage facilities located at chemical weapons destruction facilities, these storage facilities shall be subject to systematic verification in conformity with the relevant facility agreements.

64. At the end of an active destruction phase, inspectors shall make an inventory of the chemical weapons, that have been removed from the storage facility, to be destroyed. They shall verify the accuracy of the inventory of the chemical weapons remaining, employing inventory control procedures as referred to in paragraph 62.

Systematic on-site verification measures at chemical weapons destruction facilities

65. The inspectors shall be granted access to conduct their activities at the chemical weapons destruction facilities and the chemical weapons storage facilities located at such facilities during the entire active phase of destruction.

66. At each chemical weapons destruction facility, to provide assurance that no chemical weapons are diverted and that the destruction process has been completed, inspectors shall have the right to verify through their physical presence and monitoring with on-site instruments:

(a)   The receipt of chemical weapons at the facility;

(b)   The temporary holding area for chemical weapons and the specific type and quantity of chemical weapons stored in that area;

(c)   The specific type and quantity of chemical weapons being destroyed;

(d)   The process of destruction;

(e)   The end-product of destruction;

(f)   The mutilation of metal parts; and

(g)   The integrity of the destruction process and of the facility as a whole.

67.   Inspectors shall have the right to tag, for sampling, munitions, devices, or containers located in the temporary holding areas at the chemical weapons destruction facilities.

68.   To the extent that it meets inspection requirements, information from routine facility operations, with appropriate data authentication, shall be used for inspection purposes.

69.   After the completion of each period of destruction, the Technical Secretariat shall confirm the declaration of the State Party, reporting the completion of destruction of the designated quantity of chemical weapons.

70. Inspectors shall, in accordance with facility agreements:

(a) Have unimpeded access to all parts of the chemical weapons destruction facilities and the chemical weapons storage facilities located at such facilities, including any munitions, devices, bulk containers, or other containers, therein. The items to be inspected shall be chosen by the inspectors in accordance with the verification plan that has been agreed to by the inspected State Party and approved by the Executive Council;

(b) Monitor the systematic on-site analysis of samples during the destruction process; and

(c) Receive, if necessary, samples taken at their request from any devices, bulk containers and other containers at the destruction facility or the storage facility thereat.

Part IV (B)
Old chemical weapons and abandoned chemical weapons

A.   General

1.   Old chemical weapons shall be destroyed as provided for in Section B.

2.   Abandoned chemical weapons, including those which also meet the definition of Article II, paragraph 5 (b), shall be destroyed as provided for in Section C.

B.   Regime for old chemical weapons

3.   A State Party which has on its territory old chemical weapons as defined in Article II, paragraph 5 (a), shall, not later than 30 days after this Convention enters into force for it, submit to the Technical Secretariat all available relevant information, including, to the extent possible, the location, type, quantity and the present condition of these old chemical weapons.

In the case of old chemical weapons as defined in Article II, paragraph 5 (b), the State Party shall submit to the Technical Secretariat a declaration pursuant to Article III, paragraph 1 (b) (i), including, to the extent possible, the information specified in Part IV (A), paragraphs 1 to 3, of this Annex.

4.   A State Party which discovers old chemical weapons after this Convention enters into force for it shall submit to the Technical Secretariat the information specified in

paragraph 3 not later than 180 days after the discovery of the old chemical weapons.

5.   The Technical Secretariat shall conduct an initial inspection, and any further inspections as may be necessary, in order to verify the information submitted pursuant to paragraphs 3 and 4 and in particular to determine whether the chemical weapons meet the definition of old chemical weapons as specified in Article II, paragraph 5. Guidelines to determine the usability of chemical weapons produced between 1925 and 1946 shall be considered and approved by the Conference pursuant to Article VIII, paragraph 21 (i).

6.   A State Party shall treat old chemical weapons that have been confirmed by the Technical Secretariat as meeting the definition in Article II, paragraph 5 (a), as toxic waste. It shall inform the Technical Secretariat of the steps being taken to destroy or otherwise dispose of such old chemical weapons as toxic waste in accordance with its national legislation.

7.   Subject to paragraphs 3 to 5, a State Party shall destroy old chemical weapons that have been confirmed by the Technical Secretariat as meeting the definition in Article II, paragraph 5 (b), in accordance with Article IV and Part IV (A) of this Annex. Upon request of a State Party, the Executive Council may, however, modify the provisions on time-limit and order of destruction of these old chemical weapons, if it determines that doing so would not pose a risk to the object and purpose of this Convention. The request shall contain specific proposals for modification of the provisions

and a detailed explanation of the reasons for the proposed modification.

C. Regime for abandoned chemical weapons

8. A State Party on whose territory there are abandoned chemical weapons (hereinafter referred to as the "Territorial State Party") shall, not later than 30 days after this Convention enters into force for it, submit to the Technical Secretariat all available relevant information concerning the abandoned chemical weapons. This information shall include, to the extent possible, the location, type, quantity and the present condition of the abandoned chemical weapons as well as information on the abandonment.

9. A State Party which discovers abandoned chemical weapons after this Convention enters into force for it shall, not later than 180 days after the discovery, submit to the Technical Secretariat all available relevant information concerning the discovered abandoned chemical weapons. This information shall include, to the extent possible, the location, type, quantity and the present condition of the abandoned chemical weapons as well as information on the abandonment.

10. A State Party which has abandoned chemical weapons on the territory of another State Party (hereinafter referred to as the "Abandoning State Party") shall, not later than 30 days after this Convention enters into force for it, submit to the Technical Secretariat all available relevant information concerning the abandoned chemical weapons. This information shall include, to the extent possible,

the location, type, quantity as well as information on the abandonment, and the condition of the abandoned chemical weapons.

11. The Technical Secretariat shall conduct an initial inspection, and any further inspections as may be necessary, in order to verify all available relevant information submitted pursuant to paragraphs 8 to 10 and determine whether systematic verification in accordance with Part IV (A), paragraphs 41 to 43, of this Annex is required. It shall, if necessary, verify the origin of the abandoned chemical weapons and establish evidence concerning the abandonment and the identity of the Abandoning State.

12. The report of the Technical Secretariat shall be submitted to the Executive Council, the Territorial State Party, and to the Abandoning State Party or the State Party declared by the Territorial State Party or identified by the Technical Secretariat as having abandoned the chemical weapons. If one of the States Parties directly concerned is not satisfied with the report it shall have the right to settle the matter in accordance with provisions of this Convention or bring the issue to the Executive Council with a view to settling the matter expeditiously.

13. Pursuant to Article I, paragraph 3, the Territorial State Party shall have the right to request the State Party which has been established as the Abandoning State Party pursuant to paragraphs 8 to 12 to enter into consultations for the purpose of destroying the abandoned chemical weapons

in cooperation with the Territorial State Party. It shall immediately inform the Technical Secretariat of this request.

14.   Consultations between the Territorial State Party and the Abandoning State Party with a view to establishing a mutually agreed plan for destruction shall begin not later than 30 days after the Technical Secretariat has been informed of the request referred to in paragraph 13. The mutually agreed plan for destruction shall be transmitted to the Technical Secretariat not later than 180 days after the Technical Secretariat has been informed of the request referred to in paragraph 13. Upon the request of the Abandoning State Party and the Territorial State Party, the Executive Council may extend the time-limit for transmission of the mutually agreed plan for destruction.

15.   For the purpose of destroying abandoned chemical weapons, the Abandoning State Party shall provide all necessary financial, technical, expert, facility as well as other resources. The Territorial State Party shall provide appropriate cooperation.

16.   If the Abandoning State cannot be identified or is not a State Party, the Territorial State Party, in order to ensure the destruction of these abandoned chemical weapons, may request the Organization and other States Parties to provide assistance in the destruction of these abandoned chemical weapons.

17.   Subject to paragraphs 8 to 16, Article IV and Part IV (A) of this Annex shall also apply to the destruction of abandoned

chemical weapons. In the case of abandoned chemical weapons which also meet the definition of old chemical weapons in Article II, paragraph 5 (b), the Executive Council, upon the request of the Territorial State Party, individually or together with the Abandoning State Party, may modify or in exceptional cases suspend the application of provisions on destruction, if it determines that doing so would not pose a risk to the object and purpose of this Convention. In the case of abandoned chemical weapons which do not meet the definition of old chemical weapons in Article II, paragraph 5 (b), the Executive Council, upon the request of the Territorial State Party, individually or together with the Abandoning State Party, may in exceptional circumstances modify the provisions on the time-limit and the order of destruction, if it determines that doing so would not pose a risk to the object and purpose of this Convention. Any request as referred to in this paragraph shall contain specific proposals for modification of the provisions and a detailed explanation of the reasons for the proposed modification.

18. States Parties may conclude between themselves agreements or arrangements concerning the destruction of abandoned chemical weapons. The Executive Council may, upon request of the Territorial State Party, individually or together with the Abandoning State Party, decide that selected provisions of such agreements or arrangements take precedence over provisions of this Section, if it determines that the agreement or arrangement ensures the destruction of the abandoned chemical weapons in accordance with paragraph 17.

Part V
Destruction of chemical weapons production facilities and its verification pursuant to Article V

A. Declarations

Declarations of chemical weapons production facilities

1. The declaration of chemical weapons production facilities by a State Party pursuant to Article III, paragraph 1 (c) (ii), shall contain for each facility:

(a) The name of the facility, the names of the owners, and the names of the companies or enterprises operating the facility since 1 January 1946;

(b) The precise location of the facility, including the address, location of the complex, location of the facility within the complex including the specific building and structure number, if any;

(c) A statement whether it is a facility for the manufacture of chemicals that are defined as chemical weapons or whether it is a facility for the filling of chemical weapons, or both;

(d) The date when the construction of the facility was completed and the periods during which any modifications to the facility were made, including the installation of new or modified equipment, that significantly changed the production process characteristics of the facility;

(e)   Information on the chemicals defined as chemical weapons that were manufactured at the facility; the munitions, devices, and containers that were filled at the facility; and the dates of the beginning and cessation of such manufacture or filling:

(i)   For chemicals defined as chemical weapons that were manufactured at the facility, such information shall be expressed in terms of the specific types of chemicals manufactured, indicating the chemical name in accordance with the current International Union of Pure and Applied Chemistry (IUPAC) nomenclature, structural formula, and the Chemical Abstracts Service registry number, if assigned, and in terms of the amount of each chemical expressed by weight of chemical in tonnes;

(ii)   For munitions, devices and containers that were filled at the facility, such information shall be expressed in terms of the specific type of chemical weapons filled and the weight of the chemical fill per unit;

(f)   The production capacity of the chemical weapons production facility:

(i)   For a facility where chemical weapons were manufactured, production capacity shall be expressed in terms of the annual quantitative potential for manufacturing a specific substance on the basis of the technological process actually used or, in the case of processes not actually used, planned to be used at the facility;

(ii) For a facility where chemical weapons were filled, production capacity shall be expressed in terms of the quantity of chemical that the facility can fill into each specific type of chemical weapon a year;

(g) For each chemical weapons production facility that has not been destroyed, a description of the facility including:

(i) A site diagram;

(ii) A process flow diagram of the facility; and

(iii) An inventory of buildings at the facility, and specialized equipment at the facility and of any spare parts for such equipment;

(h) The present status of the facility, stating:

(i) The date when chemical weapons were last produced at the facility;

(ii) Whether the facility has been destroyed, including the date and manner of its destruction; and

(iii) Whether the facility has been used or modified before entry into force of this Convention for an activity not related to the production of chemical weapons, and if so, information on what modifications have been made, the date such non-chemical weapons related activity began and the nature of such activity, indicating, if applicable, the kind of product;

(i)   A specification of the measures that have been taken by the State Party for closure of, and a description of the measures that have been or will be taken by the State Party to inactivate the facility;

(j)   A description of the normal pattern of activity for safety and security at the inactivated facility; and

(k)   A statement as to whether the facility will be converted for the destruction of chemical weapons and, if so, the dates for such conversions.

Declarations of chemical weapons production facilities pursuant to Article III, paragraph 1 (c) (iii)

2.   The declaration of chemical weapons production facilities pursuant to Article III, paragraph 1 (c) (iii), shall contain all information specified in paragraph 1 above. It is the responsibility of the State Party on whose territory the facility is or has been located to make appropriate arrangements with the other State to ensure that the declarations are made. If the State Party on whose territory the facility is or has been located is not able to fulfil this obligation, it shall state the reasons therefor.

Declarations of past transfers and receipts

3.   A State Party that has transferred or received chemical weapons production equipment since 1 January 1946 shall declare these transfers and receipts pursuant to Article III, paragraph 1 (c) (iv), and in accordance with paragraph 5 below. When not all the specified information is available for transfer and receipt of such equipment for the period between 1 January 1946 and 1 January 1970, the State Party shall declare whatever information is still available to it and provide an explanation as to why it cannot submit a full declaration.

4.   Chemical weapons production equipment referred to in paragraph 3 means:

(a)   Specialized equipment;

(b)   Equipment for the production of equipment specifically designed for use directly in connection with chemical weapons employment; and

(c)   Equipment designed or used exclusively for producing non-chemical parts for chemical munitions.

5.   The declaration concerning transfer and receipt of chemical weapons production equipment shall specify:

(a)   Who received/transferred the chemical weapons production equipment;

(b)   The identity of such equipment;

(c) The date of transfer or receipt;

(d) Whether the equipment was destroyed, if known; and

(e) Current disposition, if known.

Submission of general plans for destruction

6. For each chemical weapons production facility, a State Party shall supply the following information:

(a) Envisaged time-frame for measures to be taken; and

(b) Methods of destruction.

7. For each chemical weapons production facility that a State Party intends to convert temporarily into a chemical weapons destruction facility, the State Party shall supply the following information:

(a) Envisaged time-frame for conversion into a destruction facility;

(b) Envisaged time-frame for utilizing the facility as a chemical weapons destruction facility;

(c) Description of the new facility;

(d) Method of destruction of special equipment;

(e) Time-frame for destruction of the converted facility after it has been utilized to destroy chemical weapons; and

(f) Method of destruction of the converted facility.

Submission of annual plans for destruction and annual reports on destruction

8. The State Party shall submit an annual plan for destruction not less than 90 days before the beginning of the coming destruction year. The annual plan shall specify:

(a) Capacity to be destroyed;

(b) Name and location of the facilities where destruction will take place;

(c) List of buildings and equipment that will be destroyed at each facility; and

(d) Planned method(s) of destruction.

9. A State Party shall submit an annual report on destruction not later than 90 days after the end of the previous destruction year. The annual report shall specify:

(a) Capacity destroyed;

(b) Name and location of each facility where destruction took place;

(c) List of buildings and equipment that were destroyed at each facility;

(d) Methods of destruction.

10. For a chemical weapons production facility declared pursuant to Article III, paragraph 1 (c) (iii), it is the responsibility of the State Party on whose territory the facility is or has been located to make appropriate arrangements to ensure that the declarations specified in paragraphs 6 to 9 above are made. If the State Party on whose territory the facility is or has been located is not able to fulfil this obligation, it shall state the reasons therefor.

B. Destruction

General principles for destruction of chemical weapons production facilities

11. Each State Party shall decide on methods to be applied for the destruction of chemical weapons production facilities, according to the principles laid down in Article V and in this Part.

Principles and methods for closure of a chemical weapons production facility

12. The purpose of the closure of a chemical weapons production facility is to render it inactive.

13. Agreed measures for closure shall be taken by a State Party with due regard to the specific characteristics of each facility. Such measures shall include, inter alia:

(a) Prohibition of occupation of the specialized buildings and standard buildings of the facility except for agreed activities;

(b) Disconnection of equipment directly related to the production of chemical weapons, including, inter alia, process control equipment and utilities;

(c) Decommissioning of protective installations and equipment used exclusively for the safety of operations of the chemical weapons production facility;

(d) Installation of blind flanges and other devices to prevent the addition of chemicals to, or the removal of chemicals from, any specialized process equipment for synthesis, separation or purification of chemicals defined as a chemical weapon, any storage tank, or any machine for filling chemical weapons, the heating, cooling, or supply of electrical or other forms of power to such equipment, storage tanks, or machines; and

(e) Interruption of rail, road and other access routes for heavy transport to the chemical weapons production facility except those required for agreed activities.

14. While the chemical weapons production facility remains closed, a State Party may continue safety and physical security activities at the facility.

Technical maintenance of chemical weapons production
facilities prior to their destruction

15. A State Party may carry out standard maintenance activities at chemical weapons production facilities only for safety reasons, including visual inspection, preventive maintenance, and routine repairs.

16. All planned maintenance activities shall be specified in the general and detailed plans for destruction. Maintenance activities shall not include:

(a)   Replacement of any process equipment;

(b)   Modification of the characteristics of the chemical process equipment;

(c)   Production of chemicals of any type.

17. All maintenance activities shall be subject to monitoring by the Technical Secretariat.

Principles and methods for temporary conversion of
chemical weapons production facilities into chemical
weapons destruction facilities

18. Measures pertaining to the temporary conversion of chemical weapons production facilities into chemical weapons destruction facilities shall ensure that the regime for the temporarily converted facilities is at least as stringent as the regime for chemical weapons production facilities that have not been converted.

19. Chemical weapons production facilities converted into chemical weapons destruction facilities before entry into force of this Convention shall be declared under the category of chemical weapons production facilities.

They shall be subject to an initial visit by inspectors, who shall confirm the correctness of the information about these facilities. Verification that the conversion of these facilities was performed in such a manner as to render them inoperable as chemical weapons production facilities shall also be required, and shall fall within the framework of measures provided for the facilities that are to be rendered inoperable not later than 90 days after entry into force of this Convention.

20. A State Party that intends to carry out a conversion of chemical weapons production facilities shall submit to the Technical Secretariat, not later than 30 days after this Convention enters into force for it, or not later than 30 days after a decision has been taken for temporary conversion, a general facility conversion plan, and subsequently shall submit annual plans.

21. Should a State Party have the need to convert to a chemical weapons destruction facility an additional chemical weapons production facility that had been closed after this Convention entered into force for it, it shall inform the Technical Secretariat thereof not less than 150 days before conversion. The Technical Secretariat, in conjunction with the State Party, shall make sure that the necessary measures

are taken to render that facility, after its conversion, inoperable as a chemical weapons production facility.

22. A facility converted for the destruction of chemical weapons shall not be more fit for resuming chemical weapons production than a chemical weapons production facility which has been closed and is under maintenance. Its reactivation shall require no less time than that required for a chemical weapons production facility that has been closed and is under maintenance.

23. Converted chemical weapons production facilities shall be destroyed not later than 10 years after entry into force of this Convention.

24. Any measures for the conversion of any given chemical weapons production facility shall be facility-specific and shall depend upon its individual characteristics.

25. The set of measures carried out for the purpose of converting a chemical weapons production facility into a chemical weapons destruction facility shall not be less than that which is provided for the disabling of other chemical weapons production facilities to be carried out not later than 90 days after this Convention enters into force for the State Party.

*Principles and methods related to destruction of a
chemical weapons production facility*

26. A State Party shall destroy equipment and buildings
covered by the definition of a chemical weapons production
facility as follows:

(a) All specialized equipment and standard equipment
shall be physically destroyed;

(b) All specialized buildings and standard buildings
shall be physically destroyed.

27. A State Party shall destroy facilities for producing
unfilled chemical munitions and equipment for chemical
weapons employment as follows:

(a) Facilities used exclusively for production of
non-chemical parts for chemical munitions or equipment
specifically designed for use directly in connection with
chemical weapons employment, shall be declared and
destroyed. The destruction process and its verification shall
be conducted according to the provisions of Article V and
this Part of this Annex that govern destruction of chemical
weapons production facilities;

(b) All equipment designed or used exclusively for
producing non-chemical parts for chemical munitions shall
be physically destroyed. Such equipment, which includes
specially designed moulds and metal-forming dies, may be
brought to a special location for destruction;

(c)   All buildings and standard equipment used for such production activities shall be destroyed or converted for purposes not prohibited under this Convention, with confirmation, as necessary, through consultations and inspections as provided for under Article IX;

(d)   Activities for purposes not prohibited under this Convention may continue while destruction or conversion proceeds.

Order of destruction

28. The order of destruction of chemical weapons production facilities is based on the obligations specified in Article I and the other Articles of this Convention, including obligations regarding systematic on-site verification. It takes into account interests of States Parties for undiminished security during the destruction period; confidence- building in the early part of the destruction stage; gradual acquisition of experience in the course of destroying chemical weapons production facilities; and applicability irrespective of the actual characteristics of the facilities and the methods chosen for their destruction. The order of destruction is based on the principle of levelling out.

29. A State Party shall, for each destruction period, determine which chemical weapons production facilities are to be destroyed and carry out the destruction in such a way that not more than what is specified in paragraphs 30 and 31 remains at the end of each destruction period. A State Party is not precluded from destroying its facilities at a faster pace.

30. The following provisions shall apply to chemical weapons production facilities that produce Schedule 1 chemicals:

(a) A State Party shall start the destruction of such facilities not later than one year after this Convention enters into force for it, and shall complete it not later than 10 years after entry into force of this Convention. For a State which is a Party at the entry into force of this Convention, this overall period shall be divided into three separate destruction periods, namely, years 2-5, years 6-8, and years 9-10. For States which become a Party after entry into force of this Convention, the destruction periods shall be adapted, taking into account paragraphs 28 and 29;

(b) Production capacity shall be used as the comparison factor for such facilities. It shall be expressed in agent tonnes, taking into account the rules specified for binary chemical weapons;

(c) Appropriate agreed levels of production capacity shall be established for the end of the eighth year after entry into force of this Convention. Production capacity that exceeds the relevant level shall be destroyed in equal increments during the first two destruction periods;

(d) A requirement to destroy a given amount of capacity shall entail a requirement to destroy any other chemical weapons production facility that supplied the Schedule 1 facility or filled the Schedule 1 chemical produced there into munitions or devices;

(e) Chemical weapons production facilities that have been converted temporarily for destruction of chemical weapons shall continue to be subject to the obligation to destroy capacity according to the provisions of this paragraph.

31. A State Party shall start the destruction of chemical weapons production facilities not covered in paragraph 30 not later than one year after this Convention enters into force for it, and complete it not later than five years after entry into force of this Convention.

Detailed plans for destruction

32. Not less than 180 days before the destruction of a chemical weapons production facility starts, a State Party shall provide to the Technical Secretariat the detailed plans for destruction of the facility, including proposed measures for verification of destruction referred to in paragraph 33 (f), with respect to, inter alia:

(a) Timing of the presence of the inspectors at the facility to be destroyed; and

(b) Procedures for verification of measures to be applied to each item on the declared inventory.

33. The detailed plans for destruction of each chemical weapons production facility shall contain:

(a) Detailed time schedule of the destruction process;

(b)   Layout of the facility;

(c)   Process flow diagram;

(d)   Detailed inventory of equipment, buildings and other items to be destroyed;

(e)   Measures to be applied to each item on the inventory;

(f)   Proposed measures for verification;

(g)   Security/safety measures to be observed during the destruction of the facility; and

(h)   Working and living conditions to be provided for inspectors.

34.   If a State Party intends to convert temporarily a chemical weapons production facility into a chemical weapons destruction facility, it shall notify the Technical Secretariat not less than 150 days before undertaking any conversion activities. The notification shall:

(a)   Specify the name, address, and location of the facility;

(b)   Provide a site diagram indicating all structures and areas that will be involved in the destruction of chemical weapons and also identify all structures of the chemical weapons production facility that are to be temporarily converted;

(c)   Specify the types of chemical weapons, and the type and quantity of chemical fill to be destroyed;

(d)   Specify the destruction method;

(e)   Provide a process flow diagram, indicating which portions of the production process and specialized equipment will be converted for the destruction of chemical weapons;

(f)   Specify the seals and inspection equipment potentially affected by the conversion, if applicable; and

(g)   Provide a schedule identifying: The time allocated to design, temporary conversion of the facility, installation of equipment, equipment check-out, destruction operations, and closure.

35.   In relation to the destruction of a facility that was temporarily converted for destruction of chemical weapons, information shall be provided in accordance with paragraphs 32 and 33.

Review of detailed plans

36.   On the basis of the detailed plan for destruction and proposed measures for verification submitted by the State Party, and on experience from previous inspections, the Technical Secretariat shall prepare a plan for verifying the destruction of the facility, consulting closely with the State Party. Any differences between the Technical Secretariat and the State Party concerning appropriate measures should be

resolved through consultations. Any unresolved matters shall be forwarded to the Executive Council for appropriate action with a view to facilitating the full implementation of this Convention.

37. To ensure that the provisions of Article V and this Part are fulfilled, the combined plans for destruction and verification shall be agreed upon between the Executive Council and the State Party. This agreement should be completed, not less than 60 days before the planned initiation of destruction.

38. Each member of the Executive Council may consult with the Technical Secretariat on any issues regarding the adequacy of the combined plan for destruction and verification. If there are no objections by any member of the Executive Council, the plan shall be put into action.

39. If there are any difficulties, the Executive Council shall enter into consultations with the State Party to reconcile them. If any difficulties remain unresolved they shall be referred to the Conference. The resolution of any differences over methods of destruction shall not delay the execution of other parts of the destruction plan that are acceptable.

40. If agreement is not reached with the Executive Council on aspects of verification, or if the approved verification plan cannot be put into action, verification of destruction shall proceed through continuous monitoring with on-site instruments and physical presence of inspectors.

41. Destruction and verification shall proceed according to the agreed plan. The verification shall not unduly interfere with the destruction process and shall be conducted through the presence of inspectors on-site to witness the destruction.

42. If required verification or destruction actions are not taken as planned, all States Parties shall be so informed.

C. Verification

Verification of declarations of chemical weapons production facilities through on-site inspection

43. The Technical Secretariat shall conduct an initial inspection of each chemical weapons production facility in the period between 90 and 120 days after this Convention enters into force for the State Party.

44. The purposes of the initial inspection shall be:

(a) To confirm that the production of chemical weapons has ceased and that the facility has been inactivated in accordance with this Convention;

(b) To permit the Technical Secretariat to familiarize itself with the measures that have been taken to cease production of chemical weapons at the facility;

(c) To permit the inspectors to install temporary seals;

(d) To permit the inspectors to confirm the inventory of buildings and specialized equipment;

(e) To obtain information necessary for planning inspection activities at the facility, including use of tamper-indicating seals and other agreed equipment, which shall be installed pursuant to the detailed facility agreement for the facility; and

(f) To conduct preliminary discussions regarding a detailed agreement on inspection procedures at the facility.

45. Inspectors shall employ, as appropriate, agreed seals, markers or other inventory control procedures to facilitate an accurate inventory of the declared items at each chemical weapons production facility.

46. Inspectors shall install such agreed devices as may be necessary to indicate if any resumption of production of chemical weapons occurs or if any declared item is removed. They shall take the necessary precaution not to hinder closure activities by the inspected State Party. Inspectors may return to maintain and verify the integrity of the devices.

47. If, on the basis of the initial inspection, the Director-General believes that additional measures are necessary to inactivate the facility in accordance with this Convention, the Director-General may request, not later than 135 days after this Convention enters into force for a State Party, that such measures be implemented by the inspected State Party not later than 180 days after this Convention enters into force for it. At its discretion, the inspected State Party may satisfy the request. If it does not satisfy the request, the

inspected State Party and the Director-General shall consult to resolve the matter.

Systematic verification of chemical weapons production facilities and cessation of their activities

48.   The purpose of the systematic verification of a chemical weapons production facility shall be to ensure that any resumption of production of chemical weapons or removal of declared items will be detected at this facility.

49.   The detailed facility agreement for each chemical weapons production facility shall specify:

(a)   Detailed on-site inspection procedures, which may include:

(i)   Visual examinations;

(ii)   Checking and servicing of seals and other agreed devices; and

(iii)   Obtaining and analysing samples;

(b)   Procedures for using tamper-indicating seals and other agreed equipment to prevent the undetected reactivation of the facility, which shall specify:

(i)   The type, placement, and arrangements for installation; and

(ii)   The maintenance of such seals and equipment; and

    (c)   Other agreed measures.

50. The seals or other approved equipment provided for in a detailed agreement on inspection measures for that facility shall be placed not later than 240 days after this Convention enters into force for a State Party. Inspectors shall be permitted to visit each chemical weapons production facility for the installation of such seals or equipment.

51. During each calendar year, the Technical Secretariat shall be permitted to conduct up to four inspections of each chemical weapons production facility.

52. The Director-General shall notify the inspected State Party of his decision to inspect or visit a chemical weapons production facility 48 hours before the planned arrival of the inspection team at the facility for systematic inspections or visits. In the case of inspections or visits to resolve urgent problems, this period may be shortened. The Director-General shall specify the purpose of the inspection or visit.

53. Inspectors shall, in accordance with the facility agreements, have unimpeded access to all parts of the chemical weapons production facilities. The items on the declared inventory to be inspected shall be chosen by the inspectors.

54. The guidelines for determining the frequency of systematic on-site inspections shall be considered and approved by the Conference pursuant to Article VIII, paragraph 21 (i). The particular production facility to be

inspected shall be chosen by the Technical Secretariat in such a way as to preclude the prediction of precisely when the facility is to be inspected.

*Verification of destruction of chemical weapons
production facilities*

55. The purpose of systematic verification of the destruction of chemical weapons production facilities shall be to confirm that the facility is destroyed in accordance with the obligations under this Convention and that each item on the declared inventory is destroyed in accordance with the agreed detailed plan for destruction.

56. When all items on the declared inventory have been destroyed, the Technical Secretariat shall confirm the declaration of the State Party to that effect. After this confirmation, the Technical Secretariat shall terminate the systematic verification of the chemical weapons production facility and shall promptly remove all devices and monitoring instruments installed by the inspectors.

57. After this confirmation, the State Party shall make the declaration that the facility has been destroyed.

*Verification of temporary conversion of a chemical
weapons production facility into a chemical weapons
destruction facility*

58. Not later than 90 days after receiving the initial notification of the intent to convert temporarily a production facility, the inspectors shall have the right to visit the facility

to familiarize themselves with the proposed temporary conversion and to study possible inspection measures that will be required during the conversion.

59.   Not later than 60 days after such a visit, the Technical Secretariat and the inspected State Party shall conclude a transition agreement containing additional inspection measures for the temporary conversion period. The transition agreement shall specify inspection procedures, including the use of seals, monitoring equipment, and inspections, that will provide confidence that no chemical weapons production takes place during the conversion process. This agreement shall remain in force from the beginning of the temporary conversion activity until the facility begins operation as a chemical weapons destruction facility.

60.   The inspected State Party shall not remove or convert any portion of the facility, or remove or modify any seal or other agreed inspection equipment that may have been installed pursuant to this Convention until the transition agreement has been concluded.

61.   Once the facility begins operation as a chemical weapons destruction facility, it shall be subject to the provisions of Part IV (A) of this Annex applicable to chemical weapons destruction facilities. Arrangements for the pre-operation period shall be governed by the transition agreement.

62.   During destruction operations the inspectors shall have access to all portions of the temporarily converted chemical

weapons production facilities, including those that are not directly involved with the destruction of chemical weapons.

63. Before the commencement of work at the facility to convert it temporarily for chemical weapons destruction purposes and after the facility has ceased to function as a facility for chemical weapons destruction, the facility shall be subject to the provisions of this Part applicable to chemical weapons production facilities.

D. Conversion of chemical weapons production facilities to purposes not prohibited under this Convention

Procedures for requesting conversion

64. A request to use a chemical weapons production facility for purposes not prohibited under this Convention may be made for any facility that a State Party is already using for such purposes before this Convention enters into force for it, or that it plans to use for such purposes.

65. For a chemical weapons production facility that is being used for purposes not prohibited under this Convention when this Convention enters into force for the State Party, the request shall be submitted to the Director-General not later than 30 days after this Convention enters into force for the State Party. The request shall contain, in addition to data submitted in accordance with paragraph 1 (h) (iii), the following information:

    (a)   A detailed justification for the request;

(b)   A general facility conversion plan that specifies:

(i)   The nature of the activity to be conducted at the facility;

(ii) If the planned activity involves production, processing, or consumption of chemicals: the name of each of the chemicals, the flow diagram of the facility, and the quantities planned to be produced, processed, or consumed annually;

(iii) Which buildings or structures are proposed to be used and what modifications are proposed, if any;

(iv) Which buildings or structures have been destroyed or are proposed to be destroyed and the plans for destruction;

(v)   What equipment is to be used in the facility;

(vi) What equipment has been removed and destroyed and what equipment is proposed to be removed and destroyed and the plans for its destruction;

(vii) The proposed schedule for conversion, if applicable; and

(viii) The nature of the activity of each other facility operating at the site; and

(c)   A detailed explanation of how measures set forth in subparagraph (b), as well as any other measures proposed by the State Party, will ensure the prevention of standby chemical weapons production capability at the facility.

66. For a chemical weapons production facility that is not being used for purposes not prohibited under this Convention when this Convention enters into force for the State Party, the request shall be submitted to the Director-General not later than 30 days after the decision to convert, but in no case later than four years after this Convention enters into force for the State Party. The request shall contain the following information:

(a) A detailed justification for the request, including its economic needs;

(b) A general facility conversion plan that specifies:

(i) The nature of the activity planned to be conducted at the facility;

(ii) If the planned activity involves production, processing, or consumption of chemicals: the name of each of the chemicals, the flow diagram of the facility, and the quantities planned to be produced, processed, or consumed annually;

(iii) Which buildings or structures are proposed to be retained and what modifications are proposed, if any;

(iv) Which buildings or structures have been destroyed or are proposed to be destroyed and the plans for destruction;

(v)   What equipment is proposed for use in the facility;

(vi) What equipment is proposed to be removed and destroyed and the plans for its destruction;

(vii) The proposed schedule for conversion; and

(viii) The nature of the activity of each other facility operating at the site; and

(c)   A detailed explanation of how the measures set forth in subparagraph (b), as well as any other measures proposed by the State Party, will ensure the prevention of standby chemical weapons production capability at the facility.

67.   The State Party may propose in its request any other measures it deems appropriate to build confidence.

Actions pending a decision

68.   Pending a decision of the Conference, a State Party may continue to use for purposes not prohibited under this Convention a facility that was being used for such purposes before this Convention enters into force for it, but only if the State Party certifies in its request that no specialized equipment and no specialized buildings are being used and that the specialized equipment and specialized buildings have been rendered inactive using the methods specified in paragraph 13.

69. If the facility, for which the request was made, was not being used for purposes not prohibited under this Convention before this Convention enters into force for the State Party, or if the certification required in paragraph 68 is not made, the State Party shall cease immediately all activity pursuant to Article V, paragraph 4. The State Party shall close the facility in accordance with paragraph 13 not later than 90 days after this Convention enters into force for it.

Conditions for conversion

70. As a condition for conversion of a chemical weapons production facility for purposes not prohibited under this Convention, all specialized equipment at the facility must be destroyed and all special features of buildings and structures that distinguish them from buildings and structures normally used for purposes not prohibited under this Convention and not involving Schedule 1 chemicals must be eliminated.

71. A converted facility shall not be used:

(a) For any activity involving production, processing, or consumption of a Schedule 1 chemical or a Schedule 2 chemical; or

(b) For the production of any highly toxic chemical, including any highly toxic organophosphorus chemical, or for any other activity that would require special equipment for handling highly toxic or highly corrosive chemicals, unless the Executive Council decides that such production or activity would pose no risk to the object and purpose of this Convention, taking into account criteria for toxicity, corrosiveness and, if applicable, other technical factors, to be considered and approved by the Conference pursuant to Article VIII, paragraph 21 (i).

72. Conversion of a chemical weapons production facility shall be completed not later than six years after entry into force of this Convention.

Decisions by the Executive Council and the Conference

73. Not later than 90 days after receipt of the request by the Director-General, an initial inspection of the facility shall be conducted by the Technical Secretariat. The purpose of this inspection shall be to determine the accuracy of the information provided in the request, to obtain information on the technical characteristics of the proposed converted facility, and to assess the conditions under which use for purposes not prohibited under this Convention may be permitted. The Director-General shall promptly submit a report to the Executive Council, the Conference, and all States Parties containing his recommendations on the measures necessary to convert the facility to purposes not prohibited under this Convention and to provide assurance that the converted facility will be used only for purposes not prohibited under this Convention.

74. If the facility has been used for purposes not prohibited under this Convention before this Convention enters into force for the State Party, and is continuing to be in operation, but the measures required to be certified

under paragraph 68 have not been taken, the Director-General shall immediately inform the Executive Council, which may require implementation of measures it deems appropriate, inter alia, shut-down of the facility and removal of specialized equipment and modification of buildings or structures. The Executive Council shall stipulate the deadline for implementation of these measures and shall suspend consideration of the request pending their satisfactory completion. The facility shall be inspected promptly after the expiration of the deadline to determine whether the measures have been implemented. If not, the State Party shall be required to shut down completely all facility operations.

75. As soon as possible after receiving the report of the Director-General, the Conference, upon recommendation of the Executive Council, shall decide, taking into account the report and any views expressed by States Parties, whether to approve the request, and shall establish the conditions upon which approval is contingent. If any State Party objects to approval of the request and the associated conditions, consultations shall be undertaken among interested States Parties for up to 90 days to seek a mutually acceptable solution. A decision on the request and associated conditions, along with any proposed modifications thereto, shall be taken, as a matter of substance, as soon as possible after the end of the consultation period.

76. If the request is approved, a facility agreement shall be completed not later than 90 days after such a decision is taken. The facility agreement shall contain the conditions

under which the conversion and use of the facility is permitted, including measures for verification. Conversion shall not begin before the facility agreement is concluded.

Detailed plans for conversion

77. Not less than 180 days before conversion of a chemical weapons production facility is planned to begin, the State Party shall provide the Technical Secretariat with the detailed plans for conversion of the facility, including proposed measures for verification of conversion, with respect to, inter alia:

(a) Timing of the presence of the inspectors at the facility to be converted; and

(b) Procedures for verification of measures to be applied to each item on the declared inventory.

78. The detailed plan for conversion of each chemical weapons production facility shall contain:

(a) Detailed time schedule of the conversion process;

(b) Layout of the facility before and after conversion;

(c) Process flow diagram of the facility before, and as appropriate, after the conversion;

(d) Detailed inventory of equipment, buildings and structures and other items to be destroyed and of the buildings and structures to be modified;

(e) Measures to be applied to each item on the inventory, if any;

(f) Proposed measures for verification;

(g) Security/safety measures to be observed during the conversion of the facility; and

(h) Working and living conditions to be provided for inspectors.

Review of detailed plans

79. On the basis of the detailed plan for conversion and proposed measures for verification submitted by the State Party, and on experience from previous inspections, the Technical Secretariat shall prepare a plan for verifying the conversion of the facility, consulting closely with the State Party. Any differences between the Technical Secretariat and the State Party concerning appropriate measures shall be resolved through consultations. Any unresolved matters shall be forwarded to the Executive Council for appropriate action with a view to facilitate the full implementation of this Convention.

80. To ensure that the provisions of Article V and this Part are fulfilled, the combined plans for conversion and verification shall be agreed upon between the Executive Council and the State Party. This agreement shall be completed not less than 60 days before conversion is planned to begin.

81. Each member of the Executive Council may consult with the Technical Secretariat on any issue regarding the adequacy of the combined plan for conversion and verification. If there are no objections by any member of the Executive Council, the plan shall be put into action.

82. If there are any difficulties, the Executive Council should enter into consultations with the State Party to reconcile them. If any difficulties remain unresolved, they should be referred to the Conference. The resolution of any differences over methods of conversion should not delay the execution of other parts of the conversion plan that are acceptable.

83. If agreement is not reached with the Executive Council on aspects of verification, or if the approved verification plan cannot be put into action, verification of conversion shall proceed through continuous monitoring with on-site instruments and physical presence of inspectors.

84. Conversion and verification shall proceed according to the agreed plan. The verification shall not unduly interfere with the conversion process and shall be conducted through the presence of inspectors to confirm the conversion.

85. For the 10 years after the Director-General certifies that conversion is complete, the State Party shall provide to inspectors unimpeded access to the facility at any time. The inspectors shall have the right to observe all areas, all activities, and all items of equipment at the facility. The inspectors shall have the right to verify that the activities at the facility are consistent with any conditions established

under this Section, by the Executive Council and the Conference. The inspectors shall also have the right, in accordance with provisions of Part II, Section E, of this Annex to receive samples from any area of the facility and to analyse them to verify the absence of Schedule 1 chemicals, their stable by-products and decomposition products and of Schedule 2 chemicals and to verify that the activities at the facility are consistent with any other conditions on chemical activities established under this Section, by the Executive Council and the Conference. The inspectors shall also have the right to managed access, in accordance with Part X, Section C, of this Annex, to the plant site at which the facility is located. During the 10-year period, the State Party shall report annually on the activities at the converted facility. Upon completion of the 10-year period, the Executive Council, taking into account recommendations of the Technical Secretariat, shall decide on the nature of continued verification measures.

86. Costs of verification of the converted facility shall be allocated in accordance with Article V, paragraph 19.

Part VI
Activities not prohibited under this Convention in accordance with Article VI

Regime for Schedule 1 chemicals and facilities related to such chemicals

A. General provisions

1.   A State Party shall not produce, acquire, retain or use Schedule 1 chemicals outside the territories of States Parties and shall not transfer such chemicals outside its territory except to another State Party.

2.   A State Party shall not produce, acquire, retain, transfer or use Schedule 1 chemicals unless:

(a)   The chemicals are applied to research, medical, pharmaceutical or protective purposes; and

(b)   The types and quantities of chemicals are strictly limited to those which can be justified for such purposes; and

(c)   The aggregate amount of such chemicals at any given time for such purposes is equal to or less than 1 tonne; and

(d)   The aggregate amount for such purposes acquired by a State Party in any year through production, withdrawal from chemical weapons stocks and transfer is equal to or less than 1 tonne.

B. Transfers

3.   A State Party may transfer Schedule 1 chemicals outside its territory only to another State Party and only for research, medical, pharmaceutical or protective purposes in accordance with paragraph 2.

4.   Chemicals transferred shall not be retransferred to a third State.

5.   Not less than 30 days before any transfer to another State Party both States Parties shall notify the Technical Secretariat of the transfer.

6.   Each State Party shall make a detailed annual declaration regarding transfers during the previous year. The declaration shall be submitted not later than 90 days after the end of that year and shall for each Schedule 1 chemical that has been transferred include the following information:

    (a) The chemical name, structural formula and Chemical Abstracts Service registry number, if assigned;

    (b) The quantity acquired from other States or transferred to other States Parties. For each transfer the quantity, recipient and purpose shall be included.

C. Production

General principles for production

7.   Each State Party, during production under paragraphs 8 to 12, shall assign the highest priority to ensuring the safety of people and to protecting the environment. Each State

Party shall conduct such production in accordance with its national standards for safety and emissions.

Single small-scale facility

8.   Each State Party that produces Schedule 1 chemicals for research, medical, pharmaceutical or protective purposes shall carry out the production at a single small-scale facility approved by the State Party, except as set forth in paragraphs 10, 11 and 12.

9.   The production at a single small-scale facility shall be carried out in reaction vessels in production lines not configurated for continuous operation. The volume of such a reaction vessel shall not exceed 100 litres, and the total volume of all reaction vessels with a volume exceeding 5 litres shall not be more than 500 litres.

Other facilities

10. Production of Schedule 1 chemicals in aggregate quantities not exceeding 10 kg per year may be carried out for protective purposes at one facility outside a single small-scale facility. This facility shall be approved by the State Party.

11. Production of Schedule 1 chemicals in quantities of more than 100 g per year may be carried out for research, medical or pharmaceutical purposes outside a single small-scale facility in aggregate quantities not exceeding 10 kg per year per facility. These facilities shall be approved by the State Party.

12.   Synthesis of Schedule 1 chemicals for research, medical or pharmaceutical purposes, but not for protective purposes, may be carried out at laboratories in aggregate quantities less than 100 g per year per facility. These facilities shall not be subject to any obligation relating to declaration and verification as specified in Sections D and E.

D.   Declarations

Single small-scale facility

13.   Each State Party that plans to operate a single small-scale facility shall provide the Technical Secretariat with the precise location and a detailed technical description of the facility, including an inventory of equipment and detailed diagrams. For existing facilities, this initial declaration shall be provided not later than 30 days after this Convention enters into force for the State Party. Initial declarations on new facilities shall be provided not less than 180 days before operations are to begin.

14.   Each State Party shall give advance notification to the Technical Secretariat of planned changes related to the initial declaration. The notification shall be submitted not less than 180 days before the changes are to take place.

15.   A State Party producing Schedule 1 chemicals at a single small-scale facility shall make a detailed annual declaration regarding the activities of the facility for the previous year. The declaration shall be submitted not later than 90 days after the end of that year and shall include:

(a)   Identification of the facility;

(b) For each Schedule 1 chemical produced, acquired, consumed or stored at the facility, the following information:

(i) The chemical name, structural formula and Chemical Abstracts Service registry number, if assigned;

(ii) The methods employed and quantity produced;

(iii) The name and quantity of precursors listed in Schedules 1, 2, or 3 used for production of Schedule 1 chemicals;

(iv) The quantity consumed at the facility and the purpose(s) of the consumption;

(v) The quantity received from or shipped to other facilities in the State Party. For each shipment the quantity, recipient and purpose should be included;

(vi) The maximum quantity stored at any time during the year; and

(vii) The quantity stored at the end of the year; and

(c) Information on any changes at the facility during the year compared to previously submitted detailed technical descriptions of the facility including inventories of equipment and detailed diagrams.

16. Each State Party producing Schedule 1 chemicals at a single small-scale facility shall make a detailed annual declaration regarding the projected activities and the

anticipated production at the facility for the coming year. The declaration shall be submitted not less than 90 days before the beginning of that year and shall include:

(a) Identification of the facility;

(b) For each Schedule 1 chemical anticipated to be produced, consumed or stored at the facility, the following information:

(i) The chemical name, structural formula and Chemical Abstracts Service registry number, if assigned;

(ii) The quantity anticipated to be produced and the purpose of the production; and

(c) Information on any anticipated changes at the facility during the year compared to previously submitted detailed technical descriptions of the facility including inventories of equipment and detailed diagrams.

Other facilities referred to in paragraphs 10 and 11

17. For each facility, a State Party shall provide the Technical Secretariat with the name, location and a detailed technical description of the facility or its relevant part(s) as requested by the Technical Secretariat. The facility producing Schedule 1 chemicals for protective purposes shall be specifically identified. For existing facilities, this initial declaration shall be provided not later than 30 days after this Convention enters into force for the State Party. Initial

declarations on new facilities shall be provided not less than 180 days before operations are to begin.

18.   Each State Party shall give advance notification to the Technical Secretariat of planned changes related to the initial declaration. The notification shall be submitted not less than 180 days before the changes are to take place.

19.   Each State Party shall, for each facility, make a detailed annual declaration regarding the activities of the facility for the previous year. The declaration shall be submitted not later than 90 days after the end of that year and shall include:

(a)   Identification of the facility;

(b)   For each Schedule 1 chemical the following information:

(i)   The chemical name, structural formula and Chemical Abstracts Service registry number, if assigned;

(ii)   The quantity produced and, in case of production for protective purposes, methods employed;

(iii)   The name and quantity of precursors listed in Schedules 1, 2, or 3, used for production of Schedule 1 chemicals;

(iv)   The quantity consumed at the facility and the purpose of the consumption;

(v)   The quantity transferred to other facilities within the State Party. For each transfer the quantity, recipient and purpose should be included;

(vi) The maximum quantity stored at any time during the year; and

(vii) The quantity stored at the end of the year; and

(c)   Information on any changes at the facility or its relevant parts during the year compared to previously submitted detailed technical description of the facility.

20.   Each State Party shall, for each facility, make a detailed annual declaration regarding the projected activities and the anticipated production at the facility for the coming year. The declaration shall be submitted not less than 90 days before the beginning of that year and shall include:

(a)   Identification of the facility;

(b)   For each Schedule 1 chemical the following information:

(i)   The chemical name, structural formula and Chemical Abstracts Service registry number, if assigned; and

(ii) The quantity anticipated to be produced, the time periods when the production is anticipated to take place and the purposes of the production; and

(c) Information on any anticipated changes at the facility or its relevant parts, during the year compared to previously submitted detailed technical descriptions of the facility.

E.   Verification

Single small-scale facility

21. The aim of verification activities at the single small-scale facility shall be to verify that the quantities of Schedule 1 chemicals produced are correctly declared and, in particular, that their aggregate amount does not exceed 1 tonne.

22. The facility shall be subject to systematic verification through on-site inspection and monitoring with on-site instruments.

23. The number, intensity, duration, timing and mode of inspections for a particular facility shall be based on the risk to the object and purpose of this Convention posed by the relevant chemicals, the characteristics of the facility and the nature of the activities carried out there. Appropriate guidelines shall be considered and approved by the Conference pursuant to Article VIII, paragraph 21 (i).

24. The purpose of the initial inspection shall be to verify information provided concerning the facility, including verification of the limits on reaction vessels set forth in paragraph 9.

25. Not later than 180 days after this Convention enters into force for a State Party, it shall conclude a

facility agreement, based on a model agreement, with the Organization, covering detailed inspection procedures for the facility.

26. Each State Party planning to establish a single small-scale facility after this Convention enters into force for it shall conclude a facility agreement, based on a model agreement, with the Organization, covering detailed inspection procedures for the facility before it begins operation or is used.

27. A model for agreements shall be considered and approved by the Conference pursuant to Article VIII, paragraph 21 (i).

Other facilities referred to in paragraphs 10 and 11

28. The aim of verification activities at any facility referred to in paragraphs 10 and 11 shall be to verify that:

(a) The facility is not used to produce any Schedule 1 chemical, except for the declared chemicals;

(b) The quantities of Schedule 1 chemicals produced, processed or consumed are correctly declared and consistent with needs for the declared purpose; and

(c) The Schedule 1 chemical is not diverted or used for other purposes.

29. The facility shall be subject to systematic verification through on-site inspection and monitoring with on-site instruments.

30. The number, intensity, duration, timing and mode of inspections for a particular facility shall be based on the risk to the object and purpose of this Convention posed by the quantities of chemicals produced, the characteristics of the facility and the nature of the activities carried out there. Appropriate guidelines shall be considered and approved by the Conference pursuant to Article VIII, paragraph 21 (i).

31. Not later than 180 days after this Convention enters into force for a State Party, it shall conclude facility agreements with the Organization, based on a model agreement covering detailed inspection procedures for each facility.

32. Each State Party planning to establish such a facility after entry into force of this Convention shall conclude a facility agreement with the Organization before the facility begins operation or is used.

Part VII
Activities not prohibited under this Convention in accordance with Article VI

Regime for Schedule 2 chemicals and facilities related to such chemicals

A.   Declarations

Declarations of aggregate national data

1.   The initial and annual declarations to be provided by each State Party pursuant to Article VI, paragraphs 7 and 8, shall include aggregate national data for the previous calendar year on the quantities produced, processed, consumed, imported and exported of each Schedule 2 chemical, as well as a quantitative specification of import and export for each country involved.

2.   Each State Party shall submit:

(a)   Initial declarations pursuant to paragraph 1 not later than 30 days after this Convention enters into force for it; and, starting in the following calendar year,

(b)   Annual declarations not later than 90 days after the end of the previous calendar year.

Declarations of plant sites producing, processing or consuming Schedule 2 chemicals

3.   Initial and annual declarations are required for all plant sites that comprise one or more plant(s) which produced, processed or consumed during any of the previous three

calendar years or is anticipated to produce, process or consume in the next calendar year more than:

(a)   1 kg of a chemical designated "*" in Schedule 2, part A;

(b)   100 kg of any other chemical listed in Schedule 2, part A; or

(c)   1 tonne of a chemical listed in Schedule 2, part B.

4.   Each State Party shall submit:

(a)   Initial declarations pursuant to paragraph 3 not later than 30 days after this Convention enters into force for it; and, starting in the following calendar year;

(b)   Annual declarations on past activities not later than 90 days after the end of the previous calendar year;

(c)   Annual declarations on anticipated activities not later than 60 days before the beginning of the following calendar year. Any such activity additionally planned after the annual declaration has been submitted shall be declared not later than five days before this activity begins.

5.   Declarations pursuant to paragraph 3 are generally not required for mixtures containing a low concentration of a Schedule 2 chemical. They are only required, in accordance with guidelines, in cases where the ease of recovery from the mixture of the Schedule 2 chemical and its total weight are deemed to pose a risk to the object and purpose of

this Convention. These guidelines shall be considered and approved by the Conference pursuant to Article VIII, paragraph 21 (i).

6.   Declarations of a plant site pursuant to paragraph 3 shall include:

(a)   The name of the plant site and the name of the owner, company, or enterprise operating it;

(b)   Its precise location including the address; and

(c)   The number of plants within the plant site which are declared pursuant to Part VIII of this Annex.

7.   Declarations of a plant site pursuant to paragraph 3 shall also include, for each plant which is located within the plant site and which falls under the specifications set forth in paragraph 3, the following information:

(a)   The name of the plant and the name of the owner, company, or enterprise operating it;

(b)   Its precise location within the plant site including the specific building or structure number, if any;

(c)   Its main activities;

(d)   Whether the plant:

(i)   Produces, processes, or consumes the declared Schedule 2 chemical(s);

(ii) Is dedicated to such activities or multi-purpose; and

(iii) Performs other activities with regard to the declared Schedule 2 chemical(s), including a specification of that other activity (e.g. storage); and

(e) The production capacity of the plant for each declared Schedule 2 chemical.

8. Declarations of a plant site pursuant to paragraph 3 shall also include the following information on each Schedule 2 chemical above the declaration threshold:

(a) The chemical name, common or trade name used by the facility, structural formula, and Chemical Abstracts Service registry number, if assigned;

(b) In the case of the initial declaration: the total amount produced, processed, consumed, imported and exported by the plant site in each of the three previous calendar years;

(c) In the case of the annual declaration on past activities: the total amount produced, processed, consumed, imported and exported by the plant site in the previous calendar year;

(d) In the case of the annual declaration on anticipated activities: the total amount anticipated to be produced, processed or consumed by the plant site in the following calendar year, including the anticipated time periods for production, processing or consumption; and

(e)   The purposes for which the chemical was or will be produced, processed or consumed:

(i)   Processing and consumption on site with a specification of the product types;

(ii)   Sale or transfer within the territory or to any other place under the jurisdiction or control of the State Party, with a specification whether to other industry, trader or other destination and, if possible, of final product types;

(iii) Direct export, with a specification of the States involved; or

(iv)   Other, including a specification of these other purposes.

Declarations on past production of Schedule 2 chemicals
for chemical weapons purposes

9.   Each State Party shall, not later than 30 days after this Convention enters into force for it, declare all plant sites comprising plants that produced at any time since 1 January 1946 a Schedule 2 chemical for chemical weapons purposes.

10.   Declarations of a plant site pursuant to paragraph 9 shall include:

(a)   The name of the plant site and the name of the owner, company, or enterprise operating it;

(b)   Its precise location including the address;

(c)   For each plant which is located within the plant site, and which falls under the specifications set forth in paragraph 9, the same information as required under paragraph 7, subparagraphs (a) to (e); and

(d)   For each Schedule 2 chemical produced for chemical weapons purposes:

(i)   The chemical name, common or trade name used by the plant site for chemical weapons production purposes, structural formula, and Chemical Abstracts Service registry number, if assigned;

(ii)   The dates when the chemical was produced and the quantity produced; and

(iii)   The location to which the chemical was delivered and the final product produced there, if known.

Information to States Parties

11.   A list of plant sites declared under this Section together with the information provided under paragraphs 6, 7 (a), 7 (c), 7 (d) (i), 7 (d) (iii), 8 (a) and 10 shall be transmitted by the Technical Secretariat to States Parties upon request.

B. Verification

General

12. Verification provided for in Article VI, paragraph 4, shall be carried out through on-site inspection at those of the declared plant sites that comprise one or more plants which produced, processed or consumed during any of the previous three calendar years or are anticipated to produce, process or consume in the next calendar year more than:

(a) 10 kg of a chemical designated "*" in Schedule 2, part A;

(b) 1 tonne of any other chemical listed in Schedule 2, part A; or

(c) 10 tonnes of a chemical listed in Schedule 2, part B.

13. The programme and budget of the Organization to be adopted by the Conference pursuant to Article VIII, paragraph 21 (a) shall contain, as a separate item, a programme and budget for verification under this Section. In the allocation of resources made available for verification under Article VI, the Technical Secretariat shall, during the first three years after the entry into force of this Convention, give priority to the initial inspections of plant sites declared under Section A. The allocation shall thereafter be reviewed on the basis of the experience gained.

14. The Technical Secretariat shall conduct initial inspections and subsequent inspections in accordance with paragraphs 15 to 22.

Inspection aims

15. The general aim of inspections shall be to verify that activities are in accordance with obligations under this Convention and consistent with the information to be provided in declarations. Particular aims of inspections at plant sites declared under Section A shall include verification of:

(a) The absence of any Schedule 1 chemical, especially its production, except if in accordance with Part VI of this Annex;

(b) Consistency with declarations of levels of production, processing or consumption of Schedule 2 chemicals; and

(c) Non-diversion of Schedule 2 chemicals for activities prohibited under this Convention.

Initial inspections

16. Each plant site to be inspected pursuant to paragraph 12 shall receive an initial inspection as soon as possible but preferably not later than three years after entry into force of this Convention. Plant sites declared after this period shall receive an initial inspection not later than one year after production, processing or consumption is first declared. Selection of plant sites for initial inspections shall be made by the Technical Secretariat in such a way as to preclude the prediction of precisely when the plant site is to be inspected.

17. During the initial inspection, a draft facility agreement for the plant site shall be prepared unless the inspected State Party and the Technical Secretariat agree that it is not needed.

18. With regard to frequency and intensity of subsequent inspections, inspectors shall during the initial inspection assess the risk to the object and purpose of this Convention posed by the relevant chemicals, the characteristics of the plant site and the nature of the activities carried out there, taking into account, inter alia, the following criteria:

(a) The toxicity of the scheduled chemicals and of the end-products produced with it, if any;

(b) The quantity of the scheduled chemicals typically stored at the inspected site;

(c) The quantity of feedstock chemicals for the scheduled chemicals typically stored at the inspected site;

(d) The production capacity of the Schedule 2 plants; and

(e) The capability and convertibility for initiating production, storage and filling of toxic chemicals at the inspected site.

Inspections

19. Having received the initial inspection, each plant site to be inspected pursuant to paragraph 12 shall be subject to subsequent inspections.

20. In selecting particular plant sites for inspection and in deciding on the frequency and intensity of inspections, the Technical Secretariat shall give due consideration to the risk to the object and purpose of this Convention posed by the relevant chemical, the characteristics of the plant site and the nature of the activities carried out there, taking into account the respective facility agreement as well as the results of the initial inspections and subsequent inspections.

21. The Technical Secretariat shall choose a particular plant site to be inspected in such a way as to preclude the prediction of exactly when it will be inspected.

22. No plant site shall receive more than two inspections per calendar year under the provisions of this Section. This, however, shall not limit inspections pursuant to Article IX.

Inspection procedures

23. In addition to agreed guidelines, other relevant provisions of this Annex and the Confidentiality Annex, paragraphs 24 to 30 below shall apply.

24. A facility agreement for the declared plant site shall be concluded not later than 90 days after completion of the initial inspection between the inspected State Party and

the Organization unless the inspected State Party and the Technical Secretariat agree that it is not needed. It shall be based on a model agreement and govern the conduct of inspections at the declared plant site. The agreement shall specify the frequency and intensity of inspections as well as detailed inspection procedures, consistent with paragraphs 25 to 29.

25. The focus of the inspection shall be the declared Schedule 2 plant(s) within the declared plant site. If the inspection team requests access to other parts of the plant site, access to these areas shall be granted in accordance with the obligation to provide clarification pursuant to Part II, paragraph 51, of this Annex and in accordance with the facility agreement, or, in the absence of a facility agreement, in accordance with the rules of managed access as specified in Part X, Section C, of this Annex.

26. Access to records shall be provided, as appropriate, to provide assurance that there has been no diversion of the declared chemical and that production has been consistent with declarations.

27. Sampling and analysis shall be undertaken to check for the absence of undeclared scheduled chemicals.

28. Areas to be inspected may include:

   (a) Areas where feed chemicals (reactants) are delivered or stored;

(b)   Areas where manipulative processes are performed upon the reactants prior to addition to the reaction vessels;

(c)   Feed lines as appropriate from the areas referred to in subparagraph (a) or subparagraph (b) to the reaction vessels together with any associated valves, flow meters, etc.;

(d)   The external aspect of the reaction vessels and ancillary equipment;

(e)   Lines from the reaction vessels leading to long- or short-term storage or to equipment further processing the declared Schedule 2 chemicals;

(f)   Control equipment associated with any of the items under subparagraphs (a) to (e);

(g)   Equipment and areas for waste and effluent handling;

(h)   Equipment and areas for disposition of chemicals not up to specification.

29.   The period of inspection shall not last more than 96 hours; however, extensions may be agreed between the inspection team and the inspected State Party.

Notification of inspection

30.   A State Party shall be notified by the Technical Secretariat of the inspection not less than 48 hours before

the arrival of the inspection team at the plant site to be inspected.

C.   Transfers to States not party to this Convention

31. Schedule 2 chemicals shall only be transferred to or received from States Parties. This obligation shall take effect three years after entry into force of this Convention.

32. During this interim three-year period, each State Party shall require an end-use certificate, as specified below, for transfers of Schedule 2 chemicals to States not Party to this Convention. For such transfers, each State Party shall adopt the necessary measures to ensure that the transferred chemicals shall only be used for purposes not prohibited under this Convention. Inter alia, the State Party shall require from the recipient State a certificate stating, in relation to the transferred chemicals:

(a)   That they will only be used for purposes not prohibited under this Convention;

(b)   That they will not be re-transferred;

(c)   Their types and quantities;

(d)   Their end-use(s); and

(e)   The name(s) and address(es) of the end-user(s).

Part VIII
Activities not prohibited under this Convention in accordance with Article VI

Regime for Schedule 3 chemicals and facilities related to such chemicals

A.   Declarations

Declarations of aggregate national data

1.   The initial and annual declarations to be provided by a State Party pursuant to Article VI, paragraphs 7 and 8, shall include aggregate national data for the previous calendar year on the quantities produced, imported and exported of each Schedule 3 chemical, as well as a quantitative specification of import and export for each country involved.

2.   Each State Party shall submit:

(a)   Initial declarations pursuant to paragraph 1 not later than 30 days after this Convention enters into force for it; and, starting in the following calendar year,

(b)   Annual declarations not later than 90 days after the end of the previous calendar year.

Declarations of plant sites producing Schedule 3 chemicals

3.   Initial and annual declarations are required for all plant sites that comprise one or more plants which produced during the previous calendar year or are anticipated to

produce in the next calendar year more than 30 tonnes of a Schedule 3 chemical.

4.   Each State Party shall submit:

(a)   Initial declarations pursuant to paragraph 3 not later than 30 days after this Convention enters into force for it; and, starting in the following calendar year;

(b)   Annual declarations on past activities not later than 90 days after the end of the previous calendar year;

(c)   Annual declarations on anticipated activities not later than 60 days before the beginning of the following calendar year. Any such activity additionally planned after the annual declaration has been submitted shall be declared not later than five days before this activity begins.

5.   Declarations pursuant to paragraph 3 are generally not required for mixtures containing a low concentration of a Schedule 3 chemical. They are only required, in accordance with guidelines, in such cases where the ease of recovery from the mixture of the Schedule 3 chemical and its total weight are deemed to pose a risk to the object and purpose of this Convention. These guidelines shall be considered and approved by the Conference pursuant to Article VIII, paragraph 21 (i).

6.   Declarations of a plant site pursuant to paragraph 3 shall include:

(a) The name of the plant site and the name of the owner, company, or enterprise operating it;

(b) Its precise location including the address; and

(c) The number of plants within the plant site which are declared pursuant to Part VII of this Annex.

7. Declarations of a plant site pursuant to paragraph 3 shall also include, for each plant which is located within the plant site and which falls under the specifications set forth in paragraph 3, the following information:

(a) The name of the plant and the name of the owner, company, or enterprise operating it;

(b) Its precise location within the plant site, including the specific building or structure number, if any;

(c) Its main activities.

8. Declarations of a plant site pursuant to paragraph 3 shall also include the following information on each Schedule 3 chemical above the declaration threshold:

(a) The chemical name, common or trade name used by the facility, structural formula, and Chemical Abstracts Service registry number, if assigned;

(b) The approximate amount of production of the chemical in the previous calendar year, or, in case of declarations on anticipated activities, anticipated for the next calendar year, expressed in the ranges: 30 to 200 tonnes, 200 to 1,000 tonnes, 1,000 to 10,000 tonnes, 10,000 to 100,000 tonnes, and above 100,000 tonnes; and

(c) The purposes for which the chemical was or will be produced.

Declarations on past production of Schedule 3 chemicals
for chemical weapons purposes

9. Each State Party shall, not later than 30 days after this Convention enters into force for it, declare all plant sites comprising plants that produced at any time since 1 January 1946 a Schedule 3 chemical for chemical weapons purposes.

10. Declarations of a plant site pursuant to paragraph 9 shall include:

(a) The name of the plant site and the name of the owner, company, or enterprise operating it;

(b) Its precise location including the address;

(c) For each plant which is located within the plant site, and which falls under the specifications set forth in paragraph 9, the same information as required under paragraph 7, subparagraphs (a) to (c); and

(d) For each Schedule 3 chemical produced for chemical weapons purposes:

(i)   The chemical name, common or trade name used by the plant site for chemical weapons production purposes, structural formula, and Chemical Abstracts Service registry number, if assigned;

(ii)   The dates when the chemical was produced and the quantity produced; and

(iii)   The location to which the chemical was delivered and the final product produced there, if known.

Information to States Parties

11.   A list of plant sites declared under this Section together with the information provided under paragraphs 6, 7 (a), 7 (c), 8 (a) and 10 shall be transmitted by the Technical Secretariat to States Parties upon request.

B.   Verification

General

12.   Verification provided for in paragraph 5 of Article VI shall be carried out through on-site inspections at those declared plant sites which produced during the previous calendar year or are anticipated to produce in the next calendar year in excess of 200 tonnes aggregate of any Schedule 3 chemical above the declaration threshold of 30 tonnes.

13.   The programme and budget of the Organization to be adopted by the Conference pursuant to Article VIII, paragraph 21 (a), shall contain, as a separate item, a

programme and budget for verification under this Section taking into account Part VII, paragraph 13, of this Annex.

14. Under this Section, the Technical Secretariat shall randomly select plant sites for inspection through appropriate mechanisms, such as the use of specially designed computer software, on the basis of the following weighting factors:

(a) Equitable geographical distribution of inspections; and

(b) The information on the declared plant sites available to the Technical Secretariat, related to the relevant chemical, the characteristics of the plant site and the nature of the activities carried out there.

15. No plant site shall receive more than two inspections per year under the provisions of this Section. This, however, shall not limit inspections pursuant to Article IX.

16. In selecting plant sites for inspection under this Section, the Technical Secretariat shall observe the following limitation for the combined number of inspections to be received by a State Party per calendar year under this Part and Part IX of this Annex: the combined number of inspections shall not exceed three plus 5 per cent of the total number of plant sites declared by a State Party under both this Part and Part IX of this Annex, or 20 inspections, whichever of these two figures is lower.

Inspection aims

17.   At plant sites declared under Section A, the general aim of inspections shall be to verify that activities are consistent with the information to be provided in declarations. The particular aim of inspections shall be the verification of the absence of any Schedule 1 chemical, especially its production, except if in accordance with Part VI of this Annex.

Inspection procedures

18.   In addition to agreed guidelines, other relevant provisions of this Annex and the Confidentiality Annex, paragraphs 19 to 25 below shall apply.

19.   There shall be no facility agreement, unless requested by the inspected State Party.

20.   The focus of the inspections shall be the declared Schedule 3 plant(s) within the declared plant site. If the inspection team, in accordance with Part II, paragraph 51, of this Annex, requests access to other parts of the plant site for clarification of ambiguities, the extent of such access shall be agreed between the inspection team and the inspected State Party.

21.   The inspection team may have access to records in situations in which the inspection team and the inspected State Party agree that such access will assist in achieving the objectives of the inspection.

22. Sampling and on-site analysis may be undertaken to check for the absence of undeclared scheduled chemicals. In case of unresolved ambiguities, samples may be analysed in a designated off-site laboratory, subject to the inspected State Party's agreement.

23. Areas to be inspected may include:

(a) Areas where feed chemicals (reactants) are delivered or stored;

(b) Areas where manipulative processes are performed upon the reactants prior to addition to the reaction vessel;

(c) Feed lines as appropriate from the areas referred to in subparagraph (a) or subparagraph (b) to the reaction vessel together with any associated valves, flow meters, etc.;

(d) The external aspect of the reaction vessels and ancillary equipment;

(e) Lines from the reaction vessels leading to long- or short-term storage or to equipment further processing the declared Schedule 3 chemicals;

(f) Control equipment associated with any of the items under subparagraphs (a) to (e);

(g) Equipment and areas for waste and effluent handling;

(h) Equipment and areas for disposition of chemicals not up to specification.

24. The period of inspection shall not last more than 24 hours; however, extensions may be agreed between the inspection team and the inspected State Party.

Notification of inspection

25. A State Party shall be notified by the Technical Secretariat of the inspection not less than 120 hours before the arrival of the inspection team at the plant site to be inspected.

C. Transfers to States not party to this Convention

26. When transferring Schedule 3 chemicals to States not Party to this Convention, each State Party shall adopt the necessary measures to ensure that the transferred chemicals shall only be used for purposes not prohibited under this Convention. Inter alia, the State Party shall require from the recipient State a certificate stating, in relation to the transferred chemicals:

(a) That they will only be used for purposes not prohibited under this Convention;

(b) That they will not be re-transferred;

(c) Their types and quantities;

(d) Their end-use(s); and

(e)   The name(s) and address(es) of the end-user(s).

27.   Five years after entry into force of this Convention, the Conference shall consider the need to establish other measures regarding transfers of Schedule 3 chemicals to States not Party to this Convention.

Part IX
Activities not prohibited under this Convention in accordance with Article VI

Regime for other chemical production facilities

A. Declarations

List of other chemical production facilities

1.   The initial declaration to be provided by each State Party pursuant to Article VI, paragraph 7, shall include a list of all plant sites that:

(a) Produced by synthesis during the previous calendar year more than 200 tonnes of unscheduled discrete organic chemicals; or

(b) Comprise one or more plants which produced by synthesis during the previous calendar year more than 30 tonnes of an unscheduled discrete organic chemical containing the elements phosphorus, sulfur or fluorine (hereinafter referred to as "PSF-plants" and "PSF-chemical").

2.   The list of other chemical production facilities to be submitted pursuant to paragraph 1 shall not include plant sites that exclusively produced explosives or hydrocarbons.

3.   Each State Party shall submit its list of other chemical production facilities pursuant to paragraph 1 as part of its initial declaration not later than 30 days after this Convention enters into force for it. Each State Party shall, not later than 90 days after the beginning of each following

calendar year, provide annually the information necessary to update the list.

4.   The list of other chemical production facilities to be submitted pursuant to paragraph 1 shall include the following information on each plant site:

(a)   The name of the plant site and the name of the owner, company, or enterprise operating it;

(b)   The precise location of the plant site including its address;

(c)   Its main activities; and

(d)   The approximate number of plants producing the chemicals specified in paragraph 1 in the plant site.

5.   With regard to plant sites listed pursuant to paragraph 1 (a), the list shall also include information on the approximate aggregate amount of production of the unscheduled discrete organic chemicals in the previous calendar year expressed in the ranges: under 1,000 tonnes, 1,000 to 10,000 tonnes and above 10,000 tonnes.

6.   With regard to plant sites listed pursuant to paragraph 1 (b), the list shall also specify the number of PSF-plants within the plant site and include information on the approximate aggregate amount of production of PSF-chemicals produced by each PSF-plant in the previous calendar year expressed in the ranges: under 200 tonnes, 200 to 1,000 tonnes, 1,000 to 10,000 tonnes and above 10,000 tonnes.

Assistance by the Technical Secretariat

7.   If a State Party, for administrative reasons, deems it necessary to ask for assistance in compiling its list of chemical production facilities pursuant to paragraph 1, it may request the Technical Secretariat to provide such assistance. Questions as to the completeness of the list shall then be resolved through consultations between the State Party and the Technical Secretariat.

Information to States Parties

8.   The lists of other chemical production facilities submitted pursuant to paragraph 1, including the information provided under paragraph 4, shall be transmitted by the Technical Secretariat to States Parties upon request.

B.   Verification

General

9.   Subject to the provisions of Section C, verification as provided for in Article VI, paragraph 6, shall be carried out through on-site inspection at:

(a)   Plant sites listed pursuant to paragraph 1 (a); and

(b)   Plant sites listed pursuant to paragraph 1 (b) that comprise one or more PSF-plants which produced during the previous calendar year more than 200 tonnes of a PSF-chemical.

10. The programme and budget of the Organization to be adopted by the Conference pursuant to Article VIII, paragraph 21 (a), shall contain, as a separate item, a programme and budget for verification under this Section after its implementation has started.

11. Under this Section, the Technical Secretariat shall randomly select plant sites for inspection through appropriate mechanisms, such as the use of specially designed computer software, on the basis of the following weighting factors:

(a) Equitable geographical distribution of inspections;

(b) The information on the listed plant sites available to the Technical Secretariat, related to the characteristics of the plant site and the activities carried out there; and

(c) Proposals by States Parties on a basis to be agreed upon in accordance with paragraph 25.

12. No plant site shall receive more than two inspections per year under the provisions of this Section. This, however, shall not limit inspections pursuant to Article IX.

13. In selecting plant sites for inspection under this Section, the Technical Secretariat shall observe the following limitation for the combined number of inspections to be received by a State Party per calendar year under this Part and Part VIII of this Annex: the combined number of inspections shall not exceed three plus 5 per cent of the total number of plant sites declared by a State Party under

both this Part and Part VIII of this Annex, or 20 inspections, whichever of these two figures is lower.

Inspection aims

14. At plant sites listed under Section A, the general aim of inspections shall be to verify that activities are consistent with the information to be provided in declarations. The particular aim of inspections shall be the verification of the absence of any Schedule 1 chemical, especially its production, except if in accordance with Part VI of this Annex.

Inspection procedures

15. In addition to agreed guidelines, other relevant provisions of this Annex and the Confidentiality Annex, paragraphs 16 to 20 below shall apply.

16. There shall be no facility agreement, unless requested by the inspected State Party.

17. The focus of inspection at a plant site selected for inspection shall be the plant(s) producing the chemicals specified in paragraph 1, in particular the PSF-plants listed pursuant to paragraph 1 (b). The inspected State Party shall have the right to manage access to these plants in accordance with the rules of managed access as specified in Part X, Section C, of this Annex. If the inspection team, in accordance with Part II, paragraph 51, of this Annex, requests access to other parts of the plant site for clarification of ambiguities, the extent of such access shall be

agreed between the inspection team and the inspected State Party.

18. The inspection team may have access to records in situations in which the inspection team and the inspected State Party agree that such access will assist in achieving the objectives of the inspection.

19. Sampling and on-site analysis may be undertaken to check for the absence of undeclared scheduled chemicals. In cases of unresolved ambiguities, samples may be analysed in a designated off-site laboratory, subject to the inspected State Party's agreement.

20. The period of inspection shall not last more than 24 hours; however, extensions may be agreed between the inspection team and the inspected State Party.

Notification of inspection

21. A State Party shall be notified by the Technical Secretariat of the inspection not less than 120 hours before the arrival of the inspection team at the plant site to be inspected.

C.   Implementation and review of Section B

Implementation

22. The implementation of Section B shall start at the beginning of the fourth year after entry into force of this Convention unless the Conference, at its regular session

in the third year after entry into force of this Convention, decides otherwise.

23.   The Director-General shall, for the regular session of the Conference in the third year after entry into force of this Convention, prepare a report which outlines the experience of the Technical Secretariat in implementing the provisions of Parts VII and VIII of this Annex as well as of Section A of this Part.

24.   At its regular session in the third year after entry into force of this Convention, the Conference, on the basis of a report of the Director-General, may also decide on the distribution of resources available for verification under Section B between "PSF-plants" and other chemical production facilities. Otherwise, this distribution shall be left to the expertise of the Technical Secretariat and be added to the weighting factors in paragraph 11.

25.   At its regular session in the third year after entry into force of this Convention, the Conference, upon advice of the Executive Council, shall decide on which basis (e.g. regional) proposals by States Parties for inspections should be presented to be taken into account as a weighting factor in the selection process specified in paragraph 11.

Review

26.   At the first special session of the Conference convened pursuant to Article VIII, paragraph 22, the provisions of this Part of the Verification Annex shall be re-examined in the light of a comprehensive review of the overall verification

regime for the chemical industry (Article VI, Parts VII to IX of this Annex) on the basis of the experience gained. The Conference shall then make recommendations so as to improve the effectiveness of the verification regime.

Part X
Challenge inspections pursuant to Article IX

A. Designation and selection of inspectors and inspection assistants

1. Challenge inspections pursuant to Article IX shall only be performed by inspectors and inspection assistants especially designated for this function. In order to designate inspectors and inspection assistants for challenge inspections pursuant to Article IX, the Director-General shall, by selecting inspectors and inspection assistants from among the inspectors and inspection assistants for routine inspection activities, establish a list of proposed inspectors and inspection assistants. It shall comprise a sufficiently large number of inspectors and inspection assistants having the necessary qualification, experience, skill and training, to allow for flexibility in the selection of the inspectors, taking into account their availability, and the need for rotation. Due regard shall be paid also to the importance of selecting inspectors and inspection assistants on as wide a geographical basis as possible. The designation of inspectors and inspection assistants shall follow the procedures provided for under Part II, Section A, of this Annex.

2. The Director-General shall determine the size of the inspection team and select its members taking into account the circumstances of a particular request. The size of the inspection team shall be kept to a minimum necessary for the proper fulfilment of the inspection mandate. No national of the requesting State Party or the inspected State Party shall be a member of the inspection team.

B.   Pre-inspection activities

3.   Before submitting the inspection request for a challenge inspection, the State Party may seek confirmation from the Director-General that the Technical Secretariat is in a position to take immediate action on the request. If the Director-General cannot provide such confirmation immediately, he shall do so at the earliest opportunity, in keeping with the order of requests for confirmation. He shall also keep the State Party informed of when it is likely that immediate action can be taken. Should the Director-General reach the conclusion that timely action on requests can no longer be taken, he may ask the Executive Council to take appropriate action to improve the situation in the future.

Notification

4.   The inspection request for a challenge inspection to be submitted to the Executive Council and the Director-General shall contain at least the following information:

(a)   The State Party to be inspected and, if applicable, the Host State;

(b)   The point of entry to be used;

(c)   The size and type of the inspection site;

(d)   The concern regarding possible non-compliance with this Convention including a specification of the relevant provisions of this Convention about which the concern has arisen, and of the nature and circumstances of the possible non-compliance as well as all appropriate information on the basis of which the concern has arisen; and

(e) The name of the observer of the requesting State Party.

The requesting State Party may submit any additional information it deems necessary.

5. The Director-General shall within one hour acknowledge to the requesting State Party receipt of its request.

6. The requesting State Party shall notify the Director-General of the location of the inspection site in due time for the Director-General to be able to provide this information to the inspected State Party not less than 12 hours before the planned arrival of the inspection team at the point of entry.

7. The inspection site shall be designated by the requesting State Party as specifically as possible by providing a site diagram related to a reference point with geographic coordinates, specified to the nearest second if possible. If possible, the requesting State Party shall also provide a map with a general indication of the inspection site and a diagram specifying as precisely as possible the requested perimeter of the site to be inspected.

8. The requested perimeter shall:

(a) Run at least a 10 metre distance outside any buildings or other structures;

(b)   Not cut through existing security enclosures; and

(c)   Run at least a 10 metre distance outside any existing security enclosures that the requesting State Party intends to include within the requested perimeter.

9.   If the requested perimeter does not conform with the specifications of paragraph 8, it shall be redrawn by the inspection team so as to conform with that provision.

10.   The Director-General shall, not less than 12 hours before the planned arrival of the inspection team at the point of entry, inform the Executive Council about the location of the inspection site as specified in paragraph 7.

11.   Contemporaneously with informing the Executive Council according to paragraph 10, the Director-General shall transmit the inspection request to the inspected State Party including the location of the inspection site as specified in paragraph 7. This notification shall also include the information specified in Part II, paragraph 32, of this Annex.

12.   Upon arrival of the inspection team at the point of entry, the inspected State Party shall be informed by the inspection team of the inspection mandate.

Entry into the territory of the inspected State Party or
the Host State

13.   The Director-General shall, in accordance with Article IX, paragraphs 13 to 18, dispatch an inspection team as soon

as possible after an inspection request has been received. The inspection team shall arrive at the point of entry specified in the request in the minimum time possible, consistent with the provisions of paragraphs 10 and 11.

14.   If the requested perimeter is acceptable to the inspected State Party, it shall be designated as the final perimeter as early as possible, but in no case later than 24 hours after the arrival of the inspection team at the point of entry. The inspected State Party shall transport the inspection team to the final perimeter of the inspection site. If the inspected State Party deems it necessary, such transportation may begin up to 12 hours before the expiry of the time period specified in this paragraph for the designation of the final perimeter. Transportation shall, in any case, be completed not later than 36 hours after the arrival of the inspection team at the point of entry.

15. For   all   declared   facilities,   the   procedures   in subparagraphs (a) and (b) shall apply. (For the purposes of this Part, "declared facility" means all facilities declared pursuant to Articles III, IV, and V. With regard to Article VI, "declared facility" means only facilities declared pursuant to Part VI of this Annex, as well as declared plants specified by declarations pursuant to Part VII, paragraphs 7 and 10 (c), and Part VIII, paragraphs 7 and 10 (c), of this Annex.)

(a)   If the requested perimeter is contained within or conforms with the declared perimeter, the declared perimeter shall be considered the final perimeter. The final perimeter may, however, if agreed by the inspected

State Party, be made smaller in order to conform with the perimeter requested by the requesting State Party.

(b) The inspected State Party shall transport the inspection team to the final perimeter as soon as practicable, but in any case shall ensure their arrival at the perimeter not later than 24 hours after the arrival of the inspection team at the point of entry.

Alternative determination of final perimeter

16. At the point of entry, if the inspected State Party cannot accept the requested perimeter, it shall propose an alternative perimeter as soon as possible, but in any case not later than 24 hours after the arrival of the inspection team at the point of entry. In case of differences of opinion, the inspected State Party and the inspection team shall engage in negotiations with the aim of reaching agreement on a final perimeter.

17. The alternative perimeter should be designated as specifically as possible in accordance with paragraph 8. It shall include the whole of the requested perimeter and should, as a rule, bear a close relationship to the latter, taking into account natural terrain features and man-made boundaries. It should normally run close to the surrounding security barrier if such a barrier exists. The inspected State Party should seek to establish such a relationship between the perimeters by a combination of at least two of the following means:

(a)   An alternative perimeter that does not extend to an area significantly greater than that of the requested perimeter;

(b)   An alternative perimeter that is a short, uniform distance from the requested perimeter;

(c)   At least part of the requested perimeter is visible from the alternative perimeter.

18. If the alternative perimeter is acceptable to the inspection team, it shall become the final perimeter and the inspection team shall be transported from the point of entry to that perimeter. If the inspected State Party deems it necessary, such transportation may begin up to 12 hours before the expiry of the time period specified in paragraph 16 for proposing an alternative perimeter. Transportation shall, in any case, be completed not later than 36 hours after the arrival of the inspection team at the point of entry.

19. If a final perimeter is not agreed, the perimeter negotiations shall be concluded as early as possible, but in no case shall they continue more than 24 hours after the arrival of the inspection team at the point of entry. If no agreement is reached, the inspected State Party shall transport the inspection team to a location at the alternative perimeter. If the inspected State Party deems it necessary, such transportation may begin up to 12 hours before the expiry of the time period specified in paragraph 16 for proposing an alternative perimeter. Transportation shall, in any case,

be completed not later than 36 hours after the arrival of the inspection team at the point of entry.

20. Once at the location, the inspected State Party shall provide the inspection team with prompt access to the alternative perimeter to facilitate negotiations and agreement on the final perimeter and access within the final perimeter.

21. If no agreement is reached within 72 hours after the arrival of the inspection team at the location, the alternative perimeter shall be designated the final perimeter.

Verification of location

22. To help establish that the inspection site to which the inspection team has been transported corresponds to the inspection site specified by the requesting State Party, the inspection team shall have the right to use approved location-finding equipment and have such equipment installed according to its directions. The inspection team may verify its location by reference to local landmarks identified from maps. The inspected State Party shall assist the inspection team in this task.

Securing the site, exit monitoring

23. Not later than 12 hours after the arrival of the inspection team at the point of entry, the inspected State Party shall begin collecting factual information of all vehicular exit activity from all exit points for all land, air, and water vehicles of the requested perimeter. It shall provide

this information to the inspection team upon its arrival at the alternative or final perimeter, whichever occurs first.

24. This obligation may be met by collecting factual information in the form of traffic logs, photographs, video recordings, or data from chemical evidence equipment provided by the inspection team to monitor such exit activity. Alternatively, the inspected State Party may also meet this obligation by allowing one or more members of the inspection team independently to maintain traffic logs, take photographs, make video recordings of exit traffic, or use chemical evidence equipment, and conduct other activities as may be agreed between the inspected State Party and the inspection team.

25. Upon the inspection team's arrival at the alternative perimeter or final perimeter, whichever occurs first, securing the site, which means exit monitoring procedures by the inspection team, shall begin.

26. Such procedures shall include: the identification of vehicular exits, the making of traffic logs, the taking of photographs, and the making of video recordings by the inspection team of exits and exit traffic. The inspection team has the right to go, under escort, to any other part of the perimeter to check that there is no other exit activity.

27. Additional procedures for exit monitoring activities as agreed upon by the inspection team and the inspected State Party may include, inter alia:

(a) Use of sensors;

(b) Random selective access;

(c) Sample analysis.

28. All activities for securing the site and exit monitoring shall take place within a band around the outside of the perimeter, not exceeding 50 metres in width, measured outward.

29. The inspection team has the right to inspect on a managed access basis vehicular traffic exiting the site. The inspected State Party shall make every reasonable effort to demonstrate to the inspection team that any vehicle, subject to inspection, to which the inspection team is not granted full access, is not being used for purposes related to the possible non-compliance concerns raised in the inspection request.

30. Personnel and vehicles entering and personnel and personal passenger vehicles exiting the site are not subject to inspection.

31. The application of the above procedures may continue for the duration of the inspection, but may not unreasonably hamper or delay the normal operation of the facility.

Pre-inspection briefing and inspection plan

32. To facilitate development of an inspection plan, the inspected State Party shall provide a safety and logistical briefing to the inspection team prior to access.

33. The pre-inspection briefing shall be held in accordance with Part II, paragraph 37, of this Annex. In the course of the pre-inspection briefing, the inspected State Party may indicate to the inspection team the equipment, documentation, or areas it considers sensitive and not related to the purpose of the challenge inspection. In addition, personnel responsible for the site shall brief the inspection team on the physical layout and other relevant characteristics of the site. The inspection team shall be provided with a map or sketch drawn to scale showing all structures and significant geographic features at the site. The inspection team shall also be briefed on the availability of facility personnel and records.

34. After the pre-inspection briefing, the inspection team shall prepare, on the basis of the information available and appropriate to it, an initial inspection plan which specifies the activities to be carried out by the inspection team, including the specific areas of the site to which access is desired. The inspection plan shall also specify whether the inspection team will be divided into subgroups. The inspection plan shall be made available to the representatives of the inspected State Party and the inspection site. Its implementation shall be consistent with the provisions of Section C, including those related to access and activities.

Perimeter activities

35. Upon the inspection team's arrival at the final or alternative perimeter, whichever occurs first, the team shall have the right to commence immediately perimeter activities in accordance with the procedures set forth under this Section, and to continue these activities until the completion of the challenge inspection.

36. In conducting the perimeter activities, the inspection team shall have the right to:

(a) Use monitoring instruments in accordance with Part II, paragraphs 27 to 30, of this Annex;

(b) Take wipes, air, soil or effluent samples; and

(c) Conduct any additional activities which may be agreed between the inspection team and the inspected State Party.

37. The perimeter activities of the inspection team may be conducted within a band around the outside of the perimeter up to 50 metres in width measured outward from the perimeter. If the inspected State Party agrees, the inspection team may also have access to any building or structure within the perimeter band. All directional monitoring shall be oriented inward. For declared facilities, at the discretion of the inspected State Party, the band could run inside, outside, or on both sides of the declared perimeter.

C.   **Conduct of inspections**

General rules

38. The inspected State Party shall provide access within the requested perimeter as well as, if different, the final perimeter. The extent and nature of access to a particular place or places within these perimeters shall be negotiated between the inspection team and the inspected State Party on a managed access basis.

39. The inspected State Party shall provide access within the requested perimeter as soon as possible, but in any case not later than 108 hours after the arrival of the inspection team at the point of entry in order to clarify the concern regarding possible non-compliance with this Convention raised in the inspection request.

40. Upon the request of the inspection team, the inspected State Party may provide aerial access to the inspection site.

41. In meeting the requirement to provide access as specified in paragraph 38, the inspected State Party shall be under the obligation to allow the greatest degree of access taking into account any constitutional obligations it may have with regard to proprietary rights or searches and seizures. The inspected State Party has the right under managed access to take such measures as are necessary to protect national security. The provisions in this paragraph may not be invoked by the inspected State Party to conceal evasion of its obligations not to engage in activities prohibited under this Convention.

42. If the inspected State Party provides less than full access to places, activities, or information, it shall be under the obligation to make every reasonable effort to provide alternative means to clarify the possible non-compliance concern that generated the challenge inspection.

43. Upon arrival at the final perimeter of facilities declared pursuant to Articles IV, V and VI, access shall be granted following the pre-inspection briefing and discussion of the inspection plan which shall be limited to the minimum necessary and in any event shall not exceed three hours. For facilities declared pursuant to Article III, paragraph 1 (d), negotiations shall be conducted and managed access commenced not later than 12 hours after arrival at the final perimeter.

44. In carrying out the challenge inspection in accordance with the inspection request, the inspection team shall use only those methods necessary to provide sufficient relevant facts to clarify the concern about possible non-compliance with the provisions of this Convention, and shall refrain from activities not relevant thereto. It shall collect and document such facts as are related to the possible non-compliance with this Convention by the inspected State Party, but shall neither seek nor document information which is clearly not related thereto, unless the inspected State Party expressly requests it to do so. Any material collected and subsequently found not to be relevant shall not be retained.

45. The inspection team shall be guided by the principle of conducting the challenge inspection in the least intrusive

manner possible, consistent with the effective and timely accomplishment of its mission. Wherever possible, it shall begin with the least intrusive procedures it deems acceptable and proceed to more intrusive procedures only as it deems necessary.

Managed access

46. The inspection team shall take into consideration suggested modifications of the inspection plan and proposals which may be made by the inspected State Party, at whatever stage of the inspection including the pre-inspection briefing, to ensure that sensitive equipment, information or areas, not related to chemical weapons, are protected.

47. The inspected State Party shall designate the perimeter entry/exit points to be used for access. The inspection team and the inspected State Party shall negotiate: the extent of access to any particular place or places within the final and requested perimeters as provided in paragraph 48; the particular inspection activities, including sampling, to be conducted by the inspection team; the performance of particular activities by the inspected State Party; and the provision of particular information by the inspected State Party.

48. In conformity with the relevant provisions in the Confidentiality Annex the inspected State Party shall have the right to take measures to protect sensitive installations and prevent disclosure of confidential information and data

not related to chemical weapons. Such measures may include, inter alia:

(a)   Removal of sensitive papers from office spaces;

(b)   Shrouding of sensitive displays, stores, and equipment;

(c)   Shrouding of sensitive pieces of equipment, such as computer or electronic systems;

(d)   Logging off of computer systems and turning off of data indicating devices;

(e)   Restriction of sample analysis to presence or absence of chemicals listed in Schedules 1, 2 and 3 or appropriate degradation products;

(f)   Using random selective access techniques whereby the inspectors are requested to select a given percentage or number of buildings of their choice to inspect; the same principle can apply to the interior and content of sensitive buildings;

(g)   In exceptional cases, giving only individual inspectors access to certain parts of the inspection site.

49.   The inspected State Party shall make every reasonable effort to demonstrate to the inspection team that any object, building, structure, container or vehicle to which the inspection team has not had full access, or which has been protected in accordance with paragraph 48, is not used for

purposes related to the possible non-compliance concerns raised in the inspection request.

50. This may be accomplished by means of, inter alia, the partial removal of a shroud or environmental protection cover, at the discretion of the inspected State Party, by means of a visual inspection of the interior of an enclosed space from its entrance, or by other methods.

51. In the case of facilities declared pursuant to Articles IV, V and VI, the following shall apply:

(a) For facilities with facility agreements, access and activities within the final perimeter shall be unimpeded within the boundaries established by the agreements;

(b) For facilities without facility agreements, negotiation of access and activities shall be governed by the applicable general inspection guidelines established under this Convention;

(c) Access beyond that granted for inspections under Articles IV, V and VI shall be managed in accordance with procedures of this section.

52. In the case of facilities declared pursuant to Article III, paragraph 1 (d), the following shall apply: if the inspected State Party, using procedures of paragraphs 47 and 48, has not granted full access to areas or structures not related to chemical weapons, it shall make every reasonable effort to demonstrate to the inspection team that such areas or

structures are not used for purposes related to the possible non-compliance concerns raised in the inspection request.

Observer

53. In accordance with the provisions of Article IX, paragraph 12, on the participation of an observer in the challenge inspection, the requesting State Party shall liaise with the Technical Secretariat to coordinate the arrival of the observer at the same point of entry as the inspection team within a reasonable period of the inspection team's arrival.

54. The observer shall have the right throughout the period of inspection to be in communication with the embassy of the requesting State Party located in the inspected State Party or in the Host State or, in the case of absence of an embassy, with the requesting State Party itself. The inspected State Party shall provide means of communication to the observer.

55. The observer shall have the right to arrive at the alternative or final perimeter of the inspection site, wherever the inspection team arrives first, and to have access to the inspection site as granted by the inspected State Party. The observer shall have the right to make recommendations to the inspection team, which the team shall take into account to the extent it deems appropriate. Throughout the inspection, the inspection team shall keep the observer informed about the conduct of the inspection and the findings.

56. Throughout the in-country period, the inspected State Party shall provide or arrange for the amenities necessary for the observer such as communication means, interpretation services, transportation, working space, lodging, meals and medical care. All the costs in connection with the stay of the observer on the territory of the inspected State Party or the Host State shall be borne by the requesting State Party.

Duration of inspection

57. The period of inspection shall not exceed 84 hours, unless extended by agreement with the inspected State Party.

D.   Post-inspection activities

Departure

58. Upon completion of the post-inspection procedures at the inspection site, the inspection team and the observer of the requesting State Party shall proceed promptly to a point of entry and shall then leave the territory of the inspected State Party in the minimum time possible.

Reports

59. The inspection report shall summarize in a general way the activities conducted by the inspection team and the factual findings of the inspection team, particularly with regard to the concerns regarding possible non-compliance with this Convention cited in the request for the challenge inspection, and shall be limited to information directly related to this Convention. It shall also include an assessment by the inspection team of the degree and nature of access

and cooperation granted to the inspectors and the extent to which this enabled them to fulfil the inspection mandate. Detailed information relating to the concerns regarding possible non-compliance with this Convention cited in the request for the challenge inspection shall be submitted as an Appendix to the final report and be retained within the Technical Secretariat under appropriate safeguards to protect sensitive information.

60. The inspection team shall, not later than 72 hours after its return to its primary work location, submit a preliminary inspection report, having taken into account, inter alia, paragraph 17 of the Confidentiality Annex, to the Director-General. The Director-General shall promptly transmit the preliminary inspection report to the requesting State Party, the inspected State Party and to the Executive Council.

61. A draft final inspection report shall be made available to the inspected State Party not later than 20 days after the completion of the challenge inspection. The inspected State Party has the right to identify any information and data not related to chemical weapons which should, in its view, due to its confidential character, not be circulated outside the Technical Secretariat. The Technical Secretariat shall consider proposals for changes to the draft final inspection report made by the inspected State Party and, using its own discretion, wherever possible, adopt them. The final report shall then be submitted not later than 30 days after the completion of the challenge inspection to the Director-General for further distribution and consideration in accordance with Article IX, paragraphs 21 to 25.

Part XI
Investigations in cases of alleged use of chemical weapons

A. General

1. Investigations of alleged use of chemical weapons, or of alleged use of riot control agents as a method of warfare, initiated pursuant to Articles IX or X, shall be conducted in accordance with this Annex and detailed procedures to be established by the Director-General.

2. The following additional provisions address specific procedures required in cases of alleged use of chemical weapons.

B. Pre-inspection activities

Request for an investigation

3. The request for an investigation of an alleged use of chemical weapons to be submitted to the Director-General, to the extent possible, should include the following information:

(a) The State Party on whose territory use of chemical weapons is alleged to have taken place;

(b) The point of entry or other suggested safe routes of access;

(c) Location and characteristics of the areas where chemical weapons are alleged to have been used;

(d)   When chemical weapons are alleged to have been used;

(e)   Types of chemical weapons believed to have been used;

(f)   Extent of alleged use;

(g)   Characteristics of the possible toxic chemicals;

(h)   Effects on humans, animals and vegetation;

(i)   Request for specific assistance, if applicable.

4.   The State Party which has requested an investigation may submit at any time any additional information it deems necessary.

Notification

5.   The Director-General shall immediately acknowledge receipt to the requesting State Party of its request and inform the Executive Council and all States Parties.

6.   If applicable, the Director-General shall notify the State Party on whose territory an investigation has been requested. The Director-General shall also notify other States Parties if access to their territories might be required during the investigation.

Assignment of inspection team

7.   The Director-General shall prepare a list of qualified experts whose particular field of expertise could be required in an investigation of alleged use of chemical weapons and constantly keep this list updated. This list shall be communicated, in writing, to each State Party not later than 30 days after entry into force of this Convention and after each change to the list. Any qualified expert included in this list shall be regarded as designated unless a State Party, not later than 30 days after its receipt of the list, declares its non-acceptance in writing.

8.   The Director-General shall select the leader and members of an inspection team from the inspectors and inspection assistants already designated for challenge inspections taking into account the circumstances and specific nature of a particular request. In addition, members of the inspection team may be selected from the list of qualified experts when, in the view of the Director-General, expertise not available among inspectors already designated is required for the proper conduct of a particular investigation.

9.   When briefing the inspection team, the Director-General shall include any additional information provided by the requesting State Party, or any other sources, to ensure that the inspection can be carried out in the most effective and expedient manner.

Dispatch of inspection team

10. Immediately upon the receipt of a request for an investigation of alleged use of chemical weapons the Director-General shall, through contacts with the relevant States Parties, request and confirm arrangements for the safe reception of the team.

11. The Director-General shall dispatch the team at the earliest opportunity, taking into account the safety of the team.

12. If the inspection team has not been dispatched within 24 hours from the receipt of the request, the Director-General shall inform the Executive Council and the States Parties concerned about the reasons for the delay.

Briefings

13. The inspection team shall have the right to be briefed by representatives of the inspected State Party upon arrival and at any time during the inspection.

14. Before the commencement of the inspection the inspection team shall prepare an inspection plan to serve, inter alia, as a basis for logistic and safety arrangements. The inspection plan shall be updated as need arises.

C. Conduct of inspections

Access

15. The inspection team shall have the right of access to any and all areas which could be affected by the alleged use

of chemical weapons. It shall also have the right of access to hospitals, refugee camps and other locations it deems relevant to the effective investigation of the alleged use of chemical weapons. For such access, the inspection team shall consult with the inspected State Party.

Sampling

16. The inspection team shall have the right to collect samples of types, and in quantities it considers necessary. If the inspection team deems it necessary, and if so requested by it, the inspected State Party shall assist in the collection of samples under the supervision of inspectors or inspection assistants. The inspected State Party shall also permit and cooperate in the collection of appropriate control samples from areas neighbouring the site of the alleged use and from other areas as requested by the inspection team.

17. Samples of importance in the investigation of alleged use include toxic chemicals, munitions and devices, remnants of munitions and devices, environmental samples (air, soil, vegetation, water, snow, etc.) and biomedical samples from human or animal sources (blood, urine, excreta, tissue etc.).

18. If duplicate samples cannot be taken and the analysis is performed at off-site laboratories, any remaining sample shall, if so requested, be returned to the inspected State Party after the completion of the analysis.

Extension of inspection site

19. If the inspection team during an inspection deems it necessary to extend the investigation into a neighbouring State Party, the Director-General shall notify that State Party about the need for access to its territory and request and confirm arrangements for the safe reception of the team.

Extension of inspection duration

20. If the inspection team deems that safe access to a specific area relevant to the investigation is not possible, the requesting State Party shall be informed immediately. If necessary, the period of inspection shall be extended until safe access can be provided and the inspection team will have concluded its mission.

Interviews

21. The inspection team shall have the right to interview and examine persons who may have been affected by the alleged use of chemical weapons. It shall also have the right to interview eyewitnesses of the alleged use of chemical weapons and medical personnel, and other persons who have treated or have come into contact with persons who may have been affected by the alleged use of chemical weapons. The inspection team shall have access to medical histories, if available, and be permitted to participate in autopsies, as appropriate, of persons who may have been affected by the alleged use of chemical weapons.

D. Reports

Procedures

22. The inspection team shall, not later than 24 hours after its arrival on the territory of the inspected State Party, send a situation report to the Director-General. It shall further throughout the investigation send progress reports as necessary.

23. The inspection team shall, not later than 72 hours after its return to its primary work location, submit a preliminary report to the Director-General. The final report shall be submitted to the Director-General not later than 30 days after its return to its primary work location. The Director-General shall promptly transmit the preliminary and final reports to the Executive Council and to all States Parties.

Contents

24. The situation report shall indicate any urgent need for assistance and any other relevant information. The progress reports shall indicate any further need for assistance that might be identified during the course of the investigation.

25. The final report shall summarize the factual findings of the inspection, particularly with regard to the alleged use cited in the request. In addition, a report of an investigation of an alleged use shall include a description of the investigation process, tracing its various stages, with special reference to:

(a)   The locations and time of sampling and on-site analyses; and

(b)   Supporting evidence, such as the records of interviews, the results of medical examinations and scientific analyses, and the documents examined by the inspection team.

26.   If the inspection team collects through, inter alia, identification of any impurities or other substances during laboratory analysis of samples taken, any information in the course of its investigation that might serve to identify the origin of any chemical weapons used, that information shall be included in the report.

E.   States not party to this Convention

27.   In the case of alleged use of chemical weapons involving a State not Party to this Convention or in territory not controlled by a State Party, the Organization shall closely cooperate with the Secretary-General of the United Nations. If so requested, the Organization shall put its resources at the disposal of the Secretary-General of the United Nations.

Annex on the protection of confidential information ("Confidentiality Annex")

Contents

A. General principles for the handling of confidential information

1. The obligation to protect confidential information shall pertain to the verification of both civil and military activities and facilities. Pursuant to the general obligations set forth in Article VIII, the Organization shall:

(a) Require only the minimum amount of information and data necessary for the timely and efficient carrying out of its responsibilities under this Convention;

(b) Take the necessary measures to ensure that inspectors and other staff members of the Technical Secretariat meet the highest standards of efficiency, competence, and integrity;

(c) Develop agreements and regulations to implement the provisions of this Convention and shall specify as precisely as possible the information to which the Organization shall be given access by a State Party.

2. The Director-General shall have the primary responsibility for ensuring the protection of confidential information. The Director-General shall establish a stringent regime governing the handling of confidential information by the Technical Secretariat, and in doing so, shall observe the following guidelines:

(a) Information shall be considered confidential if:

(i)   It is so designated by the State Party from which the information was obtained and to which the information refers; or

(ii)   In the judgement of the Director-General, its unauthorized disclosure could reasonably be expected to cause damage to the State Party to which it refers or to the mechanisms for implementation of this Convention;

(b)   All data and documents obtained by the Technical Secretariat shall be evaluated by the appropriate unit of the Technical Secretariat in order to establish whether they contain confidential information. Data required by States Parties to be assured of the continued compliance with this Convention by other States Parties shall be routinely provided to them. Such data shall encompass:

(i)   The initial and annual reports and declarations provided by States Parties under Articles III, IV, V and VI, in accordance with the provisions set forth in the Verification Annex;

(ii)   General reports on the results and effectiveness of verification activities; and

(iii)   Information to be supplied to all States Parties in accordance with the provisions of this Convention;

(c)   No information obtained by the Organization in connection with the implementation of this Convention shall be published or otherwise released, except, as follows:

(i)   General information on the implementation of this Convention may be compiled and released publicly in accordance with the decisions of the Conference or the Executive Council;

(ii)   Any information may be released with the express consent of the State Party to which the information refers;

(iii) Information classified as confidential shall be released by the Organization only through procedures which ensure that the release of information only occurs in strict conformity with the needs of this Convention. Such procedures shall be considered and approved by the Conference pursuant to Article VIII, paragraph 21 (i);

(d)   The level of sensitivity of confidential data or documents shall be established, based on criteria to be applied uniformly in order to ensure their appropriate handling and protection. For this purpose, a classification system shall be introduced, which by taking account of relevant work undertaken in the preparation of this Convention shall provide for clear criteria ensuring the inclusion of information into appropriate categories of confidentiality and the justified durability of the confidential nature of information. While providing for the necessary flexibility in its implementation the classification system shall protect the rights of States Parties providing confidential information. A classification system shall be considered and approved by the Conference pursuant to Article VIII, paragraph 21 (i);

(e) Confidential information shall be stored securely at the premises of the Organization. Some data or documents may also be stored with the National Authority of a State Party. Sensitive information, including, inter alia, photographs, plans and other documents required only for the inspection of a specific facility may be kept under lock and key at this facility;

(f) To the greatest extent consistent with the effective implementation of the verification provisions of this Convention, information shall be handled and stored by the Technical Secretariat in a form that precludes direct identification of the facility to which it pertains;

(g) The amount of confidential information removed from a facility shall be kept to the minimum necessary for the timely and effective implementation of the verification provisions of this Convention; and

(h) Access to confidential information shall be regulated in accordance with its classification. The dissemination of confidential information within the Organization shall be strictly on a need-to-know basis.

3. The Director-General shall report annually to the Conference on the implementation of the regime governing the handling of confidential information by the Technical Secretariat.

4.   Each State Party shall treat information which it receives from the Organization in accordance with the level of confidentiality established for that information. Upon request, a State Party shall provide details on the handling of information provided to it by the Organization.

B.   Employment and conduct of personnel in the Technical Secretariat

5.   Conditions of staff employment shall be such as to ensure that access to and handling of confidential information shall be in conformity with the procedures established by the Director-General in accordance with Section A.

6.   Each position in the Technical Secretariat shall be governed by a formal position description that specifies the scope of access to confidential information, if any, needed in that position.

7.   The Director-General, the inspectors and the other members of the staff shall not disclose even after termination of their functions to any unauthorized persons any confidential information coming to their knowledge in the performance of their official duties. They shall not communicate to any State, organization or person outside the Technical Secretariat any information to which they have access in connection with their activities in relation to any State Party.

8.   In the discharge of their functions inspectors shall only request the information and data which are necessary

to fulfil their mandate. They shall not make any records of information collected incidentally and not related to verification of compliance with this Convention.

9. The staff shall enter into individual secrecy agreements with the Technical Secretariat covering their period of employment and a period of five years after it is terminated.

10. In order to avoid improper disclosures, inspectors and staff members shall be appropriately advised and reminded about security considerations and of the possible penalties that they would incur in the event of improper disclosure.

11. Not less than 30 days before an employee is given clearance for access to confidential information that refers to activities on the territory or in any other place under the jurisdiction or control of a State Party, the State Party concerned shall be notified of the proposed clearance. For inspectors the notification of a proposed designation shall fulfil this requirement.

12. In evaluating the performance of inspectors and any other employees of the Technical Secretariat, specific attention shall be given to the employee's record regarding protection of confidential information.

C. Measures to protect sensitive installations and prevent disclosure of confidential data in the course of on-site verification activities

13. States Parties may take such measures as they deem necessary to protect confidentiality, provided that they fulfil their obligations to demonstrate compliance in accordance with the relevant Articles and the Verification Annex. When receiving an inspection, the State Party may indicate to the inspection team the equipment, documentation or areas that it considers sensitive and not related to the purpose of the inspection.

14. Inspection teams shall be guided by the principle of conducting on-site inspections in the least intrusive manner possible consistent with the effective and timely accomplishment of their mission. They shall take into consideration proposals which may be made by the State Party receiving the inspection, at whatever stage of the inspection, to ensure that sensitive equipment or information, not related to chemical weapons, is protected.

15. Inspection teams shall strictly abide by the provisions set forth in the relevant Articles and Annexes governing the conduct of inspections. They shall fully respect the procedures designed to protect sensitive installations and to prevent the disclosure of confidential data.

16. In the elaboration of arrangements and facility agreements, due regard shall be paid to the requirement of protecting confidential information. Agreements on

inspection procedures for individual facilities shall also include specific and detailed arrangements with regard to the determination of those areas of the facility to which inspectors are granted access, the storage of confidential information on-site, the scope of the inspection effort in agreed areas, the taking of samples and their analysis, the access to records and the use of instruments and continuous monitoring equipment.

17. The report to be prepared after each inspection shall only contain facts relevant to compliance with this Convention. The report shall be handled in accordance with the regulations established by the Organization governing the handling of confidential information. If necessary, the information contained in the report shall be processed into less sensitive forms before it is transmitted outside the Technical Secretariat and the inspected State Party.

D. Procedures in case of breaches or alleged breaches of confidentiality

18. The Director-General shall establish necessary procedures to be followed in case of breaches or alleged breaches of confidentiality, taking into account recommendations to be considered and approved by the Conference pursuant to Article VIII, paragraph 21 (i).

19. The Director-General shall oversee the implementation of individual secrecy agreements. The Director-General shall promptly initiate an investigation if, in his judgement, there is sufficient indication that obligations concerning

the protection of confidential information have been violated. The Director-General shall also promptly initiate an investigation if an allegation concerning a breach of confidentiality is made by a State Party.

20. The Director-General shall impose appropriate punitive and disciplinary measures on staff members who have violated their obligations to protect confidential information. In cases of serious breaches, the immunity from jurisdiction may be waived by the Director-General.

21. States Parties shall, to the extent possible, cooperate and support the Director-General in investigating any breach or alleged breach of confidentiality and in taking appropriate action in case a breach has been established.

22. The Organization shall not be held liable for any breach of confidentiality committed by members of the Technical Secretariat.

23. For breaches involving both a State Party and the Organization, a "Commission for the settlement of disputes related to confidentiality", set up as a subsidiary organ of the Conference, shall consider the case. This Commission shall be appointed by the Conference. Rules governing its composition and operating procedures shall be adopted by the Conference at its first session.

CONVENTIONAL ARMS

Convention on the Prohibition of the Use, Stockpiling, Production and Transfer of Anti-Personnel Mines and on their Destruction (Anti-Personnel Mine Ban Convention)

OPENED FOR SIGNATURE AT OTTAWA:
3-4 December 1997

DEPOSITARY:
Secretary-General of the United Nations

ENTERED INTO FORCE:
1 March 1999

NUMBER OF SIGNATORY STATES: 133*

NUMBER OF STATES PARTIES: 162*

* As at 28 November 2014. For the updated adherence status, see http://disarmament.un.org/treaties/.

TEXT:

Preamble

The States Parties,

Determined to put an end to the suffering and casualties caused by anti-personnel mines, that kill or maim hundreds of people every week, mostly innocent and defenceless civilians and especially children, obstruct economic development and reconstruction, inhibit the repatriation of refugees and internally displaced persons, and have other severe consequences for years after emplacement,

Believing it necessary to do their utmost to contribute in an efficient and coordinated manner to face the challenge of removing anti-personnel mines placed throughout the world, and to assure their destruction,

Wishing to do their utmost in providing assistance for the care and rehabilitation, including the social and economic reintegration of mine victims,

Recognizing that a total ban of anti-personnel mines would also be an important confidence-building measure,

Welcoming the adoption of the Protocol on Prohibitions or Restrictions on the Use of Mines, Booby-Traps and Other Devices, as amended on 3 May 1996, annexed to the Convention on Prohibitions or Restrictions on the Use of Certain Conventional Weapons Which May Be Deemed to Be Excessively Injurious or to Have Indiscriminate Effects, and calling for the early ratification of this Protocol by all States which have not yet done so,

Welcoming also United Nations General Assembly Resolution 51/45 S of 10 December 1996 urging all States to pursue vigorously an effective, legally-binding international agreement to ban the use, stockpiling, production and transfer of anti-personnel landmines,

Welcoming furthermore the measures taken over the past years, both unilaterally and multilaterally, aiming at prohibiting, restricting or suspending the use, stockpiling, production and transfer of anti-personnel mines,

Stressing the role of public conscience in furthering the principles of humanity as evidenced by the call for a total ban of anti-personnel mines and recognizing the efforts to that end undertaken by the International Red Cross and Red Crescent Movement, the International Campaign to Ban Landmines and numerous other non-governmental organizations around the world,

Recalling the Ottawa Declaration of 5 October 1996 and the Brussels Declaration of 27 June 1997 urging the international community to negotiate an international and legally binding agreement prohibiting the use, stockpiling, production and transfer of anti-personnel mines,

Emphasizing the desirability of attracting the adherence of all States to this Convention, and determined to work strenuously towards the promotion of its universalization in all relevant fora including, inter alia, the United Nations, the Conference on Disarmament, regional organizations, and groupings, and review conferences of the Convention on Prohibitions or Restrictions on the Use of Certain Conventional Weapons Which May Be Deemed to Be Excessively Injurious or to Have Indiscriminate Effects,

Basing themselves on the principle of international humanitarian law that the right of the parties to an armed conflict to choose methods or means of warfare is not unlimited, on the principle that prohibits the employment in armed conflicts of weapons, projectiles and materials and methods of warfare of a nature to cause superfluous injury or unnecessary suffering and on the principle that a distinction must be made between civilians and combatants,

Have agreed as follows:

Article 1
General Obligations

1. Each State Party undertakes never under any circumstances:

(a) To use anti-personnel mines;

(b) To develop, produce, otherwise acquire, stockpile, retain or transfer to anyone, directly or indirectly, anti-personnel mines;

(c) To assist, encourage or induce, in any way, anyone to engage in any activity prohibited to a State Party under this Convention.

2. Each State Party undertakes to destroy or ensure the destruction of all anti-personnel mines in accordance with the provisions of this Convention.

Article 2
Definitions

1. "Anti-personnel mine" means a mine designed to be exploded by the presence, proximity or contact of a person and that will incapacitate, injure or kill one or more persons. Mines designed to be detonated by the presence, proximity or contact of a vehicle as opposed to a person, that are equipped with anti-handling devices, are not considered anti-personnel mines as a result of being so equipped.

2. "Mine" means a munition designed to be placed under, on or near the ground or other surface area and to be exploded by the presence, proximity or contact of a person or a vehicle.

3. "Anti-handling device" means a device intended to protect a mine and which is part of, linked to, attached to or placed under the mine and which activates when an attempt is made to tamper with or otherwise intentionally disturb the mine.

4. "Transfer" involves, in addition to the physical movement of anti-personnel mines into or from national territory, the transfer of title to and control over the mines, but does not involve the transfer of territory containing emplaced anti-personnel mines.

5. "Mined area" means an area which is dangerous due to the presence or suspected presence of mines.

Article 3
Exceptions

1.   Notwithstanding the general obligations under Article 1, the retention or transfer of a number of anti-personnel mines for the development of and training in mine detection, mine clearance, or mine destruction techniques is permitted. The amount of such mines shall not exceed the minimum number absolutely necessary for the above-mentioned purposes.

2.   The transfer of anti-personnel mines for the purpose of destruction is permitted.

Article 4
Destruction of Stockpiled Anti-Personnel Mines

Except as provided for in Article 3, each State Party undertakes to destroy or ensure the destruction of all stockpiled anti-personnel mines it owns or possesses, or that are under its jurisdiction or control, as soon as possible but not later than four years after the entry into force of this Convention for that State Party.

Article 5
Destruction of Anti-Personnel Mines
in Mined Areas

1.   Each State Party undertakes to destroy or ensure the destruction of all anti-personnel mines in mined areas under its jurisdiction or control, as soon as possible but not later

than ten years after the entry into force of this Convention for that State Party.

2.   Each State Party shall make every effort to identify all areas under its jurisdiction or control in which anti-personnel mines are known or suspected to be emplaced and shall ensure as soon as possible that all anti-personnel mines in mined areas under its jurisdiction or control are perimeter-marked, monitored and protected by fencing or other means, to ensure the effective exclusion of civilians, until all anti-personnel mines contained therein have been destroyed. The marking shall at least be to the standards set out in the Protocol on Prohibitions or Restrictions on the Use of Mines, Booby-Traps and Other Devices, as amended on 3 May 1996, annexed to the Convention on Prohibitions or Restrictions on the Use of Certain Conventional Weapons Which May Be Deemed to Be Excessively Injurious or to Have Indiscriminate Effects.

3.   If a State Party believes that it will be unable to destroy or ensure the destruction of all anti-personnel mines referred to in paragraph 1 within that time period, it may submit a request to a Meeting of the States Parties or a Review Conference for an extension of the deadline for completing the destruction of such anti-personnel mines, for a period of up to ten years.

4.   Each request shall contain:

(a)   The duration of the proposed extension;

(b) A detailed explanation of the reasons for the proposed extension, including:

(i) The preparation and status of work conducted under national demining programs;

(ii) The financial and technical means available to the State Party for the destruction of all the anti-personnel mines; and

(iii) Circumstances which impede the ability of the State Party to destroy all the anti-personnel mines in mined areas;

(c) The humanitarian, social, economic, and environmental implications of the extension; and

(d) Any other information relevant to the request for the proposed extension.

5. The Meeting of the States Parties or the Review Conference shall, taking into consideration the factors contained in paragraph 4, assess the request and decide by a majority of votes of States Parties present and voting whether to grant the request for an extension period.

6. Such an extension may be renewed upon the submission of a new request in accordance with paragraphs 3, 4 and 5 of this Article. In requesting a further extension period a State Party shall submit relevant additional information on what has been undertaken in the previous extension period pursuant to this Article.

Article 6
International Cooperation and Assistance

1.   In fulfilling its obligations under this Convention each State Party has the right to seek and receive assistance, where feasible, from other States Parties to the extent possible.

2.   Each State Party undertakes to facilitate and shall have the right to participate in the fullest possible exchange of equipment, material and scientific and technological information concerning the implementation of this Convention. The States Parties shall not impose undue restrictions on the provision of mine clearance equipment and related technological information for humanitarian purposes.

3.   Each State Party in a position to do so shall provide assistance for the care and rehabilitation, and social and economic reintegration, of mine victims and for mine awareness programmes. Such assistance may be provided, inter alia, through the United Nations system, international, regional or national organizations or institutions, the International Committee of the Red Cross, national Red Cross and Red Crescent societies and their International Federation, non-governmental organizations, or on a bilateral basis.

4.   Each State Party in a position to do so shall provide assistance for mine clearance and related activities. Such assistance may be provided, inter alia, through the United Nations system, international or regional organizations

or institutions, non-governmental organizations or institutions, or on a bilateral basis, or by contributing to the United Nations Voluntary Trust Fund for Assistance in Mine Clearance, or other regional funds that deal with demining.

5. Each State Party in a position to do so shall provide assistance for the destruction of stockpiled anti-personnel mines.

6. Each State Party undertakes to provide information to the database on mine clearance established within the United Nations system, especially information concerning various means and technologies of mine clearance, and lists of experts, expert agencies or national points of contact on mine clearance.

7. States Parties may request the United Nations, regional organizations, other States Parties or other competent intergovernmental or non-governmental fora to assist its authorities in the elaboration of a national demining program to determine, inter alia:

(a) The extent and scope of the anti-personnel mine problem;

(b) The financial, technological and human resources that are required for the implementation of the programme;

(c) The estimated number of years necessary to destroy all anti-personnel mines in mined areas under the jurisdiction or control of the concerned State Party;

(d)   Mine awareness activities to reduce the incidence of mine-related injuries or deaths;

(e)   Assistance to mine victims;

(f)   The relationship between the Government of the concerned State Party and the relevant governmental, intergovernmental or non-governmental entities that will work in the implementation of the program.

8.   Each State Party giving and receiving assistance under the provisions of this Article shall cooperate with a view to ensuring the full and prompt implementation of agreed assistance programs.

Article 7
Transparency Measures

1.   Each State Party shall report to the Secretary-General of the United Nations as soon as practicable, and in any event not later than 180 days after the entry into force of this Convention for that State Party on:

(a)   The national implementation measures referred to in Article 9;

(b)   The total of all stockpiled anti-personnel mines owned or possessed by it, or under its jurisdiction or control, to include a breakdown of the type, quantity and, if possible, lot numbers of each type of anti-personnel mine stockpiled;

(c)   To the extent possible, the location of all mined areas that contain, or are suspected to contain, anti-personnel mines under its jurisdiction or control, to include as much detail as possible regarding the type and quantity of each type of anti-personnel mine in each mined area and when they were emplaced;

(d)   The types, quantities and, if possible, lot numbers of all anti-personnel mines retained or transferred for the development of and training in mine detection, mine clearance or mine destruction techniques, or transferred for the purpose of destruction, as well as the institutions authorized by a State Party to retain or transfer anti-personnel mines, in accordance with Article 3;

(e)   The status of programmes for the conversion or de-commissioning of anti-personnel mine production facilities;

(f)   The status of programmes for the destruction of anti-personnel mines in accordance with Articles 4 and 5, including details of the methods which will be used in destruction, the location of all destruction sites and the applicable safety and environmental standards to be observed;

(g)   The types and quantities of all anti-personnel mines destroyed after the entry into force of this Convention for that State Party, to include a breakdown of the quantity of each type of anti-personnel mine destroyed, in accordance with Articles 4 and 5, respectively, along with, if possible, the lot numbers of each type of anti-personnel mine in the case of destruction in accordance with Article 4;

(h)   The technical characteristics of each type of anti-personnel mine produced, to the extent known, and those currently owned or possessed by a State Party, giving, where reasonably possible, such categories of information as may facilitate identification and clearance of anti-personnel mines; at a minimum, this information shall include the dimensions, fusing, explosive content, metallic content, colour photographs and other information which may facilitate mine clearance; and

(i)   The measures taken to provide an immediate and effective warning to the population in relation to all areas identified under paragraph 2 of Article 5.

2.   The information provided in accordance with this Article shall be updated by the States Parties annually, covering the last calendar year, and reported to the Secretary-General of the United Nations not later than 30 April of each year.

3.   The Secretary-General of the United Nations shall transmit all such reports received to the States Parties.

Article 8
Facilitation and Clarification of Compliance

1.   The States Parties agree to consult and cooperate with each other regarding the implementation of the provisions of this Convention, and to work together in a spirit of

cooperation to facilitate compliance by States Parties with their obligations under this Convention.

2.   If one or more States Parties wish to clarify and seek to resolve questions relating to compliance with the provisions of this Convention by another State Party, it may submit, through the Secretary-General of the United Nations, a Request for Clarification of that matter to that State Party. Such a request shall be accompanied by all appropriate information. Each State Party shall refrain from unfounded Requests for Clarification, care being taken to avoid abuse. A State Party that receives a Request for Clarification shall provide, through the Secretary-General of the United Nations, within 28 days to the requesting State Party all information which would assist in clarifying this matter.

3.   If the requesting State Party does not receive a response through the Secretary-General of the United Nations within that time period, or deems the response to the Request for Clarification to be unsatisfactory, it may submit the matter through the Secretary-General of the United Nations to the next Meeting of the States Parties. The Secretary-General of the United Nations shall transmit the submission, accompanied by all appropriate information pertaining to the Request for Clarification, to all States Parties. All such information shall be presented to the requested State Party which shall have the right to respond.

4.   Pending the convening of any meeting of the States Parties, any of the States Parties concerned may request the

Secretary-General of the United Nations to exercise his or her good offices to facilitate the clarification requested.

5. The requesting State Party may propose through the Secretary-General of the United Nations the convening of a Special Meeting of the States Parties to consider the matter. The Secretary-General of the United Nations shall thereupon communicate this proposal and all information submitted by the States Parties concerned, to all States Parties with a request that they indicate whether they favour a Special Meeting of the States Parties, for the purpose of considering the matter. In the event that within 14 days from the date of such communication, at least one-third of the States Parties favours such a Special Meeting, the Secretary-General of the United Nations shall convene this Special Meeting of the States Parties within a further 14 days. A quorum for this Meeting shall consist of a majority of States Parties.

6. The Meeting of the States Parties or the Special Meeting of the States Parties, as the case may be, shall first determine whether to consider the matter further, taking into account all information submitted by the States Parties concerned. The Meeting of the States Parties or the Special Meeting of the States Parties shall make every effort to reach a decision by consensus. If despite all efforts to that end no agreement has been reached, it shall take this decision by a majority of States Parties present and voting.

7. All States Parties shall cooperate fully with the Meeting of the States Parties or the Special Meeting of the States Parties in the fulfilment of its review of the matter, including

any fact-finding missions that are authorized in accordance with paragraph 8.

8. If further clarification is required, the Meeting of the States Parties or the Special Meeting of the States Parties shall authorize a fact-finding mission and decide on its mandate by a majority of States Parties present and voting. At any time the requested State Party may invite a fact-finding mission to its territory. Such a mission shall take place without a decision by a Meeting of the States Parties or a Special Meeting of the States Parties to authorize such a mission. The mission, consisting of up to 9 experts, designated and approved in accordance with paragraphs 9 and 10, may collect additional information on the spot or in other places directly related to the alleged compliance issue under the jurisdiction or control of the requested State Party.

9. The Secretary-General of the United Nations shall prepare and update a list of the names, nationalities and other relevant data of qualified experts provided by States Parties and communicate it to all States Parties. Any expert included on this list shall be regarded as designated for all fact-finding missions unless a State Party declares its non-acceptance in writing. In the event of non-acceptance, the expert shall not participate in fact-finding missions on the territory or any other place under the jurisdiction or control of the objecting State Party, if the non-acceptance was declared prior to the appointment of the expert to such missions.

10. Upon receiving a request from the Meeting of the States Parties or a Special Meeting of the States Parties, the Secretary-General of the United Nations shall, after consultations with the requested State Party, appoint the members of the mission, including its leader. Nationals of States Parties requesting the fact-finding mission or directly affected by it shall not be appointed to the mission. The members of the fact-finding mission shall enjoy privileges and immunities under Article VI of the Convention on the Privileges and Immunities of the United Nations, adopted on 13 February 1946.

11. Upon at least 72 hours notice, the members of the fact-finding mission shall arrive in the territory of the requested State Party at the earliest opportunity. The requested State Party shall take the necessary administrative measures to receive, transport and accommodate the mission, and shall be responsible for ensuring the security of the mission to the maximum extent possible while they are on territory under its control.

12. Without prejudice to the sovereignty of the requested State Party, the fact-finding mission may bring into the territory of the requested State Party the necessary equipment which shall be used exclusively for gathering information on the alleged compliance issue. Prior to its arrival, the mission will advise the requested State Party of the equipment that it intends to utilize in the course of its fact-finding mission.

13. The requested State Party shall make all efforts to ensure that the fact-finding mission is given the opportunity to speak with all relevant persons who may be able to provide information related to the alleged compliance issue.

14. The requested State Party shall grant access for the fact-finding mission to all areas and installations under its control where facts relevant to the compliance issue could be expected to be collected. This shall be subject to any arrangements that the requested State Party considers necessary for:

(a) The protection of sensitive equipment, information and areas;

(b) The protection of any constitutional obligations the requested State Party may have with regard to proprietary rights, searches and seizures, or other constitutional rights; or

(c) The physical protection and safety of the members of the fact-finding mission.

In the event that the requested State Party makes such arrangements, it shall make every reasonable effort to demonstrate through alternative means its compliance with this Convention.

15. The fact-finding mission may remain in the territory of the State Party concerned for no more than 14 days, and at any particular site no more than 7 days, unless otherwise agreed.

16. All information provided in confidence and not related to the subject matter of the fact-finding mission shall be treated on a confidential basis.

17. The fact-finding mission shall report, through the Secretary-General of the United Nations, to the Meeting of the States Parties or the Special Meeting of the States Parties the results of its findings.

18. The Meeting of the States Parties or the Special Meeting of the States Parties shall consider all relevant information, including the report submitted by the fact-finding mission, and may request the requested State Party to take measures to address the compliance issue within a specified period of time. The requested State Party shall report on all measures taken in response to this request.

19. The Meeting of the States Parties or the Special Meeting of the States Parties may suggest to the States Parties concerned ways and means to further clarify or resolve the matter under consideration, including the initiation of appropriate procedures in conformity with international law. In circumstances where the issue at hand is determined to be due to circumstances beyond the control of the requested State Party, the Meeting of the States Parties or the Special Meeting of the States Parties may recommend appropriate measures, including the use of cooperative measures referred to in Article 6.

20. The Meeting of the States Parties or the Special Meeting of the States Parties shall make every effort to reach its

decisions referred to in paragraphs 18 and 19 by consensus, otherwise by a two-thirds majority of States Parties present and voting.

Article 9
National Implementation Measures

Each State Party shall take all appropriate legal, administrative and other measures, including the imposition of penal sanctions, to prevent and suppress any activity prohibited to a State Party under this Convention undertaken by persons or on territory under its jurisdiction or control.

Article 10
Settlement of Disputes

1.   The States Parties shall consult and cooperate with each other to settle any dispute that may arise with regard to the application or the interpretation of this Convention. Each State Party may bring any such dispute before the Meeting of the States Parties.

2.   The Meeting of the States Parties may contribute to the settlement of the dispute by whatever means it deems appropriate, including offering its good offices, calling upon the States parties to a dispute to start the settlement procedure of their choice and recommending a time-limit for any agreed procedure.

3.   This Article is without prejudice to the provisions of this Convention on facilitation and clarification of compliance.

Article 11
Meetings of the States Parties

1.   The States Parties shall meet regularly in order to consider any matter with regard to the application or implementation of this Convention, including:

(a)   The operation and status of this Convention;

(b)   Matters arising from the reports submitted under the provisions of this Convention;

(c)   International cooperation and assistance in accordance with Article 6;

(d)   The development of technologies to clear anti-personnel mines;

(e)   Submissions of States Parties under Article 8; and

(f)   Decisions relating to submissions of States Parties as provided for in Article 5.

2.   The First Meeting of the States Parties shall be convened by the Secretary-General of the United Nations within one year after the entry into force of this Convention. The subsequent meetings shall be convened by the Secretary-General of the United Nations annually until the first Review Conference.

3.   Under the conditions set out in Article 8, the Secretary-General of the United Nations shall convene a Special Meeting of the States Parties.

4.   States not parties to this Convention, as well as the United Nations, other relevant international organizations or institutions, regional organizations, the International Committee of the Red Cross and relevant non-governmental organizations may be invited to attend these meetings as observers in accordance with the agreed Rules of Procedure.

Article 12
Review Conferences

1.   A Review Conference shall be convened by the Secretary-General of the United Nations five years after the entry into force of this Convention. Further Review Conferences shall be convened by the Secretary-General of the United Nations if so requested by one or more States Parties, provided that the interval between Review Conferences shall in no case be less than five years. All States Parties to this Convention shall be invited to each Review Conference.

2.   The purpose of the Review Conference shall be:

(a)   To review the operation and status of this Convention;

(b)   To consider the need for and the interval between further Meetings of the States Parties referred to in paragraph 2 of Article 11;

(c)   To take decisions on submissions of States Parties as provided for in Article 5; and

(d)   To adopt, if necessary, in its final report conclusions related to the implementation of this Convention.

3.   States not parties to this Convention, as well as the United Nations, other relevant international organizations or institutions, regional organizations, the International Committee of the Red Cross and relevant non-governmental organizations may be invited to attend each Review Conference as observers in accordance with the agreed Rules of Procedure.

Article 13
Amendments

1.   At any time after the entry into force of this Convention any State Party may propose amendments to this Convention. Any proposal for an amendment shall be communicated to the Depositary, who shall circulate it to all States Parties and shall seek their views on whether an Amendment Conference should be convened to consider the proposal. If a majority of the States Parties notify the Depositary no later than 30 days after its circulation that they support further consideration of the proposal, the Depositary shall convene an Amendment Conference to which all States Parties shall be invited.

2.   States not parties to this Convention, as well as the United Nations, other relevant international organizations

or institutions, regional organizations, the International Committee of the Red Cross and relevant non-governmental organizations may be invited to attend each Amendment Conference as observers in accordance with the agreed Rules of Procedure.

3.   The Amendment Conference shall be held immediately following a Meeting of the States Parties or a Review Conference unless a majority of the States Parties request that it be held earlier.

4.   Any amendment to this Convention shall be adopted by a majority of two-thirds of the States Parties present and voting at the Amendment Conference. The Depositary shall communicate any amendment so adopted to the States Parties.

5.   An amendment to this Convention shall enter into force for all States Parties to this Convention which have accepted it, upon the deposit with the Depositary of instruments of acceptance by a majority of States Parties. Thereafter it shall enter into force for any remaining State Party on the date of deposit of its instrument of acceptance.

Article 14
Costs

1.   The costs of the Meetings of the States Parties, the Special Meetings of the States Parties, the Review Conferences and the Amendment Conferences shall be borne by the States Parties and States not parties to this

Convention participating therein, in accordance with the United Nations scale of assessment adjusted appropriately.

2.   The costs incurred by the Secretary-General of the United Nations under Articles 7 and 8 and the costs of any fact-finding mission shall be borne by the States Parties in accordance with the United Nations scale of assessment adjusted appropriately.

Article 15
Signature

This Convention, done at Oslo, Norway, on 18 September 1997, shall be open for signature at Ottawa, Canada, by all States from 3 December 1997 until 4 December 1997, and at the United Nations Headquarters in New York from 5 December 1997 until its entry into force.

Article 16
Ratification, Acceptance, Approval or Accession

1.   This Convention is subject to ratification, acceptance or approval of the Signatories.

2.   It shall be open for accession by any State which has not signed the Convention.

3.   The instruments of ratification, acceptance, approval or accession shall be deposited with the Depositary.

Article 17
Entry into Force

1.   This Convention shall enter into force on the first day of the sixth month after the month in which the 40th instrument of ratification, acceptance, approval or accession has been deposited.

2.   For any State which deposits its instrument of ratification, acceptance, approval or accession after the date of the deposit of the 40th instrument of ratification, acceptance, approval or accession, this Convention shall enter into force on the first day of the sixth month after the date on which that State has deposited its instrument of ratification, acceptance, approval or accession.

Article 18
Provisional Application

Any State may at the time of its ratification, acceptance, approval or accession, declare that it will apply provisionally paragraph 1 of Article 1 of this Convention pending its entry into force.

Article 19
Reservations

The Articles of this Convention shall not be subject to reservations.

Article 20
Duration and Withdrawal

1.   This Convention shall be of unlimited duration.

2.   Each State Party shall, in exercising its national sovereignty, have the right to withdraw from this Convention. It shall give notice of such withdrawal to all other States Parties, to the Depositary and to the United Nations Security Council. Such instrument of withdrawal shall include a full explanation of the reasons motivating this withdrawal.

3.   Such withdrawal shall only take effect six months after the receipt of the instrument of withdrawal by the Depositary. If, however, on the expiry of that six- month period, the withdrawing State Party is engaged in an armed conflict, the withdrawal shall not take effect before the end of the armed conflict.

4.   The withdrawal of a State Party from this Convention shall not in any way affect the duty of States to continue fulfilling the obligations assumed under any relevant rules of international law.

Article 21
Depositary

The Secretary-General of the United Nations is hereby designated as the Depositary of this Convention.

Article 22
Authentic Texts

The original of this Convention, of which the Arabic, Chinese, English, French, Russian and Spanish texts are equally authentic, shall be deposited with the Secretary-General of the United Nations.

Convention on Cluster Munitions

OPENED FOR SIGNATURE AT OSLO:
3 December 2008

ENTRY INTO FORCE:
1 August 2010

DEPOSITARY:
Secretary-General of the United Nations

NUMBER OF SIGNATORY STATES: 108*

NUMBER OF STATES PARTIES: 88*

* As at 28 November 2014. For the updated adherence status, see http://disarmament.un.org/treaties/.

TEXT:

The States Parties to this Convention,

Deeply concerned that civilian populations and individual civilians continue to bear the brunt of armed conflict,

Determined to put an end for all time to the suffering and casualties caused by cluster munitions at the time of their use, when they fail to function as intended or when they are abandoned,

Concerned that cluster munition remnants kill or maim civilians, including women and children, obstruct economic and social development, including through the loss of livelihood, impede post-conflict rehabilitation and reconstruction, delay or prevent the return of refugees and internally displaced persons, can negatively impact on national and international peace-building and humanitarian assistance efforts, and have other severe consequences that can persist for many years after use,

Deeply concerned also at the dangers presented by the large national stockpiles of cluster munitions retained for operational use and *determined* to ensure their rapid destruction,

Believing it necessary to contribute effectively in an efficient, coordinated manner to resolving the challenge of removing cluster munition remnants located throughout the world, and to ensure their destruction,

Determined also to ensure the full realization of the rights of all cluster munition victims and *recognizing* their inherent dignity,

Resolved to do their utmost in providing assistance to cluster munition victims, including medical care, rehabilitation and psychological support, as well as providing for their social and economic inclusion,

Recognizing the need to provide age- and gender-sensitive assistance to cluster munition victims and to address the special needs of vulnerable groups,

Bearing in mind the Convention on the Rights of Persons with Disabilities which, inter alia, requires that States Parties to that Convention undertake to ensure and promote the full realization of all human rights and fundamental freedoms of all persons with disabilities without discrimination of any kind on the basis of disability,

Mindful of the need to coordinate adequately efforts undertaken in various fora to address the rights and needs of victims of various types of weapons, and *resolved* to avoid discrimination among victims of various types of weapons,

Reaffirming that in cases not covered by this Convention or by other international agreements, civilians and combatants remain under the protection and authority of the principles of international law, derived from established custom, from the principles of humanity and from the dictates of public conscience,

Resolved also that armed groups distinct from the armed forces of a State shall not, under any circumstances, be permitted to engage in any activity prohibited to a State Party to this Convention,

Welcoming the very broad international support for the international norm prohibiting anti-personnel mines, enshrined in the 1997 Convention on the Prohibition of the

Use, Stockpiling, Production and Transfer of Anti-Personnel Mines and on Their Destruction,

Welcoming also the adoption of the Protocol on Explosive Remnants of War, annexed to the Convention on Prohibitions or Restrictions on the Use of Certain Conventional Weapons Which May be Deemed to be Excessively Injurious or to Have Indiscriminate Effects, and its entry into force on 12 November 2006, and *wishing* to enhance the protection of civilians from the effects of cluster munition remnants in post-conflict environments,

Bearing in mind also United Nations Security Council Resolution 1325 on women, peace and security and United Nations Security Council Resolution 1612 on children in armed conflict,

Welcoming further the steps taken nationally, regionally and globally in recent years aimed at prohibiting, restricting or suspending the use, stockpiling, production and transfer of cluster munitions,

Stressing the role of public conscience in furthering the principles of humanity as evidenced by the global call for an end to civilian suffering caused by cluster munitions and *recognizing* the efforts to that end undertaken by the United Nations, the International Committee of the Red Cross, the Cluster Munition Coalition and numerous other non-governmental organizations around the world,

Reaffirming the Declaration of the Oslo Conference on Cluster Munitions, by which, inter alia, States recognised the grave consequences caused by the use of cluster munitions and committed themselves to conclude by 2008 a legally binding instrument that would prohibit the use, production, transfer and stockpiling of cluster munitions that cause unacceptable harm to civilians, and would establish a framework for cooperation and assistance that ensures adequate provision of care and rehabilitation for victims, clearance of contaminated areas, risk reduction education and destruction of stockpiles,

Emphasizing the desirability of attracting the adherence of all States to this Convention, and *determined* to work strenuously towards the promotion of its universalization and its full implementation,

Basing themselves on the principles and rules of international humanitarian law, in particular the principle that the right of parties to an armed conflict to choose methods or means of warfare is not unlimited, and the rules that the parties to a conflict shall at all times distinguish between the civilian population and combatants and between civilian objects and military objectives and accordingly direct their operations against military objectives only, that in the conduct of military operations constant care shall be taken to spare the civilian population, civilians and civilian objects and that the civilian population and individual civilians enjoy general protection against dangers arising from military operations,

HAVE AGREED as follows:

Article 1
General obligations and scope of application

1.   Each State Party undertakes never under any circumstances to:

(a)   Use cluster munitions;

(b)   Develop, produce, otherwise acquire, stockpile, retain or transfer to anyone, directly or indirectly, cluster munitions;

(c)   Assist, encourage or induce anyone to engage in any activity prohibited to a State Party under this Convention.

2.   Paragraph 1 of this Article applies, mutatis mutandis, to explosive bomblets that are specifically designed to be dispersed or released from dispensers affixed to aircraft.

3.   This Convention does not apply to mines.

Article 2
Definitions

For the purposes of this Convention:

1.   **"Cluster munition victims"** means all persons who have been killed or suffered physical or psychological injury, economic loss, social marginalization or substantial

impairment of the realization of their rights caused by the use of cluster munitions. They include those persons directly impacted by cluster munitions as well as their affected families and communities;

2. **"Cluster munition"** means a conventional munition that is designed to disperse or release explosive submunitions each weighing less than 20 kilograms, and includes those explosive submunitions. It does not mean the following:

(a) A munition or submunition designed to dispense flares, smoke, pyrotechnics or chaff; or a munition designed exclusively for an air defence role;

(b) A munition or submunition designed to produce electrical or electronic effects;

(c) A munition that, in order to avoid indiscriminate area effects and the risks posed by unexploded submunitions, has all of the following characteristics:

(i) Each munition contains fewer than ten explosive submunitions;

(ii) Each explosive submunition weighs more than four kilograms;

(iii) Each explosive submunition is designed to detect and engage a single target object;

(iv) Each explosive submunition is equipped with an electronic self-destruction mechanism;

(v) Each explosive submunition is equipped with an electronic selfdeactivating feature;

3. **"Explosive submunition"** means a conventional munition that in order to perform its task is dispersed or released by a cluster munition and is designed to function by detonating an explosive charge prior to, on or after impact;

4. **"Failed cluster munition"** means a cluster munition that has been fired, dropped, launched, projected or otherwise delivered and which should have dispersed or released its explosive submunitions but failed to do so;

5. **"Unexploded submunition"** means an explosive submunition that has been dispersed or released by, or otherwise separated from, a cluster munition and has failed to explode as intended;

6. **"Abandoned cluster munitions"** means cluster munitions or explosive submunitions that have not been used and that have been left behind or dumped, and that are no longer under the control of the party that left them behind or dumped them. They may or may not have been prepared for use;

7. **"Cluster munition remnants"** means failed cluster munitions, abandoned cluster munitions, unexploded submunitions and unexploded bomblets;

8. **"Transfer"** involves, in addition to the physical movement of cluster munitions into or from national territory, the transfer of title to and control over cluster munitions, but does not involve the transfer of territory containing cluster munition remnants;

9. **"Self-destruction mechanism"** means an incorporated automatically-functioning mechanism which is in addition to the primary initiating mechanism of the munition and which secures the destruction of the munition into which it is incorporated;

10. **"Self-deactivating"** means automatically rendering a munition inoperable by means of the irreversible exhaustion of a component, for example a battery, that is essential to the operation of the munition;

11. **"Cluster munition contaminated area"** means an area known or suspected to contain cluster munition remnants;

12. **"Mine"** means a munition designed to be placed under, on or near the ground or other surface area and to be exploded by the presence, proximity or contact of a person or a vehicle;

13. **"Explosive bomblet"** means a conventional munition, weighing less than 20 kilograms, which is not self-propelled and which, in order to perform its task, is dispersed or released by a dispenser, and is designed to function by detonating an explosive charge prior to, on or after impact;

14. **"Dispenser"** means a container that is designed to disperse or release explosive bomblets and which is affixed to an aircraft at the time of dispersal or release;

15. **"Unexploded bomblet"** means an explosive bomblet that has been dispersed, released or otherwise separated from a dispenser and has failed to explode as intended.

Article 3
Storage and stockpile destruction

1. Each State Party shall, in accordance with national regulations, separate all cluster munitions under its jurisdiction and control from munitions retained for operational use and mark them for the purpose of destruction.

2. Each State Party undertakes to destroy or ensure the destruction of all cluster munitions referred to in paragraph 1 of this Article as soon as possible but not later than eight years after the entry into force of this Convention for that State Party. Each State Party undertakes to ensure that destruction methods comply with applicable international standards for protecting public health and the environment.

3. If a State Party believes that it will be unable to destroy or ensure the destruction of all cluster munitions referred to in paragraph 1 of this Article within eight years of entry into force of this Convention for that State Party it may submit a request to a Meeting of States Parties or a Review Conference for an extension of the deadline for

completing the destruction of such cluster munitions by a period of up to four years. A State Party may, in exceptional circumstances, request additional extensions of up to four years. The requested extensions shall not exceed the number of years strictly necessary for that State Party to complete its obligations under paragraph 2 of this Article.

4.   Each request for an extension shall set out:

(a)   The duration of the proposed extension;

(b)   A detailed explanation of the proposed extension, including the financial and technical means available to or required by the State Party for the destruction of all cluster munitions referred to in paragraph 1 of this Article and, where applicable, the exceptional circumstances justifying it;

(c)   A plan for how and when stockpile destruction will be completed;

(d)   The quantity and type of cluster munitions and explosive submunitions held at the entry into force of this Convention for that State Party and any additional cluster munitions or explosive submunitions discovered after such entry into force;

(e)   The quantity and type of cluster munitions and explosive submunitions destroyed during the period referred to in paragraph 2 of this Article; and

(f)   The quantity and type of cluster munitions and explosive submunitions remaining to be destroyed during the proposed extension and the annual destruction rate expected to be achieved.

5.   The Meeting of States Parties or the Review Conference shall, taking into consideration the factors referred to in paragraph 4 of this Article, assess the request and decide by a majority of votes of States Parties present and voting whether to grant the request for an extension. The States Parties may decide to grant a shorter extension than that requested and may propose benchmarks for the extension, as appropriate. A request for an extension shall be submitted a minimum of nine months prior to the Meeting of States Parties or the Review Conference at which it is to be considered.

6.   Notwithstanding the provisions of Article 1 of this Convention, the retention or acquisition of a limited number of cluster munitions and explosive submunitions for the development of and training in cluster munition and explosive submunition detection, clearance or destruction techniques, or for the development of cluster munition counter-measures, is permitted. The amount of explosive submunitions retained or acquired shall not exceed the minimum number absolutely necessary for these purposes.

7.   Notwithstanding the provisions of Article 1 of this Convention, the transfer of cluster munitions to another State Party for the purpose of destruction, as well as for the purposes described in paragraph 6 of this Article, is permitted.

8.   States Parties retaining, acquiring or transferring cluster munitions or explosive submunitions for the purposes described in paragraphs 6 and 7 of this Article shall submit a detailed report on the planned and actual use of these cluster munitions and explosive submunitions and their type, quantity and lot numbers. If cluster munitions or explosive submunitions are transferred to another State Party for these purposes, the report shall include reference to the receiving party. Such a report shall be prepared for each year during which a State Party retained, acquired or transferred cluster munitions or explosive submunitions and shall be submitted to the Secretary-General of the United Nations no later than 30 April of the following year.

Article 4
Clearance and destruction of cluster munition remnants and risk reduction education

1.   Each State Party undertakes to clear and destroy, or ensure the clearance and destruction of, cluster munition remnants located in cluster munition contaminated areas under its jurisdiction or control, as follows:

(a)   Where cluster munition remnants are located in areas under its jurisdiction or control at the date of entry into force of this Convention for that State Party, such clearance and destruction shall be completed as soon as possible but not later than ten years from that date;

(b)   Where, after entry into force of this Convention for that State Party, cluster munitions have become cluster munition remnants located in areas under its jurisdiction or control, such clearance and destruction must be completed as soon as possible but not later than ten years after the end of the active hostilities during which such cluster munitions became cluster munition remnants; and

(c)   Upon fulfilling either of its obligations set out in sub-paragraphs (a) and (b) of this paragraph, that State Party shall make a declaration of compliance to the next Meeting of States Parties.

2.   In fulfilling its obligations under paragraph 1 of this Article, each State Party shall take the following measures as soon as possible, taking into consideration the provisions of Article 6 of this Convention regarding international cooperation and assistance:

(a)   Survey, assess and record the threat posed by cluster munition remnants, making every effort to identify all cluster munition contaminated areas under its jurisdiction or control;

(b)   Assess and prioritise needs in terms of marking, protection of civilians, clearance and destruction, and take steps to mobilise resources and develop a national plan to carry out these activities, building, where appropriate, upon existing structures, experiences and methodologies;

(c)   Take all feasible steps to ensure that all cluster munition contaminated areas under its jurisdiction or control are perimeter-marked, monitored and protected by fencing or other means to ensure the effective exclusion of civilians. Warning signs based on methods of marking readily recognizable by the affected community should be utilised in the marking of suspected hazardous areas. Signs and other hazardous area boundary markers should, as far as possible, be visible, legible, durable and resistant to environmental effects and should clearly identify which side of the marked boundary is considered to be within the cluster munition contaminated areas and which side is considered to be safe;

(d)   Clear and destroy all cluster munition remnants located in areas under its jurisdiction or control; and

(e)   Conduct risk reduction education to ensure awareness among civilians living in or around cluster munition contaminated areas of the risks posed by such remnants.

3.   In conducting the activities referred to in paragraph 2 of this Article, each State Party shall take into account international standards, including the International Mine Action Standards (IMAS).

4.   This paragraph shall apply in cases in which cluster munitions have been used or abandoned by one State Party prior to entry into force of this Convention for that State Party and have become cluster munition remnants that are located in areas under the jurisdiction or control of another State Party at the time of entry into force of this Convention for the latter.

(a) In such cases, upon entry into force of this Convention for both States Parties, the former State Party is strongly encouraged to provide, inter alia, technical, financial, material or human resources assistance to the latter State Party, either bilaterally or through a mutually agreed third party, including through the United Nations system or other relevant organizations, to facilitate the marking, clearance and destruction of such cluster munition remnants.

(b) Such assistance shall include, where available, information on types and quantities of the cluster munitions used, precise locations of cluster munition strikes and areas in which cluster munition remnants are known to be located.

5. If a State Party believes that it will be unable to clear and destroy or ensure the clearance and destruction of all cluster munition remnants referred to in paragraph 1 of this Article within ten years of the entry into force of this Convention for that State Party, it may submit a request to a Meeting of States Parties or a Review Conference for an extension of the deadline for completing the clearance and destruction of such cluster munition remnants by a period of up to five years. The requested extension shall not exceed the number of years strictly necessary for that State Party to complete its obligations under paragraph 1 of this Article.

6. A request for an extension shall be submitted to a Meeting of States Parties or a Review Conference prior to the expiry of the time period referred to in paragraph 1 of this Article for that State Party. Each request shall be submitted

a minimum of nine months prior to the Meeting of States Parties or Review Conference at which it is to be considered. Each request shall set out:

(a)   The duration of the proposed extension;

(b)   A detailed explanation of the reasons for the proposed extension, including the financial and technical means available to and required by the State Party for the clearance and destruction of all cluster munition remnants during the proposed extension;

(c)   The preparation of future work and the status of work already conducted under national clearance and demining programmes during the initial ten year period referred to in paragraph 1 of this Article and any subsequent extensions;

(d)   The total area containing cluster munition remnants at the time of entry into force of this Convention for that State Party and any additional areas containing cluster munition remnants discovered after such entry into force;

(e)   The total area containing cluster munition remnants cleared since entry into force of this Convention;

(f)   The total area containing cluster munition remnants remaining to be cleared during the proposed extension;

(g) The circumstances that have impeded the ability of the State Party to destroy all cluster munition remnants located in areas under its jurisdiction or control during the initial ten year period referred to in paragraph 1 of this Article, and those that may impede this ability during the proposed extension;

(h) The humanitarian, social, economic and environmental implications of the proposed extension; and

(i) Any other information relevant to the request for the proposed extension.

7. The Meeting of States Parties or the Review Conference shall, taking into consideration the factors referred to in paragraph 6 of this Article, including, inter alia, the quantities of cluster munition remnants reported, assess the request and decide by a majority of votes of States Parties present and voting whether to grant the request for an extension. The States Parties may decide to grant a shorter extension than that requested and may propose benchmarks for the extension, as appropriate.

8. Such an extension may be renewed by a period of up to five years upon the submission of a new request, in accordance with paragraphs 5, 6 and 7 of this Article. In requesting a further extension a State Party shall submit relevant additional information on what has been undertaken during the previous extension granted pursuant to this Article.

Article 5
Victim assistance

1.   Each State Party with respect to cluster munition victims in areas under its jurisdiction or control shall, in accordance with applicable international humanitarian and human rights law, adequately provide age- and gender-sensitive assistance, including medical care, rehabilitation and psychological support, as well as provide for their social and economic inclusion. Each State Party shall make every effort to collect reliable relevant data with respect to cluster munition victims.

2.   In fulfilling its obligations under paragraph 1 of this Article each State Party shall:

   (a)   Assess the needs of cluster munition victims;

   (b)   Develop, implement and enforce any necessary national laws and policies;

   (c)   Develop a national plan and budget, including timeframes to carry out these activities, with a view to incorporating them within the existing national disability, development and human rights frameworks and mechanisms, while respecting the specific role and contribution of relevant actors;

   (d)   Take steps to mobilise national and international resources;

(e) Not discriminate against or among cluster munition victims, or between cluster munition victims and those who have suffered injuries or disabilities from other causes; differences in treatment should be based only on medical, rehabilitative, psychological or socio-economic needs;

(f) Closely consult with and actively involve cluster munition victims and their representative organizations;

(g) Designate a focal point within the government for coordination of matters relating to the implementation of this Article; and

(h) Strive to incorporate relevant guidelines and good practices including in the areas of medical care, rehabilitation and psychological support, as well as social and economic inclusion.

Article 6
International cooperation and assistance

1. In fulfilling its obligations under this Convention each State Party has the right to seek and receive assistance.

2. Each State Party in a position to do so shall provide technical, material and financial assistance to States Parties affected by cluster munitions, aimed at the implementation of the obligations of this Convention. Such assistance may be provided, inter alia, through the United Nations system, international, regional or national organizations

or institutions, non-governmental organizations or institutions, or on a bilateral basis.

3. Each State Party undertakes to facilitate and shall have the right to participate in the fullest possible exchange of equipment and scientific and technological information concerning the implementation of this Convention. The States Parties shall not impose undue restrictions on the provision and receipt of clearance and other such equipment and related technological information for humanitarian purposes.

4. In addition to any obligations it may have pursuant to paragraph 4 of Article 4 of this Convention, each State Party in a position to do so shall provide assistance for clearance and destruction of cluster munition remnants and information concerning various means and technologies related to clearance of cluster munitions, as well as lists of experts, expert agencies or national points of contact on clearance and destruction of cluster munition remnants and related activities.

5. Each State Party in a position to do so shall provide assistance for the destruction of stockpiled cluster munitions, and shall also provide assistance to identify, assess and prioritise needs and practical measures in terms of marking, risk reduction education, protection of civilians and clearance and destruction as provided in Article 4 of this Convention.

6.   Where, after entry into force of this Convention, cluster munitions have become cluster munition remnants located in areas under the jurisdiction or control of a State Party, each State Party in a position to do so shall urgently provide emergency assistance to the affected State Party.

7.   Each State Party in a position to do so shall provide assistance for the implementation of the obligations referred to in Article 5 of this Convention to adequately provide age- and gender-sensitive assistance, including medical care, rehabilitation and psychological support, as well as provide for social and economic inclusion of cluster munition victims. Such assistance may be provided, inter alia, through the United Nations system, international, regional or national organizations or institutions, the International Committee of the Red Cross, national Red Cross and Red Crescent Societies and their International Federation, non-governmental organizations or on a bilateral basis.

8.   Each State Party in a position to do so shall provide assistance to contribute to the economic and social recovery needed as a result of cluster munition use in affected States Parties.

9.   Each State Party in a position to do so may contribute to relevant trust funds in order to facilitate the provision of assistance under this Article.

10.   Each State Party that seeks and receives assistance shall take all appropriate measures in order to facilitate the timely and effective implementation of this Convention, including

facilitation of the entry and exit of personnel, materiel and equipment, in a manner consistent with national laws and regulations, taking into consideration international best practices.

11.   Each State Party may, with the purpose of developing a national action plan, request the United Nations system, regional organizations, other States Parties or other competent intergovernmental or non-governmental institutions to assist its authorities to determine, inter alia:

(a)   The nature and extent of cluster munition remnants located in areas under its jurisdiction or control;

(b)   The financial, technological and human resources required for the implementation of the plan;

(c)   The time estimated as necessary to clear and destroy all cluster munition remnants located in areas under its jurisdiction or control;

(d)   Risk reduction education programmes and awareness activities to reduce the incidence of injuries or deaths caused by cluster munition remnants;

(e)   Assistance to cluster munition victims; and

(f)   The coordination relationship between the government of the State Party concerned and the relevant governmental, intergovernmental or non-governmental entities that will work in the implementation of the plan.

12. States Parties giving and receiving assistance under the provisions of this Article shall cooperate with a view to ensuring the full and prompt implementation of agreed assistance programmes.

Article 7
Transparency measures

1. Each State Party shall report to the Secretary-General of the United Nations as soon as practicable, and in any event not later than 180 days after the entry into force of this Convention for that State Party, on:

(a) The national implementation measures referred to in Article 9 of this Convention;

(b) The total of all cluster munitions, including explosive submunitions, referred to in paragraph 1 of Article 3 of this Convention, to include a breakdown of their type, quantity and, if possible, lot numbers of each type;

(c) The technical characteristics of each type of cluster munition produced by that State Party prior to entry into force of this Convention for it, to the extent known, and those currently owned or possessed by it, giving, where reasonably possible, such categories of information as may facilitate identification and clearance of cluster munitions; at a minimum, this information shall include the dimensions, fusing, explosive content, metallic content, colour photographs and other information that may facilitate the clearance of cluster munition remnants;

(d)   The status and progress of programmes for the conversion or decommissioning of production facilities for cluster munitions;

(e)   The status and progress of programmes for the destruction, in accordance with Article 3 of this Convention, of cluster munitions, including explosive submunitions, with details of the methods that will be used in destruction, the location of all destruction sites and the applicable safety and environmental standards to be observed;

(f)   The types and quantities of cluster munitions, including explosive submunitions, destroyed in accordance with Article 3 of this Convention, including details of the methods of destruction used, the location of the destruction sites and the applicable safety and environmental standards observed;

(g)   Stockpiles   of   cluster   munitions,   including explosive   submunitions,   discovered   after   reported completion of the programme referred to in sub-paragraph (e) of this paragraph, and plans for their destruction in accordance with Article 3 of this Convention;

(h)   To the extent possible, the size and location of all cluster munition contaminated areas under its jurisdiction or control, to include as much detail as possible regarding the type and quantity of each type of cluster munition remnant in each such area and when they were used;

(i) The status and progress of programmes for the clearance and destruction of all types and quantities of cluster munition remnants cleared and destroyed in accordance with Article 4 of this Convention, to include the size and location of the cluster munition contaminated area cleared and a breakdown of the quantity of each type of cluster munition remnant cleared and destroyed;

(j) The measures taken to provide risk reduction education and, in particular, an immediate and effective warning to civilians living in cluster munition contaminated areas under its jurisdiction or control;

(k) The status and progress of implementation of its obligations under Article 5 of this Convention to adequately provide age- and gender-sensitive assistance, including medical care, rehabilitation and psychological support, as well as provide for social and economic inclusion of cluster munition victims and to collect reliable relevant data with respect to cluster munition victims;

(l) The name and contact details of the institutions mandated to provide information and to carry out the measures described in this paragraph;

(m) The amount of national resources, including financial, material or in kind, allocated to the implementation of Articles 3, 4 and 5 of this Convention; and

(n) The amounts, types and destinations of international cooperation and assistance provided under Article 6 of this Convention.

2. The information provided in accordance with paragraph 1 of this Article shall be updated by the States Parties annually, covering the previous calendar year, and reported to the Secretary-General of the United Nations not later than 30 April of each year.

3. The Secretary-General of the United Nations shall transmit all such reports received to the States Parties.

Article 8
Facilitation and clarification of compliance

1. The States Parties agree to consult and cooperate with each other regarding the implementation of the provisions of this Convention and to work together in a spirit of cooperation to facilitate compliance by States Parties with their obligations under this Convention.

2. If one or more States Parties wish to clarify and seek to resolve questions relating to a matter of compliance with the provisions of this Convention by another State Party, it may submit, through the Secretary-General of the United Nations, a Request for Clarification of that matter to that State Party. Such a request shall be accompanied by all appropriate information. Each State Party shall refrain from unfounded Requests for Clarification, care being taken to avoid abuse. A State Party that receives a Request for

Clarification shall provide, through the Secretary-General of the United Nations, within 28 days to the requesting State Party all information that would assist in clarifying the matter.

3.   If the requesting State Party does not receive a response through the Secretary-General of the United Nations within that time period, or deems the response to the Request for Clarification to be unsatisfactory, it may submit the matter through the Secretary-General of the United Nations to the next Meeting of States Parties. The Secretary-General of the United Nations shall transmit the submission, accompanied by all appropriate information pertaining to the Request for Clarification, to all States Parties. All such information shall be presented to the requested State Party which shall have the right to respond.

4.   Pending the convening of any Meeting of States Parties, any of the States Parties concerned may request the Secretary-General of the United Nations to exercise his or her good offices to facilitate the clarification requested.

5.   Where a matter has been submitted to it pursuant to paragraph 3 of this Article, the Meeting of States Parties shall first determine whether to consider that matter further, taking into account all information submitted by the States Parties concerned. If it does so determine, the Meeting of States Parties may suggest to the States Parties concerned ways and means further to clarify or resolve the matter under consideration, including the initiation of appropriate procedures in conformity with international law.

In circumstances where the issue at hand is determined to be due to circumstances beyond the control of the requested State Party, the Meeting of States Parties may recommend appropriate measures, including the use of cooperative measures referred to in Article 6 of this Convention.

6.   In addition to the procedures provided for in paragraphs 2 to 5 of this Article, the Meeting of States Parties may decide to adopt such other general procedures or specific mechanisms for clarification of compliance, including facts, and resolution of instances of non-compliance with the provisions of this Convention as it deems appropriate.

Article 9
National implementation measures

Each State Party shall take all appropriate legal, administrative and other measures to implement this Convention, including the imposition of penal sanctions to prevent and suppress any activity prohibited to a State Party under this Convention undertaken by persons or on territory under its jurisdiction or control.

Article 10
Settlement of disputes

1.   When a dispute arises between two or more States Parties relating to the interpretation or application of this Convention, the States Parties concerned shall consult together with a view to the expeditious settlement of the dispute by negotiation or by other peaceful means of

their choice, including recourse to the Meeting of States Parties and referral to the International Court of Justice in conformity with the Statute of the Court.

2.   The Meeting of States Parties may contribute to the settlement of the dispute by whatever means it deems appropriate, including offering its good offices, calling upon the States Parties concerned to start the settlement procedure of their choice and recommending a time-limit for any agreed procedure.

Article 11
Meetings of States Parties

1.   The States Parties shall meet regularly in order to consider and, where necessary, take decisions in respect of any matter with regard to the application or implementation of this Convention, including:

(a)   The operation and status of this Convention;

(b)   Matters arising from the reports submitted under the provisions of this Convention;

(c)   International cooperation and assistance in accordance with Article 6 of this Convention;

(d)   The development of technologies to clear cluster munition remnants;

(e)   Submissions of States Parties under Articles 8 and 10 of this Convention; and

(f) Submissions of States Parties as provided for in Articles 3 and 4 of this Convention.

2. The first Meeting of States Parties shall be convened by the Secretary-General of the United Nations within one year of entry into force of this Convention. The subsequent meetings shall be convened by the Secretary-General of the United Nations annually until the first Review Conference.

3. States not party to this Convention, as well as the United Nations, other relevant international organizations or institutions, regional organizations, the International Committee of the Red Cross, the International Federation of Red Cross and Red Crescent Societies and relevant non-governmental organizations may be invited to attend these meetings as observers in accordance with the agreed rules of procedure.

Article 12
Review Conferences

1. A Review Conference shall be convened by the Secretary-General of the United Nations five years after the entry into force of this Convention. Further Review Conferences shall be convened by the Secretary-General of the United Nations if so requested by one or more States Parties, provided that the interval between Review Conferences shall in no case be less than five years. All States Parties to this Convention shall be invited to each Review Conference.

2. The purpose of the Review Conference shall be:

(a) To review the operation and status of this Convention;

(b) To consider the need for and the interval between further Meetings of States Parties referred to in paragraph 2 of Article 11 of this Convention; and

(c) To take decisions on submissions of States Parties as provided for in Articles 3 and 4 of this Convention.

3. States not party to this Convention, as well as the United Nations, other relevant international organizations or institutions, regional organizations, the International Committee of the Red Cross, the International Federation of Red Cross and Red Crescent Societies and relevant non-governmental organizations may be invited to attend each Review Conference as observers in accordance with the agreed rules of procedure.

Article 13
Amendments

1. At any time after its entry into force any State Party may propose amendments to this Convention. Any proposal for an amendment shall be communicated to the Secretary-General of the United Nations, who shall circulate it to all States Parties and shall seek their views on whether an Amendment Conference should be convened to consider the proposal. If a majority of the States Parties notify the Secretary-General of the United Nations no later than 90 days after its circulation that they support further

consideration of the proposal, the Secretary-General of the United Nations shall convene an Amendment Conference to which all States Parties shall be invited.

2. States not party to this Convention, as well as the United Nations, other relevant international organizations or institutions, regional organizations, the International Committee of the Red Cross, the International Federation of Red Cross and Red Crescent Societies and relevant non-governmental organizations may be invited to attend each Amendment Conference as observers in accordance with the agreed rules of procedure.

3. The Amendment Conference shall be held immediately following a Meeting of States Parties or a Review Conference unless a majority of the States Parties request that it be held earlier.

4. Any amendment to this Convention shall be adopted by a majority of two-thirds of the States Parties present and voting at the Amendment Conference. The Depositary shall communicate any amendment so adopted to all States.

5. An amendment to this Convention shall enter into force for States Parties that have accepted the amendment on the date of deposit of acceptances by a majority of the States which were Parties at the date of adoption of the amendment. Thereafter it shall enter into force for any remaining State Party on the date of deposit of its instrument of acceptance.

Article 14
Costs and administrative tasks

1.   The costs of the Meetings of States Parties, the Review Conferences and the Amendment Conferences shall be borne by the States Parties and States not party to this Convention participating therein, in accordance with the United Nations scale of assessment adjusted appropriately.

2.   The costs incurred by the Secretary-General of the United Nations under Articles 7 and 8 of this Convention shall be borne by the States Parties in accordance with the United Nations scale of assessment adjusted appropriately.

3.   The performance by the Secretary-General of the United Nations of administrative tasks assigned to him or her under this Convention is subject to an appropriate United Nations mandate.

Article 15
Signature

This Convention, done at Dublin on 30 May 2008, shall be open for signature at Oslo by all States on 3 December 2008 and thereafter at United Nations Headquarters in New York until its entry into force.

Article 16
Ratification, acceptance, approval or accession

1.   This Convention is subject to ratification, acceptance or approval by the Signatories.

2.   It shall be open for accession by any State that has not signed the Convention.

3.   The instruments of ratification, acceptance, approval or accession shall be deposited with the Depositary.

Article 17
Entry into force

1.   This Convention shall enter into force on the first day of the sixth month after the month in which the thirtieth instrument of ratification, acceptance, approval or accession has been deposited.

2.   For any State that deposits its instrument of ratification, acceptance, approval or accession after the date of the deposit of the thirtieth instrument of ratification, acceptance, approval or accession, this Convention shall enter into force on the first day of the sixth month after the date on which that State has deposited its instrument of ratification, acceptance, approval or accession.

Article 18
Provisional application

Any State may, at the time of its ratification, acceptance, approval or accession, declare that it will apply provisionally Article 1 of this Convention pending its entry into force for that State.

Article 19
Reservations

The Articles of this Convention shall not be subject to reservations.

Article 20
Duration and withdrawal

1. This Convention shall be of unlimited duration.

2. Each State Party shall, in exercising its national sovereignty, have the right to withdraw from this Convention. It shall give notice of such withdrawal to all other States Parties, to the Depositary and to the United Nations Security Council. Such instrument of withdrawal shall include a full explanation of the reasons motivating withdrawal.

3. Such withdrawal shall only take effect six months after the receipt of the instrument of withdrawal by the Depositary. If, however, on the expiry of that six-month period, the withdrawing State Party is engaged in an armed

conflict, the withdrawal shall not take effect before the end of the armed conflict.

Article 21
Relations with States not party to this Convention

1.   Each State Party shall encourage States not party to this Convention to ratify, accept, approve or accede to this Convention, with the goal of attracting the adherence of all States to this Convention.

2.   Each State Party shall notify the governments of all States not party to this Convention, referred to in paragraph 3 of this Article, of its obligations under this Convention, shall promote the norms it establishes and shall make its best efforts to discourage States not party to this Convention from using cluster munitions.

3.   Notwithstanding the provisions of Article 1 of this Convention and in accordance with international law, States Parties, their military personnel or nationals, may engage in military cooperation and operations with States not party to this Convention that might engage in activities prohibited to a State Party.

4.   Nothing in paragraph 3 of this Article shall authorise a State Party:

    (a)   To develop, produce or otherwise acquire cluster munitions;

(b)   To itself stockpile or transfer cluster munitions;

(c)   To itself use cluster munitions; or

(d)   To expressly request the use of cluster munitions in cases where the choice of munitions used is within its exclusive control.

Article 22
Depository

The Secretary-General of the United Nations is hereby designated as the Depositary of this Convention.

Article 23
Authentic texts

The Arabic, Chinese, English, French, Russian and Spanish texts of this Convention shall be equally authentic.

Arms Trade Treaty

OPENED FOR SIGNATURE IN NEW YORK:
3 June 2013

ENTRY INTO FORCE:
24 December 2014

DEPOSITARY:
Secretary-General of the United Nations

NUMBER OF SIGNATORY STATES: 123*

NUMBER OF STATES PARTIES: 54*

* As at 28 November 2014. For the updated adherence status, see http://disarmament.un.org/treaties/.

TEXT:

Preamble

The States Parties to this Treaty,

Guided by the purposes and principles of the Charter of the United Nations,

Recalling Article 26 of the Charter of the United Nations which seeks to promote the establishment and maintenance of international peace and security with the least diversion for armaments of the world's human and economic resources,

Underlining the need to prevent and eradicate the illicit trade in conventional arms and to prevent their diversion to the illicit market, or for unauthorized end use and end users, including in the commission of terrorist acts,

Recognizing the legitimate political, security, economic and commercial interests of States in the international trade in conventional arms,

Reaffirming the sovereign right of any State to regulate and control conventional arms exclusively within its territory, pursuant to its own legal or constitutional system,

Acknowledging that peace and security, development and human rights are pillars of the United Nations system and foundations for collective security and recognizing that development, peace and security and human rights are interlinked and mutually reinforcing,

Recalling the United Nations Disarmament Commission Guidelines for international arms transfers in the context of General Assembly resolution 46/36H of 6 December 1991,

Noting the contribution made by the United Nations Programme of Action to Prevent, Combat and Eradicate the Illicit Trade in Small Arms and Light Weapons in All Its Aspects, as well as the Protocol against the Illicit Manufacturing of and Trafficking in Firearms, Their Parts and Components and Ammunition, supplementing the United Nations Convention against Transnational Organized Crime, and the International Instrument to Enable States to

Identify and Trace, in a Timely and Reliable Manner, Illicit Small Arms and Light Weapons,

Recognizing the security, social, economic and humanitarian consequences of the illicit and unregulated trade in conventional arms,

Bearing in mind that civilians, particularly women and children, account for the vast majority of those adversely affected by armed conflict and armed violence,

Recognizing also the challenges faced by victims of armed conflict and their need for adequate care, rehabilitation and social and economic inclusion,

Emphasizing that nothing in this Treaty prevents States from maintaining and adopting additional effective measures to further the object and purpose of this Treaty,

Mindful of the legitimate trade and lawful ownership, and use of certain conventional arms for recreational, cultural, historical, and sporting activities, where such trade, ownership and use are permitted or protected by law,

Mindful also of the role regional organizations can play in assisting States Parties, upon request, in implementing this Treaty,

Recognizing the voluntary and active role that civil society, including non-governmental organizations, and industry, can play in raising awareness of the object and purpose of this Treaty, and in supporting its implementation,

Acknowledging that regulation of the international trade in conventional arms and preventing their diversion should not hamper international cooperation and legitimate trade in materiel, equipment and technology for peaceful purposes,

Emphasizing the desirability of achieving universal adherence to this Treaty,

Determined to act in accordance with the following principles;

Principles

– The inherent right of all States to individual or collective self-defence as recognized in Article 51 of the Charter of the United Nations;

– The settlement of international disputes by peaceful means in such a manner that international peace and security, and justice, are not endangered in accordance with Article 2 (3) of the Charter of the United Nations;

– Refraining in their international relations from the threat or use of force against the territorial integrity or political independence of any State, or in any other manner inconsistent with the purposes of the United Nations in accordance with Article 2 (4) of the Charter of the United Nations;

– Non-intervention in matters which are essentially within the domestic jurisdiction of any State in accordance with Article 2 (7) of the Charter of the United Nations;

– Respecting and ensuring respect for international humanitarian law in accordance with, inter alia, the Geneva Conventions of 1949, and respecting and ensuring respect for human rights in accordance with, inter alia, the Charter of the United Nations and the Universal Declaration of Human Rights;

– The responsibility of all States, in accordance with their respective international obligations, to effectively regulate the international trade in conventional arms, and to prevent their diversion, as well as the primary responsibility of all States in establishing and implementing their respective national control systems;

– The respect for the legitimate interests of States to acquire conventional arms to exercise their right to self-defence and for peacekeeping operations; and to produce, export, import and transfer conventional arms;

– Implementing this Treaty in a consistent, objective and non-discriminatory manner,

Have agreed as follows:

Article 1
Object and Purpose

The object of this Treaty is to:

– Establish the highest possible common international standards for regulating or improving the regulation of the international trade in conventional arms;

– Prevent and eradicate the illicit trade in conventional arms and prevent their diversion;

for the purpose of:

– Contributing to international and regional peace, security and stability;

– Reducing human suffering;

– Promoting cooperation, transparency and responsible action by States Parties in the international trade in conventional arms, thereby building confidence among States Parties.

Article 2
Scope

1.   This Treaty shall apply to all conventional arms within the following categories:

(a)   Battle tanks;

(b)   Armoured combat vehicles;

(c)   Large-calibre artillery systems;

(d)   Combat aircraft;

(e)   Attack helicopters;

(f)   Warships;

(g)   Missiles and missile launchers; and

(h)   Small arms and light weapons.

2.   For the purposes of this Treaty, the activities of the international trade comprise export, import, transit, trans-shipment and brokering, hereafter referred to as "transfer".

3.   This Treaty shall not apply to the international movement of conventional arms by, or on behalf of, a State Party for its use provided that the conventional arms remain under that State Party's ownership.

Article 3
Ammunition/Munitions

Each State Party shall establish and maintain a national control system to regulate the export of ammunition/munitions fired, launched or delivered by the conventional arms covered under Article 2 (1), and shall apply the provisions of Article 6 and Article 7 prior to authorizing the export of such ammunition/munitions.

Article 4
Parts and Components

Each State Party shall establish and maintain a national control system to regulate the export of parts and components where the export is in a form that provides the capability to assemble the conventional arms covered under Article 2 (1) and shall apply the provisions of Article 6 and Article 7 prior to authorizing the export of such parts and components.

Article 5
General Implementation

1.   Each State Party shall implement this Treaty in a consistent, objective and nondiscriminatory manner, bearing in mind the principles referred to in this Treaty.

2.   Each State Party shall establish and maintain a national control system, including a national control list, in order to implement the provisions of this Treaty.

3.   Each State Party is encouraged to apply the provisions of this Treaty to the broadest range of conventional arms. National definitions of any of the categories covered under Article 2 (1) (a)-(g) shall not cover less than the descriptions used in the United Nations Register of Conventional Arms at the time of entry into force of this Treaty. For the category covered under Article 2 (1) (h), national definitions shall not cover less than the descriptions used in relevant United

Nations instruments at the time of entry into force of this Treaty.

4. Each State Party, pursuant to its national laws, shall provide its national control list to the Secretariat, which shall make it available to other States Parties. States Parties are encouraged to make their control lists publicly available.

5. Each State Party shall take measures necessary to implement the provisions of this Treaty and shall designate competent national authorities in order to have an effective and transparent national control system regulating the transfer of conventional arms covered under Article 2 (1) and of items covered under Article 3 and Article 4.

6. Each State Party shall designate one or more national points of contact to exchange information on matters related to the implementation of this Treaty. Each State Party shall notify the Secretariat, established under Article 18, of its national point(s) of contact and keep the information updated.

Article 6
Prohibitions

1. A State Party shall not authorize any transfer of conventional arms covered under Article 2 (1) or of items covered under Article 3 or Article 4, if the transfer would violate its obligations under measures adopted by the United Nations Security Council acting under Chapter VII of the Charter of the United Nations, in particular arms embargoes.

2.   A State Party shall not authorize any transfer of conventional arms covered under Article 2 (1) or of items covered under Article 3 or Article 4, if the transfer would violate its relevant international obligations under international agreements to which it is a Party, in particular those relating to the transfer of, or illicit trafficking in, conventional arms.

3.   A State Party shall not authorize any transfer of conventional arms covered under Article 2 (1) or of items covered under Article 3 or Article 4, if it has knowledge at the time of authorization that the arms or items would be used in the commission of genocide, crimes against humanity, grave breaches of the Geneva Conventions of 1949, attacks directed against civilian objects or civilians protected as such, or other war crimes as defined by international agreements to which it is a Party.

Article 7
Export and Export Assessment

1.   If the export is not prohibited under Article 6, each exporting State Party, prior to authorization of the export of conventional arms covered under Article 2 (1) or of items covered under Article 3 or Article 4, under its jurisdiction and pursuant to its national control system, shall, in an objective and non-discriminatory manner, taking into account relevant factors, including information provided by the importing State in accordance with Article 8 (1), assess the potential that the conventional arms or items:

(a) would contribute to or undermine peace and security;

(b) could be used to:

(i) commit or facilitate a serious violation of international humanitarian law;

(ii) commit or facilitate a serious violation of international human rights law;

(iii) commit or facilitate an act constituting an offence under international conventions or protocols relating to terrorism to which the exporting State is a Party; or

(iv) commit or facilitate an act constituting an offence under international conventions or protocols relating to transnational organized crime to which the exporting State is a Party.

2.   The exporting State Party shall also consider whether there are measures that could be undertaken to mitigate risks identified in (a) or (b) in paragraph 1, such as confidence-building measures or jointly developed and agreed programmes by the exporting and importing States.

3.   If, after conducting this assessment and considering available mitigating measures, the exporting State Party determines that there is an overriding risk of any of the negative consequences in paragraph 1, the exporting State Party shall not authorize the export.

4.   The exporting State Party, in making this assessment, shall take into account the risk of the conventional arms covered under Article 2 (1) or of the items covered under Article 3 or Article 4 being used to commit or facilitate serious acts of gender-based violence or serious acts of violence against women and children.

5.   Each exporting State Party shall take measures to ensure that all authorizations for the export of conventional arms covered under Article 2 (1) or of items covered under Article 3 or Article 4 are detailed and issued prior to the export.

6.   Each exporting State Party shall make available appropriate information about the authorization in question, upon request, to the importing State Party and to the transit or trans-shipment States Parties, subject to its national laws, practices or policies.

7.   If, after an authorization has been granted, an exporting State Party becomes aware of new relevant information, it is encouraged to reassess the authorization after consultations, if appropriate, with the importing State.

Article 8
Import

1.   Each importing State Party shall take measures to ensure that appropriate and relevant information is provided, upon request, pursuant to its national laws, to the exporting State Party, to assist the exporting State

Party in conducting its national export assessment under Article 7. Such measures may include end use or end user documentation.

2. Each importing State Party shall take measures that will allow it to regulate, where necessary, imports under its jurisdiction of conventional arms covered under Article 2 (1). Such measures may include import systems.

3. Each importing State Party may request information from the exporting State Party concerning any pending or actual export authorizations where the importing State Party is the country of final destination.

Article 9
Transit or Trans-shipment

Each State Party shall take appropriate measures to regulate, where necessary and feasible, the transit or trans-shipment under its jurisdiction of conventional arms covered under Article 2 (1) through its territory in accordance with relevant international law.

Article 10
Brokering

Each State Party shall take measures, pursuant to its national laws, to regulate brokering taking place under its jurisdiction for conventional arms covered under Article 2 (1). Such measures may include requiring brokers to register or obtain written authorization before engaging in brokering.

Article 11
Diversion

1.   Each State Party involved in the transfer of conventional arms covered under Article 2 (1) shall take measures to prevent their diversion.

2.   The exporting State Party shall seek to prevent the diversion of the transfer of conventional arms covered under Article 2 (1) through its national control system, established in accordance with Article 5 (2), by assessing the risk of diversion of the export and considering the establishment of mitigation measures such as confidence-building measures or jointly developed and agreed programmes by the exporting and importing States. Other prevention measures may include, where appropriate: examining parties involved in the export, requiring additional documentation, certificates, assurances, not authorizing the export or other appropriate measures.

3.   Importing, transit, trans-shipment and exporting States Parties shall cooperate and exchange information, pursuant to their national laws, where appropriate and feasible, in order to mitigate the risk of diversion of the transfer of conventional arms covered under Article 2 (1).

4.   If a State Party detects a diversion of transferred conventional arms covered under Article 2 (1), the State

Party shall take appropriate measures, pursuant to its national laws and in accordance with international law, to address such diversion. Such measures may include alerting potentially affected States Parties, examining diverted shipments of such conventional arms covered under Article 2 (1), and taking follow-up measures through investigation and law enforcement.

5.   In order to better comprehend and prevent the diversion of transferred conventional arms covered under Article 2 (1), States Parties are encouraged to share relevant information with one another on effective measures to address diversion. Such information may include information on illicit activities including corruption, international trafficking routes, illicit brokers, sources of illicit supply, methods of concealment, common points of dispatch, or destinations used by organized groups engaged in diversion.

6.   States Parties are encouraged to report to other States Parties, through the Secretariat, on measures taken in addressing the diversion of transferred conventional arms covered under Article 2 (1).

Article 12
Record Keeping

1.   Each State Party shall maintain national records, pursuant to its national laws and regulations, of its issuance of export authorizations or its actual exports of the conventional arms covered under Article 2 (1).

2.   Each State Party is encouraged to maintain records of conventional arms covered under Article 2 (1) that are transferred to its territory as the final destination or that are authorized to transit or trans-ship territory under its jurisdiction.

3.   Each State Party is encouraged to include in those records: the quantity, value, model/type, authorized international transfers of conventional arms covered under Article 2 (1), conventional arms actually transferred, details of exporting State(s), importing State(s), transit and trans-shipment State(s), and end users, as appropriate.

4.   Records shall be kept for a minimum of ten years.

Article 13
Reporting

1.   Each State Party shall, within the first year after entry into force of this Treaty for that State Party, in accordance with Article 22, provide an initial report to the Secretariat of measures undertaken in order to implement this Treaty, including national laws, national control lists and other regulations and administrative measures. Each State Party shall report to the Secretariat on any new measures undertaken in order to implement this Treaty, when appropriate. Reports shall be made available, and distributed to States Parties by the Secretariat.

2.   States Parties are encouraged to report to other States Parties, through the Secretariat, information on measures

taken that have been proven effective in addressing the diversion of transferred conventional arms covered under Article 2 (1).

3.   Each State Party shall submit annually to the Secretariat by 31 May a report for the preceding calendar year concerning authorized or actual exports and imports of conventional arms covered under Article 2 (1). Reports shall be made available, and distributed to States Parties by the Secretariat. The report submitted to the Secretariat may contain the same information submitted by the State Party to relevant United Nations frameworks, including the United Nations Register of Conventional Arms. Reports may exclude commercially sensitive or national security information.

Article 14
Enforcement

Each State Party shall take appropriate measures to enforce national laws and regulations that implement the provisions of this Treaty.

Article 15
International Cooperation

1.   States Parties shall cooperate with each other, consistent with their respective security interests and national laws, to effectively implement this Treaty.

2.   States Parties are encouraged to facilitate international cooperation, including exchanging information on matters

of mutual interest regarding the implementation and application of this Treaty pursuant to their respective security interests and national laws.

3.　States Parties are encouraged to consult on matters of mutual interest and to share information, as appropriate, to support the implementation of this Treaty.

4.　States Parties are encouraged to cooperate, pursuant to their national laws, in order to assist national implementation of the provisions of this Treaty, including through sharing information regarding illicit activities and actors and in order to prevent and eradicate diversion of conventional arms covered under Article 2 (1).

5.　States Parties shall, where jointly agreed and consistent with their national laws, afford one another the widest measure of assistance in investigations, prosecutions and judicial proceedings in relation to violations of national measures established pursuant to this Treaty.

6.　States Parties are encouraged to take national measures and to cooperate with each other to prevent the transfer of conventional arms covered under Article 2 (1) becoming subject to corrupt practices.

7.　States Parties are encouraged to exchange experience and information on lessons learned in relation to any aspect of this Treaty.

Article 16
International Assistance

1.   In implementing this Treaty, each State Party may seek assistance including legal or legislative assistance, institutional capacity-building, and technical, material or financial assistance. Such assistance may include stockpile management, disarmament, demobilization and reintegration programmes, model legislation, and effective practices for implementation. Each State Party in a position to do so shall provide such assistance, upon request.

2.   Each State Party may request, offer or receive assistance through, inter alia, the United Nations, international, regional, subregional or national organizations, non-governmental organizations, or on a bilateral basis.

3.   A voluntary trust fund shall be established by States Parties to assist requesting States Parties requiring international assistance to implement this Treaty. Each State Party is encouraged to contribute resources to the fund.

Article 17
Conference of States Parties

1.   A Conference of States Parties shall be convened by the provisional Secretariat, established under Article 18, no later than one year following the entry into force of this Treaty and thereafter at such other times as may be decided by the Conference of States Parties.

2.   The Conference of States Parties shall adopt by consensus its rules of procedure at its first session.

3.   The Conference of States Parties shall adopt financial rules for itself as well as governing the funding of any subsidiary bodies it may establish as well as financial provisions governing the functioning of the Secretariat. At each ordinary session, it shall adopt a budget for the financial period until the next ordinary session.

4.   The Conference of States Parties shall:

(a)   Review the implementation of this Treaty, including developments in the field of conventional arms;

(b)   Consider and adopt recommendations regarding the implementation and operation of this Treaty, in particular the promotion of its universality;

(c)   Consider amendments to this Treaty in accordance with Article 20;

(d)   Consider issues arising from the interpretation of this Treaty;

(e)   Consider and decide the tasks and budget of the Secretariat;

(f)   Consider the establishment of any subsidiary bodies as may be necessary to improve the functioning of this Treaty; and

(g) Perform any other function consistent with this Treaty.

5. Extraordinary meetings of the Conference of States Parties shall be held at such other times as may be deemed necessary by the Conference of States Parties, or at the written request of any State Party provided that this request is supported by at least two-thirds of the States Parties.

Article 18
Secretariat

1. This Treaty hereby establishes a Secretariat to assist States Parties in the effective implementation of this Treaty. Pending the first meeting of the Conference of States Parties, a provisional Secretariat will be responsible for the administrative functions covered under this Treaty.

2. The Secretariat shall be adequately staffed. Staff shall have the necessary expertise to ensure that the Secretariat can effectively undertake the responsibilities described in paragraph 3.

3. The Secretariat shall be responsible to States Parties. Within a minimized structure, the Secretariat shall undertake the following responsibilities:

(a) Receive, make available and distribute the reports as mandated by this Treaty;

(b) Maintain and make available to States Parties the list of national points of contact;

(c) Facilitate the matching of offers of and requests for assistance for Treaty implementation and promote international cooperation as requested;

(d) Facilitate the work of the Conference of States Parties, including making arrangements and providing the necessary services for meetings under this Treaty; and

(e) Perform other duties as decided by the Conferences of States Parties.

Article 19
Dispute Settlement

1. States Parties shall consult and, by mutual consent, cooperate to pursue settlement of any dispute that may arise between them with regard to the interpretation or application of this Treaty including through negotiations, mediation, conciliation, judicial settlement or other peaceful means.

2. States Parties may pursue, by mutual consent, arbitration to settle any dispute between them, regarding issues concerning the interpretation or application of this Treaty.

Article 20
Amendments

1. Six years after the entry into force of this Treaty, any State Party may propose an amendment to this Treaty. Thereafter, proposed amendments may only be considered by the Conference of States Parties every three years.

2. Any proposal to amend this Treaty shall be submitted in writing to the Secretariat, which shall circulate the proposal to all States Parties, not less than 180 days before the next meeting of the Conference of States Parties at which amendments may be considered pursuant to paragraph 1. The amendment shall be considered at the next Conference of States Parties at which amendments may be considered pursuant to paragraph 1 if, no later than 120 days after its circulation by the Secretariat, a majority of States Parties notify the Secretariat that they support consideration of the proposal.

3. The States Parties shall make every effort to achieve consensus on each amendment. If all efforts at consensus have been exhausted, and no agreement reached, the amendment shall, as a last resort, be adopted by a three-quarters majority vote of the States Parties present and voting at the meeting of the Conference of States Parties. For the purposes of this Article, States Parties present and voting means States Parties present and casting an affirmative or negative vote. The Depositary shall communicate any adopted amendment to all States Parties.

4.   An amendment adopted in accordance with paragraph 3 shall enter into force for each State Party that has deposited its instrument of acceptance for that amendment, ninety days following the date of deposit with the Depositary of the instruments of acceptance by a majority of the number of States Parties at the time of the adoption of the amendment. Thereafter, it shall enter into force for any remaining State Party ninety days following the date of deposit of its instrument of acceptance for that amendment.

Article 21
Signature, Ratification, Acceptance, Approval or Accession

1.   This Treaty shall be open for signature at the United Nations Headquarters in New York by all States from 3 June 2013 until its entry into force.

2.   This Treaty is subject to ratification, acceptance or approval by each signatory State.

3.   Following its entry into force, this Treaty shall be open for accession by any State that has not signed the Treaty.

4.   The instruments of ratification, acceptance, approval or accession shall be deposited with the Depositary.

Article 22
Entry into Force

1.   This Treaty shall enter into force ninety days following the date of the deposit of the fiftieth instrument of ratification, acceptance or approval with the Depositary.

2.   For any State that deposits its instrument of ratification, acceptance, approval or accession subsequent to the entry into force of this Treaty, this Treaty shall enter into force for that State ninety days following the date of deposit of its instrument of ratification, acceptance, approval or accession.

Article 23
Provisional Application

Any State may at the time of signature or the deposit of instrument of its of ratification, acceptance, approval or accession, declare that it will apply provisionally Article 6 and Article 7 pending the entry into force of this Treaty for that State.

Article 24
Duration and Withdrawal

1.   This Treaty shall be of unlimited duration.

2.   Each State Party shall, in exercising its national sovereignty, have the right to withdraw from this Treaty. It shall give notification of such withdrawal to the Depositary,

which shall notify all other States Parties. The notification of withdrawal may include an explanation of the reasons for its withdrawal. The notice of withdrawal shall take effect ninety days after the receipt of the notification of withdrawal by the Depositary, unless the notification of withdrawal specifies a later date.

3.   A State shall not be discharged, by reason of its withdrawal, from the obligations arising from this Treaty while it was a Party to this Treaty, including any financial obligations that it may have accrued.

Article 25
Reservations

1.   At the time of signature, ratification, acceptance, approval or accession, each State may formulate reservations, unless the reservations are incompatible with the object and purpose of this Treaty.

2.   A State Party may withdraw its reservation at any time by notification to this effect addressed to the Depositary.

Article 26
Relationship with Other International Agreements

1.   The implementation of this Treaty shall not prejudice obligations undertaken by States Parties with regard to existing or future international agreements, to which they are parties, where those obligations are consistent with this Treaty.

2.   This Treaty shall not be cited as grounds for voiding defence cooperation agreements concluded between States Parties to this Treaty.

Article 27
Depositary

The Secretary-General of the United Nations shall be the Depositary of this Treaty.

Article 28
Authentic Texts

The original text of this Treaty, of which the Arabic, Chinese, English, French, Russian and Spanish texts are equally authentic, shall be deposited with the Secretary-General of the United Nations.

NUCLEAR-WEAPON-FREE ZONES

Note: Certain treaties that establish nuclear-weapon-free zones (Bangkok Treaty, Treaty on a Nuclear-Weapon-Free Zone in Central Asia, Pelindaba Treaty, Rarotonga Treaty and Treaty of Tlatelolco) have associated protocols concerning security guarantees from the nuclear-weapon States and some also have protocols for States outside the zone of application, but which have some territory within the zone. They are at different stages with regard to signature, ratification and entry into force. Full details can be found at http://disarmament.un.org/treaties/.

Treaty for the Prohibition of Nuclear Weapons in Latin America and the Caribbean (Treaty of Tlatelolco)

OPENED FOR SIGNATURE AT MEXICO CITY:
14 February 1967

ENTERED INTO FORCE:
For each Government individually

DEPOSITARY GOVERNMENT:
Mexico

AGENCY:
Agency for the Prohibition of Nuclear Weapons in Latin America and the Caribbean (OPANAL)

NUMBER OF SIGNATORY STATES: 33

NUMBER OF STATES PARTIES: 33

˙ As at 28 November 2014. For the updated adherence status, see http://disarmament.un.org/treaties/.

TEXT:[1]

Preamble

In the name of their peoples and faithfully interpreting their desires and aspirations, the Governments of the States

---

[1] With the Amendments adopted by the General Conference Articles 7, 14, 15, 16, 19, 20 and 25.

which sign the Treaty for the Prohibition of Nuclear Weapons in Latin America and the Caribbean;

Desiring to contribute, so far as lies in their power, towards ending the armaments race, especially in the field of nuclear weapons, and towards strengthening a world at peace, based on the sovereign equality of States, mutual respect and good neighborliness;

Recalling that the United Nations General Assembly, in its Resolution 808 (IX), unanimously adopted as one of the three points of a coordinated programme of disarmament "the total prohibition of the use and manufacture of nuclear weapons and weapons of mass destruction of every type";

Recalling that militarily denuclearized zones are not an end in themselves but rather a means for achieving general and complete disarmament at a later stage;

Recalling United Nations General Assembly Resolution 1911 (XVIII), which established that the measures that should be agreed upon for the denuclearization of Latin America and the Caribbean should be taken "in the light of the principles of the Charter of the United Nations and of regional agreements";

Recalling United Nations General Assembly Resolution 2028 (XX), which established the principle of an acceptable balance of mutual responsibilities and duties for the nuclear and non-nuclear powers, and

Recalling that the Charter of the Organization of American States proclaims that it is an essential purpose of the Organization to strengthen the peace and security of the hemisphere,

Convinced:

That the incalculable destructive power of nuclear weapons has made it imperative that the legal prohibition of war should be strictly observed in practice if the survival of civilization and of mankind itself is to be assured;

That nuclear weapons, whose terrible effects are suffered, indiscriminately and inexorably, by military forces and civilian population alike, constitute, through the persistence of the radioactivity they release, an attack on the integrity of the human species and ultimately may even render the whole earth uninhabitable;

That general and complete disarmament under effective international control is a vital matter which all the peoples of the world equally demand;

That the proliferation of nuclear weapons, which seems inevitable unless States, in the exercise of their sovereign rights, impose restrictions on themselves in order to prevent it, would make any agreement on disarmament enormously difficult and would increase the danger of the outbreak of a nuclear conflagration;

That the establishment of militarily denuclearized zones is closely linked with the maintenance of peace and security in the respective regions;

That the military denuclearization of vast geographical zones, adopted by the sovereign decision of the States comprised therein, will exercise a beneficial influence on other regions where similar conditions exist;

That the privileged situation of the Signatory States, whose territories are wholly free from nuclear weapons, imposes upon them the inescapable duty of preserving that situation both in their own interests and for the good of mankind;

That the existence of nuclear weapons in any country of Latin America and the Caribbean would make it a target for possible nuclear attacks and would inevitably set off, throughout the region, a ruinous race in nuclear weapons which would involve the unjustifiable diversion, for warlike purposes, of the limited resources required for economic and social development;

That the foregoing reasons, together with the traditional peace loving outlook of Latin America and the Caribbean, give rise to an inescapable necessity that nuclear energy should be used in that region exclusively for peaceful purposes, and that the Latin American and Caribbean countries should use their right to the greatest and most equitable possible access to this new source of energy in order to expedite the economic and social development of their peoples,

Convinced finally:

That the military denuclearization of Latin America and the Caribbean -being understood to mean the undertaking entered into internationally in this Treaty to keep their territories forever free from nuclear weapons- will constitute a measure which will spare their peoples from the squandering of their limited resources on nuclear armaments and will protect them against possible nuclear attacks on their territories, and will also constitute a significant contribution towards preventing the proliferation of nuclear weapons and a powerful factor for general and complete disarmament, and

That Latin America and the Caribbean, faithful to their tradition of universality, must not only endeavor to banish from their homelands the scourge of a nuclear war, but also strive to promote the well-being and advancement of their peoples, at the same time co-operating in the fulfillment of the ideals of mankind, that is to say, in the consolidation of a permanent peace based on equal rights, economic fairness and social justice for all, in accordance with the principles and purposes set forth in the Charter of the United Nations and in the Charter of the Organization of American States,

Have agreed as follows:

Obligations
Article 1

1.   The Contracting Parties hereby undertake to use exclusively for peaceful purposes the nuclear material and facilities which are under their jurisdiction, and to prohibit and prevent in their respective territories:

a.   The testing, use, manufacture, production or acquisition by any means whatsoever of any nuclear weapons, by the Parties themselves, directly or indirectly, on behalf of anyone else or in any other way, and

b.   The receipt, storage, installation, deployment and any form of possession of any nuclear weapons, directly or indirectly, by the Parties themselves, by anyone on their behalf or in any other way.

2.   The Contracting Parties also undertake to refrain from engaging in, encouraging or authorizing, directly or indirectly, or in any way participating in the testing, use, manufacture, production, possession or control of any nuclear weapon.

Definition of the Contracting Parties
Article 2

For the purposes of this Treaty, the Contracting Parties are those for whom the Treaty is in force.

Definition of territory
Article 3

For the purposes of this Treaty, the term "territory" shall include the territorial sea, air space and any other space over which the State exercises sovereignty in accordance with its own legislation.

Zone of Application
Article 4

1.   The Zone of application of this Treaty is the whole of the territories for which the Treaty is in force.

2.   Upon fulfillment of the requirements of Article 29, paragraph 1, the Zone of Application of this Treaty shall also be that which is situated in the western hemisphere within the following limits (except the continental part of the territory of the United States of America and its territorial waters): starting at a point located at 35° north latitude, 75° west longitude; from this point directly southward to a point at 30° north latitude, 75° west longitude; from there, directly eastward to a point at 30° north latitude, 50° west longitude; from there, along a loxodromic line to a point at 5° north latitude, 20° west longitude; from there, directly southward to a point at 60° south latitude, 20° west longitude; from there, directly westward to a point at 60° south latitude, 115° west longitude; from there, directly northward to a point at 0° latitude, 115° west longitude; from there, along a loxodromic line to a point at 35° north latitude, 150° west

longitude; from there, directly eastward to a point at 35° north latitude, 75° west longitude.

Definition of nuclear weapons
Article 5

For the purposes of this Treaty, a nuclear weapon is any device which is capable of releasing nuclear energy in an uncontrolled manner and which has a group of characteristics that are appropriate for use for warlike purposes. An instrument that may be used for the transport or propulsion of the device is not included in this definition if it is separable from the device and not an indivisible part thereof.

Meeting of Signatories
Article 6

At the request of any of the Signatory States or if the Agency established by Article 7 should so decide, a meeting of all the Signatories may be convoked to consider in common questions which may affect the very essence of this instrument, including possible amendments to it. In either case, the meeting will be convoked by the Secretary General.

Organization
Article 7

1.   In order to ensure compliance with the obligations of this Treaty, the Contracting Parties hereby establish an international organization to be known as the "Agency for

the Prohibition of Nuclear Weapons in Latin America and the Caribbean", hereinafter referred to as "the Agency". Only the Contracting Parties shall be affected by its decisions.

2.   The Agency shall be responsible for the holding of periodic or extraordinary consultations among Member States on matters relating to the purposes, measures and procedures set forth in this Treaty and to the supervision of compliance with the obligations arising there from.

3.   The Contracting Parties agree to extend to the Agency full and prompt co-operation in accordance with the provisions of this Treaty, of any agreements they may conclude with the Agency and of any agreements the Agency may conclude with any other international organization or body.

4.   The headquarters of the Agency shall be in Mexico City.

Organs
Article 8

1.   There are hereby established as principal organs of the Agency: a General Conference, a Council and a Secretariat.

2.   Such subsidiary organs as are considered necessary by the General Conference may be established within the purview of this Treaty.

The General Conference
Article 9

1.   The General Conference, the supreme organ of the Agency, shall be composed of all the Contracting Parties; it shall hold regular sessions every two years, and may also hold special sessions whenever this Treaty so provides or, in the opinion of the Council, the circumstances so require.

2.   The General Conference:

a.   May consider and decide on any matters or questions covered by this Treaty, within the limits thereof, including those referring to powers and functions of any organ provided for in this Treaty.

b.   Shall establish procedures for the Control System to ensure observance of this Treaty in accordance with its provisions.

c.   Shall elect the Members of the Council and the Secretary General.

d.   May remove the Secretary General from office if the proper functioning of the Agency so requires.

e.   Shall receive and consider the biennial and special reports submitted by the Council and the Secretary General.

f.   Shall initiate and consider studies designed to facilitate the optimum fulfillment of the aims of this Treaty, without prejudice to the power of the Secretary General independently to carry out similar studies for submission to and consideration by the Conference.

g. Shall be the organ competent to authorize the conclusion of agreements with Governments and other international organizations and bodies.

3. The General Conference shall adopt the Agency's budget and fix the scale of financial contributions to be paid by Member States, taking into account the systems and criteria used for the same purpose by the United Nations.

4. The General Conference shall elect its officers for each session and may establish such subsidiary organs as it deems necessary for the performance of its functions.

5. Each Member of the Agency shall have one vote. The decisions of the General Conference shall be taken by a two-thirds majority of the Members present and voting in the case of matters relating to the Control System and measures referred to in Article 20, the admission of new Members, the election or removal of the Secretary General, adoption of the budget and matters related thereto. Decisions on other matters, as well as procedural questions and also determination of which questions must be decided by a two-thirds majority, shall be taken by a simple majority of the Members present and voting.

6. The General Conference shall adopt its own Rules of Procedure.

The Council
Article 10

1.   The Council shall be composed of five Members of the Agency elected by the General Conference from among the Contracting Parties, due account being taken of equitable geographic distribution.

2.   The Members of the Council shall be elected for a term of four years. However, in the first election three will be elected for two years. Outgoing Members may not be re-elected for the following period unless the limited number of States for which the Treaty is in force so requires.

3.   Each Member of the Council shall have one representative.

4.   The Council shall be so organized as to be able to function continuously.

5.   In addition to the functions conferred upon it by this Treaty and to those which may be assigned to it by the General Conference, the Council shall, through the Secretary General, ensure the proper operation of the Control System in accordance with the provisions of this Treaty and with the decisions adopted by the General Conference.

6.   The Council shall submit an annual report on its work to the General Conference as well as such special reports as it deems necessary or which the General Conference requests of it.

7.   The Council shall elect its officers for each session.

8.   The decisions of the Council shall be taken by a simple majority of its Members present and voting.

9.   The Council shall adopt its own Rules of Procedure.

The Secretariat
Article 11

1.   The Secretariat shall consist of a Secretary General, who shall be the chief administrative officer of the Agency, and of such staff as the Agency may require. The term of office of the Secretary General shall be four years and he may be re-elected for a single additional term. The Secretary General may not be a national of the country in which the Agency has its headquarters. In case the office of Secretary General becomes vacant, a new election shall be held to fill the office for the remainder of the term.

2.   The staff of the Secretariat shall be appointed by the Secretary General, in accordance with rules laid down by the General Conference.

3.   In addition to the functions conferred upon him by this Treaty and to those which may be assigned to him by the General Conference, the Secretary General shall ensure, as provided by Article 10, paragraph 5, the proper operation of the Control System established by this Treaty, in accordance with the provisions of the Treaty and the decisions taken by the General Conference.

4.   The Secretary General shall act in that capacity in all meetings of the General Conference and of the Council and shall make an annual report to both bodies on the work of the Agency and any special reports requested by the General Conference or the Council or which the Secretary General may deem desirable.

5.   The Secretary General shall establish the procedures for distributing to all Contracting Parties information received by the Agency from governmental sources and such information from non-governmental sources as may be of interest to the Agency.

6.   In the performance of their duties the Secretary General and the staff shall not seek or receive instructions from any Government or from any other authority external to the Agency and shall refrain from any action which might reflect on their position as international officials responsible only to the Agency; subject to their responsibility to the Agency, they shall not disclose any industrial secrets or other confidential information coming to their knowledge by reason of their official duties in the Agency.

7.   Each of the Contracting Parties undertakes to respect the exclusively international character of the responsibilities of the Secretary General and the staff and not to seek to influence them in the discharge of their responsibilities.

Control System
Article 12

1.   For the purpose of verifying compliance with the obligations entered into by the Contracting Parties in accordance with Article 1, a Control System shall be established which shall be put into effect in accordance with the provisions of Articles 13-18 of this Treaty.

2.   The Control System shall be used in particular for the purpose of verifying:

a.   That devices, services and facilities intented for peaceful uses of nuclear energy are not used in the testing or manufacture of nuclear weapons,

b.   That none of the activities prohibited in Article I of this Treaty are carried out in the territory of the Contracting Parties with nuclear materials or weapons introduced from abroad, and

c.   That explosions for peaceful purposes are compatible with Article 18 of this Treaty.

IAEA Safeguards
Article 13

Each Contracting Party shall negotiate multilateral or bilateral agreements with the International Atomic Energy Agency for the application of its safeguards to its nuclear activities. Each Contracting Party shall initiate negotiations within a period of 180 days after the date of the deposit of its instrument of ratification of this Treaty. These agreements shall enter into force, for each Party, not later than eighteen months after the date of the initiation of such negotiations except in case of unforeseen circumstances or force majeure.

Reports of the Contracting Parties
Article 14

1. The Contracting Parties shall submit to the Agency and to the International Atomic Energy Agency, for their information, semi-annual reports stating that no activity prohibited under this Treaty has occurred in their respective territories.

2. The Contracting Parties to the Treaty shall simultaneously transmit to the Agency a copy of the reports submitted to the International Atomic Energy Agency which relate to matters subject of this Treaty that are relevant to the work of the Agency.

3. The information furnished by the Contracting Parties shall not be, totally or partially, disclosed or transmitted to third parties, by the addressees of the reports, except when the Contracting Parties give their express consent.

Complementary or supplementary information
Article 15

1. At the request of any of the Contracting Parties and with the authorization of the Council, the Secretary General may request any of the Contracting Parties to provide the

Agency with complementary or supplementary information regarding any extraordinary event or circumstance which affects the compliance with this Treaty, explaining his reasons. The Contracting Parties undertake to co-operate promptly and fully with the Secretary General.

2.   The Secretary General shall inform the Council and the Contracting Parties forthwith of such requests and of the respective replies.

Special inspections
Article 16

1.   The International Atomic Energy Agency has the power of carrying out special inspections in accordance with Article 12 and with the agreements referred to in Article 13 of this Treaty.

2.   At the request of any of the Contracting Parties and in accordance with the procedures established in Article 15 of this Treaty, the Council may submit for the consideration of the International Atomic Energy Agency a request that the necessary mechanisms be put into operation to carry out a special inspection.

3.   The Secretary General shall request the Director General of the International Atomic Energy Agency to transmit to him in a timely manner the information forwarded to the Board of Governors of the IAEA relating to the conclusion of the special inspection. The Secretary General shall make this information available to the Council promptly.

4. The Council, through the Secretary General shall transmit this information to all the Contracting Parties.

Use of nuclear energy for peaceful purposes
Article 17

Nothing in the provisions of this Treaty shall prejudice the rights of the Contracting Parties, in conformity with this Treaty, to use nuclear energy for peaceful purposes, in particular for their economic development and social progress.

Explosions for peaceful purposes
Article 18

1. The Contracting Parties may carry out explosions of nuclear devices for peaceful purposes -including explosions which involve devices similar to those used in nuclear weapons- or collaborate with third parties for the same purpose, provided that they do so in accordance with the provisions of this Article and the other articles of the Treaty, particularly Articles 1 and 5.

2. Contracting Parties intending to carry out, or to co-operate in carrying out, such an explosion shall notify the Agency and the International Atomic Energy Agency, as far in advance as the circumstances require, of the date of the explosion and shall at the same time provide the following information:

a. The nature of the nuclear device and the source from which it was obtained,

b. The place and purpose of the planned explosion,

c. The procedures which will be followed in order to comply with paragraph 3 of this Article,

d. The expected force of the device, and

e. The fullest possible information on any possible radioactive fall-out that may result from the explosion or explosions, and measures which will be taken to avoid danger to the population, flora, fauna and territories of any other Party or Parties.

3. The Secretary General and the technical personnel designated by the Council and the International Atomic Energy Agency may observe all the preparations, including the explosion of the device, and shall have unrestricted access to any area in the vicinity of the site of the explosion in order to ascertain whether the device and the procedures followed during the explosion are in conformity with the information supplied under paragraph 2 of this Article and the other provisions of this Treaty.

4. The Contracting Parties may accept the collaboration of third parties for the purpose set forth in paragraph 1 of the present Article, in accordance with paragraphs 2 and 3 thereof.

Relations with the International Atomic Energy Agency
Article 19

The Agency may conclude such agreements with the International Atomic Energy Agency as are authorized by the General Conference and as it considers likely to facilitate the efficient operation of the Control System established by this Treaty.

Relations with other international organizations
Article 20

1.   The Agency may also enter into relations with any international organization or body, especially any which may be established in the future to supervise disarmament or measures for the control of armaments in any part of the world.

2.   The Contracting Parties may, if they see fit, request the advice of the Inter-American Nuclear Energy Commission on all technical matters connected with the application of this Treaty with which the Commission is competent to deal under its Statute.

Measures in the event of violation of the Treaty
Article 21

1.   The General Conference shall take note of all cases in which, in its opinion, any Contracting Party is not complying fully with its obligations under this Treaty and shall draw the

matter to the attention of the Party concerned, making such recommendations as it deems appropriate.

2. If, in its opinion, such non-compliance constitutes a violation of this Treaty which might endanger peace and security, the General Conference shall report thereon simultaneously to the United Nations Security Council and the General Assembly through the Secretary General of the United Nations, and to the Council of the Organization of American States. The General Conference shall likewise report to the International Atomic Energy Agency for such purposes as are relevant in accordance with its Statute.

United Nations and Organization of American States
Article 22

None of the provisions of this Treaty shall be construed as impairing the rights and obligations of the Parties under the Charter of the United Nations or, in the case of State Members of the Organization of American States, under existing regional treaties.

Privileges and immunities
Article 23

1. The Agency shall enjoy in the territory of each of the Contracting Parties such legal capacity and such privileges and immunities as may be necessary for the exercise of its functions and the fulfillment of its purposes.

2.   Representatives of the Contracting Parties accredited to the Agency and officials of the Agency shall similarly enjoy such privileges and immunities as are necessary for the performance of their functions.

3.   The Agency may conclude agreements with the Contracting Parties with a view to determining the details of the application of paragraphs 1 and 2 of this Article.

Notification of other agreements
Article 24

Once this Treaty has entered into force, the Secretariat shall be notified immediately of any international agreement concluded by any of the Contracting Parties on matters with which this Treaty is concerned; the Secretariat shall register it and notify the other Contracting Parties.

Settlement of disputes
Article 25

Unless the Parties concerned agree on another mode of peaceful settlement, any question or dispute concerning the interpretation or application of this Treaty which is not settled shall be referred to the International Court of Justice with the prior consent of the Parties to the controversy.

Signature
Article 26

1.   This Treaty shall be open indefinitely for signature by:

a. All the Latin American Republics, and the Caribbean.

b. All other sovereign States in the western hemisphere situated in their entirety south of parallel 35° north latitude; and, except as provided in paragraph 2 of this Article, all such States when they have been admitted by the General Conference.

2. The condition of State Party to the Treaty of Tlatelolco shall be restricted to Independent States which are situated within the Zone of application of the Treaty in accordance with Article 4 of same, and with paragraph I of the present Article, and which were Members of the United Nations as of December 10, 1985 as well as to the non-autonomous territories mentioned in document OEA/CER.P, AG/doc. 1939/ 85 of November 5, 1985, once they attain their independence.

Ratification and deposit
Article 27

1. This Treaty shall be subject to ratification by Signatory States in accordance with their respective constitutional procedures.

2. This Treaty and the instruments of ratification shall be deposited with the Government of the Mexican United States, which is hereby designated the Depositary Government.

3.   The Depositary Government shall send certified copies of this Treaty to the Governments of Signatory States and shall notify them of the deposit of each instrument of ratification.

Reservations
Article 28

This Treaty shall not be subject to reservations.

Entry into force
Article 29

1.   Subject to the provisions of paragraph 2 of this Article, this Treaty shall enter into force among the States that have ratified it as soon as the following requirements have been met:

a.   Deposit of the instruments of ratification of this Treaty with the Depositary Government by the Governments of the States mentioned in Article 26 which are in existence on the date when this Treaty is opened for signature and which are not affected by the provisions of Article 26, paragraph 2;

b.   Signature and ratification of Additional Protocol I annexed to this Treaty by all extra-continental or continental States having de jure or de facto international responsibility for territories situated in the Zone of Application of the Treaty;

c.   Signature and ratification of the Additional Protocol II annexed to this Treaty by all powers possessing nuclear weapons;

d.   Conclusion of bilateral or multilateral agreements on the application of the Safeguards System of the International Atomic Energy Agency in accordance with Article 13 of this Treaty.

2.   All Signatory States shall have the imprescriptible right to waive, wholly or in part, the requirements laid down in the preceding paragraph. They may do so by means of a declaration which shall be annexed to their respective instrument of ratification and which may be formulated at the time of deposit of the instrument or subsequently. For those States which exercise this right, this Treaty shall enter into force upon deposit of the declaration, or as soon as those requirements have been met which have not been expressly waived.

3.   As soon as this Treaty has entered into force in accordance with the provisions of paragraph 2 for eleven States, the Depositary Government shall convene a preliminary meeting of those States in order that the Agency may be set up and commence its work.

4.   After the entry into force of this Treaty for all the countries of the Zone, the rise of a new power possessing nuclear weapons shall have the effect of suspending the execution of this Treaty for those countries which have ratified it without waiving requirements of paragraph 1,

subparagraph c) of this Article, and which request such suspension; the Treaty shall remain suspended until the new power, on its own initiative or upon request by the General Conference, ratifies the annexed Additional Protocol II.

Amendments
Article 30

1.   Any Contracting Party may propose amendments to this Treaty and shall submit its proposals to the Council through the Secretary General, who shall transmit them to all the other Contracting Parties and, in addition, to all other Signatories in accordance with Article 6. The Council through the Secretary General, shall immediately following the meeting of Signatories convene a Special Session of the General Conference to examine the proposals made, for the adoption of which a two-thirds majority of the Contracting Parties present and voting shall be required.

2.   Amendments adopted shall enter into force as soon as the requirements set forth in Article 29 of this Treaty have been complied with.

Duration and denunciation
Article 31

1.   This Treaty shall be of a permanent nature and shall remain in force indefinitely, but any Party may denounce it by notifying the Secretary General of the Agency if, in the opinion of the denouncing State, there have arisen or may arise circumstances connected with the content of this

Treaty or of the annexed Additional Protocols I and II which affect its supreme interests or the peace and security of one or more Contracting Parties.

2. The denunciation shall take effect three months after the delivery to the Secretary General of the Agency of the notification by the Government of the Signatory State concerned. The Secretary General shall immediately communicate such notification to the other Contracting Parties and to the Secretary General of the United Nations for the information of the United Nations Security Council and the General Assembly. He shall also communicate it to the Secretary General of the Organization of American States.

Authentic texts and registration
Article 32

This Treaty, of which the Spanish, Chinese, English, French, Portuguese and Russian texts are equally authentic, shall be registered by the Depositary Government in accordance with Article 102 of the United Nations Charter. The Depositary Government shall notify the Secretary General of the United Nations of the signatures, ratifications and amendments relating to this Treaty and shall communicate them to the Secretary General of the Organization of American States for its information.

Transitional Article

Denunciation of the declaration referred to in Article 29, paragraph 2, shall be subject to the same procedures as the denunciation of this Treaty, except that it will take effect on the date of delivery of the respective notification.

In witness whereof *the undersigned Plenipotentiaries, having deposited their full powers, found in good and due form, sign this Treaty on behalf of their respective Governments.*

Done *at Mexico, Distrito Federal, on the fourteenth day of February, one thousand nine hundred and sixty-seven.*

Additional Protocol I

The undersigned Plenipotentiaries, furnished with full powers by their respective Governments,

Convinced that the Treaty for the Prohibition of Nuclear Weapons in Latin America and the Caribbean, negotiated and signed in accordance with the recommendations of the General Assembly of the United Nations in Resolution 1911 (XVIII) of 27 November 1963, represents an important step towards ensuring the non-proliferation of nuclear weapons,

Aware that the non-proliferation of nuclear weapons is not an end in itself but, rather, a means of achieving general and complete disarmament at a later stage, and

Desiring to contribute, so far as lies in their power, towards ending the armaments race, especially in the field of nuclear weapons, and towards strengthening a world at peace, based on mutual respect and sovereign equality of States,

Have agreed as follows:

Article 1

To undertake to apply the statute of denuclearization in respect of warlike purposes as defined in Articles 1, 3, 5 and 13 of the Treaty for the Prohibition of Nuclear Weapons in Latin America and the Caribbean in territories for which, de jure or de facto, they are internationally responsible and which lie within the limits of the geographical Zone established in that Treaty.

Article 2

The duration of this Protocol shall be the same as that of the Treaty for the Prohibition of Nuclear Weapons in Latin America and the Caribbean of which this Protocol is an annex, and the provisions regarding ratification and denunciation contained in the Treaty shall be applicable to it.

Article 3

This Protocol shall enter into force, for the States which have ratified it, on the date of the deposit of their respective instruments of ratification.

In witness whereof the undersigned Plenipotentiaries, having deposited their full powers, found in good and due form, sign this Protocol on behalf of their respective Governments.

Additional Protocol II

The undersigned Plenipotentiaries, furnished with full powers by their respective Governments,

Convinced that the Treaty for the Prohibition of Nuclear Weapons in Latin America and the Caribbean negotiated and signed in accordance with the recommendations of the General Assembly of the United Nations in Resolution 1911 (XVIII) of 27 November 1963, represents an important step towards ensuring the non-proliferation of nuclear weapons,

Aware that the non-proliferation of nuclear weapons is not an end in itself but, rather, a means of achieving general and complete disarmament at a later stage, and

Desiring to contribute, so far as lies in their power, towards ending the armaments race, especially in the field of nuclear weapons, and towards promoting and strengthening a world at peace, based on mutual respect and sovereign equality of States,

Have agreed as follows:

Article 1

The statute of denuclearization of Latin America and the Caribbean in respect of warlike purposes, as defined, delimited and set forth in the Treaty for the Prohibition of Nuclear Weapons in Latin America and the Caribbean of which this instrument is an annex, shall be fully respected by the Parties to this Protocol in all its express aims and provisions.

Article 2

The Governments represented by the undersigned Plenipotentiaries undertake, therefore, not to contribute in any way to the performance of acts involving a violation of the obligations of Article 1 of the Treaty in the territories to which the Treaty applies in accordance with Article 4 thereof.

Article 3

The Governments represented by the undersigned Plenipotentiaries also undertake not to use or threaten to use nuclear weapons against the Contracting Parties of the Treaty for the Prohibition of Nuclear Weapons in Latin America and the Caribbean.

Article 4

The duration of this Protocol shall be the same as that of the Treaty for the Prohibition of Nuclear Weapons in Latin America and the Caribbean of which this Protocol is an annex, and the definitions of territory and nuclear weapons set forth in Articles 3 and 5 of the Treaty shall be applicable to this Protocol, as well as the provisions regarding ratification, reservations, denunciation, authentic texts and registration contained in Articles 27, 28, 31 and 32 of the Treaty.

Article 5

This Protocol shall enter into force, for the States which have ratified it, on the date of the deposit of their respective instruments of ratification.

In witness whereof the undersigned Plenipotentiaries, having deposited their full powers found to be in good and due form, hereby sign this Additional Protocol on behalf of their respective Governments.

Annex 1

Map of the Treaty of Tlatelolco
(Zone of Application—Article 4)

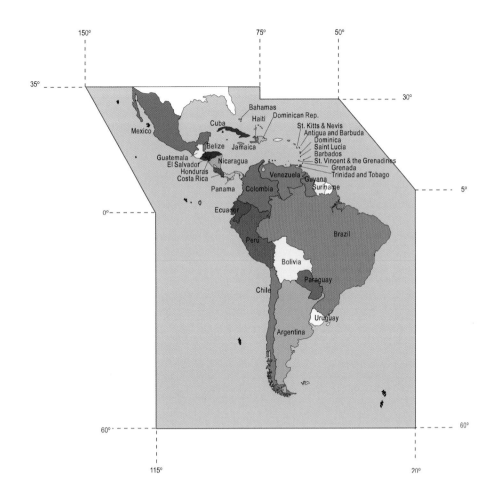

South Pacific Nuclear Free Zone Treaty (Rarotonga Treaty)

SIGNED AT RAROTONGA:
6 August 1985

ENTERED INTO FORCE:
11 December 1986

DEPOSITARY:
Secretary-General, Pacific Islands Forum Secretariat

NUMBER OF SIGNATORY STATES: 13*

NUMBER OF STATES PARTIES: 13*

* As at 28 November 2014. For the updated adherence status, see http://disarmament.un.org/treaties/.

TEXT:

The Parties to this Treaty

UNITED in their commitment to a world at peace;

GRAVELY CONCERNED that the continuing nuclear arms race presents the risk of nuclear war which would have devastating consequences for all people;

CONVINCED that all countries have an obligation to make every effort to achieve the goal of eliminating nuclear weapons, the terror which they hold for humankind and the threat which they pose to life on earth;

BELIEVING that regional arms control measures can contribute to global efforts to reverse the nuclear arms race and promote the national security of each country in the region and the common security of all;

DETERMINED to ensure, so far as lies within their power, that the bounty and beauty of the land and sea in their region shall remain the heritage of their peoples and their descendants in perpetuity to be enjoyed by all in peace;

REAFFIRMING the importance of the Treaty on the Non-Proliferation of Nuclear Weapons (NPT) in preventing the proliferation of nuclear weapons and in contributing to world security;

NOTING, in particular, that Article VII of the NPT recognises the right of any group of States to conclude regional treaties in order to assure the total absence of nuclear weapons in their respective territories;

NOTING that the prohibitions of emplantation and emplacement of nuclear weapons on the seabed and the ocean floor and in the subsoil thereof contained in the Treaty on the Prohibition of the Emplacement of Nuclear Weapons and Other Weapons of Mass Destruction on the Seabed and the Ocean Floor and in the Subsoil Thereof apply in the South Pacific;

NOTING also that the prohibition of testing of nuclear weapons in the atmosphere or under water, including territorial waters or high seas, contained in the Treaty Banning Nuclear Weapon Tests in the Atmosphere, in Outer Space and Under Water applies in the South Pacific;

DETERMINED to keep the region free of environmental pollution by radioactive wastes and other radioactive matter;

GUIDED by the decision of the Fifteenth South Pacific Forum at Tuvalu that a nuclear free zone should be established in the region at the earliest possible opportunity in accordance with the principles set out in the communiqué of that meeting;

AGREED as follows:

Article 1
Usage of terms

For the purpose of this Treaty and its Protocols:

(a) "South Pacific Nuclear Free Zone" means the areas described in Annex 1 as illustrated by the map attached to that Annex;

(b) "territory" means internal waters, territorial sea and archipelagic waters, the seabed and subsoil beneath, the land territory and the airspace above them;

(c) "nuclear explosive device" means any nuclear weapon or other explosive device capable of releasing nuclear energy, irrespective of the purpose for which it could be used. The term includes such a weapon or device in unassembled and partly assembled forms, but does not include the means of transport or delivery of such a weapon or device if separable from and not an indivisible part of it;

(d) "stationing" means emplantation, emplacement, transportation on land or inland waters, stockpiling, storage, installation and deployment.

Article 2
Application of the Treaty

1. Except where otherwise specified, this Treaty and its Protocols shall apply to territory within the South Pacific Nuclear Free Zone.

2. Nothing in this Treaty shall prejudice or in any way affect the rights, or the exercise of the rights, of any State under international law with regard to freedom of the seas.

Article 3
Renunciation of nuclear explosive devices

Each Party undertakes:

(a) not to manufacture or otherwise acquire, possess or have control over any nuclear explosive device by any means anywhere inside or outside the South Pacific Nuclear Free Zone;

(b) not to seek or receive any assistance in the manufacture or acquisition of any nuclear explosive device;

(c) not to take any action to assist or encourage the manufacture or acquisition of any nuclear explosive device by any State.

Article 4
Peaceful nuclear activities

Each Party undertakes:

(a) not to provide source or special fissionable material, or equipment or material especially designed or prepared for the processing, use or production of special fissionable material for peaceful purposes to:

(i) any non-nuclear-weapon State unless subject to the safeguards required by Article III.1 of the NPT, or

(ii) any nuclear-weapon State unless subject to applicable safeguards agreements with the International Atomic Energy Agency (IAEA).

Any such provision shall be in accordance with strict non-proliferation measures to provide assurance of exclusively peaceful non-explosive use;

(b) to support the continued effectiveness of the international non-proliferation system based on the NPT and the IAEA safeguards system.

Article 5
Prevention of stationing of nuclear explosive devices

1.   Each Party undertakes to prevent in its territory the stationing of any nuclear explosive device.

2.   Each Party in the exercise of its sovereign rights remains free to decide for itself whether to allow visits by foreign ships and aircraft to its ports and airfields, transit of its airspace by foreign aircraft, and navigation by foreign ships in its territorial sea or archipelagic waters in a manner not covered by the rights of innocent passage, archipelagic sea lane passage or transit passage of straits.

Article 6
Prevention of testing of nuclear explosive devices

Each Party undertakes:

(a)   to prevent in its territory the testing of any nuclear explosive device;

(b)   not to take action to assist or encourage the testing of any nuclear explosive device by any State.

Article 7
Prevention of dumping

1.   Each Party undertakes:

(a) not to dump radioactive wastes and other radioactive matter at sea anywhere within the South Pacific Nuclear Free Zone;

(b) to prevent the dumping of radioactive wastes and other radioactive matter by anyone in its territorial sea;

(c) not to take any action to assist or encourage the dumping by anyone of radioactive wastes and other radioactive matter at sea anywhere within the South Pacific Nuclear Free Zone;

(d) to support the conclusion as soon as possible of the proposed Convention relating to the protection of the natural resources and environment of the South Pacific region and its Protocol for the prevention of pollution of the South Pacific region by dumping, with the aim of precluding dumping at sea of radioactive wastes and other radioactive matter by anyone anywhere in the region.

2. Paragraphs 1(a) and 1(b) of this Article shall not apply to areas of the South Pacific Nuclear Free Zone in respect of which such a Convention and Protocol have entered into force.

Article 8
Control system

1. The Parties hereby establish a control system for the purpose of verifying compliance with their obligations under this Treaty.

2.   The control system shall comprise:

(a)   reports and exchange of information as provided for in Article 9;

(b)   consultations as provided for in Article 10 and Annex 4(1);

(c)   the application to peaceful nuclear activities of safeguards by the IAEA as provided for in Annex 2;

(d)   a complaints procedure as provided for in Annex 4.

Article 9
Reports and exchanges of information

1.   Each Party shall report to the Director of the South Pacific Bureau for Economic Cooperation (the Director) as soon as possible any significant event within its jurisdiction affecting the implementation of this Treaty. The Director shall circulate such reports promptly to all Parties.

2.   The Parties shall endeavour to keep each other informed on matters arising under or in relation to this Treaty. They may exchange information by communicating it to the Director, who shall circulate it to all Parties.

3.   The Director shall report annually to the South Pacific Forum on the status of this Treaty and matters arising under or in relation to it, incorporating reports and communications made under paragraphs 1 and 2 of this

Article and matters arising under Articles 8(2)(d) and 10 and Annex 2(4).

Article 10
Consultations and review

Without prejudice to the conduct of consultations among Parties by other means, the Director, at the request of any Party, shall convene a meeting of the Consultative Committee established by Annex 3 for consultation and co-operation on any matter arising in relation to this Treaty or for reviewing its operation.

Article 11
Amendment

The Consultative Committee shall consider proposals for amendment of the provisions of this Treaty proposed by any Party and circulated by the Director to all Parties not less than three months prior to the convening of the Consultative Committee for this purpose. Any proposal agreed upon by consensus by the Consultative Committee shall be communicated to the Director who shall circulate it for acceptance to all Parties. An amendment shall enter into force thirty days after receipt by the depositary of acceptances from all Parties.

Article 12
Signature and ratification

1.   This Treaty shall be open for signature by any Member of the South Pacific Forum.

2.   This Treaty shall be subject to ratification. Instruments of ratification shall be deposited with the Director who is hereby designated depositary of this Treaty and its Protocols.

3.   If a Member of the South Pacific Forum whose territory is outside the South Pacific Nuclear Free Zone becomes a Party to this Treaty, Annex 1 shall be deemed to be amended so far as is required to enclose at least the territory of that Party within the boundaries of the South Pacific Nuclear Free Zone. The delineation of any area added pursuant to this paragraph shall be approved by the South Pacific Forum.

Article 13
Withdrawal

1.   This Treaty is of a permanent nature and shall remain in force indefinitely, provided that in the event of a violation by any Party of a provision of this Treaty essential to the achievement of the objectives of the Treaty or of the spirit of the Treaty, every other Party shall have the right to withdraw from the Treaty.

2.   Withdrawal shall be effected by giving notice twelve months in advance to the Director who shall circulate such notice to all other Parties.

Article 14
Reservations

This Treaty shall not be subject to reservations.

Article 15
Entry into force

1.   This Treaty shall enter into force on the date of deposit of the eighth instrument of ratification.

2.   For a signatory which ratifies this Treaty after the date of deposit of the eighth instrument of ratification, the Treaty shall enter into force on the date of deposit of its instrument of ratification.

Article 16
Depositary functions

The depositary shall register this Treaty and its Protocols pursuant to Article 102 of the Charter of the United Nations and shall transmit certified copies of the Treaty and its Protocols to all Members of the South Pacific Forum and all States eligible to become Party to the Protocols to the Treaty and shall notify them of signatures and ratifications of the Treaty and its Protocols.

IN WITNESS WHEREOF the undersigned, being duly authorized by their Governments, have signed this Treaty.

DONE at Rarotonga, this Sixth day of August, One thousand nine hundred and eighty-five, in a single original in the English language.

Annex 1
South Pacific Nuclear Free Zone

A.   The area bounded by a line-

(1)   commencing at the point of intersection of the Equator by the maritime boundary between Indonesia and Papua New Guinea;

(2)   running thence northerly along that maritime boundary to its intersection by the outer limit of the Exclusive Economic Zone of Papua New Guinea;

(3)   thence generally north-easterly, easterly and south-easterly along that outer limit to its intersection by the Equator;

(4)   thence east along the Equator to its intersection by the meridian of Longitude 163 degrees East;

(5)   thence north along that meridian to its intersection by the parallel of Latitude 3 degrees North;

(6)   thence east along that parallel to its intersection by the meridian of Longitude 171 degrees East;

(7)   thence north along that meridian to its intersection by the parallel of Latitude 4 degrees North;

(8)   thence east along that parallel to its intersection by the meridian of Longitude 180 degrees East;

(9) thence south along that meridian to its intersection by the Equator;

(10) thence east along the Equator to its intersection by the meridian of Longitude 165 degrees West;

(11) thence north along that meridian to its intersection by the parallel of Latitude 5 degrees 30 minutes North;

(12) thence east along that parallel to its intersection by the meridian of Longitude 154 degrees West;

(13) thence south along that meridian to its intersection by the Equator;

(14) thence east along the Equator to its intersection by the meridian of Longitude 115 degrees West;

(15) thence south along that meridian to its intersection by the parallel of Latitude 60 degrees South;

(16) thence west along that parallel to its intersection by the meridian of Longitude 115 degrees East;

(17) thence north along the meridian to its southernmost intersection by the outer limit of the territorial sea of Australia;

(18) thence generally northerly and easterly along the outer limit of the territorial sea of Australia to its intersection by the meridian of Longitude 136 degrees 45 minutes East;

(19) thence north-easterly along the geodesic to the point of Latitude 10 degrees 50 minutes South, Longitude 139 degrees 12 minutes East;

(20) thence north-easterly along the maritime boundary between Indonesia and Papua New Guinea to where it joins the land border between those two countries;

(21) thence generally northerly along the land border to where it joins the maritime boundary between Indonesia and Papua New Guinea, on the northern coastline of Papua New Guinea; and

(22) thence generally northerly along that boundary to the point of commencement.

B.   The areas within the outer limits of the territorial seas of all Australian islands lying westward of the area described in paragraph A and north of Latitude 60 degrees South, provided that any such areas shall cease to be part of the South Pacific Nuclear Free Zone upon receipt by the depositary of written notice from the Government of Australia stating that the areas have become subject to another treaty having an object and purpose substantially the same as that of this Treaty.

Attachment to Annex 1 to the South Pacific Nuclear Free Zone Treaty: illustrative map

(Australian islands in the Indian Ocean, which are also part of the South Pacific Nuclear Free Zone, are not shown.)

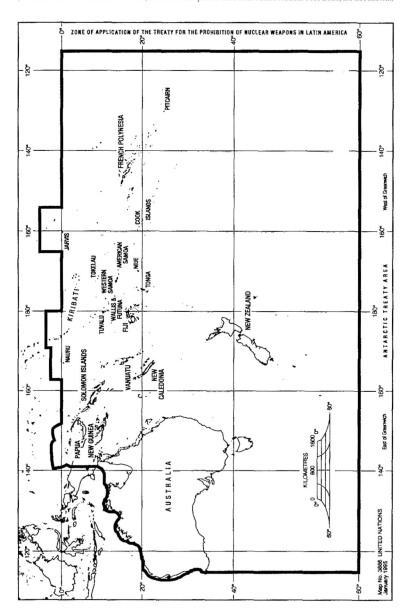

Annex 2
IAEA Safeguards

1.   The safeguards referred to in Article 8 shall in respect of each Party be applied by the IAEA as set forth in an agreement negotiated and concluded with the IAEA on all source or special fissionable material in all peaceful nuclear activities within the territory of the Party, under its jurisdiction or carried out under its control anywhere.

2.   The agreement referred to in paragraph 1 shall be, or shall be equivalent in its scope and effect to, an agreement required in connection with the NPT on the basis of the material reproduced in document INFCIRC/153 (Corrected) of the IAEA. Each Party shall take all appropriate steps to ensure that such agreement is in force for it not later than eighteen months after the date of entry into force for that Party of this Treaty.

3.   For the purposes of this Treaty, the safeguards referred to in paragraph 1 shall have as their purpose the verification of the non-diversion of nuclear material from peaceful nuclear activities to nuclear explosive devices.

4.   Each Party agrees upon the request of any other Party to transmit to that Party and to the Director for the information of all Parties a copy of the overall conclusions of the most recent report by the IAEA on its inspection activities in the territory of the Party concerned, and to advise the Director promptly of any subsequent findings of the Board of Governors of the IAEA in relation to those conclusions for the information of all Parties.

Annex 3
Consultative Committee

1.   There is hereby established a Consultative Committee which shall be convened by the Director from time to time pursuant to Articles 10 and 11 and Annex 4 (2). The Consultative Committee shall be constituted of representatives of the Parties, each Party being entitled to appoint one representative who may be accompanied by advisers. Unless otherwise agreed, the Consultative Committee shall be chaired at any given meeting by the representative of the Party which last hosted the meeting of Heads of Government of Members of the South Pacific Forum. A quorum shall be constituted by representatives of half the Parties. Subject to the provisions of Article 11, decisions of the Consultative Committee shall be taken by consensus or, failing consensus, by a two-thirds majority of those present and voting. The Consultative Committee shall adopt such other rules of procedure as it sees fit.

2.   The costs of the Consultative Committee, including the costs of special inspections pursuant to Annex 4, shall be borne by the South Pacific Bureau for Economic Cooperation. It may seek special funding should this be required.

Annex 4
Complaints Procedure

1.   A Party which considers that there are grounds for a complaint that another Party is in breach of its obligations under this Treaty shall, before bringing such a complaint to the Director, bring the subject matter of the complaint to the attention of the Party complained of and shall allow the latter reasonable opportunity to provide it with an explanation and to resolve the matter.

2.   If the matter is not so resolved, the complainant Party may bring the complaint to the Director with a request that the Consultative Committee be convened to consider it. Complaints shall be supported by an account of evidence of breach of obligations known to the complainant Party. Upon receipt of a complaint the Director shall convene the Consultative Committee as quickly as possible to consider it.

3.   The Consultative Committee, taking account of efforts made under paragraph 1, shall afford the Party complained of a reasonable opportunity to provide it with an explanation of the matter.

4.   If, after considering any explanation given to it by the representatives of the Party complained of, the Consultative Committee decides that there is sufficient substance in the complaint to warrant a special inspection in the territory of that Party or elsewhere, the Consultative Committee shall direct that such special inspection be made as quickly as possible by a special inspection team of three suitably qualified special inspectors appointed by the Consultative

Committee in consultation with the complained of and complainant Parties, provided that no national of either Party shall serve on the special inspection team. If so requested by the Party complained of, the special inspection team shall be accompanied by representatives of that Party. Neither the right of consultation on the appointment of special inspectors, nor the right to accompany special inspectors, shall delay the work of the special inspection team.

5.   In making a special inspection, special inspectors shall be subject to the direction only of the Consultative Committee and shall comply with such directives concerning tasks, objectives, confidentiality and procedures as may be decided upon by it. Directives shall take account of the legitimate interests of the Party complained of in complying with its other international obligations and commitments and shall not duplicate safeguards procedures to be undertaken by the IAEA pursuant to agreements referred to in Annex 2 (1). The special inspectors shall discharge their duties with due respect for the laws of the Party complained of.

6.   Each Party shall give to special inspectors full and free access to all information and places within its territory which may be relevant to enable the special inspectors to implement the directives given to them by the Consultative Committee.

7.   The Party complained of shall take all appropriate steps to facilitate the special inspection, and shall grant to

special inspectors privileges and immunities necessary for the performance of their functions, including inviolability for all papers and documents and immunity from arrest, detention and legal process for acts done and words spoken and written, for the purpose of the special inspection.

8.   The special inspectors shall report in writing as quickly as possible to the Consultative Committee, outlining their activities, setting out relevant facts and information as ascertained by them, with supporting evidence and documentation as appropriate, and stating their conclusions. The Consultative Committee shall report fully to all Members of the South Pacific Forum, giving its decision as to whether the Party complained of is in breach of its obligations under this Treaty.

9.   If the Consultative Committee has decided that the Party complained of is in breach of its obligations under this Treaty, or that the above provisions have not been complied with, or at any time at the request of either the complainant or complained of Party, the Parties shall meet promptly at a meeting of the South Pacific Forum.

Protocol 1

The Parties to this Protocol

NOTING the South Pacific Nuclear Free Zone Treaty (the Treaty)

HAVE AGREED as follows:

Article 1

Each Party undertakes to apply, in respect of the territories for which it is internationally responsible situated within the South Pacific Nuclear Free Zone, the prohibitions contained in Articles 3, 5 and 6, insofar as they related to the manufacture, stationing and testing of any nuclear explosive device within those territories, and the safeguards specified in Article 8(2)(c) and Annex 2 of the Treaty.

Article 2

Each Party may, by written notification to the depositary, indicate its acceptance from the date of such notification of any alteration to its obligation under this Protocol brought about by the entry into force of an amendment to the Treaty pursuant to Article 11 of the Treaty.

Article 3

This Protocol shall be open for signature by the French Republic, the United Kingdom of Great Britain and Northern Ireland and the United States of America.

Article 4

This Protocol shall be subject to ratification.

Article 5

This Protocol is of a permanent nature and shall remain in force indefinitely, provided that each Party shall, in exercising its national sovereignty, have the right to withdraw from this Protocol if it decides that extraordinary events, related to the subject matter of this Protocol, have jeopardised its supreme interests. It shall give notice of such withdrawal to the depositary three months in advance. Such notice shall include a statement of the extraordinary events it regards as having jeopardised its supreme interests.

Article 6

This Protocol shall enter into force for each State on the date of its deposit with the depositary of its instrument of ratification.

IN WITNESS WHEREOF the undersigned, being duly authorized by their Governments, have signed this Protocol.

DONE at Suva, this Eighth day of August, One thousand nine hundred and eighty-six, in a single original in the English language.

Protocol 2

The Parties to this Protocol

NOTING the South Pacific Nuclear Free Zone Treaty (the Treaty)

HAVE AGREED as follows:

Article 1

Each Party undertakes not to use or threaten to use any nuclear explosive device against:

(a)   Parties to the Treaty; or

(b)   any territory within the South Pacific Nuclear Free Zone for which a State that has become a Party to Protocol 1 is internationally responsible.

Article 2

Each Party undertakes not to contribute to any act of a Party to the Treaty which constitutes a violation of the Treaty, or to any act of another Party to a Protocol which constitutes a violation of a Protocol.

Article 3

Each Party may, by written notification to the depositary, indicate its acceptance from the date of such notification of any alteration to its obligation under this

Protocol brought about by the entry into force of an amendment to the Treaty pursuant to Article 11 of the Treaty or by the extension of the South Pacific Nuclear Free Zone pursuant to Article 12(3) of the Treaty.

Article 4

This Protocol shall be open for signature by the French Republic, the People's Republic of China, the Union of Soviet Socialist Republics, the United Kingdom of Great Britain and Northern Ireland and the United States of America.

Article 5

This Protocol shall be subject to ratification.

Article 6

This Protocol is of a permanent nature and shall remain in force indefinitely, provided that each Party shall, in exercising its national sovereignty, have the right to withdraw from this Protocol if it decides that extraordinary events, related to the subject matter of this Protocol, have jeopardised its supreme interests. It shall give notice of such withdrawal to the depositary three months in advance. Such notice shall include a statement of the extraordinary events it regards as having jeopardised its supreme interests.

Article 7

This Protocol shall enter into force for each State on the date of its deposit with the depositary of its instrument of ratification.

IN WITNESS WHEREOF the undersigned, being duly authorized by their Governments, have signed this Protocol.

DONE at Suva, this Eighth day of August, One thousand nine hundred and eighty-six, in a single original in the English language.

Protocol 3

The Parties to this Protocol

NOTING the South Pacific Nuclear Free Zone Treaty (the Treaty)

HAVE AGREED as follows:

Article 1

Each Party undertakes not to test any nuclear explosive device anywhere within the South Pacific Nuclear Free Zone.

Article 2

Each Party may, by written notification to the depositary, indicate its acceptance from the date of such notification of any alteration to its obligation under this Protocol brought about by the entry into force of an amendment to the Treaty pursuant to Article 11 of the Treaty or by the extension of the South Pacific Nuclear Free Zone pursuant to Article 12(3) of the Treaty.

Article 3

This Protocol shall be open for signature by the French Republic, the People's Republic of China, the Union of Soviet Socialist Republics, the United Kingdom of Great Britain and Northern Ireland and the United States of America.

Article 4

This Protocol shall be subject to ratification.

Article 5

This Protocol is of a permanent nature and shall remain in force indefinitely, provided that each Party shall, in exercising its national sovereignty, have the right to withdraw from this Protocol if it decides that extraordinary events, related to the subject matter of this Protocol, have jeopardised its supreme interests. It shall give notice of such withdrawal to the depositary three months in advance. Such notice shall include a statement of the extraordinary events it regards as having jeopardised its supreme interests.

Article 6

This Protocol shall enter into force for each State on the date of its deposit with the depositary of its instrument of ratification.

IN WITNESS WHEREOF the undersigned, being duly authorised by their Governments, have signed this Protocol.

DONE at Suva this Eighth day of August, One thousand nine hundred and eighty-six, in a single original in the English language.

Treaty on the Southeast Asia Nuclear Weapon-Free Zone (Bangkok Treaty)

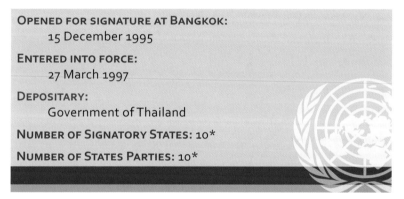

OPENED FOR SIGNATURE AT BANGKOK:
15 December 1995

ENTERED INTO FORCE:
27 March 1997

DEPOSITARY:
Government of Thailand

NUMBER OF SIGNATORY STATES: 10*

NUMBER OF STATES PARTIES: 10*

* As at 28 November 2014. For the updated adherence status, see http://disarmament.un.org/treaties/.

TEXT:

The States Parties to this Treaty:

DESIRING to contribute to the realization of the purposes and principles of the Charter of the United Nations;

DETERMINED to take concrete action which will contribute to the progress towards general and complete disarmament of nuclear weapons, and to the promotion of international peace and security;

REAFFIRMING the desire of the Southeast Asian States to maintain peace and stability in the region in the spirit of peaceful coexistence and mutual understanding and cooperation as enunciated in various communiqués, declarations and other legal instruments;

RECALLING the Declaration on the Zone of Peace, Freedom and Neutrality (ZOPFAN) signed in Kuala Lumpur on 27 November 1971 and the Programme of Action on ZOPFAN adopted at the 26th ASEAN Ministerial Meeting in Singapore in July 1993;

CONVINCED that the establishment of a Southeast Asia Nuclear Weapon-Free Zone, as an essential component of the ZOPFAN, will contribute towards strengthening the security of States within the Zone and towards enhancing international peace and security as a whole;

REAFFIRMING the importance of the Treaty on the Non-Proliferation of Nuclear Weapons (NPT) in preventing the proliferation of nuclear weapons and in contributing towards international peace and security;

RECALLING Article VII of the NPT which recognizes the right of any group of States to conclude regional treaties in order to assure the total absence of nuclear weapons in their respective territories;

RECALLING the Final Document of the Tenth Special Session of the United Nations General Assembly which encourages the establishment of nuclear weapon-free zones;

RECALLING the Principles and Objectives for Nuclear Non-Proliferation and Disarmament, adopted at the 1995 Review and Extension Conference of the Parties to the NPT, that the cooperation of all the nuclear-weapon States and their respect and support for the relevant protocols is important for the maximum effectiveness of this nuclear weapon-free zone treaty and its relevant protocols.

DETERMINED to protect the region from environmental pollution and the hazards posed by radioactive wastes and other radioactive material;

HAVE AGREED as follows:

Article 1
Use of Terms

For the purposes of this Treaty and its Protocol:

(a) "Southeast Asia Nuclear Weapon-Free Zone", hereinafter referred to as the "Zone", means the area comprising the territories of all States in Southeast Asia, namely, Brunei Darussalam, Cambodia, Indonesia, Laos, Malaysia, Myanmar, Philippines, Singapore, Thailand and Vietnam, and their respective continental shelves and Exclusive Economic Zones (EEZ);

(b) "territory" means the land territory, internal waters, territorial sea, archipelagic waters, the seabed and the subsoil thereof and the airspace above them;

(c) "nuclear weapon" means any explosive device capable of releasing nuclear energy in an uncontrolled manner but does not include the means of transport or delivery of such device if separable from and not an indivisible part thereof;

(d) "station" means to deploy, emplace, implant, install, stockpile or store;

(e) "radioactive material" means material that contains radionuclides above clearance or exemption levels recommended by the International Atomic Energy Agency (IAEA);

(f) "radioactive wastes" means material that contains or is contaminated with radionuclides at concentrations or activities greater than clearance levels recommended by the IAEA and for which no use is foreseen; and

(g) "dumping" means

(i) any deliberate disposal at sea, including seabed and subsoil insertion, of radioactive wastes or other matter from vessels, aircraft, platforms or other man-made structures at sea, and

(ii) any deliberate disposal at sea, including seabed and subsoil insertion, of vessels, aircraft, platforms or other man-made structures at sea, containing radioactive material,

but does not include the disposal of wastes or other matter incidental to, or derived from the normal operations of vessels, aircraft, platforms or other man-made structures at sea and their equipment, other than wastes or other matter transported by or to vessels, aircraft, platforms or other man-made structures at sea, operating for the purpose of disposal of such matter or derived from the treatment of such wastes or other matter on such vessels, aircraft, platforms or structures.

Article 2
Application of the Treaty

1.   This Treaty and its Protocol shall apply to the territories, continental shelves, and EEZ of the States Parties within the Zone in which this Treaty is in force.

2.   Nothing in this Treaty shall prejudice the rights or the exercise of these rights by any State under the provisions of the United Nations Convention on the Law of the Sea of 1982, in particular with regard to freedom of the high seas, rights of innocent passage, archipelagic sea lanes passage or transit passage of ships and aircraft, and consistent with the Charter of the United Nations.

Article 3
Basic Undertakings

1.   Each State Party undertakes not to, anywhere inside or outside the Zone:

(a)   develop, manufacture or otherwise acquire, possess or have control over nuclear weapons;

(b)   station or transport nuclear weapons by any means; or

(c)   test or use nuclear weapons.

2.   Each State Party also undertakes not to allow, in its territory, any other State to:

(a)   develop, manufacture or otherwise acquire, possess or have control over nuclear weapons;

(b)   station nuclear weapons; or

(c)   test or use nuclear weapons.

3.   Each State Party also undertakes not to:

(a)   dump at sea or discharge into the atmosphere anywhere within the Zone any radioactive material or wastes;

(b)   dispose radioactive material or wastes on land in the territory of or under the jurisdiction of other States except as stipulated in Paragraph 2 (e) of Article 4; or

(c)   allow, within its territory, any other State to dump at sea or discharge into the atmosphere any radioactive material or wastes.

4.   Each State Party undertakes not to:

(a)   seek or receive any assistance in the commission of any act in violation of the provisions of Paragraphs 1, 2 and 3 of this Article; or

(b)   take any action to assist or encourage the commission of any act in violation of the provisions of Paragraphs 1, 2 and 3 of this Article.

Article 4
Use of Nuclear Energy for Peaceful Purposes

1.   Nothing in this Treaty shall prejudice the right of the States Parties to use nuclear energy, in particular for their economic development and social progress.

2.   Each State Party therefore undertakes:

(a)   to use exclusively for peaceful purposes nuclear material and facilities which are within its territory and areas under its jurisdiction and control;

(b)   prior to embarking on its peaceful nuclear energy programme, to subject its programme to rigorous nuclear safety assessment conforming to guidelines and standards recommended by the IAEA for the protection of health and minimization of danger to life and property in accordance with Paragraph 6 of Article III of the Statute of the IAEA;

(c)   upon request, to make available to another State Party the assessment except information relating to personal data, information protected by intellectual property rights or by industrial or commercial confidentiality, and information relating to national security;

(d)   to support the continued effectiveness of the international non-proliferation system based on the Treaty on the Non-Proliferation of Nuclear Weapons (NPT) and the IAEA safeguards system; and

(e)   to dispose radioactive wastes and other radioactive material in accordance with IAEA standards and procedures on land within its territory or on land within the territory of another State which has consented to such disposal.

3.   Each State Party further undertakes not to provide source or special fissionable material, or equipment or material especially designed or prepared for the processing, use or production of special fissionable material to:

(a)   any non-nuclear-weapon State except under conditions subject to the safeguards required by Paragraph 1 of Article III of the NPT; or

(b)   any nuclear-weapon State except in conformity with applicable safeguards agreements with the IAEA.

Article 5
IAEA Safeguards

Each State Party which has not done so shall conclude an agreement with the IAEA for the application of full scope safeguards to its peaceful nuclear activities not later than eighteen months after the entry into force for that State Party of this Treaty.

Article 6
Early Notification of a Nuclear Accident

Each State Party which has not acceded to the Convention on Early Notification of a Nuclear Accident shall endeavour to do so.

Article 7
Foreign Ships and Aircraft

Each State Party, on being notified, may decide for itself whether to allow visits by foreign ships and aircraft to its ports and airfields, transit of its airspace by foreign aircraft, and navigation by foreign ships through its territorial sea or archipelagic waters and overflight of foreign aircraft above those waters in a manner not governed by the rights of innocent passage, archipelagic sea lanes passage or transit passage.

Article 8
Establishment of the Commission for the Southeast Asia Nuclear Weapon-Free Zone

1.   There is hereby established a Commission for the Southeast Asia Nuclear Weapon-Free Zone, hereinafter referred to as the "Commission".

2.   All States Parties are ipso facto members of the Commission. Each State Party shall be represented by its Foreign Minister or his representative accompanied by alternates and advisers.

3.   The function of the Commission shall be to oversee the implementation of this Treaty and ensure compliance with its provisions.

4.   The Commission shall meet as and when necessary in accordance with the provisions of this Treaty including upon the request of any State Party. As far as possible, the Commission shall meet in conjunction with the ASEAN Ministerial Meeting.

5.   At the beginning of each meeting, the Commission shall elect its Chairman and such other officers as may be required. They shall hold office until a new Chairman and other officers are elected at the next meeting.

6.   Unless otherwise provided for in this Treaty, two-thirds of the members of the Commission shall be present to constitute a quorum.

7.   Each member of the Commission shall have one vote.

8.   Except as provided for in this Treaty, decisions of the Commission shall be taken by consensus or, failing consensus, by a two-thirds majority of the members present and voting.

9.   The Commission shall, by consensus, agree upon and adopt rules of procedure for itself as well as financial rules governing its funding and that of its subsidiary organs.

Article 9
The Executive Committee

1.   There is hereby established, as a subsidiary organ of the Commission, the Executive Committee.

2.   The Executive Committee shall be composed of all States Parties to this Treaty. Each State Party shall be represented by one senior official as its representative, who may be accompanied by alternates and advisers.

3.   The functions of the Executive Committee shall be to:

(a)   ensure the proper operation of verification measures in accordance with the provisions on the Control System as stipulated in Article 10;

(b)   consider and decide on requests for clarification and for a fact-finding mission;

(c)   set up a fact-finding mission in accordance with the Annex of this Treaty;

(d)   consider and decide on the findings of a fact-finding mission and report to the Commission;

(e)   request the Commission to convene a meeting when appropriate and necessary;

(f)   conclude such agreements with the IAEA or other international organizations as referred to in Article 18 on behalf of the Commission after being duly authorized to do so by the Commission; and

(g)   carry out such other tasks as may, from time to time, be assigned by the Commission.

4.   The Executive Committee shall meet as and when necessary for the efficient exercise of its functions. As far as possible, the Executive Committee shall meet in conjunction with the ASEAN Senior Officials Meeting.

5.   The Chairman of the Executive Committee shall be the representative of the Chairman of the Commission. Any submission or communication made by a State Party to the Chairman of the Executive Committee shall be disseminated to the other members of the Executive Committee.

6.   Two-thirds of the members of the Executive Committee shall be present to constitute a quorum.

7. Each member of the Executive Committee shall have one vote.

8. Decisions of the Executive Committee shall be taken by consensus or, failing consensus, by a two-thirds majority of the members present and voting.

Article 10
Control System

1. There is hereby established a control system for the purpose of verifying compliance with the obligations of the States Parties under this Treaty.

2. The Control System shall comprise:

(a) the IAEA safeguards system as provided for in Article 5;

(b) report and exchange of information as provided for in Article 11;

(c) request for clarification as provided for in Article 12; and

(d) request and procedures for a fact-finding mission as provided for in Article 13.

Article 11
Report and Exchange of Information

1.   Each State Party shall submit reports to the Executive Committee on any significant event within its territory and areas under its jurisdiction and control affecting the implementation of this Treaty.

2.   The States Parties may exchange information on matters arising under or in relation to this Treaty.

Article 12
Request for Clarification

1.   Each State Party shall have the right to request another State Party for clarification concerning any situation which may be considered ambiguous or which may give rise to doubts about the compliance of that State Party with this Treaty. It shall inform the Executive Committee of such a request. The requested State Party shall duly respond by providing without delay the necessary information and inform the Executive Committee of its reply to the requesting State Party.

2.   Each State Party shall have the right to request the Executive Committee to seek clarification from another State Party concerning any situation which may be considered ambiguous or which may give rise to doubts about compliance of that State Party with this Treaty. Upon receipt of such a request, the Executive Committee shall consult the

State Party from which clarification is sought for the purpose of obtaining the clarification requested.

Article 13
Request for a Fact-Finding Mission

A State Party shall have the right to request the Executive Committee to send a fact-finding mission to another State Party in order to clarify and resolve a situation which may be considered ambiguous or which may give rise to doubts about compliance with the provisions of this Treaty, in accordance with the procedure contained in the Annex to this Treaty.

Article 14
Remedial Measures

1.   In case the Executive Committee decides in accordance with the Annex that there is a breach of this Treaty by a State Party, that State Party shall, within a reasonable time, take all steps necessary to bring itself in full compliance with this Treaty and shall promptly inform the Executive Committee of the action taken or proposed to be taken by it.

2.   Where a State Party fails or refuses to comply with the provisions of Paragraph 1 of this Article, the Executive Committee shall request the Commission to convene a meeting in accordance with the provisions of Paragraph 3 (e) of Article 9.

3. At the meeting convened pursuant to Paragraph 2 of this Article, the Commission shall consider the emergent situation and shall decide on any measure it deems appropriate to cope with the situation, including the submission of the matter to the IAEA and, where the situation might endanger international peace and security, the Security Council and the General Assembly of the United Nations.

4. In the event of breach of the Protocol attached to this Treaty by a State Party to the Protocol, the Executive Committee shall convene a special meeting of the Commission to decide on appropriate measures to be taken.

Article 15
Signature, Ratification, Accession, Deposit and Registration

1. This Treaty shall be open for signature by all States in Southeast Asia, namely, Brunei Darussalam, Cambodia, Indonesia, Laos, Malaysia, Myanmar, Philippines, Singapore, Thailand and Vietnam.

2. This Treaty shall be subject to ratification in accordance with the constitutional procedure of the signatory States. The instruments of ratification shall be deposited with the Government of the Kingdom of Thailand which is hereby designated as the Depositary State.

3. This Treaty shall be open for accession. The instruments of accession shall be deposited with the Depositary State.

4. The Depositary State shall inform the other States Parties to this Treaty on the deposit of instruments of ratification or accession.

5. The Depositary State shall register this Treaty and its Protocol pursuant to Article 102 of the Charter of the United Nations.

Article 16
Entry into Force

1. This Treaty shall enter into force on the date of the deposit of the seventh instrument of ratification and/or accession.

2. For States which ratify or accede to this Treaty after the date of this seventh instrument of ratification or accession, this Treaty shall enter into force on the date of deposit of its instrument of ratification or accession.

Article 17
Reservations

This Treaty shall not be subject to reservations.

Article 18
Relations with Other International Organizations

The Commission may conclude such agreements with the IAEA or other international organizations as it considers likely to facilitate the efficient operation of the Control System established by this Treaty.

Article 19
Amendments

1.   Any State Party may propose amendments to this Treaty and its Protocol and shall submit its proposals to the Executive Committee, which shall transmit them to all the other States Parties. The Executive Committee shall immediately request the Commission to convene a meeting to examine the proposed amendments. The quorum required for such a meeting shall be all the members of the Commission. Any amendment shall be adopted by a consensus decision of the Commission.

2.   Amendments adopted shall enter into force 30 days after the receipt by the Depositary State of the seventh instrument of acceptance from the States Parties.

Article 20
Review

Ten years after this Treaty enters into force, a meeting of the Commission shall be convened for the purpose of reviewing the operation of this Treaty. A meeting of the Commission for the same purpose may also be convened at anytime thereafter if there is consensus among all its members.

Article 21
Settlement of Disputes

Any dispute arising from the interpretation of the provisions of this Treaty shall be settled by peaceful means as may be agreed upon by the States Parties to the dispute. If within one month, the parties to the dispute are unable to achieve a peaceful settlement of the dispute by negotiation, mediation, enquiry or conciliation, any of the parties concerned shall, with the prior consent of the other parties concerned, refer the dispute to arbitration or to the International Court of Justice.

Article 22
Duration and Withdrawal

1.   This Treaty shall remain in force indefinitely.

2.   In the event of a breach by any State Party of this Treaty essential to the achievement of the objectives of this Treaty, every other State Party shall have the right to withdraw from this Treaty.

3.   Withdrawal under Paragraph 2 of Article 22, shall be effected by giving notice twelve months in advance to the members of the Commission.

IN WITNESS WHEREOF, the undersigned have signed this Treaty.

DONE at Bangkok, this fifteenth day of December, one thousand nine hundred and ninety-five, in one original in the English language.

Annex
Procedure for a Fact-Finding Mission

1.   The State Party requesting a fact-finding mission as provided in Article 13, hereinafter referred to as the "requesting State", shall submit the request to the Executive Committee specifying the following:

(a)   the doubts or concerns and the reasons for such doubts or concerns;

(b)   the location in which the situation which gives rise to doubts has allegedly occurred;

(c)   the relevant provisions of this Treaty about which doubts of compliance have arisen; and

(d)   any other relevant information.

2.   Upon receipt of a request for a fact-finding mission, the Executive Committee shall:

(a)   immediately inform the State Party to which the fact-finding mission is requested to be sent, hereinafter referred to as the "receiving State", about the receipt of the request; and

(b)   not later than 3 weeks after receiving the request, decide if the request complies with the provisions of Paragraph 1 and whether or not it is frivolous, abusive or clearly beyond the scope of this Treaty. Neither the requesting nor receiving State Party shall participate in such decisions.

3.   In case the Executive Committee decides that the request does not comply with the provisions of Paragraph 1, or that it is frivolous, abusive or clearly beyond the scope of this Treaty, it shall take no further action on the request and inform the requesting State and the receiving State accordingly.

4.   In the event that the Executive Committee decides that the request complies with the provisions of Paragraph 1, and that it is not frivolous, abusive or clearly beyond the scope of this Treaty, it shall immediately forward the request for a fact-finding mission to the receiving State, indicating, inter alia, the proposed date for sending the mission. The proposed date shall not be later than 3 weeks from the time the receiving State receives the request for a fact-finding mission. The Executive Committee shall also immediately set up a fact-finding mission consisting of 3 inspectors from the IAEA who are neither nationals of the requesting nor receiving State.

5.   The receiving State shall comply with the request for a fact-finding mission referred to in Paragraph 4. It shall cooperate with the Executive Committee in order to facilitate the effective functioning of the fact-finding mission, inter alia, by promptly providing unimpeded access of the fact-finding mission to the location in question. The receiving State shall accord to the members of the fact-finding mission such privileges and immunities as are necessary for them to

exercise their functions effectively, including inviolability of all papers and documents and immunity from arrest, detention and legal process for acts done and words spoken for the purpose of the mission.

6. The receiving State shall have the right to take measures to protect sensitive installations and to prevent disclosures of confidential information and data not related to this Treaty.

7. The fact-finding mission, in the discharge of its functions, shall:

(a) respect the laws and regulations of the receiving State;

(b) refrain from activities inconsistent with the objectives and purposes of this Treaty;

(c) submit preliminary or interim reports to the Executive Committee; and

(d) complete its task without undue delay and shall submit its final report to the Executive Committee within a reasonable time upon completion of its work.

8. The Executive Committee shall:

(a) consider the reports submitted by the fact-finding mission and reach a decision on whether or not there is a breach of this Treaty;

(b) immediately communicate its decision to the requesting State and the receiving State; and

(c) present a full report on its decision to the Commission.

9.   In the event that the receiving State refuses to comply with the request for a fact-finding mission in accordance with Paragraph 4, the requesting State through the Executive Committee shall have the right to request for a meeting of the Commission. The Executive Committee shall immediately request the Commission to convene a meeting in accordance with Paragraph 3(e) of Article 9.

Protocol to the Treaty on the Southeast Asia Nuclear Weapon-Free Zone

The States Parties to this Protocol,

DESIRING to contribute to efforts towards achieving general and complete disarmament of nuclear weapons, and thereby ensuring international peace and security, including in Southeast Asia;

NOTING the Treaty on the Southeast Asia Nuclear Weapon-Free Zone, signed at Bangkok on the fifteenth day of December, one thousand nine hundred and ninety-five;

HAVE AGREED as follows:

Article 1

Each State Party undertakes to respect the Treaty on the Southeast Asia Nuclear Weapon-Free Zone, hereinafter referred to as the "Treaty", and not to contribute to any act which constitutes a violation of the Treaty or its Protocol by States Parties to them.

Article 2

Each State Party undertakes not to use or threaten to use nuclear weapons against any State Party to the Treaty. It further undertakes not to use or threaten to use nuclear weapons within the Southeast Asia Nuclear Weapon-Free Zone.

Article 3

This Protocol shall be open for signature by the People's Republic of China, the French Republic, the Russian Federation, the United Kingdom of Great Britain and Northern Ireland and the United States of America.

Article 4

Each State Party undertakes, by written notification to the Depositary State, to indicate its acceptance or otherwise of any alteration to its obligation under this Protocol that may be brought about by the entry into force of an amendment to the Treaty pursuant to Article 19 thereof.

Article 5

This Protocol is of a permanent nature and shall remain in force indefinitely, provided that each State Party shall, in exercising its national sovereignty, have the right to withdraw from this Protocol if it decides that extraordinary events, related to the subject-matter of this Protocol, have jeopardized its supreme national interests. It shall give notice of such withdrawal to the Depositary State twelve months in advance. Such notice shall include a statement of the extraordinary events it regards as having jeopardized its supreme national interests.

Article 6

This Protocol shall be subject to ratification.

Article 7

This Protocol shall enter into force for each State Party on the date of its deposit of its instrument of ratification with the Depositary State. The Depositary State shall inform the other States Parties to the Treaty and to this Protocol on the deposit of instruments of ratification.

IN WITNESS WHEREOF the undersigned, being duly authorized by their Governments, have signed this Protocol.

DONE at Bangkok this fifteenth day of December, one thousand nine hundred and ninety-five, in one original in the English language.

African Nuclear Weapon-Free Zone Treaty (Treaty of Pelindaba)

SIGNED AT CAIRO:
   11 April 1996

ENTERED INTO FORCE:
   15 July 2009

DEPOSITARY:
   African Union

NUMBER OF SIGNATORY STATES: 50*

NUMBER OF STATES PARTIES: 37*

˙ As at 28 November 2014. For the updated adherence status, see http://disarmament.un.org/treaties/.

TEXT:

The Parties to this Treaty,

Guided by the Declaration on the Denuclearization of Africa, adopted by the Assembly of Heads of State and Government of the Organization of African Unity (hereinafter referred to as OAU) at its first ordinary session, held at Cairo from 17 to 21 July 1964 (AHG/Res.11(1)), in which they solemnly declared their readiness to undertake, through an international agreement to be concluded under

United Nations auspices, not to manufacture or acquire control of nuclear weapons,

Guided also, by the resolutions of the fifty-fourth and fifty-sixth ordinary sessions of the Council of Ministers of OAU, held at Abuja from 27 May to 1 June 1991 and at Dakar from 22 to 28 June 1992 respectively (CM/Res.1342 (LIV) and CM/Res.1395 (LVI)), which affirmed that the evolution of the international situation was conducive to the implementation of the Cairo Declaration, as well as the relevant provisions of the 1986 OAU Declaration on Security, Disarmament and Development,

Recalling United Nations General Assembly resolution 3472 B (XXX) of 11 December 1975, in which it considered nuclear-weapon-free zones one of the most effective means for preventing the proliferation, both horizontal and vertical, of nuclear weapons,

Convinced of the need to take all steps in achieving the ultimate goal of a world entirely free of nuclear weapons, as well as of the obligations of all States to contribute to this end,

Convinced also that the African nuclear-weapon-free zone will constitute an important step towards strengthening the non-proliferation regime, promoting cooperation in the peaceful uses of nuclear energy, promoting general and complete disarmament and enhancing regional and international peace and security.

Aware that regional disarmament measures contribute to global disarmament efforts,

Believing that the African nuclear-weapon-free zone will protect African States against possible nuclear attacks on their territories,

Noting with satisfaction existing NWFZs and recognizing that the establishment of other NWFZs, especially in the Middle East, would enhance the security of States Parties to the African NWFZ,

Reaffirming the importance of the Treaty on the Non-Proliferation of Nuclear Weapons (hereinafter referred to as the NPT) and the need for the implementation of all its provisions,

Desirous of taking advantage of article IV of the NPT, which recognizes the inalienable right of all States Parties to develop research on, production and use of nuclear energy for peaceful purposes without discrimination and to facilitate the fullest possible exchange of equipment, materials and scientific and technological information for such purposes,

Determined to promote regional cooperation for the development and practical application of nuclear energy for peaceful purposes in the interest of sustainable social and economic development of the African continent,

Determined to keep Africa free of environmental pollution by radioactive wastes and other radioactive matter,

Welcoming the cooperation of all States and governmental and non-governmental organizations for the attainment of these objectives,

Have decided by this Treaty to establish the African NWFZ and hereby agree as follows:

Article 1
Definition/Usage of terms

For the purpose of this Treaty and its Protocols:

(a) "African nuclear-weapon-free zone" means the territory of the continent of Africa, islands States members of OAU and all islands considered by the Organization of African Unity in its resolutions to be part of Africa;

(b) "Territory" means the land territory, internal waters, territorial seas and archipelagic waters and the airspace above them as well as the sea bed and subsoil beneath;

(c) "Nuclear explosive device" means any nuclear weapon or other explosive device capable of releasing nuclear energy, irrespective of the purpose for which it could be used. The term includes such a weapon or device in unassembled and partly assembled forms, but does not include the means of transport or delivery of such a weapon or device if separable from and not an indivisible part of it;

(d) "Stationing" means implantation, emplacement, transport on land or inland waters, stockpiling, storage, installation and deployment;

(e) "Nuclear installation" means a nuclear-power reactor, a nuclear research reactor, a critical facility, a conversion plant, a fabrication plant, a reprocessing plant, an isotope separation plant, a separate storage installation and any other installation or location in or at which fresh or irradiated nuclear material or significant quantities of radioactive materials are present.

(f) "Nuclear material" means any source material or special fissionable material as defined in Article XX of the Statute of the International Atomic Energy Agency (IAEA) and as amended from time to time by the IAEA.

Article 2
Application of the Treaty

1. Except where otherwise specified, this Treaty and its Protocols shall apply to the territory within the African nuclear-weapon-free zone, as illustrated in the map in Annex I.

2. Nothing in this Treaty shall prejudice or in any way affect the rights, or the exercise of the rights, of any State under international law with regards to freedom of the seas.

Article 3
Renunciation of nuclear explosive devices

Each Party undertakes:

(a) Not to conduct research on, develop, manufacture, stockpile or otherwise acquire, possess or have control over any nuclear explosive device by any means anywhere;

(b) Not to seek or receive any assistance in the research on, development, manufacture, stockpiling or acquisition, or possession of any nuclear explosive device;

(c) Not to take any action to assist or encourage the research on, development, manufacture, stockpiling or acquisition, or possession of any nuclear explosive device.

Article 4
Prevention of stationing of nuclear explosive devices

1. Each Party undertakes to prohibit, in its territory, the stationing of any nuclear explosive device.

2. Without prejudice to the purposes and objectives of the treaty, each Party in the exercise of its sovereign rights remains free to decide for itself whether to allow visits by foreign ships and aircraft to its ports and airfields, transit of its airspace by foreign aircraft, and navigation by foreign ships in its territorial sea or archipelagic waters in a manner not covered by the rights of innocent passage, archipelagic sea lane passage or transit passage of straits.

Article 5
Prohibition of testing of nuclear explosive devices

Each Party undertakes:

(a)   Not to test any nuclear explosive device;

(b)   To prohibit in its territory the testing of any nuclear explosive device;

(c)   Not to assist or encourage the testing of any nuclear explosive device by any State anywhere.

Article 6
Declaration, dismantling, destruction or conversion of nuclear explosive devices and the facilities for their manufacture

Each Party undertakes:

(a)   To declare any capability for the manufacture of nuclear explosive devices;

(b)   To dismantle and destroy any nuclear explosive device that it has manufactured prior to the coming into force of this Treaty;

(c)   To destroy facilities for the manufacture of nuclear explosive devices or, where possible, to convert them to peaceful uses;

(d)   To permit the International Atomic Energy Agency (hereinafter referred to as IAEA) and the Commission established in article 12 to verify the processes of dismantling and destruction of the nuclear explosive devices, as well as the destruction or conversion of the facilities for their production.

Article 7
Prohibition of dumping of radioactive wastes

Each Party undertakes:

(a)   To effectively implement or to use as guidelines the measures contained in the Bamako Convention on the Ban of the Import into Africa and Control of Transboundary Movement and Management of Hazardous Wastes within Africa in so far as it is relevant to radioactive waste;

(b)   Not to take any action to assist or encourage the dumping of radioactive wastes and other radioactive matter anywhere within the African nuclear-weapon-free zone.

Article 8
Peaceful nuclear activities

1.   Nothing in this Treaty shall be interpreted as to prevent the use of nuclear sciences and technology for peaceful purposes.

2.   As part of their efforts to strengthen their security, stability and development, the Parties undertake to promote

individually and collectively the use of nuclear science and technology for economic and social development. To this end they undertake to establish and strengthen mechanisms for cooperation at the bilateral, subregional and regional levels.

3. Parties are encouraged to make use of the programme of assistance available in IAEA and, in this connection, to strengthen cooperation under the African Regional Cooperation Agreement for Research, Training and Development Related to Nuclear Science and Technology (hereinafter referred to as AFRA).

Article 9
Verification of peaceful uses

Each Party undertakes:

(a) To conduct all activities for the peaceful use of nuclear energy under strict non-proliferation measures to provide assurance of exclusively peaceful uses;

(b) To conclude a comprehensive safeguards agreement with IAEA for the purpose of verifying compliance with the undertakings in subparagraph (a) of this article;

(c) Not to provide source or special fissionable material, or equipment or material especially designed or prepared for the processing, use or production of special fissionable material for peaceful purposes to any non-nuclear-weapon State unless subject to a comprehensive safeguards agreement concluded with IAEA.

Article 10
Physical protection of nuclear materials and facilities

Each Party undertakes to maintain the highest standards of security and effective physical protection of nuclear materials, facilities and equipment to prevent theft or unauthorized use and handling. To that end each Party, inter alia, undertakes to apply measures of physical protection equivalent to those provided for in the Convention on Physical Protection of Nuclear Material and in recommendations and guidelines developed by IAEA for that purpose.

Article 11
Prohibition of armed attack on nuclear installations

Each Party undertakes not to take, or assist, or encourage any action aimed at an armed attack by conventional or other means against nuclear installations in the African nuclear-weapon-free zone.

Article 12
Mechanism for compliance

1.   For the purpose of ensuring compliance with their undertakings under this Treaty, the Parties agree to establish the African Commission on Nuclear Energy (hereinafter referred to as the Commission) as set out in Annex III.

2.   The Commission shall be responsible inter alia for:

(a) Collating the reports and the exchange of information as provided for in article 13;

(b) Arranging consultations as provided for in Annex IV, as well as convening conferences of Parties on the concurrence of simple majority of States Parties on any matter arising from the implementation of the Treaty;

(c) Reviewing the application to peaceful nuclear activities of safeguards by IAEA as elaborated in Annex II;

(d) Bringing into effect the complaints procedure elaborated in Annex IV;

(e) Encouraging regional and sub-regional programmes for cooperation in the peaceful uses of nuclear science and technology;

(f) Promoting international cooperation with extra-zonal States for the peaceful uses of nuclear science and technology.

3. The Commission shall meet in ordinary session once a year, and may meet in extraordinary session as may be required by the complaints and settlement of disputes procedure in Annex IV.

Article 13
Report and exchanges of information

1. Each Party shall submit an annual report to the Commission on its nuclear activities as well as other matters

relating to the Treaty, in accordance with the format for reporting to be developed by the Commission.

2. Each Party shall promptly report to the Commission any significant event affecting the implementation of the Treaty.

3. The Commission shall request the IAEA to provide it with an annual report on the activities of AFRA.

Article 14
Conference of Parties

1. A Conference of all Parties to the Treaty shall be convened by the Depositary as soon as possible after the entry into force of the Treaty to, inter alia, elect members of the Commission and determine its headquarters. Further conferences of States Parties shall be held as necessary and at least every two years, and convened in accordance with paragraph 2 (b) of article 12.

2. The Conference of all Parties to the Treaty shall adopt the Commission's budget and a scale of assessment to be paid by the States Parties.

Article 15
Interpretation of the Treaty

Any dispute arising out of the interpretation of the Treaty shall be settled by negotiation, by recourse to the Commission or another procedure agreed to by the Parties, which may include recourse to an arbitral panel or to the International Court of Justice.

Article 16
Reservations

This Treaty shall not be subject to reservations.

Article 17
Duration

This Treaty shall be of unlimited duration and shall remain in force indefinitely.

Article 18
Signature, ratification and entry into force

1.   This Treaty shall be open for signature by any State in the African nuclear-weapon-free zone. It shall be subject to ratification.

2.   It shall enter into force on the date of deposit of the twenty-eighth instrument of ratification.

3.   For a signatory that ratifies this Treaty after the date of the deposit of the twenty-eighth instrument of ratification, it shall enter into force for that signatory on the date of deposit of its instrument of ratification.

Article 19
Amendments

1.   Any amendments to the Treaty proposed by a Party shall be submitted to the Commission, which shall circulate it to all Parties.

2.   Decision on the adoption of such an amendment shall be taken by a two-thirds majority of the Parties either through written communication to the Commission or through a conference of Parties convened upon the concurrence of a simple majority.

3.   An amendment so adopted shall enter into force for all parties after receipt by the Depositary of the instrument of ratification by the majority of Parties.

Article 20
Withdrawal

1.   Each Party shall, in exercising its national sovereignty, have the right to withdraw from this Treaty if it decides that extraordinary events, related to the subject-matter of this Treaty, have jeopardized its supreme interests.

2.   Withdrawal shall be effected by a Party giving notice, which includes a statement of the extraordinary events it regards as having jeopardized its supreme interest, twelve months in advance to the Depositary. The Depositary shall circulate such notice to all other parties.

Article 21
Depositary functions

1. This Treaty, of which the Arabic, English, French and Portuguese texts are equally authentic, shall be deposited with the Secretary-General of OAU, who is hereby designated as Depositary of the Treaty.

2. The Depositary shall:

    (a) Receive instruments of ratification;

    (b) Register this Treaty and its Protocols pursuant to Article 102 of the Charter of the United Nations;

    (c) Transmit certified copies of the Treaty and its Protocols to all States in the African nuclear-weapon-free zone and to all States eligible to become party to the Protocols to the Treaty, and shall notify them of signatures and ratification of the Treaty and its Protocols.

Article 22
Status of the annexes

The annexes form an integral part of the Treaty. Any reference to this Treaty includes the annexes.

In witness whereof the undersigned, being duly authorized by their Governments, have signed this Treaty.

Annex I
Map of an African
Nuclear-Weapon-Free Zone

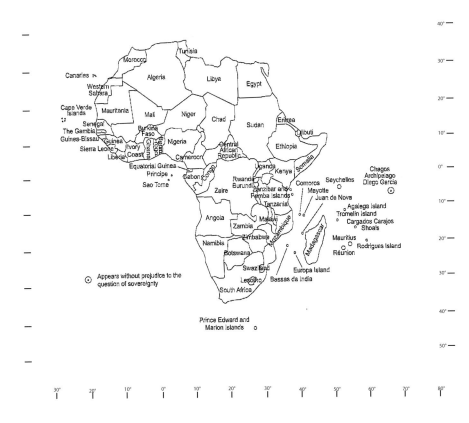

Annex II
Safeguards of the International Atomic Energy Agency

1.   The safeguards referred to in subparagraph (b) of the article 9 shall in respect of each Party be applied by the International Atomic Energy Agency as set forth in an agreement negotiated and concluded with the Agency on all source or special fissionable material in all nuclear activities within the territory of the Party, under its jurisdiction or carried out under its control anywhere.

2.   The Agreement referred to in paragraph 1 above shall be, or shall be equivalent in its scope and effect to, the agreement required in connection with the Treaty on the Non-Proliferation of Nuclear Weapons (INFCIRC/153 corrected). A party that has already entered into a safeguards agreement with the IAEA is deemed to have already complied with the requirement. Each Party shall take all appropriate steps to ensure that the Agreement referred to in paragraph 1 is in force for it not later than eighteen months after the date of entry into force for that Party of this Treaty.

3.   For the purpose of this Treaty, the safeguards referred to in paragraph 1 above shall have as their purpose the verification of the non-diversion of nuclear material from peaceful nuclear activities to nuclear explosive devices or for purposes unknown.

4.   Each Party shall include in its annual report to the Commission, in conformity with article 13, for its information and review, a copy of the overall conclusions of

the most recent report by the International Atomic Energy Agency on its inspection activities in the territory of the Party concerned, and advise the Commission promptly of any change in those conclusions. The information furnished by a Party shall not be, totally or partially, disclosed or transmitted to third parties, by the addressees of the reports, except when that Party gives its express consent.

Annex III
African Commission on Nuclear Energy

1.   The Commission established in article 12 shall be composed of twelve Members elected by Parties to the Treaty for a three-year period, bearing in mind the need for equitable geographical distribution as well as to include Members with advanced nuclear programmes. Each Member shall have one representative nominated with particular regard for his/her expertise in the subject of the Treaty.

2.   The Commission shall have a Bureau consisting of the Chairman, the Vice-Chairman and the Executive Secretary. It shall elect its Chairman and Vice-Chairman. The Secretary-General of the Organization of African Unity, at the request of Parties to the Treaty and in consultation with the Chairman, shall designate the Executive Secretary of the Commission. For the first meeting a quorum shall be constituted by representatives of two thirds of the Members of the Commission. For that meeting decisions of the Commission shall be taken as far as possible by consensus or otherwise by a two-thirds majority of the Members of the Commission. The Commission shall adopt its rules of procedure at that meeting.

3.   The Commission shall develop a format for reporting by States as required under articles 12 and 13.

4.(a) The budget of the Commission, including the costs of inspections pursuant to Annex IV to this Treaty, shall be borne by the Parties to the Treaty in accordance with a scale of assessment to be determined by the Parties;

(b)   The Commission may also accept additional funds from other sources provided such donations are consistent with the purposes and objectives of the Treaty;

Annex IV
Complaints procedure and settlement of disputes

1.   A Party which considers that there are grounds for a complaint that another Party or a Party to Protocol II is in breach of its obligations under this Treaty shall bring the subject-matter of the complaint to the attention of the Party complained of and shall allow the latter thirty days to provide it with an explanation and to resolve the matter. This may include technical visits agreed upon between the Parties.

2.   If the matter is not so resolved, the complaint Party may bring this complaint to the Commission.

3.   The Commission, taking account of efforts made under paragraph 1 above, shall afford the Party complained of forty-five days to provide it with an explanation of the matter.

4.   If, after considering any explanation given to it by the representatives of the Party complained of, the Commission considers that there is sufficient substance in the complaint to warrant an inspection in the territory of that Party or territory of a party to Protocol III, the Commission may request the International Atomic Energy Agency to conduct such inspection as soon as possible. The Commission may also designate its representatives to accompany the Agency's inspectorate team.

(a) The request shall indicate the tasks and objectives of such inspection, as well as any confidentiality requirements;

(b) If the Party complained of so requests, the inspection team shall be accompanied by representatives of that Party provided that the inspectors shall not be thereby delayed or otherwise impeded in the exercise of their functions;

(c) Each Party shall give the inspection team full and free access to all information and places within each territory that may be deemed relevant by the inspectors to the implementation of the inspection;

(d) The Party complained of shall take all appropriate steps to facilitate the work of the inspection team, and shall accord them the same privileges and immunities as those set forth in the relevant provisions of the Agreement on the Privileges and Immunities of the International Atomic Energy Agency;

(e) The International Atomic Energy Agency shall report its findings in writing as quickly as possible to the Commission, outlining its activities, setting out relevant facts and information as ascertained by it, with supporting evidence and documentation as appropriate, and stating its conclusions. The Commission shall report fully to all States Parties to the Treaty giving its decision as to whether the Party complained of is in breach of its obligations under this Treaty;

(f) If the Commission considers that the Party complained of is in breach of its obligations under this Treaty, or that the above provisions have not been complied with, States Parties to the Treaty shall meet in extraordinary session to discuss the matter;

(g) The States Parties convened in extraordinary session may as necessary, make recommendations to the Party held to be in breach of its obligations and to the Organization of African Unity. The Organization of African Unity may, if necessary, refer the matter to the United Nations Security Council;

(h) The costs involved in the procedure outlined above shall be borne by the Commission. In the case of abuse, the Commission shall decide whether the requesting State Party should bear any of the financial implications.

5. The Commission may also establish its own inspection mechanism.

Protocol I

The Parties to this Protocol

Convinced of the need to take all steps in achieving the ultimate goal of a world entirely free of nuclear weapons as well as the obligations of all States to contribute to this end,

Convinced also that the African Nuclear-Weapon-Free Zone Treaty, negotiated and signed in accordance with the Declaration on the Denuclearization of Africa (AHG/Res.II(1)) of 1964, resolutions CM/Res.1342 (LIV) of 1991 and CM/Res.1395 (LVI) Rev.1 of 1992 of the Council of Ministers of the Organization of African Unity and United Nations General Assembly Resolution 48/86 of 16 December 1993, constitutes an important measure towards ensuring the non-proliferation of nuclear weapons, promoting cooperation in the peaceful uses of nuclear energy, promoting general and complete disarmament, and enhancing regional and international peace and security,

Desirous of contributing in all appropriate manners to the effectiveness of the Treaty,

Have agreed as follows:

Article 1

Each Protocol Party undertakes not to use or threaten to use a nuclear explosive device against:

(a)   Any Party to the Treaty; or

(b)   Any territory within the African nuclear-weapon-free zone for which a State that has become a Party to Protocol III is internationally responsible as defined in Annex I.

Article 2

Each Protocol Party undertakes not to contribute to any act that constitutes a violation of the Treaty or of this Protocol.

Article 3

Each Protocol Party undertakes, by written notification to the Depositary, to indicate its acceptance or otherwise of any alteration to its obligation under this Protocol that may be brought about by the entry into force of an amendment to the Treaty pursuant to article 19 of the Treaty.

Article 4

This Protocol shall be open for signature by China, France, the Russian Federation, the United Kingdom of Great Britain and Northern Ireland and the United States of America.

Article 5

This Protocol shall be subject to ratification.

Article 6

This Protocol is of a permanent nature and shall remain in force indefinitely, provided that each Party shall, in exercising its national sovereignty, have the right to withdraw from this Protocol if it decides that extraordinary events, related to the subject–matter of this Protocol, have jeopardized its supreme interests. It shall give notice of such withdrawal to the Depositary twelve months in advance. Such notice shall include a statement of the extraordinary events it regards as having jeopardized its supreme interests.

Article 7

This Protocol shall enter into force for each State on the date of its deposit with the Depositary of its instrument of ratification or the date of entry into force of the Treaty, whichever is later.

In witness whereof the undersigned, being duly authorized by their Governments, have signed this Protocol.

Protocol II

The Parties to this Protocol,

Convinced of the need to take all steps in achieving the ultimate goal of a world entirely free of nuclear weapons as well as the obligations of all States to contribute to this end,

Convinced also that the African Nuclear-Weapon-Free Zone Treaty, negotiated and signed in accordance with the Declaration on the Denuclearization of Africa (AHG/Res.11(1)) of 1964, resolutions CM/Res.1342 (LIV) of 1991 and CM/Res.1395 (LVI)/Rev.1 of 1992 of the Council of Ministers of the Organization of African Unity and United Nations General Assembly resolution 48/86 of 16 December 1993, constitutes an important measure towards ensuring the non-proliferation of nuclear weapons, promoting cooperation in the peaceful uses of nuclear energy, promoting general and complete disarmament, and enhancing regional and international peace and security,

Desirous of contributing in all appropriate manners to the effectiveness of the Treaty,

Bearing in mind the objective of concluding a treaty banning all nuclear tests,

Have agreed as follows:

Article 1

Each Protocol Party undertakes not to test or assist or encourage the testing of any nuclear explosive device anywhere within the African nuclear-weapon-free zone.

Article 2

Each Protocol Party undertakes not to contribute to any act that constitutes a violation of the Treaty or of this Protocol.

Article 3

Each Protocol Party undertakes, by written notification to the Depositary, to indicate its acceptance or otherwise of any alteration to its obligation under this Protocol that may be brought about by the entry into force of an amendment to the Treaty pursuant to article 20 of the Treaty.

Article 4

This Protocol shall be open for signature by China, France, the Russian Federation, the United Kingdom of Great Britain and Northern Ireland and the United States of America.

Article 5

This Protocol shall be subject to ratification.

Article 6

This Protocol is of a permanent nature and shall remain in force indefinitely, provided that each Party shall, in exercising its national sovereignty, have the right to withdraw from this Protocol if it decides that extraordinary events, related to the subject-matter of this Protocol, have jeopardized its supreme interests. It shall give notice of such withdrawal to the Depositary twelve months in advance. Such notice shall include a statement of the extraordinary events it regards as having jeopardized its supreme interests.

Article 7

This Protocol shall enter into force for each State on the date of its deposit with the Depositary of its instrument of ratification or the date of entry into force of the Treaty, whichever is later.

In witness whereof the undersigned, being duly authorized by their Governments, have signed this Protocol.

Protocol III

The Parties to this Protocol,

Convinced of the need to take all steps in achieving the ultimate goal of a world entirely free of nuclear weapons as well as the obligations of all States to contribute to this end,

Convinced also that the African Nuclear-Weapon-Free Zone Treaty, negotiated and signed in accordance with the Declaration on the Denuclearization of Africa (AHG/Res.11(1)) of 1964, resolutions CM/Res.1342 (LIV) of 1991 and CM/Res.1395 (LVI)/Rev.1 of 1992 of the Council of Ministers of the Organization of African Unity and United Nations General Assembly resolution 48/86 of 16 December 1993, constitutes an important measure towards ensuring the non-proliferation of nuclear weapons, promoting cooperation in the peaceful uses of nuclear energy, promoting general and complete disarmament, and enhancing regional and international peace and security,

Desirous of contributing in all appropriate manners to the effectiveness of the Treaty,

Have agreed as follows:

Article 1

Each Protocol Party undertakes to apply, in respect of the territories for which it is de jure or de facto internationally responsible situated within the African nuclear-weapon-free zone, the provisions contained in articles 3, 4, 5, 6, 7, 8, 9 and 10 of the Treaty and to ensure the application of safeguards specified in Annex II of the Treaty.

Article 2

Each Protocol Party undertakes not to contribute to any act that constitutes a violation of the Treaty or of this Protocol.

Article 3

Each Protocol Party undertakes, by written notification to the Depositary, to indicate its acceptance or otherwise of any alterations to its obligation under this Protocol that may be brought about by the entry into force of an amendment to the Treaty pursuant to article 20 of the Treaty.

Article 4

This Protocol shall be open for signature by France and Spain.

Article 5

This Protocol shall be subject to ratification.

Article 6

This Protocol is of a permanent nature and shall remain in force indefinitely provided that each Party shall, in exercising its national sovereignty have the right to withdraw from this Protocol if it decides that extraordinary events, related to the subject-matter of this Protocol, have jeopardized its supreme interests. It shall give notice of such withdrawal to the Depositary twelve months in advance. Such notice shall include a statement of the extraordinary events it regards as having jeopardized its supreme interests.

Article 7

This Protocol shall enter into force for each State on the date of its deposit with the Depositary of its instrument of ratification or the date of entry into force of the Treaty, whichever is later.

In witness whereof the undersigned, being duly authorized by their Governments have signed this Protocol.

Treaty on a Nuclear-Weapon-Free Zone in Central Asia

OPENED FOR SIGNATURE AT SEMIPALATINSK:
8 September 2006

ENTERED INTO FORCE:
21 March 2009

DEPOSITARY:
Government of Kyrgyzstan

NUMBER OF SIGNATORY STATES: 5*

NUMBER OF STATES PARTIES: 5*

* As at 28 November 2014. For the updated adherence status, see http://disarmament.un.org/treaties/.

TEXT:

The Parties to this Treaty,

Guided by the Almaty Declaration of the Heads of State of the Central Asian States adopted on 28 February 1997; the Statement of the Ministers of Foreign Affairs of the five States of the region adopted at Tashkent on 15 September 1997; the United Nations General Assembly resolutions and decisions 52/38 S of 9 December 1997, 53/77 A of 4 December 1998, 55/33 W of 20 December 2000, 57/69 of 22 November 2002, 58/518 of 8 December 2003, 59/513 of

3 December 2004 and 60/516 of 8 December 2005, entitled "Establishment of a nuclear-weapon-free zone in Central Asia", and the Communiqué of the Consultative Meeting of Experts of the Central Asian Countries, the Nuclear-Weapon States and the United Nations adopted at Bishkek on 9 July 1998,

Stressing the need for continued systematic and consistent efforts to reduce nuclear weapons globally, with the ultimate goal of eliminating those weapons, and of general and complete disarmament under strict and effective international control, and *convinced* that all states are obliged to contribute to that end,

Convinced that a Central Asian Nuclear-Weapon-Free Zone will constitute an important step toward strengthening the nuclear non-proliferation regime, promoting cooperation in the peaceful uses of nuclear energy, promoting cooperation in the environmental rehabilitation of territories affected by radioactive contamination, and enhancing regional and international peace and security,

Believing that a Central Asian Nuclear-Weapon-Free Zone will help to promote the security of Central Asian States, particularly if the five Nuclear-Weapon States, as recognized under the Treaty on the Non-Proliferation of Nuclear Weapons of 1968 (hereafter referred to as the NPT) adhere to the accompanying Protocol on security assurances,

Recognizing that a number of regions, including Latin America and the Caribbean, the South Pacific, South-East

Asia and Africa, have created nuclear-weapon-free zones, in which the possession of nuclear weapons, their development, production, introduction and deployment as well as use or threat of use, are prohibited, and *striving* to broaden such regime throughout the planet for the good of all living things,

Reaffirming the obligations set out in the NPT, the Principles and Objectives for Nuclear Non-Proliferation and Disarmament, adopted by the 1995 Review and Extension Conference of the Parties to the NPT, and the Final Document of the 2000 Review Conference of the Parties to the NPT, as well as the principles and objectives set out in the Comprehensive Nuclear-Test-Ban Treaty of 1996 (hereafter referred to as the CTBT),

Have decided to establish a nuclear-weapon-free zone in Central Asia and *have agreed* as follows:

Article 1
Definitions and Usage of Terms

For the purposes of this Treaty and its Protocol:

(a) The "Central Asian Nuclear-Weapon-Free Zone" includes: the Republic of Kazakhstan, the Kyrgyz Republic, the Republic of Tajikistan, Turkmenistan and the Republic of Uzbekistan;

(b) "Nuclear weapon or other nuclear explosive device" means any weapon or other explosive device capable of releasing nuclear energy, irrespective of the military or civilian purpose for which the weapon or device could be used. The term includes such a weapon or device in unassembled or partly assembled forms, but does not include the means of transport or delivery of such a weapon or device if separable from and not an indivisible part of it;

(c) "Stationing" means implantation, emplacement stockpiling, storage, installation and deployment;

(d) "Nuclear material" means any source material or special fissionable material as defined in Article XX of the Statute of the International Atomic Energy Agency (hereinafter referred to as the IAEA), as amended from time to time by the IAEA;

(e) "Radioactive waste" means any radioactive material, i.e. any substance containing radionuclides, that will be or has already been removed and is no longer utilized, at activities and activity concentrations of radionuclides greater than the exemption levels established in international standards issued by the IAEA;

(f) "Facility" means:

(i) a reactor, a critical facility, a conversion plant, a fabrication plant, a reprocessing plant, an isotope separation plant or a separate storage installation; or

(ii) any location where nuclear material in amounts greater than one effective kilogram is customarily used.

Article 2
Application of the Treaty

(a)   The scope of application of a Central Asian Nuclear-Weapon-Free Zone is defined exclusively for the purposes of this Treaty as the land territory, all waters (harbors, lakes, rivers and streams) and the air space above them, which belong to the Republic of Kazakhstan, the Kyrgyz Republic, the Republic of Tajikistan, Turkmenistan and the Republic of Uzbekistan;

(b)   Nothing in this Treaty shall prejudice or in any way affect the rights of any Central Asian States in any dispute concerning the ownership of or sovereignty over lands or waters that may or may not be included within this zone.

Article 3
Basic Obligations

1.   Each Party undertakes:

(a)   Not to conduct research on, develop, manufacture, stockpile or otherwise acquire, possess or have control over any nuclear weapon or other nuclear explosive device by any means anywhere;

(b)   Not to seek or receive any assistance in research on, development, manufacture, stockpiling, acquisition, possession or obtaining control over any nuclear weapon or other nuclear explosive device;

(c) Not to take any action to assist or encourage the conduct of research on, development, manufacture, stockpiling, acquisition or possession of any nuclear weapon or other nuclear explosive device;

(d) Not to allow in its territory:

(i) The production, acquisition, stationing, storage or use, of any nuclear weapon or other nuclear explosive device;

(ii) The receipt, storage, stockpiling, installation or other form of possession of or control over any nuclear weapon or other nuclear explosive device;

(iii) Any actions, by anyone, to assist or encourage the development, production, stockpiling, acquisition, possession of or control over any nuclear weapon or other nuclear explosive device.

2.   Each Party undertakes not to allow the disposal in its territory of radioactive waste of other States.

Article 4
Foreign Ships, Aircraft, and Ground Transportation

Without prejudice to the purposes and objectives of this Treaty, each Party, in the exercise of its sovereign rights, is free to resolve issues related to transit through its territory by air, land or water, including visits by foreign ships to its ports and landing of foreign aircraft at its airfields.

Article 5
Prohibition of Testing of Nuclear Weapons or Other Nuclear Explosive Devices

Each Party undertakes, in accordance with the CTBT:

(a)   Not to carry out any nuclear weapon test explosion or any other nuclear explosion;

(b)   To prohibit and prevent any such nuclear explosion at any place under its jurisdiction or control;

(c)   To refrain from causing, encouraging, or in any way participating in the carrying out of any nuclear weapon test explosion or any other nuclear explosion.

Article 6
Environmental Security

Each Party undertakes to assist any efforts toward the environmental rehabilitation of territories contaminated as a result of past activities related to the development, production or storage of nuclear weapons or other nuclear explosive devices, in particular uranium tailings storage sites and nuclear test sites.

Article 7
Use of Nuclear Energy for Peaceful Purposes

No provision of this Treaty shall prejudice the rights of the Parties to use nuclear energy for peaceful purposes.

Article 8
IAEA Safeguards

Each Party undertakes:

(a) To use for exclusively peaceful purposes the nuclear material and facilities which are within its territory, under its jurisdiction, or under its control anywhere;

(b) To conclude with the IAEA and bring into force, if it has not already done so, an agreement for the application of safeguards in accordance with the NPT (INFCIRC/153 (Corr.)), and an Additional Protocol (INFCIRC/540 (Corr.)) not later than 18 months after the entry into force of this Treaty;

(c) Not to provide: (i) source or special fissionable material or (ii) equipment or material especially designed or prepared for the processing, use or production of special fissionable material, to any non-nuclear-weapon State, unless that State has concluded with the IAEA a comprehensive safeguards agreement and its Additional Protocol referred to in paragraph (b) of this article.

Article 9
Physical Protection of Nuclear Material and Equipment

Each Party undertakes to maintain effective standards of physical protection of nuclear material, facilities and equipment to prevent its unauthorized use or handling or theft. To that end, each Party undertakes to apply measures of physical protection to nuclear material in domestic use, transport and storage, to nuclear material in international transport, and to nuclear facilities within its territory at least as effective as those called for by the Convention on Physical Protection of Nuclear Material of 1987 and by the recommendations and guidelines developed by the IAEA for physical protection.

Article 10
Consultative Meetings

The Parties agree to hold annual meetings of their representatives, on a rotating basis, as well as extraordinary meetings, at the request of any Party, in order to review compliance with this Treaty or other matters related to its implementation.

Article 11
Settlement of Disputes

Disputes between the Parties involving the interpretation or application of this Treaty shall be settled through negotiations or by other means as may be deemed necessary by the Parties.

Article 12
Other Agreements

This Treaty does not affect the rights and obligations of the Parties under other international treaties which they may have concluded prior to the date of the entry into force of this Treaty.

The Parties shall take all necessary measures for effective implementation of the purposes and objectives of this Treaty in accordance with the main principles contained therein.

Article 13
Reservations

This Treaty shall not be subject to reservations.

Article 14
Signature and Ratification

(a) This Treaty shall be open for signature at Semipalatinsk, the Republic of Kazakhstan, by all States of the Central Asian Nuclear-Weapon-Free Zone: the Republic of Kazakhstan, the Kyrgyz Republic, the Republic of Tajikistan, Turkmenistan and the Republic of Uzbekistan.

(b) This Treaty shall be subject to ratification.

Article 15
Entry into Force and Duration

(a) This Treaty shall enter into force 30 days after the date of the deposit of the fifth instrument of ratification.

(b) This Treaty shall be of unlimited duration.

Article 16
Withdrawal from the Treaty

(a)   Any Party may, by written notification addressed to the Depositary, withdraw from the Treaty if it decides that extraordinary events, related to the subject-matter of this Treaty, have jeopardized its supreme national interests. Such notification shall include a statement of the extraordinary events it regards as having jeopardized its supreme national interests.

(b)   Withdrawal shall take effect 12 months after the date of receipt of the notification by the Depositary, who shall circulate such notification to all Parties to the Treaty and to the signatories of the Protocol.

Article 17
Amendments

(a)   Any amendment to this Treaty, proposed by a Party, shall be circulated by it to all Parties and submitted to the Consultative Meeting at least 90 days before the Meeting.

(b)   Decisions on the adoption of such an amendment shall be taken by consensus of the Parties.

(c)   An amendment so adopted shall enter into force for all Parties after receipt by the Depositary of the instrument of ratification of this amendment from all Parties.

Article 18
Depositary

(a)   This Treaty shall be deposited with the Kyrgyz Republic, which is hereby designated as Depositary of this Treaty.

(b)   The Depositary shall, inter alia:

(i)   Provide an opportunity to sign this Treaty and its Protocol and receive instruments of ratification of this Treaty and its Protocol;

(ii)   Register this Treaty and its Protocol pursuant to Article 102 of the Charter of the United Nations;

(iii) Transmit certified copies of this Treaty and its Protocol to all Parties and to all Parties to its Protocol, and notify them of signatures and ratifications of this Treaty and its Protocol.

In witness whereof, the undersigned, being duly authorized, have signed this Treaty.

Done at Semipalatinsk, the Republic of Kazakhstan, this eighth day of September, two thousand six, in one copy in the English and Russian languages, both texts being equally authentic.

Protocol to the Treaty on a Nuclear-Weapon-Free Zone in Central Asia

The Parties to this Protocol,

Recalling the Almaty Declaration of the Heads of State of the Central Asian States adopted on 28 February 1997; the Statement of the Ministers of Foreign Affairs of the five States of the region adopted at Tashkent on 15 September 1997; the United Nations General Assembly resolutions and decisions 52/38 S of 9 December 1997, 53/77 A of 4 December 1998, 55/33 W of 20 November 2000, 57/69 of 22 November 2002, 58/518 of 8 December 2003, 59/513 of 3 December 2004 and 60/516 of 8 December 2005, entitled "Establishment of a nuclear-weapon-free zone in Central Asia"; and the Communiqué of the Consultative Meeting of Experts of the Central Asian Countries, the Nuclear-Weapon States and the United Nations adopted at Bishkek on 9 July 1998,

Convinced of the need to take all steps in achieving the ultimate goal of a world entirely free of nuclear weapons and that all States are obliged to contribute to that goal,

Striving therefore to support the establishment of a Nuclear-Weapon-Free Zone in Central Asia,

Have agreed as follows:

Article 1
Negative Security Assurances

Each Party undertakes not to use or threaten to use a nuclear weapon or other nuclear explosive device against any Party to the Treaty on a nuclear-weapon-free zone in Central Asia (hereinafter referred to as "the Treaty").

Article 2
Not Contributing to Violations

Each Party undertakes not to contribute to any act that constitutes a violation of the Treaty or of this Protocol by Parties to them.

Article 3
Effect of Treaty Amendments

Each Party undertakes, by written notification to the Depositary, to indicate its acceptance or otherwise of any alteration to its obligations under this Protocol that may be brought about by the entry into force of amendments to the Treaty pursuant to Article 17 of the Treaty.

Article 4
Signature

This Protocol shall be open for signature by the People's Republic of China, the French Republic, the Russian Federation, the United Kingdom of Great Britain and Northern Ireland and the United States of America.

Article 5
Ratification

This Protocol shall be subject to ratification.

Article 6
Duration of and Withdrawal from the Protocol

1.   This Protocol is of a permanent nature and shall remain in force indefinitely.

2.   Any Party may, by written notification addressed to the Depositary, withdraw from this Protocol if it decides that extraordinary events, related to the subject-matter of this Protocol, have jeopardized its supreme national interests. Such notification shall include a statement of the extraordinary events it regards as having jeopardized its supreme national interests.

3.   Withdrawal shall take effect 12 months after the date of receipt of the notification by the Depositary, who shall circulate such notification to all Parties to the Treaty and to the signatories of this Protocol.

Article 7
Entry into Force

This Protocol shall enter into force for each Party on the date of its deposit with the Depositary of its instrument of ratification.

In witness whereof, the undersigned, duly authorized by their respective Governments, have signed this Protocol.

DONE at New York, this 6th day of May, 2014, in one original, in the Chinese, English, French and Russian languages, each text being equally authentic. The original of this Protocol shall be deposited with the Kyrgyz Republic.

RELATED TREATIES

Antarctic Treaty

SIGNED AT WASHINGTON:
  1 December 1959

ENTERED INTO FORCE:
  23 June 1961

DEPOSITARY:
  Government of the United States of America

NUMBER OF SIGNATORY STATES: 12*

NUMBER OF STATES PARTIES: 50*

* As at 28 November 2014. For the updated adherence status, see http://disarmament.un.org/treaties/.

TEXT:

The Governments of Argentina, Australia Belgium, Chile, the French Republic, Japan, New Zealand, Norway, the Union of South Africa, the Union of Soviet Socialist Republics, the United Kingdom of Great Britain and Northern Ireland and the United States of America,

Recognizing that it is in the interest of all mankind that Antarctica shall continue forever to be used exclusively for peaceful purposes and shall not become the scene or object of international discord;

Acknowledging the substantial contributions to scientific knowledge resulting from international cooperation in scientific investigation in Antarctica;

Convinced that the establishment of a firm foundation for the continuation and development of such cooperation on the basis of freedom of scientific investigation in Antarctica as applied during the International Geophysical Year accords with the interests of science and the progress of all mankind;

Convinced also that a treaty ensuring the use of Antarctica for peaceful purposes only and the continuance of international harmony in Antarctica will further the purposes and principles embodied in the Charter of the United Nations;

Have agreed as follows:

Article I

1.   Antarctica shall be used for peaceful purposes only. There shall be prohibited, inter alia, any measures of a military nature, such as the establishment of military bases and fortifications, the carrying out of military maneuvers, as well as the testing of any type of weapons.

2.   The present Treaty shall not prevent the use of military personnel or equipment for scientific research or for any other peaceful purpose.

Article II

Freedom of scientific investigation in Antarctica and cooperation toward that end, as applied during the International Geophysical Year, shall continue, subject to the provisions of the present Treaty.

Article III

1. In order to promote international cooperation in scientific investigation in Antarctica, as provided for in Article II of the present Treaty, the Contracting Parties agree that, to the greatest extent feasible and practicable:

(a) information regarding plans for scientific programs in Antarctica shall be exchanged to permit maximum economy and efficiency of operations;

(b) scientific personnel shall be exchanged in Antarctica between expeditions and stations;

(c) scientific observations and results from Antarctica shall be exchanged and made freely available.

2. In implementing this Article, every encouragement shall be given to the establishment of cooperative working relations with those Specialized Agencies of the United Nations and other international organizations having a scientific or technical interest in Antarctica.

Article IV

1.   Nothing contained in the present Treaty shall be interpreted as:

(a)   a renunciation by any Contracting Party of previously asserted rights of or claims to territorial sovereignty in Antarctica;

(b)   a renunciation or diminution by any Contracting Party of any basis of claim to territorial sovereignty in Antarctica which it may have whether as a result of its activities or those of its nationals in Antarctica, or otherwise;

(c)   prejudicing the position of any Contracting Party as regards its recognition or non-recognition of any other State's right of or claim or basis of claim to territorial sovereignty in Antarctica.

2.   No acts or activities taking place while the present Treaty is in force shall constitute a basis for asserting, supporting or denying a claim to territorial sovereignty in Antarctica or create any rights of sovereignty in Antarctica. No new claim, or enlargement of an existing claim, to territorial sovereignty in Antarctica shall be asserted while the present Treaty is in force.

Article V

1.   Any nuclear explosions in Antarctica and the disposal there of radioactive waste material shall be prohibited.

2. In the event of the conclusion of international agreements concerning the use of nuclear energy, including nuclear explosions and the disposal of radioactive waste material, to which all of the Contracting Parties whose representatives are entitled to participate in the meetings provided for under Article IX are parties, the rules established under such agreements shall apply in Antarctica.

Article VI

The provisions of the present Treaty shall apply to the area south of 60° South Latitude, including all ice shelves, but nothing in the present Treaty shall prejudice or in any way affect the rights, or the exercise of the rights, of any State under international law with regard to the high seas within that area.

Article VII

1. In order to promote the objectives and ensure the observance of the provisions of the present Treaty, each Contracting Party whose representatives are entitled to participate in the meetings referred to in Article IX of the Treaty shall have the right to designate observers to carry out any inspection provided for by the present Article. Observers shall be nationals of the Contracting Parties which designate them. The names of observers shall be communicated to every other Contracting Party having the right to designate observers, and like notice shall be given of the termination of their appointment.

2.   Each observer designated in accordance with the provisions of paragraph 1 of this Article shall have complete freedom of access at any time to any or all areas of Antarctica.

3.   All areas of Antarctica, including all stations, installations and equipment within those areas, and all ships and aircraft at points of discharging or embarking cargoes or personnel in Antarctica, shall be open at all times to inspection by any observers designated in accordance with paragraph 1 of this Article.

4.   Aerial observation may be carried out at any time over any or all areas of Antarctica by any of the Contracting Parties having the right to designate observers.

5.   Each Contracting Party shall, at the time when the present Treaty enters into force for it, inform the other Contracting Parties, and thereafter shall give them notice in advance, of

(a)   all expeditions to and within Antarctica, on the part of its ships or nationals, and all expeditions to Antarctica organized in or proceeding from its territory;

(b)   all stations in Antarctica occupied by its nationals; and

(c)   any military personnel or equipment intended to be introduced by it into Antarctica subject to the conditions prescribed in paragraph 2 of Article I of the present Treaty.

Article VIII

1. In order to facilitate the exercise of their functions under the present Treaty, and without prejudice to the respective positions of the Contracting Parties relating to jurisdiction over all other persons in Antarctica, observers designated under paragraph 1 of Article VII and scientific personnel exchanged under subparagraph 1 (b) of Article III of the Treaty, and members of the staffs accompanying any such persons, shall be subject only to the jurisdiction of the Contracting Party of which they are nationals in respect of all acts or omissions occurring while they are in Antarctica for the purpose of exercising their functions.

2. Without prejudice to the provisions of paragraph 1 of this Article, and pending the adoption of measures in pursuance of subparagraph 1 (e) of Article IX, the Contracting Parties concerned in any case of dispute with regard to the exercise of jurisdiction in Antarctica shall immediately consult together with a view to reaching a mutually acceptable solution.

Article IX

1. Representatives of the Contracting Parties named in the preamble to the present Treaty shall meet at the City of Canberra within two months after the date of entry into force of the Treaty, and thereafter at suitable intervals and places, for the purpose of exchanging information, consulting together on matters of common interest pertaining to Antarctica, and formulating and considering,

and recommending to their Governments, measures in furtherance of the principles and objectives of the Treaty, including measures regarding:

(a)   use of Antarctica for peaceful purposes only;

(b)   facilitation of scientific research in Antarctica;

(c)   facilitation of international scientific cooperation in Antarctica;

(d)   facilitation of the exercise of the rights of inspection provided for in Article VII of the Treaty;

(e)   questions relating to the exercise of jurisdiction in Antarctica;

(f)   preservation and conservation of living resources in Antarctica.

2.   Each Contracting Party which has become a party to the present Treaty by accession under Article XIII shall be entitled to appoint representatives to participate in the meetings referred to in paragraph 1 of the present Article, during such time as that Contracting Party demonstrates its interest in Antarctica by conducting substantial scientific research activity there, such as the establishment of a scientific station or the despatch of a scientific expedition.

3.   Reports from the observers referred to in Article VII of the present Treaty shall be transmitted to the representatives

of the Contracting Parties participating in the meetings referred to in paragraph 1 of the present Article.

4.   The measures referred to in paragraph 1 of this Article shall become effective when approved by all the Contracting Parties whose representatives were entitled to participate in the meetings held to consider those measures.

5.   Any or all of the rights established in the present Treaty may be exercised as from the date of entry into force of the Treaty whether or not any measures facilitating the exercise of such rights have been proposed, considered or approved as provided in this Article.

Article X

Each of the Contracting Parties undertakes to exert appropriate efforts, consistent with the Charter of the United Nations, to the end that no one engages in any activity in Antarctica contrary to the principles or purposes of the present Treaty.

Article XI

1.   If any dispute arises between two or more of the Contracting Parties concerning the interpretation or application of the present Treaty, those Contracting Parties shall consult among themselves with a view to having the dispute resolved by negotiation, inquiry, mediation, conciliation, arbitration, judicial settlement or other peaceful means of their own choice.

2.   Any dispute of this character not so resolved shall, with the consent, in each case, of all parties to the dispute, be referred to the International Court of Justice for settlement; but failure to reach agreement on reference to the International Court shall not absolve parties to the dispute from the responsibility of continuing to seek to resolve it by any of the various peaceful means referred to in paragraph 1 of this Article.

Article XII

1.   (a)   The present Treaty may be modified or amended at any time by unanimous agreement of the Contracting Parties whose representatives are entitled to participate in the meetings provided for under Article IX. Any such modification or amendment shall enter into force when the depositary Government has received notice from all such Contracting Parties that they have ratified it.

(b)   Such modification or amendment shall thereafter enter into force as to any other Contracting Party when notice of ratification by it has been received by the depositary Government. Any such Contracting Party from which no notice of ratification is received within a period of two years from the date of entry into force of the modification or amendment in accordance with the provisions of subparagraph 1(a) of this Article shall be deemed to have withdrawn from the present Treaty on the date of the expiration of such period.

2.   (a)   If after the expiration of thirty years from the date of entry into force of the present Treaty, any of the Contracting Parties whose representatives are entitled to participate in the meetings provided for under Article IX so requests by a communication addressed to the depositary Government, a Conference of all the Contracting Parties shall be held as soon as practicable to review the operation of the Treaty.

(b)   Any modification or amendment to the present Treaty which is approved at such a Conference by a majority of the Contracting Parties there represented, including a majority of those whose representatives are entitled to participate in the meetings provided for under Article IX, shall be communicated by the depositary Government to all the Contracting Parties immediately after the termination of the Conference and shall enter into force in accordance with the provisions of paragraph 1 of the present Article.

(c)   If any such modification or amendment has not entered into force in accordance with the provisions of subparagraph 1(a) of this Article within a period of two years after the date of its communication to all the Contracting Parties, any Contracting Party may at any time after the expiration of that period give notice to the depositary Government of its withdrawal from the present Treaty; and such withdrawal shall take effect two years after the receipt of the notice by the depositary Government.

Article XIII

1.   The present Treaty shall be subject to ratification by the signatory States. It shall be open for accession by any State which is a Member of the United Nations, or by any other State which may be invited to accede to the Treaty with the consent of all the Contracting Parties whose representatives are entitled to participate in the meetings provided for under Article IX of the Treaty.

2.   Ratification of or accession to the present Treaty shall be effected by each State in accordance with its constitutional processes.

3.   Instruments of ratification and instruments of accession shall be deposited with the Government of the United States of America, hereby designated as the depositary Government.

4.   The depositary Government shall inform all signatory and acceding States of the date of each deposit of an instrument of ratification or accession, and the date of entry into force of the Treaty and of any modification or amendment thereto.

5.   Upon the deposit of instruments of ratification by all the signatory States, the present Treaty shall enter into force for those States and for States which have deposited instruments of accession. Thereafter the Treaty shall enter into force for any acceding State upon the deposit of its instrument of accession.

6. The present Treaty shall be registered by the depositary Government pursuant to Article 102 of the Charter of the United Nations.

Article XIV

The present Treaty, done in the English, French, Russian and Spanish languages, each version being equally authentic, shall be deposited in the archives of the Government of the United States of America, which shall transmit duly certified copies thereof to the Governments of the signatory and acceding States.

IN WITNESS WHEREOF the undersigned Plenipotentiaries, duly authorized, have signed the present Treaty.

DONE at Washington this first day of December, one thousand nine hundred and fifty-nine.

Agreement Governing the Activities of States on the Moon and Other Celestial Bodies (Moon Treaty)

OPENED FOR SIGNATURE AT NEW YORK:
18 December 1979

ENTERED INTO FORCE:
11 July 1984

DEPOSITARY:
Secretary-General of the United Nations

NUMBER OF SIGNATORY STATES: 11*

NUMBER OF STATES PARTIES: 16*

* As at 28 November 2014. For the updated adherence status, see http://disarmament.un.org/treaties/.

TEXT:

The States Parties to this Agreement,

Noting the achievements of States in the exploration and use of the moon and other celestial bodies,

Recognizing that the moon, as a natural satellite of the earth, has an important role to play in the exploration of outer space,

Determined to promote on the basis of equality the further development of co-operation among States in the exploration and use of the moon and other celestial bodies,

Desiring to prevent the moon from becoming an area of international conflict,

Bearing in mind the benefits which may be derived from the exploitation of the natural resources of the moon and other celestial bodies,

Recalling the Treaty on Principles Governing the Activities of States in the Exploration and Use of Outer Space, including the Moon and Other Celestial Bodies, the Agreement on the Rescue of Astronauts, the Return of Astronauts and the Return of Objects Launched into Outer Space, the Convention on International Liability for Damage Caused by Space Objects, and the Convention on Registration of Objects Launched into Outer Space,

Taking into account the need to define and develop the provisions of these international instruments in relation to the moon and other celestial bodies, having regard to further progress in the exploration and use of outer space,

Have agreed on the following:

Article 1

1.   The provisions of this Agreement relating to the moon shall also apply to other celestial bodies within the solar

system, other than the earth, except in so far as specific legal norms enter into force with respect to any of these celestial bodies.

2.   For the purposes of this Agreement reference to the moon shall include orbits around or other trajectories to or around it.

3.   This Agreement does not apply to extraterrestrial materials which reach the surface of the earth by natural means.

Article 2

All activities on the moon, including its exploration and use, shall be carried out in accordance with international law, in particular the Charter of the United Nations, and taking into account the Declaration on Principles of International Law concerning Friendly Relations and Co-operation among States in accordance with the Charter of the United Nations, adopted by the General Assembly on 24 October 1970, in the interests of maintaining international peace and security and promoting international co-operation and mutual understanding, and with due regard to the corresponding interests of all other States Parties.

Article 3

1.   The moon shall be used by all States Parties exclusively for peaceful purposes.

2.   Any threat or use of force or any other hostile act or threat of hostile act on the moon is prohibited. It is likewise prohibited to use the moon in order to commit any such act or to engage in any such threat in relation to the earth, the moon spacecraft, the personnel of spacecraft or man-made space objects.

3.   States Parties shall not place in orbit around or other trajectory to or around the moon objects carrying nuclear weapons or any other kind of weapons of mass destruction or place or use such weapons on or in the moon.

4.   The establishment of military bases, installations and fortifications, the testing of any type of weapons and the conduct of military manoeuvres on the moon shall be forbidden. The use of military personnel for scientific research or for any other peaceful purposes shall not be prohibited. The use of any equipment or facility necessary for peaceful exploration and use of the moon shall also not be prohibited.

Article 4

1.   The exploration and use of the moon shall be the province of all mankind and shall be carried out for the benefit and in the interests of all countries, irrespective of their degree of economic or scientific development. Due regard shall be paid to the interests of present and future generations as well as to the need to promote higher standards of living and conditions of economic and social

progress and development in accordance with the Charter of the United Nations.

2. States Parties shall be guided by the principle of co-operation and mutual assistance in all their activities concerning the exploration and use of the moon. International co-operation in pursuance of this Agreement should be as wide as possible and may take place on a multilateral basis, on a bilateral basis or through international intergovernmental organizations.

Article 5

1. States Parties shall inform the Secretary-General of the United Nations as well as the public and the international scientific community, to the greatest extent feasible and practicable, of their activities concerned with the exploration and use of the moon. Information on the time, purposes, locations, orbital parameters and duration shall be given in respect of each mission to the moon as soon as possible after launching, while information on the results of each mission, including scientific results, shall be furnished upon completion of the mission. In the case of a mission lasting more than sixty days, information on conduct of the mission, including any scientific results, shall be given periodically at thirty days' intervals. For missions lasting more than six months, only significant additions to such information need be reported thereafter.

2. If a State Party becomes aware that another State Party plans to operate simultaneously in the same area of or in the

same orbit around or trajectory to or around the moon, it shall promptly inform the other State of the timing of and plans for its own operations.

3.   In carrying out activities under this Agreement, States Parties shall promptly inform the Secretary-General, as well as the public and the international scientific community, of any phenomena they discover in outer space, including the moon, which could endanger human life or health, as well as of any indication of organic life.

Article 6

1.   There shall be freedom of scientific investigation on the moon by all States Parties without discrimination of any kind, on the basis of equality and in accordance with international law.

2.   In carrying out scientific investigations and in furtherance of the provisions of this Agreement, the States Parties shall have the right to collect on and remove from the moon samples of its mineral and other substances. Such samples shall remain at the disposal of those States Parties which caused them to be collected and may be used by them for scientific purposes. States Parties shall have regard to the desirability of making a portion of such samples available to other interested States Parties and the international scientific community for scientific investigation. States Parties may in the course of scientific investigations also use mineral and other substances of the moon in quantities appropriate for the support of their missions.

3.   States Parties agree on the desirability of exchanging scientific and other personnel on expeditions to or installations on the moon to the greatest extent feasible and practicable.

Article 7

1.   In exploring and using the moon, States Parties shall take measures to prevent the disruption of the existing balance of its environment, whether by introducing adverse changes in that environment, by its harmful contamination through the introduction of extra-environmental matter or otherwise. States Parties shall also take measures to avoid harmfully affecting the environment of the earth through the introduction of extraterrestrial matter or otherwise.

2.   States Parties shall inform the Secretary-General of the United Nations of the measures being adopted by them in accordance with paragraph 1 of this article and shall also, to the maximum extent feasible, notify him in advance of all placements by them of radio-active materials on the moon and of the purposes of such placements.

3.   States Parties shall report to other States Parties and to the Secretary-General concerning areas of the moon having special scientific interest in order that, without prejudice to the rights of other States Parties, consideration may be given to the designation of such areas as international scientific preserves for which special protective arrangements are to be agreed upon in consultation with the competent bodies of the United Nations.

Article 8

1.   States Parties may pursue their activities in the exploration and use of the moon anywhere on or below its surface, subject to the provisions of this Agreement.

2.   For these purposes States Parties may, in particular:

(a)   Land their space objects on the moon and launch them from the moon;

(b)   Place their personnel, space vehicles, equipment, facilities, stations and installations anywhere on or below the surface of the moon.

Personnel, space vehicles, equipment, facilities, stations and installations may move or be moved freely over or below the surface of the moon.

3.   Activities of States Parties in accordance with paragraphs 1 and 2 of this article shall not interfere with the activities of other States Parties on the moon. Where such interference may occur, the States Parties concerned shall undertake consultations in accordance with article 15, paragraphs 2 and 3 of this Agreement.

Article 9

1.   States Parties may establish manned and unmanned stations on the moon. A State Party establishing a station shall use only that area which is required for the needs of the station and shall immediately inform the Secretary-General

of the United Nations of the location and purposes of that station. Subsequently, at annual intervals that State shall likewise inform the Secretary-General whether the station continues in use and whether its purposes have changed.

2.   Stations shall be installed in such a manner that they do not impede the free access to all areas of the moon by personnel, vehicles and equipment of other States Parties conducting activities on the moon in accordance with the provisions of this Agreement or of article I of the Treaty on Principles Governing the Activities of States in the Exploration and Use of Outer Space, including the Moon and Other Celestial Bodies.

Article 10

1.   States Parties shall adopt all practicable measures to safeguard the life and health of persons on the moon. For this purpose they shall regard any person on the moon as an astronaut within the meaning of article V of the Treaty on Principles Governing the Activities of States in the Exploration and Use of Outer Space, including the Moon and Other Celestial Bodies and as part of the personnel of a spacecraft within the meaning of the Agreement on the Rescue of Astronauts, the Return of Astronauts and the Return of Objects Launched into Outer Space.

2.   States Parties shall offer shelter in their stations, installations, vehicles and other facilities to persons in distress on the moon.

Article 11

1.   The moon and its natural resources are the common heritage of mankind, which finds its expression in the provisions of this Agreement and in particular in paragraph 5 of this article.

2.   The moon is not subject to national appropriation by any claim of sovereignty, by means of use or occupation, or by any other means.

3.   Neither the surface nor the subsurface of the moon, nor any part thereof or natural resources in place, shall become property of any State, international intergovernmental or non-governmental organization, national organization or non-governmental entity or of any natural person. The placement of personnel, space vehicles, equipment, facilities, stations and installations on or below the surface of the moon, including structures connected with its surface or subsurface, shall not create a right of ownership over the surface or the subsurface of the moon or any areas thereof. The foregoing provisions are without prejudice to the international regime referred to in paragraph 5 of this article.

4.   States Parties have the right to exploration and use of the moon without discrimination of any kind, on a basis of equality and in accordance with international law and the terms of this Agreement.

5.   States Parties to this Agreement hereby undertake to establish an international regime, including appropriate

procedures, to govern the exploitation of the natural resources of the moon as such exploitation is about to become feasible. This provision shall be implemented in accordance with article 18 of this Agreement.

6.   In order to facilitate the establishment of the international regime referred to in paragraph 5 of this article, States Parties shall inform the Secretary-General of the United Nations as well as the public and the international scientific community, to the greatest extent feasible and practicable, of any natural resources they may discover on the moon.

7.   The main purposes of the international regime to be established shall include:

(a)   The orderly and safe development of the natural resources of the moon;

(b)   The rational management of those resources;

(c)   The expansion of opportunities in the use of those resources;

(d)   An equitable sharing by all States Parties in the benefits derived from those resources, whereby the interests and needs of the developing countries, as well as the efforts of those countries which have contributed either directly or indirectly to the exploration of the moon, shall be given special consideration.

8. All the activities with respect to the natural resources of the moon shall be carried out in a manner compatible with the purposes specified in paragraph 7 of this article and the provisions of article 6, paragraph 2, of this Agreement.

Article 12

1. States Parties shall retain jurisdiction and control over their personnel, vehicles, equipment, facilities, stations and installations on the moon. The ownership of space vehicles, equipment, facilities, stations and installations shall not be affected by their presence on the moon.

2. Vehicles, installations and equipment or their component parts found in places other than their intended location shall be dealt with in accordance with article 5 of the Agreement on Rescue of Astronauts, the Return of Astronauts and the Return of Objects Launched into Outer Space.

3. In the event of an emergency involving a threat to human life, States Parties may use the equipment, vehicles, installations, facilities or supplies of other States Parties on the moon. Prompt notification of such use shall be made to the Secretary-General of the United Nations or the State Party concerned.

Article 13

A State Party which learns of the crash landing, forced landing or other unintended landing on the moon of a space object, or its component parts, that were not launched by it, shall promptly inform the launching State Party and the Secretary-General of the United Nations.

Article 14

1.   States Parties to this Agreement shall bear international responsibility for national activities on the moon, whether such activities are carried on by governmental agencies or by non-governmental entities, and for assuring that national activities are carried out in conformity with the provisions set forth in this Agreement. States Parties shall ensure that non-governmental entities under their jurisdiction shall engage in activities on the moon only under the authority and continuing supervision of the appropriate State Party.

2.   States Parties recognize that detailed arrangements concerning liability for damage caused on the moon, in addition to the provisions of the Treaty on Principles Governing the Activities of States in the Exploration and Use of Outer Space, including the Moon and Other Celestial Bodies and the Convention on International Liability for Damage Caused by Space Objects, may become necessary as a result of more extensive activities on the moon. Any such arrangements shall be elaborated in accordance with the procedure provided for in article 18 of this Agreement.

Article 15

1.   Each State Party may assure itself that the activities of other States Parties in the exploration and use of the moon

are compatible with the provisions of this Agreement. To this end, all space vehicles, equipment, facilities, stations and installations on the moon shall be open to other States Parties. Such States Parties shall give reasonable advance notice of a projected visit, in order that appropriate consultations may be held and that maximum precautions may be taken to assure safety and to avoid interference with normal operations in the facility to be visited. In pursuance of this article, any State Party may act on its own behalf or with the full or partial assistance of any other State Party or through appropriate international procedures within the framework of the United Nations and in accordance with the Charter.

2.   A State Party which has reason to believe that another State Party is not fulfilling the obligations incumbent upon it pursuant to this Agreement or that another State Party is interfering with the rights which the former State has under this Agreement may request consultations with that State Party. A State Party receiving such a request shall enter into such consultations without delay. Any other State Party which requests to do so shall be entitled to take part in the consultations. Each State Party participating in such consultations shall seek a mutually acceptable resolution of any controversy and shall bear in mind the rights and interests of all States Parties. The Secretary-General of the United Nations shall be informed of the results of the consultations and shall transmit the information received to all States Parties concerned.

3.   If the consultations do not lead to a mutually acceptable settlement which has due regard for the rights and interests of all States Parties, the parties concerned shall take all measures to settle the dispute by other peaceful means of their choice appropriate to the circumstances and the nature of the dispute. If difficulties arise in connexion with the opening of consultations or if consultations do not lead to a mutually acceptable settlement, any State Party may seek the assistance of the Secretary-General, without seeking the consent of any other State Party concerned, in order to resolve the controversy. A State Party which does not maintain diplomatic relations with another State Party concerned shall participate in such consultations, at its choice, either itself or through another State Party or the Secretary-General as intermediary.

Article 16

With the exception of articles 17 to 21, references in this Agreement to States shall be deemed to apply to any international intergovernmental organization which conducts space activities if the organization declares its acceptance of the rights and obligations provided for in this Agreement and if a majority of the States members of the organization are States Parties to this Agreement and to the Treaty on Principles Governing the Activities of States in the Exploration and Use of Outer Space, including the Moon and Other Celestial Bodies. States members of any such organization which are States Parties to this Agreement shall take all appropriate steps to ensure that the organization makes a declaration in accordance with the foregoing.

Article 17

Any State Party to this Agreement may propose amendments to the Agreement. Amendments shall enter into force for each State Party to the Agreement accepting the amendments upon their acceptance by a majority of the States Parties to the Agreement and thereafter for each remaining State Party to the Agreement on the date of acceptance by it.

Article 18

Ten years after the entry into force of this Agreement, the question of the review of the Agreement shall be included in the provisional agenda of the General Assembly of the United Nations in order to consider, in the light of past application of the Agreement, whether it requires revision. However, at any time after the Agreement has been in force for five years, the Secretary-General of the United Nations, as depositary, shall, at the request of one third of the States Parties to the Agreement and with the concurrence of the majority of the States Parties, convene a conference of the States Parties to review this Agreement. A review conference shall also consider the question of the implementation of the provisions of article 11, paragraph 5, on the basis of the principle referred to in paragraph 1 of that article and taking into account in particular any relevant technological developments.

Article 19

1.   This Agreement shall be open for signature by all States at United Nations Headquarters in New York.

2.   This Agreement shall be subject to ratification by signatory States. Any State which does not sign this Agreement before its entry into force in accordance with paragraph 3 of this article may accede to it at any time. Instruments of ratification or accession shall be deposited with the Secretary-General of the United Nations.

3.   This Agreement shall enter into force on the thirtieth day following the date of deposit of the fifth instrument of ratification.

4.   For each State depositing its instrument of ratification or accession after the entry into force of this Agreement, it shall enter into force on the thirtieth day following the date of deposit of any such instrument.

5.   The Secretary-General shall promptly inform all signatory and acceding States of the date of each signature, the date of deposit of each instrument of ratification or accession to this Agreement, the date of its entry into force and other notices.

Article 20

Any State Party to this Agreement may give notice of its withdrawal from the Agreement one year after its entry into force by written notification to the Secretary-General of the

United Nations. Such withdrawal shall take effect one year from the date of receipt of this notification.

Article 21

The original of this Agreement, of which the Arabic, Chinese, English, French, Russian and Spanish texts are equally authentic, shall be deposited with the Secretary-General of the United Nations, who shall send certified copies thereof to all signatory and acceding States.

IN WITNESS WHEREOF the undersigned, being duly authorized thereto by their respective Governments, have signed this Agreement, opened for signature at New York on 18 December 1979.

Treaty on Principles Governing the Activities of States in the Exploration and Use of Outer Space, including the Moon and Other Celestial Bodies (Outer Space Treaty)

OPENED FOR SIGNATURE AT LONDON, MOSCOW AND WASHINGTON:
27 January 1967

ENTERED INTO FORCE:
10 October 1967

DEPOSITARY GOVERNMENTS:
Russian Federation
United Kingdom of Great Britain and Northern Ireland
United States of America

NUMBER OF SIGNATORY STATES: 89*

NUMBER OF STATES PARTIES: 102*

* As at 28 November 2014. For the updated adherence status, see http://disarmament.un.org/treaties/.

TEXT:

The States Parties to this Treaty,

Inspired by the great prospects opening up before mankind as a result of man's entry into outer space,

Recognizing the common interest of all mankind in the progress of the exploration and use of outer space for peaceful purposes,

Believing that the exploration and use of outer space should be carried on for the benefit of all peoples irrespective of the degree of their economic or scientific development,

Desiring to contribute to broad international co-operation in the scientific as well as the legal aspects of the exploration and use of outer space for peaceful purposes,

Believing that such co-operation will contribute to the development of mutual understanding and to the strengthening of friendly relations between States and peoples,

Recalling resolution 1962 (XVIII), entitled "Declaration of Legal Principles Governing the Activities of States in the Exploration and Use of Outer Space", which was adopted unanimously by the United Nations General Assembly on 13 December 1963,

Recalling resolution 1884 (XVIII), calling upon States to refrain from placing in orbit around the earth any objects carrying nuclear weapons or any other kinds of weapons of mass destruction or from installing such weapons on celestial bodies, which was adopted unanimously by the United Nations General Assembly on 17 October 1963,

Taking account of United Nations General Assembly resolution 110 (II) of 3 November 1947, which condemned propaganda designed or likely to provoke or encourage any threat to the peace, breach of the peace or act of aggression, and considering that the aforementioned resolution is applicable to outer space,

Convinced that a Treaty on Principles Governing the Activities of States in the Exploration and Use of Outer Space, including the moon and Other Celestial Bodies, will further the Purposes and Principles of the Charter of the United Nations,

Have agreed on the following:

Article I

The exploration and use of outer space, including the moon and other celestial bodies, shall be carried out for the benefit and in the interests of all countries, irrespective of their degree of economic or scientific development, and shall be the province of all mankind.

Outer space, including the moon and other celestial bodies, shall be free for exploration and use by all States without discrimination of any kind, on a basis of equality and in accordance with international law, and there shall be free access to all areas of celestial bodies.

There shall be freedom of scientific investigation in outer space, including the moon and other celestial bodies, and States shall facilitate and encourage international co-operation in such investigation.

Article II

Outer space, including the moon and other celestial bodies, is not subject to national appropriation by claim of sovereignty, by means of use or occupation, or by any other means.

Article III

States Parties to the Treaty shall carry on activities in the exploration and use of outer space, including the moon and other celestial bodies, in accordance with international law, including the Charter of the United Nations, in the interest of maintaining international peace and security and promoting international co-operation and understanding.

Article IV

States Parties to the Treaty undertake not to place in orbit around the earth any objects carrying nuclear weapons or any other kinds of weapons of mass destruction, instal such weapons on celestial bodies, or station such weapons in outer space in any other manner.

The moon and other celestial bodies shall be used by all States Parties to the Treaty exclusively for peaceful purposes. The establishment of military bases, installations and fortifications, the testing of any type of weapons and the conduct of military manoeuvres on celestial bodies shall be forbidden. The use of military personnel for scientific research or for any other peaceful purposes shall not be prohibited. The use of any equipment or facility necessary for peaceful exploration of the moon and other celestial bodies shall also not be prohibited.

Article V

States Parties to the Treaty shall regard astronauts as envoys of mankind in outer space and shall render to them all possible assistance in the event of accident, distress, or emergency landing on the territory of another State Party or on the high seas. When astronauts make such a landing, they shall be safely and promptly returned to the State of registry of their space vehicle.

In carrying on activities in outer space and on celestial bodies, the astronauts of one State Party shall render all possible assistance to the astronauts of other States Parties.

States Parties to the Treaty shall immediately inform the other States Parties to the Treaty or the Secretary-General of the United Nations of any phenomena they discover in outer space, including the moon and other celestial bodies, which could constitute a danger to the life or health of astronauts.

Article VI

States Parties to the Treaty shall bear international responsibility for national activities in outer space, including the moon and other celestial bodies, whether such activities are carried on by governmental agencies or by non-governmental entities, and for assuring that national activities are carried out in conformity with the provisions set forth in the present Treaty. The activities of non-governmental entities in outer space, including the moon and other celestial bodies, shall require authorization and continuing supervision by the appropriate State Party to the Treaty. When activities are carried on in outer space, including the moon and other celestial bodies, by an international organization, responsibility for compliance with this Treaty shall be borne both by the international organization and by the States Parties to the Treaty participating in such organization.

Article VII

Each State Party to the Treaty that launches or procures the launching of an object into outer space, including the moon and other celestial bodies, and each State Party from whose territory or facility an object is launched, is internationally liable for damage to another State Party to the Treaty or to its natural or juridical persons by such object or its component parts on the earth, in air space or in outer space, including the moon and other celestial bodies.

Article VIII

A State Party to the Treaty on whose registry an object launched into outer space is carried shall retain jurisdiction and control over such object, and over any personnel thereof, while in outer space or on a celestial body. Ownership of objects launched into outer space, including objects landed or constructed on a celestial body, and of their component parts, is not affected by their presence in outer space or on a celestial body or by their return to the earth. Such objects or component parts found beyond the limits of the State Party to the Treaty on whose registry they are carried shall be returned to that State Party, which shall, upon request, furnish identifying data prior to their return.

Article IX

In the exploration and use of outer space, including the moon and other celestial bodies, States Parties to the Treaty shall be guided by the principle of co-operation and mutual assistance and shall conduct all their activities in outer space, including the moon and other celestial bodies, with due regard to the corresponding interests of all other States Parties to the Treaty. States Parties to the Treaty shall pursue studies of outer space, including the moon and other celestial bodies, and conduct exploration of them so as to avoid their harmful contamination and also adverse changes in the environment of the earth resulting from the introduction of extraterrestrial matter and, where necessary, shall adopt appropriate measures for this purpose. If a State Party to the Treaty has reason to believe that an activity or experiment planned by it or its nationals in outer space, including the moon and other celestial bodies, would cause potentially harmful interference with activities of other States Parties in the peaceful exploration and use of outer space, including the moon and other celestial bodies, it shall undertake appropriate international consultations before proceeding with any such activity or experiment. A State Party to the Treaty which has reason to believe that an activity or experiment planned by another State Party in outer space, including the moon and other celestial bodies, would cause potentially harmful interference with activities in the peaceful exploration and use of outer space, including the moon and other celestial bodies, may request consultation concerning the activity or experiment.

Article X

In order to promote international co-operation in the exploration and use of outer space, including the moon and other celestial bodies, in conformity with the purposes of this Treaty, the States Parties to the Treaty shall consider on a basis of equality any requests by other States Parties to the Treaty to be afforded an opportunity to observe the flight of space objects launched by those States.

The nature of such an opportunity for observation and the conditions under which it could be afforded shall be determined by agreement between the States concerned.

Article XI

In order to promote international co-operation in the peaceful exploration and use of outer space, States Parties to the Treaty conducting activities in outer space, including the moon and other celestial bodies, agree to inform the Secretary-General of the United Nations as well as the public and the international scientific community, to the greatest extent feasible and practicable, of the nature, conduct, locations and results of such activities. On receiving the said information, the Secretary-General of the United Nations should be prepared to disseminate it immediately and effectively.

Article XII

All stations, installations, equipment and space vehicles on the moon and other celestial bodies shall be open to representatives of other States Parties to the Treaty on a basis of reciprocity. Such representatives shall give reasonable advance notice of a projected visit, in order that appropriate consultations may be held and that maximum precautions may be taken to assure safety and to avoid interference with normal operations in the facility to be visited.

Article XIII

The provisions of this Treaty shall apply to the activities of States Parties to the Treaty in the exploration and use of outer space, including the moon and other celestial bodies, whether such activities are carried on by a single State Party to the Treaty or jointly with other States, including cases where they are carried on within the framework of international inter-governmental organizations.

Any practical questions arising in connection with activities carried on by international inter-governmental organizations in the exploration and use of outer space, including the moon and other celestial bodies, shall be resolved by the States Parties to the Treaty either with the appropriate international organization or with one or more States members of that international organization, which are Parties to this Treaty.

Article XIV

1. This Treaty shall be open to all States for signature. Any State which does not sign this Treaty before its entry into force in accordance with paragraph 3 of this Article may accede to it at any time.

2. This Treaty shall be subject to ratification by signatory States. Instruments of ratification and instruments of accession shall be deposited with the Governments of the United Kingdom of Great Britain and Northern Ireland, the Union of Soviet Socialist Republics and the United States of America, which are hereby designated the Depositary Governments.

3. This Treaty shall enter into force upon the deposit of instruments of ratification by five Governments including the Governments designated as Depositary Governments under this Treaty.

4. For States whose instruments of ratification or accession are deposited subsequent to the entry into force of this Treaty, it shall enter into force on the date of the deposit of their instruments of ratification or accession.

5.   The Depositary Governments shall promptly inform all signatory and acceding States of the date of each signature, the date of deposit of each instrument of ratification of and accession to this Treaty, the date of its entry into force and other notices.

6.   This Treaty shall be registered by the Depositary Governments pursuant to Article 102 of the Charter of the United Nations.

Article XV

Any State Party to the Treaty may propose amendments to this Treaty. Amendments shall enter into force for each State Party to the Treaty accepting the amendments upon their acceptance by a majority of the States Parties to the Treaty and thereafter for each remaining State Party to the Treaty on the date of acceptance by it.

Article XVI

Any State Party to the Treaty may give notice of its withdrawal from the Treaty one year after its entry into force by written notification to the Depositary Governments. Such withdrawal shall take effect one year from the date of receipt of this notification.

Article XVII

This Treaty, of which the English, Russian, French, Spanish and Chinese texts are equally authentic, shall be deposited in the archives of the Depositary Governments. Duly certified copies of this Treaty shall be transmitted by the Depositary Governments to the Governments of the signatory and acceding States.

IN WITNESS WHEREOF the undersigned, duly authorised, have signed this Treaty.

DONE in triplicate, at the cities of London, Moscow and Washington, the twenty-seventh day of January, one thousand nine hundred and sixty-seven.

Treaty on the Prohibition
of the Emplacement of Nuclear Weapons
and Other Weapons of Mass Destruction
on the Sea-Bed and the Ocean Floor
and in the Subsoil Thereof (Sea-bed Treaty)

OPENED FOR SIGNATURE AT LONDON, MOSCOW AND WASHINGTON:
11 February 1971

ENTERED INTO FORCE:
18 May 1972

DEPOSITARY GOVERNMENTS:
Russian Federation
United Kingdom of Great Britain and Northern Ireland
United States of America

NUMBER OF SIGNATORY STATES: 84*

NUMBER OF STATES PARTIES: 94*

* As at 28 November 2014. For the updated adherence status, see http://disarmament.un.org/treaties/.

TEXT:

The States Parties to this Treaty,

Recognizing the common interest of mankind in the progress of the exploration and use of the sea-bed and the ocean floor for peaceful purposes,

Considering that the prevention of a nuclear arms race on the sea-bed and the ocean floor serves the interests of maintaining world peace, reduces international tensions and strengthens friendly relations among States,

Convinced that this Treaty constitutes a step towards the exclusion of the sea-bed, the ocean floor and the subsoil thereof from the arms race,

Convinced that this Treaty constitutes a step towards a treaty on general and complete disarmament under strict and effective international control, and determined to continue negotiations to this end,

Convinced that this Treaty will further the purposes and principles of the Charter of the United Nations, in a manner consistent with the principles of international law and without infringing the freedoms of the high seas,

Have agreed as follows:

Article I

1.   The States Parties to this Treaty undertake not to emplant or emplace on the sea-bed and the ocean floor and in the subsoil thereof beyond the outer limit of a sea-bed zone, as defined in article II, any nuclear weapons or any other types of weapons of mass destruction as well as structures, launching installations or any other facilities specifically designed for storing, testing or using such weapons.

2.   The undertakings of paragraph 1 of this article shall also apply to the sea-bed zone referred to in the same paragraph, except that within such sea-bed zone, they shall not apply either to the coastal State or to the sea-bed beneath its territorial waters.

3.   The States Parties to this Treaty undertake not to assist, encourage or induce any State to carry out activities referred to in paragraph 1 of this article and not to participate in any other way in such actions.

Article II

For the purpose of this Treaty, the outer limit of the sea-bed zone referred to in article I shall be coterminous with the twelve-mile outer limit of the zone referred to in part II of the Convention on the Territorial Sea and the Contiguous Zone, signed at Geneva on April 29, 1958, and shall be measured in accordance with the provisions of part I, section II, of that Convention and in accordance with international law.

Article III

1.   In order to promote the objectives of and insure compliance with the provisions of this Treaty, each State Party to the Treaty shall have the right to verify through observation the activities of other States Parties to the Treaty on the sea-bed and the ocean floor and in the subsoil thereof beyond the zone referred to in article I, provided that observation does not interfere with such activities.

2.   If after such observation reasonable doubts remain concerning the fulfillment of the obligations assumed under the Treaty, the State Party having such doubts and the State Party that is responsible for the activities giving rise to the doubts shall consult with a view to removing the doubts. If the doubts persist, the State Party having such doubts shall notify the other States Parties, and the Parties concerned shall cooperate on such further procedures for verification as may be agreed, including appropriate inspection of objects, structures, installations or other facilities that reasonably may be expected to be of a kind described in article I. The Parties in the region of the activities, including any coastal State, and any other Party so requesting, shall be entitled to participate in such consultation and cooperation. After completion of the further procedures for verification, an appropriate report shall be circulated to other Parties by the Party that initiated such procedures.

3.   If the State responsible for the activities giving rise to the reasonable doubts is not identifiable by observation of the object, structure, installation or other facility, the State Party having such doubts shall notify and make appropriate inquiries of States Parties in the region of the activities and of any other State Party. If it is ascertained through these inquiries that a particular State Party is responsible for the activities, that State Party shall consult and cooperate with other Parties as provided in paragraph 2 of this article. If the identity of the State responsible for the activities cannot be ascertained through these inquiries, then further verification procedures, including inspection, may be undertaken by the inquiring State Party, which shall invite the participation

of the Parties in the region of the activities, including any coastal State, and of any other Party desiring to cooperate.

4.   If consultation and cooperation pursuant to paragraphs 2 and 3 of this article have not removed the doubts concerning the activities and there remains a serious question concerning fulfillment of the obligations assumed under this Treaty, a State Party may, in accordance with the provisions of the Charter of the United Nations, refer the matter to the Security Council, which may take action in accordance with the Charter.

5.   Verification pursuant to this article may be undertaken by any State Party using its own means, or with the full or partial assistance of any other State Party, or through appropriate international procedures within the framework of the United Nations and in accordance with its Charter.

6.   Verification activities pursuant to this Treaty shall not interfere with activities of other States Parties and shall be conducted with due regard for rights recognized under international law, including the freedoms of the high seas and the rights of coastal States with respect to the exploration and exploitation of their continental shelves.

Article IV

Nothing in this Treaty shall be interpreted as supporting or prejudicing the position of any State Party with respect to existing international conventions, including the 1958 Convention on the Territorial Sea and the

Contiguous Zone, or with respect to rights or claims which such State Party may assert, or with respect to recognition or non-recognition of rights or claims asserted by any other State, related to waters off its coasts, including, inter alia, territorial seas and contiguous zones, or to the sea-bed and the ocean floor, including continental shelves.

Article V

The Parties to this Treaty undertake to continue negotiations in good faith concerning further measures in the field of disarmament for the prevention of an arms race on the sea-bed, the ocean floor and the subsoil thereof.

Article VI

Any State Party may propose amendments to this Treaty. Amendments shall enter into force for each State Party accepting the amendments upon their acceptance by a majority of the States Parties to the Treaty and, thereafter, for each remaining State Party on the date of acceptance by it.

Article VII

Five years after the entry into force of this Treaty, a conference of Parties to the Treaty shall be held at Geneva, Switzerland, in order to review the operation of this Treaty with a view to assuring that the purposes of the preamble and the provisions of the Treaty are being realized. Such review shall take into account any relevant technological developments. The review conference shall determine, in accordance with the views of a majority of those Parties attending, whether and when an additional review conference shall be convened.

Article VIII

Each State Party to this Treaty shall in exercising its national sovereignty have the right to withdraw from this Treaty if it decides that extraordinary events related to the subject-matter of this Treaty have jeopardized the supreme interests of its country. It shall give notice of such withdrawal to all other States Parties to the Treaty and to the United Nations Security Council three months in advance. Such notice shall include a statement of the extraordinary events it considers to have jeopardized its supreme interests.

Article IX

The provisions of this Treaty shall in no way affect the obligations assumed by States Parties to the Treaty under international instruments establishing zones free from nuclear weapons.

Article X

1.   This Treaty shall be open for signature to all States. Any State which does not sign the Treaty before its entry

into force in accordance with paragraph 3 of this article may accede to it at any time.

2.   This Treaty shall be subject to ratification by signatory States. Instruments of ratification and of accession shall be deposited with the Governments of the United States of America, the United Kingdom of Great Britain and Northern Ireland, and the Union of Soviet Socialist Republics, which are hereby designated the Depositary Governments.

3.   This Treaty shall enter into force after the deposit of instruments of ratification by twenty-two Governments, including the Governments designated as Depositary Governments of this Treaty.

4.   For States whose instruments of ratification or accession are deposited after the entry into force of this Treaty, it shall enter into force on the date of the deposit of their instruments of ratification or accession.

5.   The Depositary Governments shall promptly inform the Governments of all signatory and acceding States of the date of each signature, of the date of deposit of each instrument of ratification or of accession, of the date of the entry into force of this Treaty, and of the receipt of other notices.

6.   This Treaty shall be registered by the Depositary Governments pursuant to Article 102 of the Charter of the United Nations.

Article XI

This Treaty, the English, Russian, French, Spanish and Chinese texts of which are equally authentic, shall be deposited in the archives of the Depositary Governments. Duly certified copies of this Treaty shall be transmitted by the Depositary Governments to the Governments of the States signatory and acceding thereto.

IN WITNESS WHEREOF the undersigned, being duly authorized thereto, have signed this Treaty.

DONE in triplicate, at the cities of Washington, London, and Moscow, this eleventh day of February, one thousand nine hundred seventy-one.